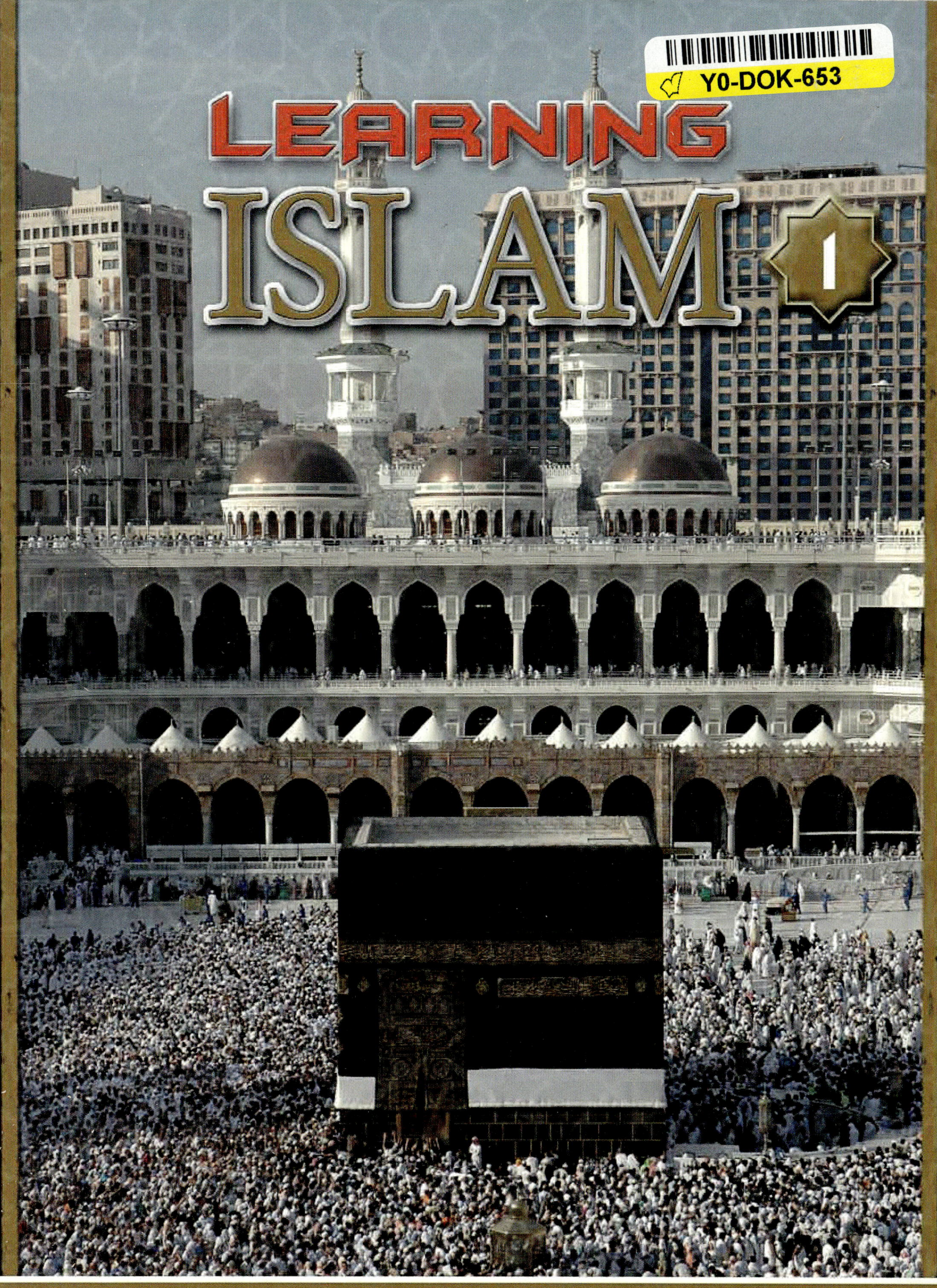

Y0-DOK-653

Islamic Studies Textbook Series
Level One

Learning Islam 1

بسم الله الرحمن الرحيم

In the Name of Allah, Most Compassionate, Most Merciful

Learning Islam © is a series of Islamic studies textbooks that introduces Muslim students to the essentials of their faith, and brings to light the historic and cultural aspects of Islam in elaborate manner. The series may be used for middle school and/or highschool grades. Each level is served by a student textbook and workbook, as well as a teacher's guide. This series builds upon the ISF's primary series "I Love Islam" which covers grades one through five.

The Islamic Services Foundation is undertaking this project in collaboration with Brighter Horizons Academy in Dallas, Texas. Extensive efforts have been made to review the enclosed material. However, constructive suggestions and comments that would enrich the content of this work are welcome.

All Praise is due to Allah (God), for providing us with the resources that have enabled us to complete the first part of this series. This is an ongoing project, and it is our sincere wish and hope that it will impact our Muslim children today, and for many years to come.

Copyright © 2019 by Islamic Services Foundation

ISBN 1-933301-40-2

All rights reserved. No part of this publication may be reproduced or transmitted in any form or by any means, electronic or mechanical, including photocopy, recording, or any information storage and retrieval system, without permission in writing from the publisher.

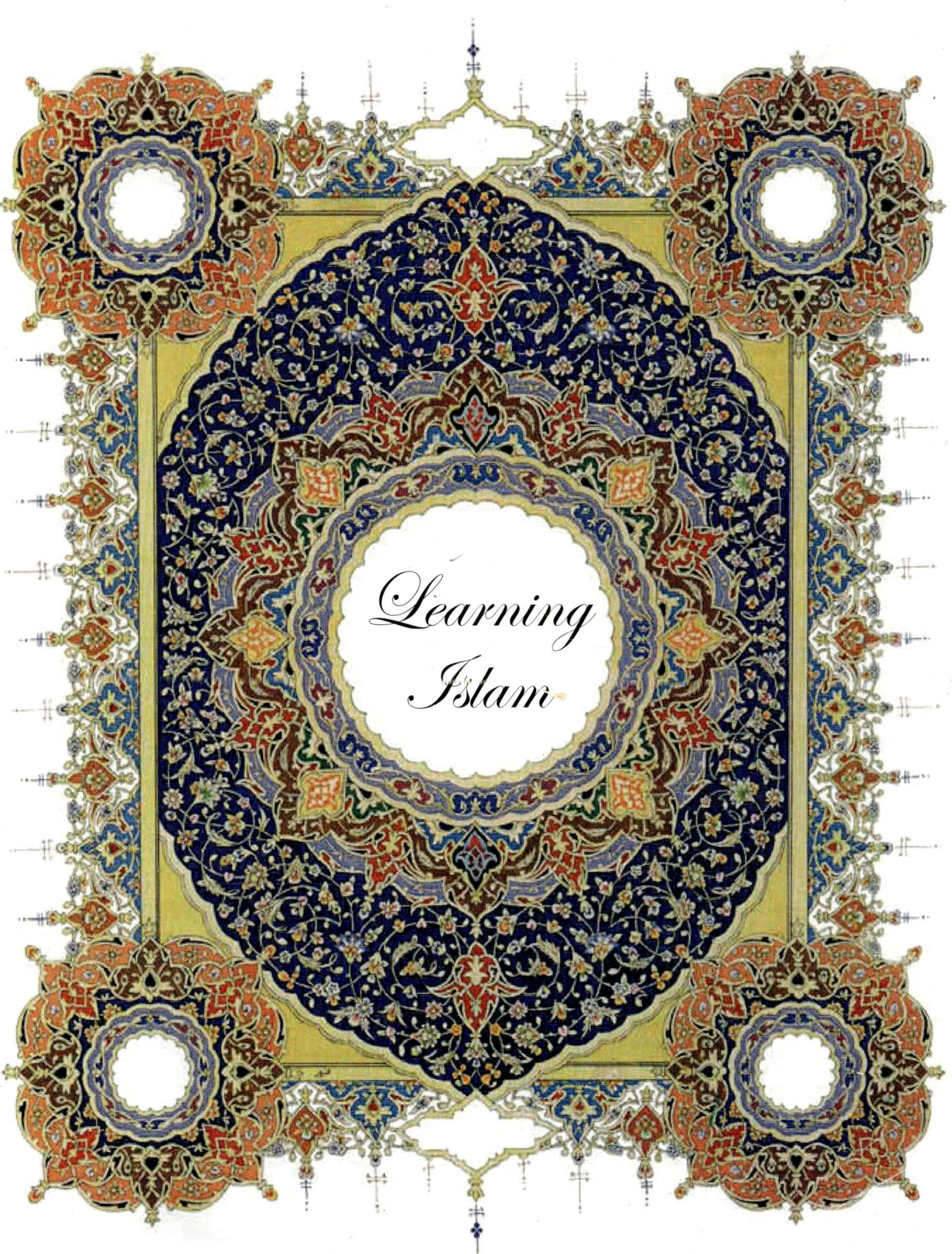
Learning
Islam

PROGRAM DIRECTOR *

Nabil Sadoun, Ed.D.

WRITING TEAM

Suad Abu Amarah
Ummukulthum Al-Maawiy
Lena Dirbashi
Nabil Sadoun, Ed.D.
Omar Tarazi

REVIEWERS AND ADVISORS

Susan Douglass
Freda Shamma, Ph.D.

CONTRIBUTORS

Dianna Abdul-Qadir
Sumayah Al-Khatib
Lana Baghal Dasti
Romana El-Rouby
Nicholas Howard
Hayah Sharif
Menat Zihni

CURRICULUM DESIGN

Nabil Sadoun, Ed.D.
Majida Salem

GRAPHIC DESIGN

Mohammed Eid Mubarak

ILLUSTRATIONS

Raed Abdulwahid
Mahmood Al-Halabi
Ramendranath Sarkar

PHOTOGRAPHY

Al-Anwar Designs

PUBLISHER AND OWNER

Islamic Services Foundation

Islamic Services Foundation
P.O. Box 451623
Garland, TX 75045
Tel: 972-414-5090
Fax: 972-414-5640
www.myislamicbooks.com

* Names are in alphabetical order of the last names.

The Wonderful Unseen World

Faith and Miracles: The Story of Prophet Musa

Al-Qur'an-ul-Kareem: The Last Holy Book

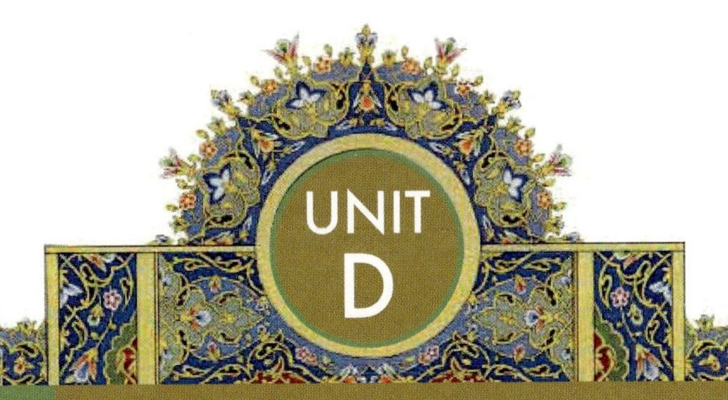

Prophet Muhammad Calls for Peace

Prayer is Light

The Wonderful Unseen World

CHAPTER OUTLINE

1. Belief in the unseen.
2. Some evidence on the existence of the unseen world.
3. How to maintain unshakable faith in Allah and the unseen.

VOCABULARY

Al-Ghayb الغَـيْب

Fitrah فِطرة

"Seeing is believing," this is what people say. This proverb means that one will not believe in the existence of something without actually seeing it. It also means that we would have stronger belief if we see with our own eyes what we are supposed to believe in.

This sounds true, but we believe in many things without having to see them. We don't see electricity, air, gravity and many other things. Still we believe in them because we feel their effects on us. We also see many signs that lead us to believe in the existence of these important things in our life.

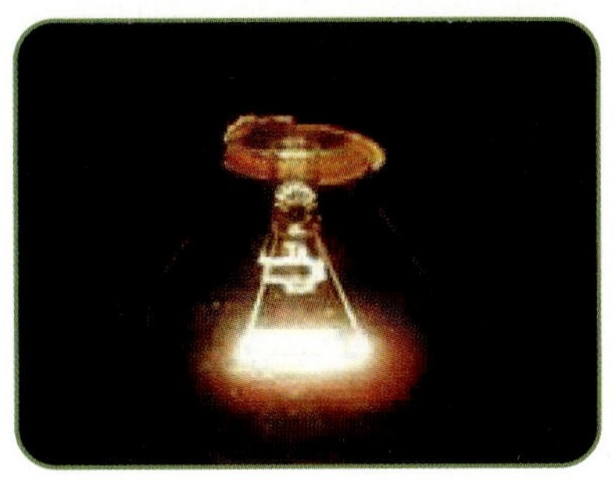

Glowing light bulbs, color TV, the voice of a talk show host on the radio, and the noise of our washer and dryer among, other things, let us know for sure that there is electric current running in the wires. This current these devices and machines to work.

When trees move around, sail boats travel in the oceans, and our kites fly high, we know for sure that air and wind are causing all that to happen.

Football players take it for granted that when they kick the ball up high it must come back down, so they run to catch it. They don't think twice about the role of gravity in bringing that ball to the ground again, but they depend on it.

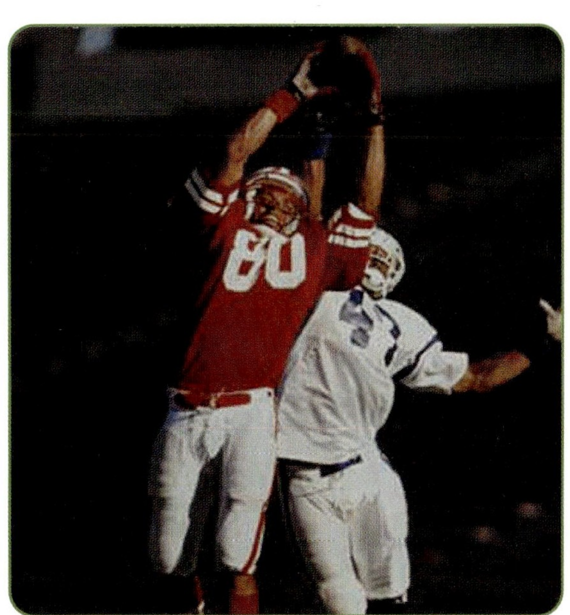

We firmly believe that electric power, air and gravity are there although we don't see them. We just see or feel their effects.

We all also believe that there were famous artists like Monet, Leonardo Da Vinci, and Van Gogh although we did not see them.

We only learned about them in art and social studies books and saw photos of their art. This made us firmly believe that these artists existed. We also believe that they are not alive now because we are told that they died and we do not see any more of their work.

What lessons can we draw from the above observations?

We learn that "seeing is believing" is not always true. We believe in things although we do not see them. Belief in Al-Ghayb الغَيب ,or the Unseen, is a necessity of life.

Logic Leads to Existence of God and the Unseen World.

What do you think about when you come home and see a freshly baked cake? Do you not say, "Hmm, my mother has baked a cake?" This means that if there is something concrete that we can see, then, there must have been someone who made it. If someone told you, "No one baked that cake in the kitchen; it baked itself by accident," you would probably say, "What nonsense! Could a cake bake itself? Someone must have baked it."

What if the person next to you still insists and says: "The screws of the kitchen cupboards became loose and the cupboards started to rock. During this rocking, the flour, butter, sugar, and cocoa fell from them and mixed. They mixed in just the right proportions. That is to say that everything was just the right amount, the sugar, the cocoa...etc. While the mix was falling off the cupboard, it just happened to directly fall into a baking dish that was standing exactly at the point of their fall. Just at that moment, an earthquake took place, and I don't know how the dish got into the oven, but it just did. Even all these coincidences are still not enough to bake the cake. There had to be another coincidence and that is that the oven had to be at the correct temperature setting. Right then, another thing happened by chance; the oven's dial turned on and then later it turned off by itself at the exact moment the cake was done, and so the oven turned itself off before the cake was burned."

Do you think that anyone would believe such a story? Of course, nobody would!

Think for a moment:: to make the sun, stars, seas, lakes, mountains, fish, cats, rabbits and human beings is a lot harder and more complex than producing a cake, but even a cake could not occur by itself through chance. Then to say that the sun or humans have come about on their own is very foolish. If there is someone baking the cake, then there is a very Intelligent Being Who has created the sun and humans. This Being is Allah, our Lord.

The Universe Tells About Allah

When we look at the living things, we learn that there are two dimensions to their existence,

* Material or physical dimension
* Spiritual or meta-physical dimension.

We see their bodies, the material or physical side of their existence, but it is not all that they are made of. The unseen side of their beings is even more important, and that is the soul. Without this unseen soul, living things would not survive. Similarly, we see this great universe which includes the Earth, the planets and amazing galaxies. That is the material side of our world, but we don't see the much greater unseen force that keeps our universe alive. That unseen force is the Creator and the Sustainer of every atom in this great universe; Allah or God.

We do not see God, but we see and feel the signs and evidences of His existence every second of our lives. We feel it in our heartbeats, with every breath we take and with every blink of our eyes. We see these signs when we see babies born, flowers spread their colors and scents, birds fly up high, animals roaming forests and deserts, and amazing fish swimming down deep in rivers, seas, and oceans. We see great evidence of God's existence in billions and billions of stars and planets traveling the endless space for billions of years without crashing into each other.

This seen universe is great, but it is nothing compared to the greatness of its maker, Allah the unseen God. Let's ponder on the following verses of the Qur'an:

﴿أَفَلَا يَنظُرُونَ إِلَى ٱلۡإِبِلِ كَيۡفَ خُلِقَتۡ ١٧ وَإِلَى
ٱلسَّمَآءِ كَيۡفَ رُفِعَتۡ ١٨ وَإِلَى ٱلۡجِبَالِ كَيۡفَ نُصِبَتۡ ١٩
وَإِلَى ٱلۡأَرۡضِ كَيۡفَ سُطِحَتۡ ٢٠﴾

الغاشية: ١٧ - ٢٠

Do they not look at the camels, how they are made?

And at the sky, how it is raised high?

And the mountains, how they are set up?

And the Earth, how it is spread?* Remind them, for you are just a reminder. [88:17-20]

﴿فَلۡيَنظُرِ ٱلۡإِنسَٰنُ إِلَىٰ طَعَامِهِۦٓ ٢٤ أَنَّا صَبَبۡنَا ٱلۡمَآءَ صَبّٗا ٢٥
ثُمَّ شَقَقۡنَا ٱلۡأَرۡضَ شَقّٗا ٢٦ فَأَنۢبَتۡنَا فِيهَا حَبّٗا ٢٧ وَعِنَبٗا وَقَضۡبٗا
٢٨ وَزَيۡتُونٗا وَنَخۡلٗا ٢٩ وَحَدَآئِقَ غُلۡبٗا ٣٠ وَفَٰكِهَةٗ وَأَبّٗا
٣١ مَّتَٰعٗا لَّكُمۡ وَلِأَنۡعَٰمِكُمۡ ٣٢﴾

عبس: ٢٤ - ٣٢

Then let man look at his food,
How We pour water in showers
Then split the Earth in clefts
And cause the grain to grow therein
And grapes and nutritious plants,
And olive-trees and palm-trees
And enclosed gardens, dense with lofty trees,
And fruits and grasses:
A convenience for you and for your cattle. [80:24-32]

Worshipping Allah is an expression of gratefulness to Allah. It also connects us with our Creator and brings peace and happiness into our hearts.

Belief in the unseen is the central part of faith in Islam. It is also something we are born with. Allah created us in a fashion that enables us to feel deep in our hearts and minds that we are created by one great God, Allah. This profound feeling is called Fitrah فِطرة . Fitrah inspires us from within to believe in our Creator, love and obey Him, follow His guidance and do good deeds.

To be a Muslim, one has to believe in God, His angels, His books, His messengers, the Day of Judgment, and Al-Qadar. As you learned during the past years, these are called Arkan-ul-Iman meaning "the Pillars of Faith." Almost all of these pillars are unseen to mankind. Only a small percentage of human beings have seen the prophets, and the rest of us can see only one pillar, the Qur'an. The rest of the pillars of Faith are unseen to us in this world.

Allah expects us to believe firmly in Him and the unseen world. This belief requires us to love, obey and worship Him.

سورة البقرة
Surat-ul-Baqarah 1-5

الٓمّ ﴿١﴾ ذَٰلِكَ ٱلْكِتَٰبُ لَا رَيْبَ ۛ فِيهِ ۛ هُدًى لِّلْمُتَّقِينَ ﴿٢﴾ ٱلَّذِينَ يُؤْمِنُونَ بِٱلْغَيْبِ وَيُقِيمُونَ ٱلصَّلَوٰةَ وَمِمَّا رَزَقْنَٰهُمْ يُنفِقُونَ ﴿٣﴾ وَٱلَّذِينَ يُؤْمِنُونَ بِمَآ أُنزِلَ إِلَيْكَ وَمَآ أُنزِلَ مِن قَبْلِكَ وَبِٱلْءَاخِرَةِ هُمْ يُوقِنُونَ ﴿٤﴾ أُو۟لَٰٓئِكَ عَلَىٰ هُدًى مِّن رَّبِّهِمْ ۖ وَأُو۟لَٰٓئِكَ هُمُ ٱلْمُفْلِحُونَ ﴿٥﴾

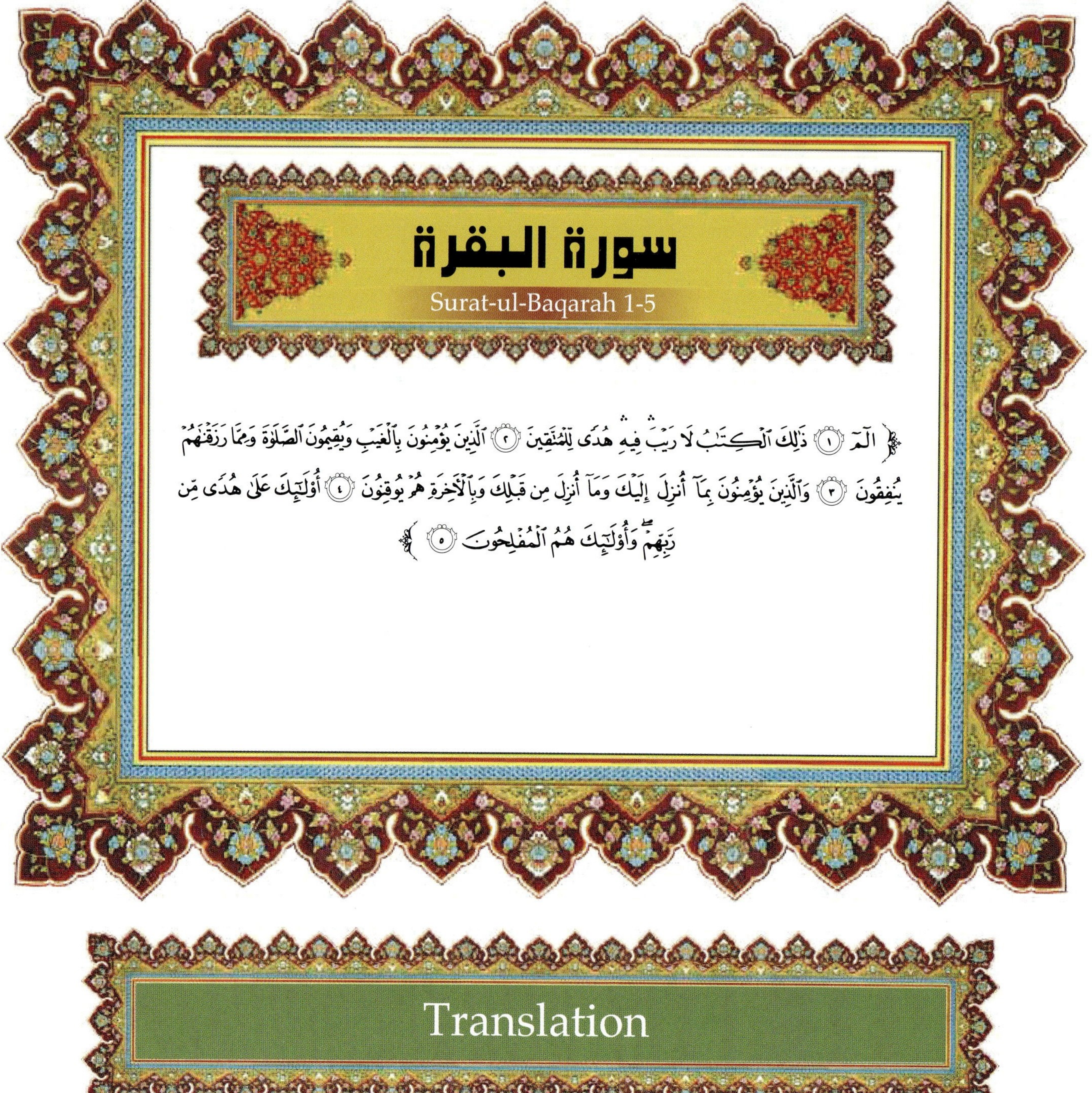

Translation

[2:1] Alif Lam Mim.

[2:2] This is the Book, there is no doubt in it, it is a guide to those who are pious.

[2:3] Those who believe in the unseen and keep up prayer and spend out of what We have given them.

[2:4] And [those] who believe in what has been revealed to you and that which was revealed before you and they firmly believe in the Hereafter.

[2:5] These are on a right guidance from their Lord and they shall be successful [in this life and the next].

How to Believe in the Unseen

Frail belief is not accepted in matters of religion. True believers carry in their hearts and minds unshakable belief in God and the unseen world. Prophet Muhammad taught early Muslims how to develop strong faith.

One day, Rasoolullah was sitting in the masjid when a man called Harithah came. The Prophet asked Harithah: "How are you this morning?"

"I am a true believer, today," Harithah replied.

"This needs to be proved," the Prophet contended.

"Oh Rasoolullah, I believe in Allah as if I see Him with my own eyes on His throne. I believe in the Paradise as if I see people in it visiting each other. And I believe in Hell as if I actually see and hear its people fighting each other in it."

Then the Prophet said to Harithah "You truly know how to believe [in the unseen], so keep up."

Faith in Islam doesn't only mean that you believe in God. Faith also means that you love, glorify, obey and worship Allah. Faith, love, obedience, worship and good actions are inseparable in Islam.

99 Names of Allah

الباطن

Al-Batin

Al-Batin الباطِن , the Unseen. He cannot be seen by his servants in this life but they see his power, greatness, mercy, compassion and marvelous creation in this world. And that is why He is also called Ath-Thahir الظاهر , The Obvious or The Evident. His works, miracles and blessings are evident everywhere and cannot be ignored. He is Unseen, but our eyes see the evidence of his existence wherever we look.

Allah says in Surat-ul-Hadeed,

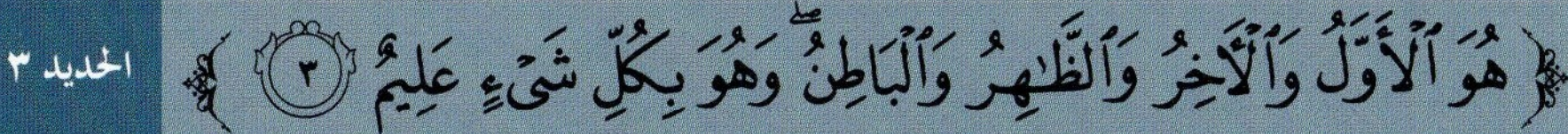

﴿ هُوَ ٱلْأَوَّلُ وَٱلْـَٔاخِرُ وَٱلظَّـٰهِرُ وَٱلْبَاطِنُ ۖ وَهُوَ بِكُلِّ شَىْءٍ عَلِيمٌ ۝٣ ﴾

الحديد ٣

He is the First and the Last and the Evident and the Unseen, and He is knowledgeable of all things. [57:3]

Selected Story

Zaid went once to a museum about world religions. As he was browsing around the museum, he saw the museum guide talking about God to a group of boys and girls. The man was saying that there is no God. Zaid listened to the following discussion:
Guide: Do you see this wall?
Students: Yes!
Guide: So the wall exists. Do you see that window?
Students: Yes!
Guide: So the window exists. Do you see the sky from that window?
Students: Yes!
Guide: So the sky exists. How about the trees outside?
Students: Yes, we see them.
Guide: So the trees exist. Now do you see angels anywhere?
Students: No
Guide: Angels do not exist. How about devils?
Students: No, not really!
Guide: So, devils also do not exist. Now, the big question. Do you see God?
The young students got totally confused. They could not give an answer.
The guide now insisted on his tricky question.
Guide: Tell me, do you see God.
Students: (Reluctantly) Not really.
Guide: Then, God does not exist. There is no God at all.

Now Zaid got really nervous. He realized that the wicked guide was trying to brainwash the tender minds of those young students. Zaid stepped ahead and asked the permission of the guide to speak. The guide agreed. Zaid now started to ask the young students a few similar questions. He pointed at the guide and asked, Friends, do you see this respected gentleman?
Students: Sure!
Zaid: So, he definitely exists. Do you see his green jacket?
Students: Yeah, we see it.
Zaid: Then, his green jacket exists. How about his glasses?
Students: Yeah.
Zaid: Then, they exist. They are a little funny though.
The students started to laugh.
Zaid: Now the big question, do you see his mind?
Students: No, not really.
Zaid: So, this gentleman has no mind!!

The students exploded laughing.

Then Zaid told the students. God does exist. He created this world and all of us. The fact that we do not see him does not mean he is not there.

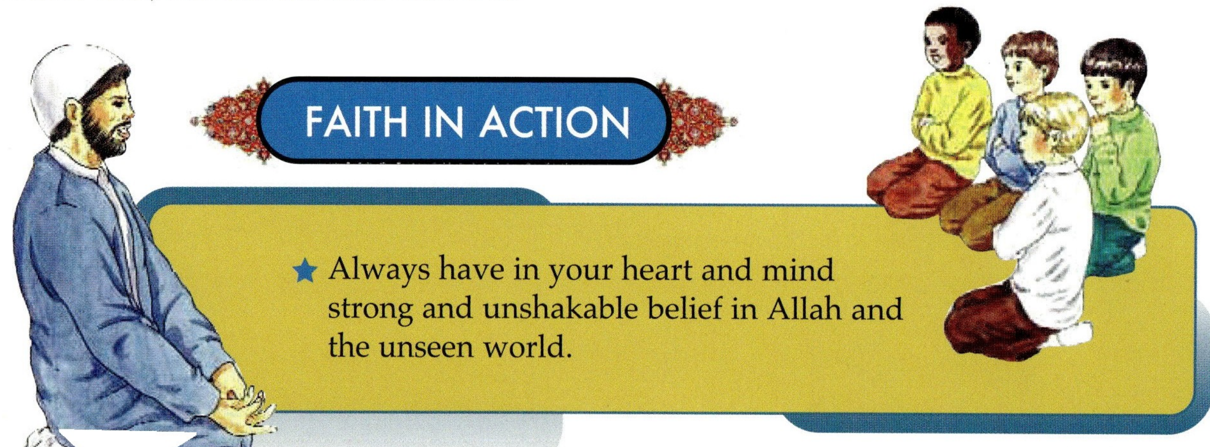

FAITH IN ACTION

★ Always have in your heart and mind strong and unshakable belief in Allah and the unseen world.

CHAPTER REVIEW

Projects and Activities

1. Watch the documentary "God Known through Reason" by Harun Yahya.

2. Write a letter to a friend, who doesn't believe in the spiritual world, trying to persuade him or her to believe in God and the unseen world.

Stretch Your Mind

1. Why do you think some people only believe in the material world and disbelieve in the spiritual unseen world?

2. "Allah is unseen, but He is obvious." Explain this statement.

Study Questions

1. This world we live in is divided into two important sides or dimensions. What are they?
2. Define: a. Al-Ghayb b. Fitrah c. Ath-Thahir
3. List three things in our life that we do not see but we know that they exist.
4. What are some proofs of strong belief in the unseen, as shown in the story of Harithah with Rasoolullah?
5. What is the name of Allah that means "The Unseen"? Write one ayah that includes that name in Arabic and English.

CHAPTER OUTLINE

1. Who is Allah?
2. Allah is the Creator of the universe.
3. Allah is the Creator of mankind.
4. Why did Allah create us?
5. The names and attributes of God.

VOCABULARY

Ayat-ul-Kursi	آية الكرسي
Tawheed	توحيد
Tawheed-ul-Khaliq	توحيد الخالق
Tawheed-ul-Ibadah	توحيد العبادة
Tawheed-ul-Asmaa'	توحيد الأسماء
was-Sifaat	والصفات

Allah, by far, is the greatest of the unseen world. He is the source and the Creator of the seen and unseen sides of the universe. In this chapter we are going to learn about our great Creator in some detailed manner. Perhaps the best way to learn about Him is through learning how He described Himself. The best description of Allah can be found in Al-Qur'an.

Who is Allah?

The greatest Ayah in Al-Qur'an is Ayat-ul-Kursi, which is ayah 255 in Surat-ul-Baqarah. Prophet Muhammad recommended that we should at least read it in the morning and the evening. He even recommended that we read it after every salah.

﴿ ٱللَّهُ لَآ إِلَٰهَ إِلَّا هُوَ ٱلۡحَيُّ ٱلۡقَيُّومُۚ لَا تَأۡخُذُهُۥ سِنَةٞ وَلَا نَوۡمٞۚ لَّهُۥ مَا فِي ٱلسَّمَٰوَٰتِ وَمَا فِي ٱلۡأَرۡضِۗ مَن ذَا ٱلَّذِي يَشۡفَعُ عِندَهُۥٓ إِلَّا بِإِذۡنِهِۦۚ يَعۡلَمُ مَا بَيۡنَ أَيۡدِيهِمۡ وَمَا خَلۡفَهُمۡۖ وَلَا يُحِيطُونَ بِشَيۡءٖ مِّنۡ عِلۡمِهِۦٓ إِلَّا بِمَا شَآءَۚ وَسِعَ كُرۡسِيُّهُ ٱلسَّمَٰوَٰتِ وَٱلۡأَرۡضَۖ وَلَا يَـُٔودُهُۥ حِفۡظُهُمَاۚ وَهُوَ ٱلۡعَلِيُّ ٱلۡعَظِيمُ ٢٥٥ ﴾

البقرة: ٢٥٥

Allah! There is no god but He, the alive, the Eternal. No slumber can overtake Him nor sleep. His are all things in the Heavens and on Earth. Who is there that can intercede in His presence except as He permits? He knows everything that appears to His creations and what is beyond them. They cannot comprehend anything out of His knowledge except what He wants them to know. His throne extends over the Heavens and the Earth, and He feels no fatigue in guarding and preserving them for He is the Most High, the Great. [2:255]

In this Ayah, Allah presented the following facts about Himself:

1. His name is Allah
2. He is the only God of the universe.

3. He has no weaknesses or deficiencies, like getting tired and needing rest.
4. He owns and controls the Earth, the Heavens and the whole universe.
5. No one can do anything in this universe without His permission.
6. His knowledge covers and encompasses every single thing in the universe.
7. Nobody can learn anything in this world without Allah's approval.
8. His throne extends over the Heavens and Earth.
9. Allah controls the universe and protects it without any difficulty.
10. Allah is the Supreme Being and the Great Lord of the Universe.

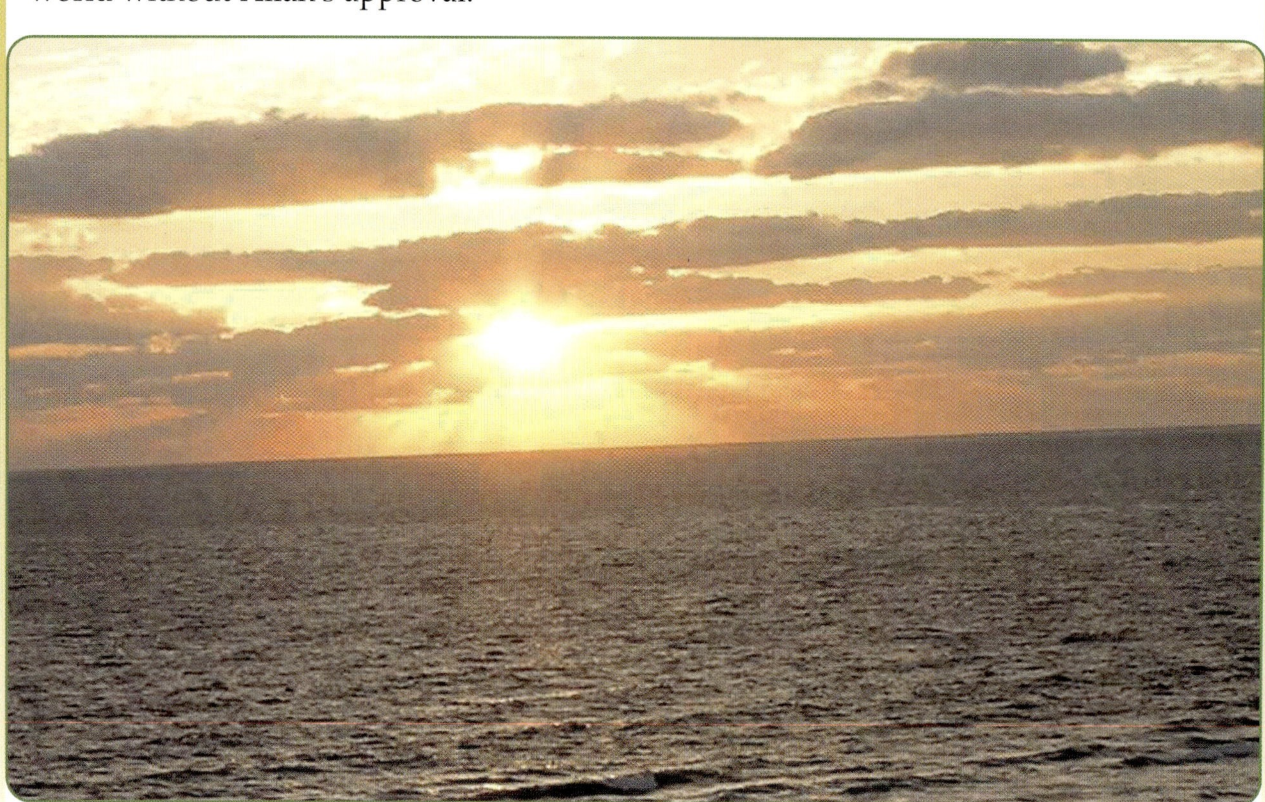

Allah is the Creator of the Universe

There is only one creator of this universe; God or Allah سبحانه وتعالى. No one has the power to create anything from nothing except Him. Listen to what Allah says in Surat-ul-A'raf:

﴿إِنَّ رَبَّكُمُ ٱللَّهُ ٱلَّذِى خَلَقَ ٱلسَّمَٰوَٰتِ وَٱلْأَرْضَ فِى
سِتَّةِ أَيَّامٍ ثُمَّ ٱسْتَوَىٰ عَلَى ٱلْعَرْشِ يُغْشِى ٱلَّيْلَ ٱلنَّهَارَ
يَطْلُبُهُۥ حَثِيثًا وَٱلشَّمْسَ وَٱلْقَمَرَ وَٱلنُّجُومَ مُسَخَّرَٰتٍۭ
بِأَمْرِهِۦٓ ۗ أَلَا لَهُ ٱلْخَلْقُ وَٱلْأَمْرُ ۗ تَبَارَكَ ٱللَّهُ رَبُّ ٱلْعَٰلَمِينَ

﴾

الأعراف: ٥٤

Surely your Lord is Allah, Who created the Heavens and the Earth in six days, then He mounted the Throne; He covers the day with the night, which follows it in a fast manner, and (He created) the sun and the moon and the stars, they all follow His order; surely His is all the power to create and command; blessed is Allah, the Lord of the worlds. [7:54]

This beautiful ayah leads us to the following conclusions:

1. Allah created the Heavens and the Earth in six days.
2. Allah is in the Heavens on His throne.
3. And He reaches everywhere with powers and blessings.
4. He created the sun, the moon and the stars.
5. He controls night and day.
6. Allah controls the affairs of the world.
7. He is full of blessings.
8. He is the only Lord of all the worlds.

ALLAH THE MAKER

Everything that we see around us,
Allah made it for us.
Allah made the sky and the land,
Allah made the sea and the sand.
Allah made the plants and the trees,
Allah made the birds and the bees.
Allah made the hills and the rivers,
Allah made the beautiful flowers.
Allah made the sun to give us heat and light,
Allah made the moon to brighten the sky at night.
Allah made the twinkling stars,
Allah made us as we are.

Allah is the Creator of Mankind

Yet, many people ask this question, “Where did we come from?” They ask about the maker of the whole human race. The Qur'an answers in Surat As-Sajdah:

﴿ ذَٰلِكَ عَٰلِمُ ٱلۡغَيۡبِ وَٱلشَّهَٰدَةِ ٱلۡعَزِيزُ ٱلرَّحِيمُ ٦
ٱلَّذِيٓ أَحۡسَنَ كُلَّ شَيۡءٍ خَلَقَهُۥۖ وَبَدَأَ خَلۡقَ ٱلۡإِنسَٰنِ مِن
طِينٖ ٧ ﴾

السجدة: ٦ - ٧

This is the Knower of the unseen and the seen, the Almighty the Merciful, who perfected everything that He has created, and He began the creation of man from clay. [32:6-7]

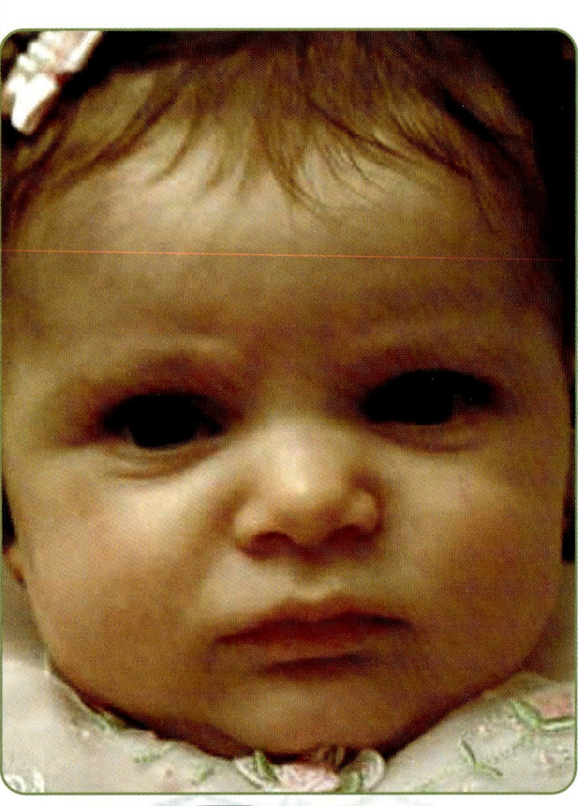

﴿ يَٰٓأَيُّهَا ٱلنَّاسُ ٱتَّقُواْ رَبَّكُمُ ٱلَّذِي خَلَقَكُم مِّن نَّفۡسٖ وَٰحِدَةٖ وَخَلَقَ
مِنۡهَا زَوۡجَهَا وَبَثَّ مِنۡهُمَا رِجَالٗا كَثِيرٗا وَنِسَآءٗۚ وَٱتَّقُواْ ٱللَّهَ ٱلَّذِي
تَسَآءَلُونَ بِهِۦ وَٱلۡأَرۡحَامَۚ إِنَّ ٱللَّهَ كَانَ عَلَيۡكُمۡ رَقِيبٗا ١ ﴾

النساء: ١

Oh people! fear your Lord, Who created you from a single person [Adam] and created its mate of the same (kind) and spread from these two, many men and women; and fear Allah, by Whom you ask your rights from others, and be careful of the ties of relationship; surely Allah ever watches over you. [4:1]

﴿ وَلَقَدۡ خَلَقۡنَا ٱلۡإِنسَٰنَ مِن سُلَٰلَةٖ مِّن طِينٖ ١٢ ثُمَّ
جَعَلۡنَٰهُ نُطۡفَةٗ فِي قَرَارٖ مَّكِينٖ ١٣ ثُمَّ خَلَقۡنَا ٱلنُّطۡفَةَ
عَلَقَةٗ فَخَلَقۡنَا ٱلۡعَلَقَةَ مُضۡغَةٗ فَخَلَقۡنَا ٱلۡمُضۡغَةَ
عِظَٰمٗا فَكَسَوۡنَا ٱلۡعِظَٰمَ لَحۡمٗا ثُمَّ أَنشَأۡنَٰهُ خَلۡقًا ءَاخَرَۚ
فَتَبَارَكَ ٱللَّهُ أَحۡسَنُ ٱلۡخَٰلِقِينَ ١٤ ﴾

المؤمنون: ١٢ - ١٤

Verily We created man from a product of wet earth;

Then placed him as a drop in a safe and fixed place (the womb);

Then We made the drop a clot of blood, then We made the clot a chewed lump- like of flesh, then We made (in) the lump of flesh bones, then We clothed the bones with flesh, then We caused it to grow into another creation, so blessed be Allah, the best of the creators![23:12-14]

The previous ayaat teach us the following lessons:

1. Allah first created Adam from a kind of clay. Adam was the first human to be created.

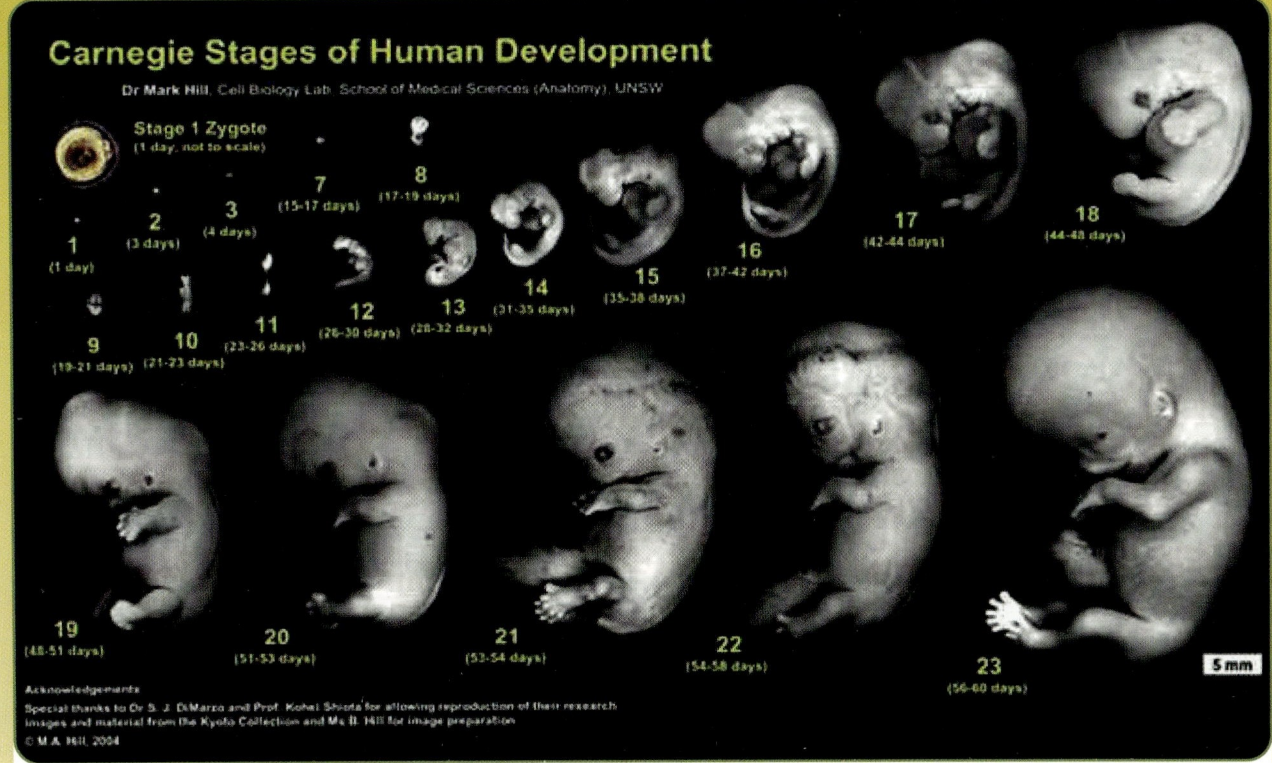

This shows when the embryo (baby in the womb) is in the Mudghah or chewed-like lump

2. Allah created the first female human from Adam. Prophet Muhammad said she was created from Adam's rib. Ancient books give her the name Eve, or Hawwaa' in Arabic.
3. All human beings are the descendants of Adam and Eve. Some scholars call Adam the "Father of all humans."
4. Every human being starts as a drop in the womb of a female. Then the drop becomes a clot of blood, and then the clot becomes a tissue that looks like a chewed curvy gum. Later, very tiny bones grow in the tissue and the bones are covered by more flesh. Then this will be fashioned as a little baby and is born as a new human being.

Why Did Allah Create Us?

Allah answers this question very clearly in Surat-uth-Thariyat:

﴿ وَمَا خَلَقْتُ ٱلْجِنَّ وَٱلْإِنسَ إِلَّا لِيَعْبُدُونِ ﴿٥٦﴾ ﴾

الذاريات: ٥٦

I created the jinn and mankind only to worship Me. [51:56]

Then in Surat-ul-Mulk, he says:

﴿ تَبَٰرَكَ ٱلَّذِى بِيَدِهِ ٱلْمُلْكُ وَهُوَ عَلَىٰ كُلِّ شَىْءٍ قَدِيرٌ ﴿١﴾ ٱلَّذِى خَلَقَ ٱلْمَوْتَ وَٱلْحَيَوٰةَ لِيَبْلُوَكُمْ أَيُّكُمْ أَحْسَنُ عَمَلًا ۚ وَهُوَ ٱلْعَزِيزُ ٱلْغَفُورُ ﴿٢﴾ ﴾

الملك: ١ - ٢

Blessed is He in Whose hand is the kingdom, and He has power over all things,

Who created death and life that He may test you-- which of you is best in deeds; and He is the Mighty, the Forgiving. [67:1-2]

We learn from the above ayaat the following lessons:

1. God created us so we would worship and serve Him.
2. He wanted to test humans and make them compete in doing the best deeds they can do.

If people obey Allah and do exactly what He created them for, they will become pious and well-behaved human beings. They will serve Allah and His creation in a sincere and continuous manner. Thus they will enjoy living together on this Earth and deserve to go back to the wonderful Jannah, their original home. This is exactly what Allah wants. He wants Adam and all his offspring to enjoy living in Paradise for eternity, except those who refuse to do so. You might ask, "Who in the world would refuse to go to Jannah?" The answer to this question is in the following Hadeeth:

Hadeeth Shareef

عَنْ أبي هُرَيْرَة رَضِيَ اللهُ عَنْهُ قالَ : قالَ رَسولُ اللهِ صَلى اللهُ عليْه وسَلّم :

"كُلُّ أمّتي يَدْخلون الجَنَّة إلا مَنْ أبى"

"قالوا: وَمَنْ يأبى يا رَسولَ الله ؟"

"قالَ: مَنْ أطاعَني دخَلَ الجَنَّة ، وَمَنْ عَصاني فَقَدْ أبى"

رواه البخاري

Abu Hurayrah رضي الله عنه narrated, that Rasoolullah said, "All of my people will enter Paradise except those who refuse."

"Who would refuse?" The Sahabah asked.

"Whoever obeys me will enter Paradise, and those who disobey me are refusing [to enter it], the Prophet explained.

Reported in Saheeh Al-Bukhari

The Names and Attributes of Allah

﴿ هُوَ ٱللَّهُ ٱلَّذِى لَآ إِلَٰهَ إِلَّا هُوَ ۖ عَٰلِمُ ٱلْغَيْبِ
وَٱلشَّهَٰدَةِ ۖ هُوَ ٱلرَّحْمَٰنُ ٱلرَّحِيمُ (٢٢) هُوَ ٱللَّهُ ٱلَّذِى
لَآ إِلَٰهَ إِلَّا هُوَ ٱلْمَلِكُ ٱلْقُدُّوسُ ٱلسَّلَٰمُ ٱلْمُؤْمِنُ
ٱلْمُهَيْمِنُ ٱلْعَزِيزُ ٱلْجَبَّارُ ٱلْمُتَكَبِّرُ ۚ سُبْحَٰنَ
ٱللَّهِ عَمَّا يُشْرِكُونَ (٢٣) هُوَ ٱللَّهُ ٱلْخَٰلِقُ ٱلْبَارِئُ
ٱلْمُصَوِّرُ ۖ لَهُ ٱلْأَسْمَآءُ ٱلْحُسْنَىٰ ۚ يُسَبِّحُ لَهُۥ مَا فِى ٱلسَّمَٰوَٰتِ
وَٱلْأَرْضِ ۖ وَهُوَ ٱلْعَزِيزُ ٱلْحَكِيمُ (٢٤) ﴾

الحشر: ٢٢ - ٢٤

He is Allah! There is no god but He; the Knower of the unseen and the seen; He is Most Gracious, Most Merciful.

He is Allah! There is no god but He; the King, the Holy, the Giver of Peace, the Giver of Faith, Guardian Over All, the Mighty, the Supreme, the Possessor of Every Greatness, Glory be to Allah above the false gods they attribute to Him.

He is Allah the Creator, the Maker, the Fashioner; His are the most beautiful names; all that is in the Heavens and the Earth glorifies Him; and He is the Mighty, the Wise. [59:22-24]

Tawheed: The Oneness of Allah

From the above, we learn three major lessons:

1. God is the only God and creator of this universe. No one has the right to claim that he created this universe or even parts of it except Allah Almighty. We have to adopt this belief wholeheartedly if we want to be true believers. This belief is called in Islam توحيد الخالق "Tawheed-ul-Khaliq", which means believing in one Creator or believing in one Lord. Scholars also call this type of Tawheed, "Tawheed-ur-Ruboobiyyah" which is derived from the Arabic word "Rabb," meaning Lord.

2. No one is worthy of worship except God, our Creator and the creator of the universe. Worshipping Allah in fact is a must on us. This belief is called توحيد العبادة "Tawheed-ul-Ibadah," which means the belief in only worshipping the One True God. Scholars also call this type of Tawheed, "Tawheed-ul-Uloohiyyah" which is derived from the Arabic word "Ilah," meaning God.

3. God has the highest and greatest names and attributes. No one has these great names and attributes except Allah the creator. This belief is called in Islam توحيد الأسماء والصفات Tawheed-ul-Asmaa' was-Sifat. It means that only God has all the great names and attributes. He is free of all weaknesses and deficiencies.

Types of Tawheed:

1 **Tawheed-ul-Khaliq**

Believing in The One True Creator

توحيد الخالق (الربوبية)

2 **Tawheed-ul-Ibadah**

Worshipping The One True Creator

توحيد العبادة (الألوهية)

3 **Tawheed-ul-Asmaa' Was-Sifat**

Believing in The Unique Attributes of Allah

توحيد الأسماء والصفات

A Poem

YA ALLAH!

When Adam ate the forbidden fruit, he cried, "Ya Allah!"
So Allah forgave him and erased his sin.
When Abraham was thrown into the fire, he cried, "Ya Allah!"
So Allah saved him and made the fire cool.
When ordered to sacrifice his son, he cried, "Ya Allah!"
So Allah replaced his son with a mountain goat.
When Hagar had nothing to feed her baby, she cried, "Ya Allah!"
So Allah burst forth for her the Spring of Zamzam.

When Joseph was thrown into the well, he cried, "Ya Allah!"
So Allah reassured him of His help and victory.
When Jacob became blind at the grief of his missing son, he cried, "Ya Allah!"
So Allah restored his sight and returned to him his son.
When Musa fled his land in fear, he cried, "Ya Allah!"
So Allah gave him safety in the farmer's house.
When Phir'oun's army closed in on them, he cried, "Ya Allah!"
So Allah parted the sea for them and drowned their enemy.

When Job was stricken with distress, he cried, "Ya Allah!"
So Allah restored for him his health and wealth.
When Jonah lay at the bottom of the sea, he cried, "Ya Allah!"
So Allah ordered the whale to bring him to shore.
When David met Goliath, he cried, "Ya Allah!"
So Allah gave him victory and Goliath was slain.
When they tried to crucify Jesus, he cried, "Ya Allah!"
So Allah raised him up and saved him from crucifixion.

When Muhammad's followers were tortured, he cried, "Ya Allah!"
So Allah opened for them the way to Madinah.
When he was nearly captured in the cave, he cried, "Ya Allah!"
So Allah's spider spun a web and concealed him.
When his army was outnumbered at Badr, he cried, "Ya Allah!"
So Allah sent down angels to rout his foe.
When his Companions were massacred at Mauna, he cried, "Ya Allah!"
So Allah avenged their deaths and destroyed the oppressors.

When a ship is tossed by a storm, they cry, "Ya Allah!"
So Allah brings them safely to land.
When trapped in a dark hole, they cry, "Ya Allah!"
So Allah enlightens them with an opening.
When the rope becomes too tight, they cry, "Ya Allah!"

99 Names of Allah

البديع

Al-Badee'

Allah is Al-Badee' البديع, The Innovative
Creator. He creates things without any pre-existing
mode. His creation is beautiful, magnificent and marvelous.
Allah says in Surat-ul-An'aam,

[He is the] Wonderful Originator of the Heavens and the Earth, and
when He decides on doing something, He only says to it, be, so there it is.
[2:117]

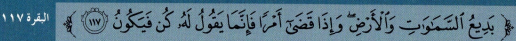

{ بَدِيعُ ٱلسَّمَٰوَٰتِ وَٱلْأَرْضِ ۖ وَإِذَا قَضَىٰ أَمْرًا فَإِنَّمَا يَقُولُ لَهُۥ كُن فَيَكُونُ ﴿١١٧﴾ } البقرة ١١٧

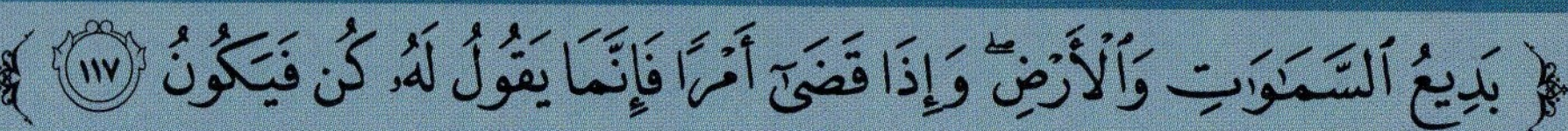

FAITH IN ACTION

★ 1. Always have a firm and unshakable
belief in Allah as the one and only Creator
of the Universe.

★ 2. Always worship Allah alone and serve His cause.

★ 3. Always learn and remember the great attributes of Allah.
Glorify and praise Him in your heart, mind, tongue and
actions.

CHAPTER REVIEW

Projects and Activities

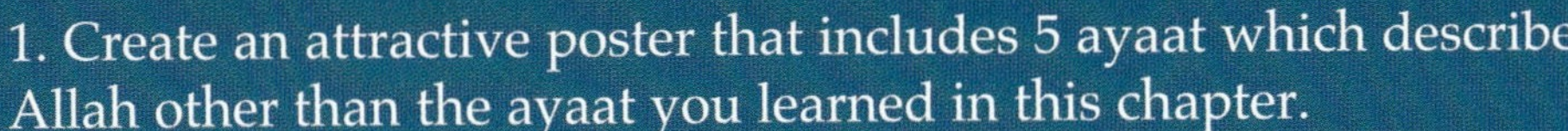

1. Create an attractive poster that includes 5 ayaat which describe Allah other than the ayaat you learned in this chapter.

2. Write a 500-word essay titled "Allah as I Know Him."

Stretch Your Mind

1. Why do you think Allah did not want us to see Him with our eyes in this life?

2. What are the differences between God and powerful people?

Study Questions

1. List three of the special qualities of Allah that make Him so great.
2. Where is Allah?
3. If a confused person asked you, "where did we come from?" How would you answer him or her?
4. Why did Allah create us? Support your answer with evidence from Al-Qur'an.
5. What is the Arabic word for believing in One God?
6. What are the three important ways of believing in One God? Explain each of these ways.
7. List and define ten of the names of Allah.

CHAPTER OUTLINE

1. Think about the World
2. The World of Harmony
3. Signs of the One Great God
4. Many Creations: One God
5. Atheism, Polytheism and Monotheism

VOCABULARY

- Tafakkur تـفـكـّر
- Tawakkul توكُّل

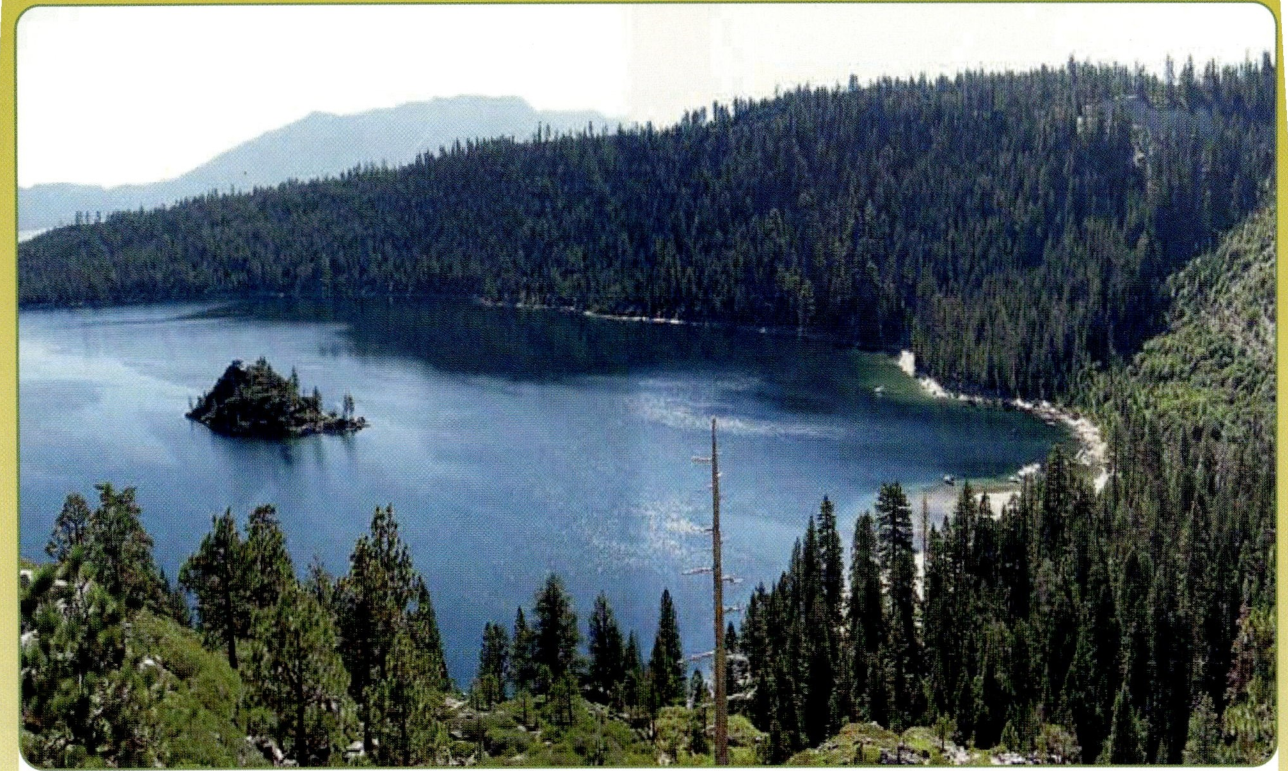

Think about the World

Have you ever wondered how everything around you is made in the most perfect form, balance and harmony? Harmony means that everything is in agreement with each other. The harmony in the world and the universe leads to a grand fact; this universe is the creation of the One and Only God; Allah. The Universe Speaks Tawheed!

In the Qur'an Allah says about the believing people:

﴿ إِنَّ فِي خَلْقِ ٱلسَّمَٰوَٰتِ وَٱلْأَرْضِ وَٱخْتِلَٰفِ ٱلَّيْلِ وَٱلنَّهَارِ لَءَايَٰتٍ لِّأُو۟لِى ٱلْأَلْبَٰبِ ﴿١٩٠﴾ ٱلَّذِينَ يَذْكُرُونَ ٱللَّهَ قِيَٰمًا وَقُعُودًا وَعَلَىٰ جُنُوبِهِمْ وَيَتَفَكَّرُونَ فِي خَلْقِ ٱلسَّمَٰوَٰتِ وَٱلْأَرْضِ رَبَّنَا مَا خَلَقْتَ هَٰذَا بَٰطِلًا سُبْحَٰنَكَ فَقِنَا عَذَابَ ٱلنَّارِ ﴿١٩١﴾ ﴾

آل عمران: ١٩٠ - ١٩١

In the creation of the Heavens and the Earth, and the alternation of night and day, there are Signs for wise people. Those who remember God standing, sitting and lying on their sides, and deeply think about the creation of the Heavens and the Earth, [and say]: "Our Lord, You did not create this for nothing. Glory be to You! So guard us from the punishment of the Fire. [2: 190-191]

The Worship of Tafakkur

This exercise of wondering about the world is called تفكّر Tafakkur as you learned in the above ayah. It means "deep thinking." Tafakkur is an act of worship in Islam because it draws our hearts closer to Allah. Prior to his becoming a prophet, Rasoolullah used to do lot of Tafakkur. As you learned in previous years, Prophet Muhammad used to go up to the mountain of Hiraa' near Makkah and think deeply about the universe and its creator. His heart used to connecﷻrongly with his Creator, Allah .

The people of Quraysh in Makkah used to worship many gods beside Allah, the One True Creator. They set up many idols around Al-Ka'bah and worshipped them. They thought that these stone gods would lead them closer to Allah. Prophet Muhammad never liked what his tribe and other tribes around Arabia did and never worshipped their false gods. Instead, he used to go out in the wilderness and reflect about the universe and its True Creator. Later Allah guided the Prophet to the true faith and made him the last messenger to mankind.

A World of Harmony

When you wake up in the morning is it by chance that breakfast is ready on the table or is it because somebody prepared it? If something as simple as breakfast on the table cannot occur by chance then what about your body, the world, and the whole universe! Surely it did not occur by chance.

Everything in the world and the universe is the Creation of Allah. Not only is Allah the Creator of the universe, but He is also the One and Only Creator.

Look at the perfect human body. You will notice that everything is in its proper place. People can do amazing things using their physical and cognitive powers. Every thing in the human body is designed in the best form. Allah said,

﴿ لَقَدْ خَلَقْنَا ٱلْإِنسَٰنَ فِىٓ أَحْسَنِ تَقْوِيمٍ ﴿٤﴾ ﴾

التين: ٤

Certainly We created man in the best form. [95:4]

Imagine if your eyes are in the back of your head, or your nose is placed by your feet! How annoying and inconvenient that would be. Allah fashioned us in a very intelligent way so we can live happily and interact very well with the world around us.

Now, look at the world around you. You will see how the sun rises from the east and sets in the west every day with amazing accuracy and harmony. The sun makes things warm during the day while at night things cool, and the cycle continues. The sun also brightens the world during the day so people can work and see things easily, while it disappears and causes darkness so we can sleep and rest. Imagine if the sun remains up during the night or disappears during the day all the time. What do you think will happen?

Listen to what Allah says in Surat-ul-Qasas,

﴿ قُلْ أَرَءَيْتُمْ إِن جَعَلَ ٱللَّهُ عَلَيْكُمُ ٱلَّيْلَ سَرْمَدًا إِلَىٰ يَوْمِ
ٱلْقِيَٰمَةِ مَنْ إِلَٰهٌ غَيْرُ ٱللَّهِ يَأْتِيكُم بِضِيَآءٍ أَفَلَا تَسْمَعُونَ
﴿٧١﴾ قُلْ أَرَءَيْتُمْ إِن جَعَلَ ٱللَّهُ عَلَيْكُمُ ٱلنَّهَارَ سَرْمَدًا
إِلَىٰ يَوْمِ ٱلْقِيَٰمَةِ مَنْ إِلَٰهٌ غَيْرُ ٱللَّهِ يَأْتِيكُم بِلَيْلٍ
تَسْكُنُونَ فِيهِ أَفَلَا تُبْصِرُونَ ﴿٧٢﴾ ﴾

القصص: ٧١ - ٧٢

Say: If Allah were to make the night to continue incessantly on you till the day of resurrection, who is the god besides Allah that could bring you light? Do you not then hear? Say: Tell me, if Allah were to make the day to continue incessantly on you till the day of resurrection, who is the god besides Allah that could bring you the night in which you take rest? Do you not then see? [28:71-72]

Allah mentions in the Qur'an that an unbeliever is the one that does not appreciate the signs of Allah. A true believer in God has the ability to see the signs and proofs of Allah's existence, greatness and oneness. A believer can begin to understand the power of Allah through His signs.

Look at the trees in the forest how they provide oxygen for us to breathe while they use the carbon dioxide we exhale. What do you think would happen if trees stopped producing oxygen or if they needed oxygen like we need it?

Go beyond the world around you; look at the stars at night and how brightly they shine. There are trillions and trillions of stars up there. They all travel around in perfect harmony without colliding with each other. Admire the harmony of the universe and how the different planets rotate around the sun. Some people believe that everything in the universe and the world happened by chance. Now, ask yourself can everything that you see around you come into existence by chance? Can this world have this amazing perfection, balance and harmony without the creation and control of a great Lord?

Did You Know?

This exercise of wondering about the world is called تفكّر Tafakkur, and it means "deep thinking." Tafakkur is an act of worship in Islam because it draws our hearts closer to Allah.

Signs of the One Great God

The Miracle of the Brain

Scatter puzzle pieces on the floor and suppose they are the entire knowledge about the world. For instance, let some pieces represent light, some represent colors and let others represent sounds. Now take these pieces one by one and start reassembling them to form the picture. What you can do with the puzzle in a matter of minutes is done hundreds of times in a second by your brain, which works by Allah's inspiration. Do you wonder how?

The brain gathers the information received from the eyes, nose, ears, skin, mouth etc. and interprets that information. What makes this interpretation is a collection of 100 billion nerve cells in your brain. These cells operate continuously and enable you to see the color of the apple you eat, to recognize the voice of your best friend and to perceive the smell of hot chocolate.

The brain consists of nerve cells, which can be seen only under a microscope. Do you think nerve cells can see your favorite toy or taste the flavor of chocolate ice cream? Certainly not! That is because nerve cells are composed of fine pieces of flesh. That's why there must be another being with supreme power that created this wonderful world. This being is Allah. Allah, the possessor of everything, creates everything perfectly and presents each of us with a beautiful life. What we should do in return is to be thankful to our Lord. Allah has given us the abilities of hearing, seeing, smelling, and other senses and powers. He has told us to obey, worship and appreciate Him for all the gifts he bestowed upon us:

﴿ وَهُوَ ٱلَّذِىٓ أَنشَأَ لَكُمُ ٱلسَّمْعَ وَٱلْأَبْصَـٰرَ وَٱلْأَفْـِٔدَةَ ۚ قَلِيلًا مَّا تَشْكُرُونَ ﴿٧٨﴾ ﴾

المؤمنون: ٧٨

It is He Who has created hearing, sight and hearts for you. What little thanks you show! (23: 78)

Ears without any Crackl

﴿ وَٱللَّهُ أَخْرَجَكُم مِّنۢ بُطُونِ أُمَّهَـٰتِكُمْ لَا تَعْلَمُونَ شَيْـًٔا وَجَعَلَ لَكُمُ ٱلسَّمْعَ وَٱلْأَبْصَـٰرَ وَٱلْأَفْـِٔدَةَ ۙ لَعَلَّكُمْ تَشْكُرُونَ ﴿٧٨﴾ ﴾

النحل: ٧٨

And Allah has brought you forth from the wombs of your mothers-- you did not know anything-- and He gave you hearing and sight and hearts that you may give thanks. [16:78]

God has created our ears perfectly just like our eyes. Imagine a stereo, for instance. Even if you turn on the best of stereos, you hear some crackling and hissing sounds. Radio channels often become mixed up. Right now, don't talk but just listen! Do you hear any hissing? Your ears never produce any. You hear the sounds marvelously clearly. Well don't you think that your ears could

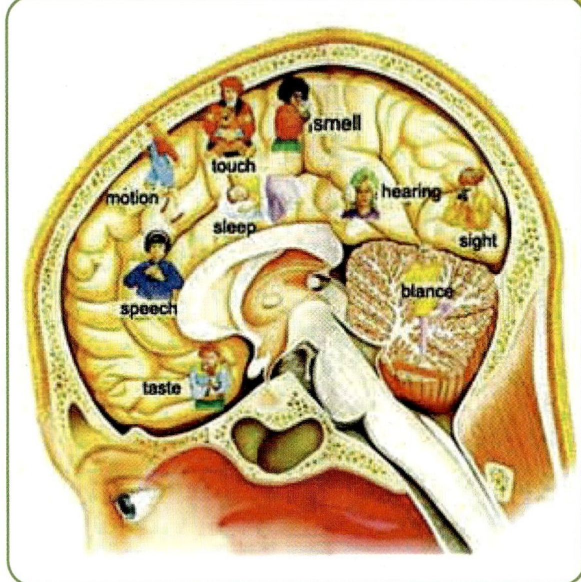

Human Brain

also have produced crackling just like stereos or radios? God has created our ears perfectly and we are able to hear the sounds around us without experiencing any distortion.

God has created our ears in such a way that we are unable to hear certain sounds that would disturb us. The blood in our body, for instance, flows very fast and it makes a lot of noise during its circulation. However, our ears do not hear the noise that it makes. Our planet also produces quite a strong noise while it spins. Nevertheless, God has created our ears so ideally that we don't hear this noise. God is very caring towards us. This is the reason why, throughout our lives, He doesn't let us hear noises that will disturb us. The noises that hurt us are only the noises that we humans create like extra loud music, or machine noise.

This is why we should thank God for His great kindness and invaluable gifts.

Tiny Seeds, Tall Trees

﴿إِنَّ ٱللَّهَ فَالِقُ ٱلْحَبِّ وَٱلنَّوَىٰ ۖ يُخْرِجُ ٱلْحَىَّ مِنَ ٱلْمَيِّتِ
وَمُخْرِجُ ٱلْمَيِّتِ مِنَ ٱلْحَىِّ ۚ ذَٰلِكُمُ ٱللَّهُ ۖ فَأَنَّىٰ تُؤْفَكُونَ ﴿٩٥﴾﴾

الأنعام: ٩٥

"It is God Who causes the seed-grain and the date-stone to split and sprout. He causes the living to come out from the dead, and He is the one to cause the dead to come out from the living. That is God: then how do you distort the truth?" [Surat-ul-An'aam, 6:95]

﴿هُوَ ٱلَّذِىٓ أَنزَلَ مِنَ ٱلسَّمَآءِ مَآءً ۖ لَّكُم مِّنْهُ شَرَابٌ
وَمِنْهُ شَجَرٌ فِيهِ تُسِيمُونَ ﴿١٠﴾ يُنۢبِتُ لَكُم بِهِ ٱلزَّرْعَ
وَٱلزَّيْتُونَ وَٱلنَّخِيلَ وَٱلْأَعْنَٰبَ وَمِن كُلِّ ٱلثَّمَرَٰتِ ۗ إِنَّ فِى
ذَٰلِكَ لَءَايَةً لِّقَوْمٍ يَتَفَكَّرُونَ ﴿١١﴾﴾

النحل: ١٠ - ١١

He sends down water from the cloud for you; it gives drink, and by it (grow) the plants and trees upon which you fodder.

With it He produces for you plants, olives, date-palms, grapes and every kind of fruit: verily in this is a sign for those who think deeply. [Surat-un-Nahl, 16:10-11]

Let's think about the date palm tree mentioned in the verse above. A palm tree is very tall with very big leaves. This huge tree grows from a very small seed planted in the earth. How can a seed know how to make a tree? How can the seed know what type of shape the tree should become? For a plant to

grow it needs certain types of nutrients from the earth. The seed must have some type of intelligence for it to make a tree. How can a seed have intelligence you ask? From the beginning when a seed is created it is programmed to make a tree. Every seed on Earth grows within Allah's knowledge. It is Allah who created the seed and made it able to produce a new tree.

Planet Earth

You may not have thought about it but everything needed to maintain Planet Earth is in perfect balance. The 77% of nitrogen, 21% of oxygen and 1% of carbon dioxide and other gases in the atmosphere represent the exact amount needed for living creatures to survive. Oxygen is a gas that is important for living creatures; it helps burn the food in our bodies to convert to energy. If the amount of oxygen in the air was greater than 21% then the cells in our body would suffer great damage and so would all the other living things that depend on oxygen. The same thing goes for the other gases in the atmosphere. All of them have to be in perfect balance and harmony in order for living things to survive.

A Poem

A Great Place to Stay - Earth!

They call it the "Third rock from the sun" -
and it's the place where we live, work and have fun.
Our lives are all balanced in a delicate theme --
Allah is the Planner and Creator, it is all in His scheme.
If we were just ten degrees closer to His creation, the sun--
by the increase in heat, we'd all be WELL DONE!
And if then from the sun, we were only ten degrees farther away--
only on solid ice would we find any place to stay!
Allah gives us plenty of water and air--
not found anywhere else in the universe - Not anywhere!
Who, but Allah could plan and maintain without any goof--
such a place for us to live and offer so much proof
We can see and enjoy Allah's creation of earth--
but to Allah, we only have any value and worth,
If we acknowledge Him, alone as Creator and Sustainer of all--
then thank and worship Him Alone, -- without any partners at all.

By Yousuf Estes

The Water Cycle

The sun heats the surfaces of large bodies of water and this causes evaporation to occur. The warm air filled with this moisture rises up to the sky, then it cools in the low temperatures there and forms what we call clouds. Winds normally blow these clouds inland. When the temperatures cool off the moisture turns back into water and falls to Earth as rain. Some of this rain gives the soil important nutrients. This revives the plants and the rest falls back into the oceans and rivers. Then the cycle begins again! Can you imagine that this perfect planning can happen by chance? Definitely not! This is another proof or sign of the existence of the One Great Creator. Allah, the only Creator of the whole universe, commands all different forces of nature to work together in perfect harmony and co-ordination.

Suppose that water is available only in seas and oceans. This would make it very hard for people to get water to drink and water their fields and gardens. Allah is merciful, so he brought water out of springs and made it gush into rivers and streams. This way we can get water with some ease. Allah made rivers, streams and valleys everywhere around earth to allow people and animals to drink. This makes people able to grow plants and crops for their food. So rivers and streams act like arteries and veins in the human body. Through blood, they feed body tissues and organs with nutrients and water. Imagine what would happen if blood was kept in one place in your body.

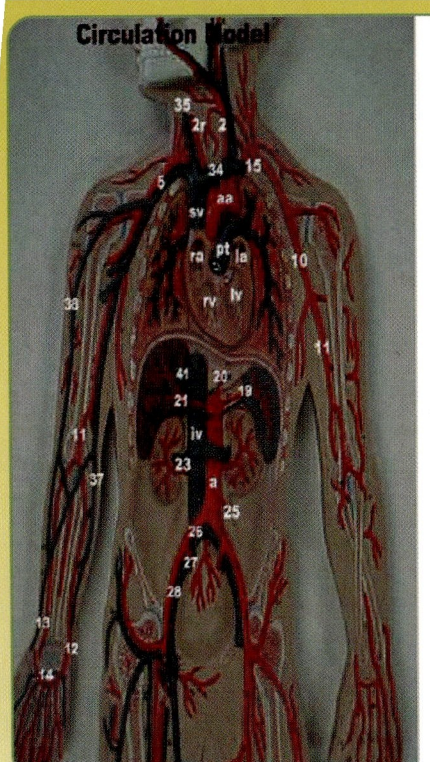

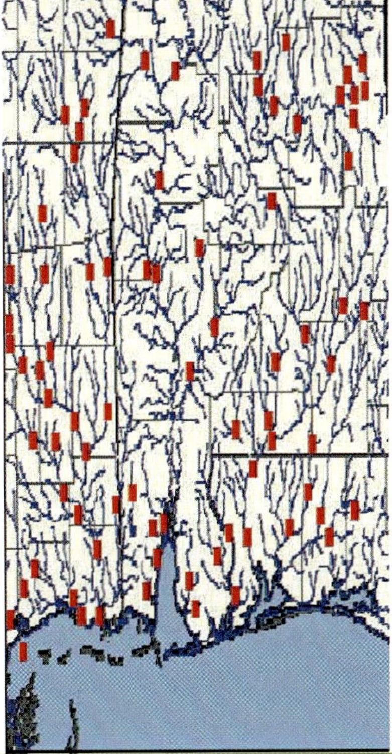

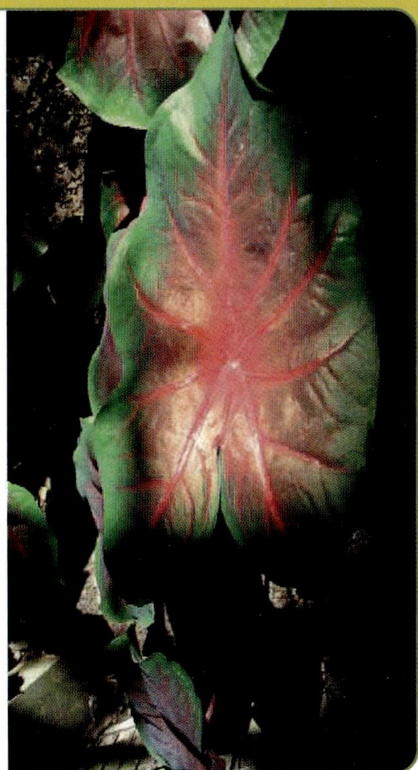

Veins in human body, rivers and streams on a part of Earth, and nutrient arteries in a leaf: signs to One Creator of the different creations in the universe.

Many Creations: One God

In this life, for example, parts made by Ford Company cannot be used for cars manufactured by Toyota. That is because Ford and Toyota are different cars made by different manufacturers who think differently.

Suppose that the creator of man is different than the creator of Earth or its atmosphere. The Earth and its atmosphere in that case would not be suitable to man's life and health. The living conditions on Earth might not allow human beings and other living things to live if the creators of man and Earth were different. The air, water or food on earth might not be good for people.

This is not the case in our universe al-hamdulillah. The Creator is the same for all creation and He provides balance and harmony in the world. This is only one example of many which proves that this universe has one great creator; Allah سبحانه وتعالى.

Atheists, Polytheists and Monotheists

You may think that no one in his right mind would not believe in God or question His oneness. Unfortunately this is not the case. Many people in this world don't believe in God. As you learned in an earlier lesson, they think this amazing universe just happened by chance or coincidence. This is called Atheism and the people who believe that are called Atheists. Unfortunately, most books of science support this false claim. You do not see the name of God appear in any of the science books taught in schools. When you learn about biology, astronomy, physics, chemistry and other fields of science, the books seem to tell about everything except God, the True Creator. He is the One who started the process and made the scientific rules that this creation follows. Some people do not want to accept the plain truth. They say that, "everything happened on its own."

Allah says in Surat-ut-Toor,Were

﴿ أَمْ خُلِقُوا۟ مِنْ غَيْرِ شَىْءٍ أَمْ هُمُ ٱلْخَٰلِقُونَ ﴿٣٥﴾ أَمْ خَلَقُوا۟ ٱلسَّمَٰوَٰتِ وَٱلْأَرْضَ ۚ بَل لَّا يُوقِنُونَ ﴿٣٦﴾ ﴾

الطور: ٣٥ - ٣٦

they created of nothing, or are they the creators? Or did they create the Heavens and the Earth? Nay! They have no firm belief. [52:35-36]

The opposite of Atheism is Polytheism. Polytheists are those who believe in more than one god. Some claim that there is a god for the sun, another for the winds, a third for oceans and many other gods and goddesses. They may build many statues and idols that represent these many gods. You learned about ancient Arabs who worshipped hundreds of idols in Makkah and Arabia. Polytheism was also common in India, Persia, the Roman Empire, Greece, Africa and other parts of the world. Polytheism is still the faith of millions of people around the globe today. There are, for example, millions of people around the world who worship many gods like Hindus and others.

Just imagine if there were many gods for this universe! Then every god would want to do things his own way. One god might want people to be able to think, while another god wants them to be like robots. Imagine the confusion! Allah in the Qur'an explains how there can be only One God:

﴿ أَمِ ٱتَّخَذُوٓا۟ ءَالِهَةً مِّنَ ٱلْأَرْضِ هُمْ يُنشِرُونَ ﴿٢١﴾ لَوْ كَانَ فِيهِمَآ ءَالِهَةٌ إِلَّا ٱللَّهُ لَفَسَدَتَا ۚ فَسُبْحَٰنَ ٱللَّهِ رَبِّ ٱلْعَرْشِ عَمَّا يَصِفُونَ ﴿٢٢﴾ ﴾

الأنبياء: ٢١ - ٢٢

Or have they taken many gods from the Earth who can raise (the dead). If there were, in the Heavens and the earth, other gods besides Allah, there would have been confusion in both! but glory to Allah, the Lord on the Throne: (High is He) above what they claim to Him! [Surat-ul-Anbiyaa' 21:21-22]

Both Atheists and Polytheists miss the truth. Islam teaches us the middle way. We do not deny God nor do we claim that there are many gods. The truth is something in between. There is just One great Creator for the whole universe. In Arabic, the language of the Qur'an, He is Allah. However, different people around the world give him different names like God in English, Elohim in Hebrew, and Dios in Spanish. As you learned earlier, the belief in one God is called Tawheed. The best available English word for it is Monotheism.

A Poem

The True Creator

Look at the stars at night;
Look at an eagle in flight;
Look in the mirror to see
how nicely Allah made you and me;
Look at the mountains;
Look at the geysers which gush out as fountains;
Look at the sky;
Look at a tiny fly;
Look at a huge whale;
Look at the colors on a sail;
Look at all the flowers;
Look into the clouds when it showers;
Look at the fingerprints on your hand;
Look at a small grain of sand;
Look at how the rivers flow;
Look at a turtle walking so slow;
Look at the fish in the sea;
Look at the stripes on a bee;
Look at an orange carrot;
Look at a colorful parrot;
Look at the beauty of the moon;
Look at a sand dune;
Look at a brown Grizzly bear;
Look at a snow colored hare;
Look at the sea shells on the shore;
Look at the water pour;
Look at the sun;
Look at a cheetah run;
Look at a bird's nest;
Look at the lions while they rest;
Look at a huge redwood tree;
Look at your own knee;
Look at cardinal's red feather;
Look at the patterns of the weather;
Look at a dog chasing a cat;
Look at a cat pouncing on a rat;
Look at the shape of an apple seed;
Look at a weed;
Look at the beauty of a rose;
Look at how slow a plant grows;
Look at all those ants;
Look at the green plants;
Look at a gurgling stream;
Look at a blue jay scream;
Look at your feet;
Look at a grain of wheat;
Look at how a bird flies;
Look at how an animal dies;
Look at a piece of grass;
Look at an elephant's mass;
Look at the geese head south;
Allah created everything, no doubt!

Sabahat Syed
(13 years old)

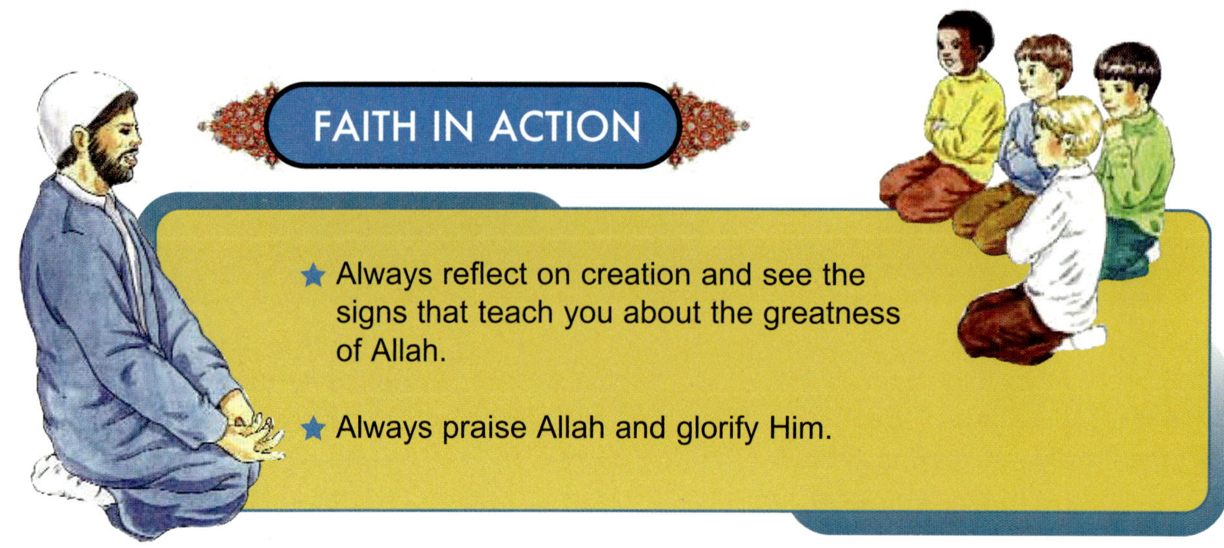

FAITH IN ACTION
Always reflect on creation and see the signs that teach you about the greatness of Allah.
Always praise Allah and glorify Him.

Selected Story

The Honorable Joha, Mulla Nasruddin Hodja and the Pumpkin Tree

"And God knows what is on the land and in the sea; and not a single leaf falls but God knows it."

Mulla Nasruddin was involved in what he did best - relaxing under the shade of a walnut tree. Greeting friends as they walked by and enjoying his lunch of rice and lamb, he still found time to contemplate the wonders of Allah.

How generous is Allah, he thought, to provide such food as pumpkins and corn and even the walnuts in the tree above. He smiled while picking up a walnut on the ground and examining it. He looked over at the large garden of vegetables nearby. Take the pumpkin for example. It is huge fruit on a plant with no strength to hold it, while the tiny walnut comes from a tree with enough strength to hold a donkey. I wonder why didn't Allah switch them and made pumpkin grow on trees.

Just then he felt a tap on his head as a walnut fell from the tree. Looking at the object which had hit him, Mulla Nasruddin exclaimed, "Oh Allah, with what wisdom did You put walnuts on that tree. If it had been pumpkins I would be sitting here with a huge lump on my head!

Source: Dr. Freda Shamma, *Ayat Jamilah*

CHAPTER REVIEW

Projects and Activities

1. Write a letter to an atheist person trying to persuade him or her that there is a Creator of this world.
2. Write a 700 word essay that refutes the belief in many gods.
3. Conduct with your classmates a debate about the existence of God. Let one act as an atheist and you be the believer. Have fun!
4. Write a poem about Allah and His creation.

Stretch Your Mind

1. Infer signs, additional to those presented in this chapter, of the oneness of God from the universe.

2. Atheism, Polytheism and Monotheism refer to different beliefs about God. Explain the differences among these beliefs.

Study Questions

1. Harmony in the creation of the universe leads to the belief in One God. Give two examples.
2. What is the brain made up of?
3. How did Allah create our ears in a special way?
4. What is the percentage of oxygen, nitrogen, and carbon dioxide in the air? Explain what would happen if the gases were in different proportions?
5. Explain briefly how the water cycle works? Do you think it could just happen by chance?
6. Define: a. Atheism b. Polytheism c. Monotheism
7. Explain how reflection about the universe leads us to the belief in one God.

The World of The Angels

CHAPTER OUTLINE

1. What are angels?
2. How important is the belief in angels?
3. What are angels made of?
4. What do angels do in this life and in the Hereafter?
5. Who are the main angels?

VOCABULARY

Malak مَلَك	Meeka'eel مِيكائيل
Mala'ikah مَلائِكَة	Munkar مُنْكَرْ
The Hafathah الحَفَظَة	Nakeer نكير
Al-Katabah الكَتَبَة	Ard-ul-Mahshar أرْضُ المَحْشَر
Malak-ul-Mawt مَلَكُ المَوت	Hamalat-ul-Arsh حَمَلة العَرْش
Jibreel جبريل	Khazin-ul-Jannah خازنُ الجنة
Israfeel إسْرافيل	Khazin-un-Nar خازنُ النار

Introduction

﴿ ٱلْحَمْدُ لِلَّهِ فَاطِرِ ٱلسَّمَٰوَٰتِ وَٱلْأَرْضِ جَاعِلِ ٱلْمَلَٰٓئِكَةِ
رُسُلًا أُو۟لِىٓ أَجْنِحَةٍ مَّثْنَىٰ وَثُلَٰثَ وَرُبَٰعَ ۚ يَزِيدُ فِى ٱلْخَلْقِ مَا
يَشَآءُ ۚ إِنَّ ٱللَّهَ عَلَىٰ كُلِّ شَىْءٍ قَدِيرٌ ﴿١﴾ ﴾

فاطر: ١

All praise is due to Allah, the Creator of the Heavens and the Earth, the Maker of the angels, messengers flying on wings, two, and three, and four; He increases in creation what He pleases; surely Allah has power over all things. [35:1]

The belief in angels is very important in Islam. In fact, it is one of the six pillars of iman, or faith.

Therefore, disbelieving in angels is considered to be kufr, or disbelief. The Arabic word for angel is مَلَك Malak and the plural is مَلائكة Mala'ikah. Angels are part of the unseen world. Although we don't see them, they are always around us. They watch every single action we do and hear every word we utter. In fact, they live with us, walk with us and join us in almost every activity we do. Let's learn more about these amazing creatures. The most important among these angels is the Angel Jibreel for his important tasks that he oversees.

Made of Light

While humans are made from clay, angels are made from light. Most of the time they are invisible to us, however, they can be visible sometimes. They can appear in different forms including the human form.

Unlike us, angels don't eat, drink, sleep, get tired, become sick or die. Although they don't need food or drink for energy, they can travel and fly as fast as light and faster. This activity does not cause them to get tired, become exhausted or to pass out.

We humans may commit mistakes and sins but angels never do. We go about our lives, studying, working, playing, having fun, and worshipping Allah only some of our time. Angels, on the other hand, worship Allah and serve him all the time; twenty four-seven!

In other faiths and cultures, it is common to draw angels as babies or beautiful ladies with wings. In Islam, we are not allowed to portray angels in any shape or form. Because we do not see them, we do not know how they look, so we should not portray them. Artists will never accurately paint the beauty that Allah has given to angels.

Since angels can change the shape we see them in, they do not have a human shape that we can identify as a particular angel. Jibreel, for example, filled the entire sky when he first appeared to Prophet Muhammad, but appeared as a normal sized man when he appeared to Maryam, mother of Isa.

Some scriptures claim that angels sin and commit evil actions. This claim is far from the truth.

According to the Qur'an and the Sunnah, angels are incapable of sin or disobedience. However, even though they are mistake free, they are not divine. They are true and devout servants of Allah.

What do Angels do?

Allah created angels for one main purpose and some other secondary purposes. The main purpose is to worship and serve God. Allah says in the Qur'an:

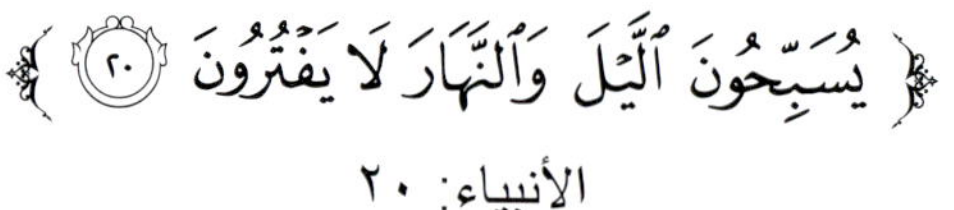
﴿ يُسَبِّحُونَ ٱلَّيۡلَ وَٱلنَّهَارَ لَا يَفۡتُرُونَ ﴿٢٠﴾ ﴾

الأنبياء: ٢٠

They glorify (Him) by night and day; they never stop. [21:20]

Learn from angels, worship and praise Allah as much as you can!

Angels also do different jobs in this universe including, but not limited to:

- Taking care of human beings

- Executing Allah's commands around the universe

- Serving Allah in the Hereafter

Angels and Humans

Angels are always around us from the time we are given life to the time of death, and even after that.

They also take good care of us throughout our lives.

Allah loves mankind and honors all children of Adam. He wants us to be happy and safe in this life and the next. So, He assigns angels to protect us and to record our deeds. Allah wants us to know for sure that angels guard us against the harms of the Shayateen, and that His angels write down every deed we do. This encourages us to watch our behavior and do all the good deeds we can so we will deserve to go back to Jannah, our original home.

The Angel of Life

Our special relationship with the angels starts even before our date of birth. When we are still a piece of flesh in our mothers' wombs, angels come and give us the breath of life; our soul. They do that upon orders from Allah. Let's learn from Rasoolullah what happens in the womb:

Hadeeth Shareef

عن أبي عبد الرحمن عبد الله بن مسعود رضي الله عنه، قال : حدثنا رسول الله صلي الله عليه وسلم ـ وهو الصادق المصدوق ـ :

(إنَّ أحَدَكُمْ يُجْمَعُ خَلْقُهُ في بَطْنِ أمِّهِ أرْبَعينَ يَوْماً ، ثمَّ يَكونُ عَلَقة مِثلَ ذلكَ، ثمَّ يَكونُ مُضْغَة مِثلَ ذلكَ ، ثمَّ يُبعث إليهِ مَلكاً، فَينْفُخُ فيهِ الرُّوحَ، ثمَّ يُؤمَرُ بأرْبعِ كَلِماتٍ : بكَتْبِ رِزْقِهِ، وأجَلِهِ، وعَمَلِهِ، وشَقِيٌّ أمْ سَعيد.)

`Abdullaah ibn Mas`ood narrated: The Messenger of Allah and he is truthful, the believed, narrated to us:
"Verily the creation of each one of you is brought together in the mother's belly for forty days in the form of a liquid seed, then he is a clot of blood, then a crumb of flesh, then there is sent to him the angel who blows the soul into him and who is commanded about four matters: to write down his wealth, his life span, his actions, and whether happy or unhappy. "

Main Lessons

1. The angel of life blows the soul into the fetus in the womb. This brings life to the baby in the belly of the mother.

2. Each born child has the following things recorded even before birth:

   1. Wealth,
   2. Life span,
   3. Deeds
   4. Destination; in Paradise or in Hell.

3. Allah alone decides on two important things; our lives and our wealth. That is how long we live and how much we will earn in this life.

4. On the other hand, we decide what kind of deeds we want to do; good deeds or bad deeds. Our deeds with the will and mercy of Allah will lead us to Jannah or Jahannam.

5. Since Allah knows what will happen in the future, He knows what choices we are going to make in our life. Therefore, He can figure out our deeds even before we are born. Since He knows how we will act, then He also knows from our beginning if we are to win Jannah or be punished in Jahannam.

The Hafathah الحفظة : Guardian Angels

At least three ayaat in the Qur'an assure us that Allah assigns angels to protect every human being.

Allah says:

﴿ لَهُۥ مُعَقِّبَٰتٌ مِّنۢ بَيْنِ يَدَيْهِ وَمِنْ خَلْفِهِۦ يَحْفَظُونَهُۥ مِنْ أَمْرِ ٱللَّهِ ﴾

الرعد: ١١

For his (man's) sake there are angels following one another, before him and behind him, who guard him by Allah's will. [13:11]

These angels are positioned in front and in the back of every person. They protect people against the harms of devils and evil jinn. If Allah wills that a person may be hurt for certain wisdom, this will happen.

Sometimes people are hurt as a punishment for their sins. In other times, calamities come to test the faith and patience of the Muslim or to grant him great rewards.

Al-Katabah:

The Honorable Record Keepers

Allah says in Surat-ul-Infitar:

﴿ وَإِنَّ عَلَيْكُمْ لَحَٰفِظِينَ ۝١٠ كِرَامًا كَٰتِبِينَ ۝١١ يَعْلَمُونَ مَا تَفْعَلُونَ ۝١٢ ﴾

الانفطار: ١٠ - ١٢

And most surely there are keepers over you. Honorable recorders. They know what you do [82:10-12]

And in Surat Qaf, He says:

﴿ إِذْ يَتَلَقَّى ٱلْمُتَلَقِّيَانِ عَنِ ٱلْيَمِينِ وَعَنِ ٱلشِّمَالِ قَعِيدٌ ۝١٧ مَّا يَلْفِظُ مِن قَوْلٍ إِلَّا لَدَيْهِ رَقِيبٌ عَتِيدٌ ۝١٨ ﴾

ق: ١٧ - ١٨

When the two writing angels receivers receive man's actions, sitting on the right and on the left. He utters not a word but there is by him a watcher at hand. [50:17-18]

Based on these ayaat, it is clear that our every action and every word will be recorded, whether good or bad. The latter ayah names the two writing angels as "Raqeeb" and "Ateed" meaning that they are watching and ready to write. If we do a good deed or say a good word, the angels will write it for us and we will be granted ten hasanat, or rewards, for it. But, when a Muslim commits a sin, he or she will only be charged for a single bad deed. This is just one sign of Allah's profound mercy.

عَن عبدِ الله بن عمرو رَضِيَ اللهُ عنهُ قال:
قالَ رَسولُ اللهِ صَلّى اللهُ عَليْهِ وسَلّم :

"...الحَسَنة بعَشْرِ أمْثالِها..." رواه البخاري

Abdullah Ibn Amro رضي الله عنه narrated that Rasoolulluh said:

"A single good deed is rewarded ten fold."

Reported in Al-Bukhari

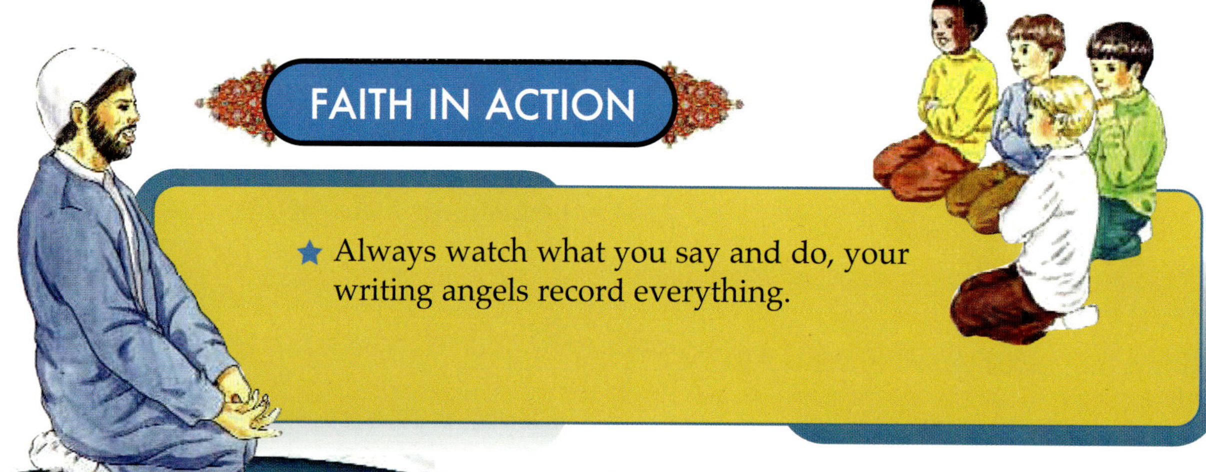

FAITH IN ACTION

- Always watch what you say and do, your writing angels record everything.

Do you know that every day you greet the angels around you at least five times a day? When you make tasleem you say "Assalamu Alaykum wa Rahmatullah" to the writing and the guardian angels, at the end of all daily prayers.

Angels Support and Defend the Believers:

Allah commands angels to support and defend the believers when they need help. We learn from the Qur'an and Hadeeth that the angels fought on the side of Muslims in many battles. The Qur'an says that Allah provided soldiers from among the believers with the angels to fight against the pagans in Badr, Al-Khandaq and Hunayn battles. Allah describes what happened in the Battle of Badr in Surat-ul-Anfal:

﴿ إِذْ يُوحِى رَبُّكَ إِلَى ٱلْمَلَٰٓئِكَةِ أَنِّى مَعَكُمْ فَثَبِّتُوا۟
ٱلَّذِينَ ءَامَنُوا۟ ۚ سَأُلْقِى فِى قُلُوبِ ٱلَّذِينَ كَفَرُوا۟
ٱلرُّعْبَ فَٱضْرِبُوا۟ فَوْقَ ٱلْأَعْنَاقِ وَٱضْرِبُوا۟ مِنْهُمْ
كُلَّ بَنَانٍ ﴿١٢﴾ ﴾

الأنفال: ١٢

When your Lord revealed to the angels: I am with you, therefore support those who believed. I will cast fear into the hearts of the pagans. Therefore strike off their heads and strike off every fingertip of them.[8:12]

In Surat Al-Ahzab, Allah also describes what happened in the Battle of Al-Khandaq:

﴿ يَٰٓأَيُّهَا ٱلَّذِينَ ءَامَنُوا۟ ٱذْكُرُوا۟ نِعْمَةَ ٱللَّهِ عَلَيْكُمْ إِذْ
جَآءَتْكُمْ جُنُودٌ فَأَرْسَلْنَا عَلَيْهِمْ رِيحًا وَجُنُودًا لَّمْ تَرَوْهَا ۚ
وَكَانَ ٱللَّهُ بِمَا تَعْمَلُونَ بَصِيرًا ﴿٩﴾ ﴾

الأحزاب: ٩

O you who believe! Remember the favor of Allah to you when armies came down upon you, so We sent against them a strong wind and soldiers, that you didn't see, and Allah is All-Seeing. [33:9]

Not only during battles, Allah has supported the believers with angels in other situations too.

According to the Qur'an, Allah sent His angels down to protect Prophet Muhammad ﷺ during Al-Hijrah. As a result, the pagans of the

Quraysh could not locate or capture the Prophet ﷺ and his companions.

Angels also defend and protect the believers at all times and in all places. There are many stories that bear witness to this fact.

Malak-ul-Mawt

Malak-ul-Mawt, or the Angel of Death, along with his helper angels, is responsible for taking away the soul of the human from the body. This is the main cause of death and that is why this angel is called "Angel of Death." Allah says in the Qur'an:

﴿ قُلْ يَتَوَفَّىٰكُم مَّلَكُ ٱلْمَوْتِ ٱلَّذِى وُكِّلَ بِكُمْ ثُمَّ إِلَىٰ رَبِّكُمْ تُرْجَعُونَ ﴿١١﴾ ﴾

السجدة: ١١

Say: The angel of death who is given charge of you shall cause you to die, then to your Lord you shall be brought back.

The time of death is naturally a painful one for all people, believers and disbelievers. But it will be much easier and more peaceful for the believer than for the disbeliever or a Muslim who has commited many evil deeds. Even Prophet Muhammad ﷺ experienced some pain at the time of his death. According to some Ahadeeth, we learn that the Angel of Death will take the soul of the believer in an easy and soft manner, like a drip of water dripping from a glass. However, the disbeliever's soul will be ripped away in a painful way.

Some ancient books call the Angel of Death Azrael, or Izrael, and it means "Helped by God." Muslims do not use this name as it is not mentioned in the Qur'an nor in the Sunnah.

Munkar and Nakeer : Angels in the grave

As soon as the dead person is placed in the grave, two angels of bluish and black colors come in and awake him or her. Allah then returns the soul to the dead person in the grave in a special way. Let us learn from Rasoolullah ﷺ what happens in the grave:

"When the dead person is buried two black-blue angels come to him, one called مُنكر Munkar and the other called نكير Nakeer."

According to this Hadeeth, the angels will ask the dead person about his Lord, his Prophet, and his religion. The believers will answer confidently and correctly, therefore, they will enjoy a happy time in the grave. On the other hand, the disbelievers will not be able to give good answers, thus, they will suffer a severe punishment in the grave.

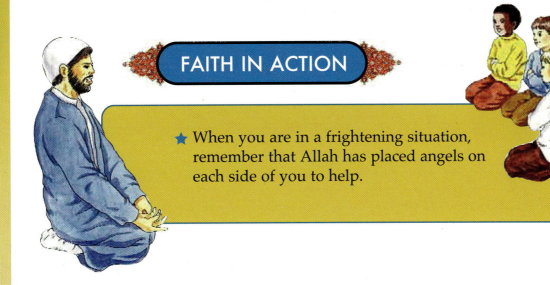

FAITH IN ACTION

★ When you are in a frightening situation, remember that Allah has placed angels on each side of you to help.

Angels and the Hereafter

In this life, generally angels cannot be seen. This is not the case in the Hereafter. We will be able to see angels as soon as we are brought alive out of our graves. They will be visible all around. Let's learn about what angels do in the Hereafter.

Israfeel إسرافيل , the Blower of the Horn

Upon an order from Allah, Angel إسرافيل Israfeel will blow a horn creating a blaring siren heralding the Hereafter. This will bring total destruction to the whole world.

Sometime later Israfeel will blow the horn again. This second deafening tone will cause the resurrection of all mankind from death and the Day of Judgment will then start.

Allah says in Surat-uz-Zumar:,

﴿ وَنُفِخَ فِي ٱلصُّورِ فَصَعِقَ مَن فِي ٱلسَّمَٰوَٰتِ وَمَن فِي ٱلْأَرْضِ إِلَّا مَن شَآءَ ٱللَّهُۖ ثُمَّ نُفِخَ فِيهِ أُخْرَىٰ فَإِذَا هُمْ قِيَامٌ يَنظُرُونَ ﴿٦٨﴾ ﴾

الزمر: ٦٨

And the horn shall be blown, so all those in the Heavens and in the Earth shall pass out, except such as Allah pleases; then it shall be blown again, then they shall stand up awaiting. [39:68]

The Carriers of the Throne

After resurrection, or life after death, all people will be gathered in one vast place; Ard-ul-Mahshar أرضُ المَحشَر , or the Land of Gathering. All the people will be guided by angels towards Allah ﷻ

who will then account for everyone's deeds. Allah will be on His majestic throne, which will be carried by eight great angels or eight groups of angels called Hamalat-ul-Arsh حملة العرش, or the Carriers of the Throne. Allah says in Surat-ul-Haqqah,

﴿ وَيَحْمِلُ عَرْشَ رَبِّكَ فَوْقَهُمْ يَوْمَئِذٍ ثَمَٰنِيَةٌ ﴿١٧﴾ يَوْمَئِذٍ تُعْرَضُونَ لَا تَخْفَىٰ مِنكُمْ خَافِيَةٌ ﴿١٨﴾ ﴾

الحاقة: ١٧ - ١٨

And the angels shall be all around; and above them eight [angels] shall bear on that day your Lord's throne. On that day you shall be exposed to view-- no secret of yours shall remain hidden. [69:17-18]

Prophet Muhammad ﷺ described these angels as so grand, "...the distance between one's ear and neck is like the distance traveled over seven hundred years."

On that special day, which will be fifty thousand years long, everyone will receive the records of his or her deeds. Good people will receive it in their right hands and others will receive it in the left. Angels will then call people by their names to be questioned about their deeds. The believers will experience very mild questioning or no questions at all and be graciously welcomed by angels into Jannah. Disbelievers and sinful Muslims, on the other hand, will face humiliating treatment and get dragged by angels to Jahannam.

The Keepers of Paradise

There are keepers of Paradise who guard its eight gates and serve the people therein. Allah says in Surat-uz-Zumar,

﴿ وَسِيقَ ٱلَّذِينَ ٱتَّقَوْا۟ رَبَّهُمْ إِلَى ٱلْجَنَّةِ زُمَرًا حَتَّىٰٓ إِذَا جَآءُوهَا وَفُتِحَتْ أَبْوَٰبُهَا وَقَالَ لَهُمْ خَزَنَتُهَا سَلَٰمٌ عَلَيْكُمْ طِبْتُمْ فَٱدْخُلُوهَا خَٰلِدِينَ ﴿٧٣﴾ ﴾

الزمر: ٧٣

And those who are mindful of their Lord shall be guided to the garden in groups; when they come to it, and its doors shall be opened, and the keepers of it shall say to them: Peace be on you, you shall be happy; therefore enter it to live in for eternity. [39:73]

It is narrated that Khazin-ul-Jannah خازن الجنة the head of all the keepers in Jannah is named Ridwan.

Always do good deeds that lead to Jannah

The Keepers of Hellfire

There are also keepers of Jahannam, or Hellfire. Angel Malik is خازن النار Khazin-un-Nar, or the main keeper of Jahannam. Allah says in Surat-uz-Zukhruf [43:74-78]:

﴿إِنَّ ٱلْمُجْرِمِينَ فِى عَذَابِ جَهَنَّمَ خَٰلِدُونَ ﴿٧٤﴾ لَا يُفَتَّرُ
عَنْهُمْ وَهُمْ فِيهِ مُبْلِسُونَ ﴿٧٥﴾ وَمَا ظَلَمْنَٰهُمْ وَلَٰكِن كَانُوا۟ هُمُ
ٱلظَّٰلِمِينَ ﴿٧٦﴾ وَنَادَوْا۟ يَٰمَٰلِكُ لِيَقْضِ عَلَيْنَا رَبُّكَ قَالَ إِنَّكُم
مَّٰكِثُونَ ﴿٧٧﴾ لَقَدْ جِئْنَٰكُم بِٱلْحَقِّ وَلَٰكِنَّ أَكْثَرَكُمْ لِلْحَقِّ
كَٰرِهُونَ ﴿٧٨﴾﴾

الزخرف: ٧٤ - ٧٨

[74] Surely the guilty shall dwell in the punishment of Hell.
[75] It shall not be reduced from them and they shall therein lose hope.
[76] And We are not unjust to them, but they themselves were unjust.
[77] And they shall call out: O Malik! let your Lord make an end to us. He shall say: Surely you shall stay.
[78] Certainly We have brought you the truth, but most of you dislike the truth.

Under Malik, there are nineteen other angels that guard Jahannam. They are also helped by countless other angels who oversee punishment of the disbelievers and the sinful there. Allah says in Surat-ul-Muddathir [74:27-30]:

﴿وَمَآ أَدْرَىٰكَ مَا سَقَرُ ﴿٢٧﴾ لَا تُبْقِى وَلَا تَذَرُ ﴿٢٨﴾ لَوَّاحَةٌ لِّلْبَشَرِ
﴿٢٩﴾ عَلَيْهَا تِسْعَةَ عَشَرَ ﴿٣٠﴾﴾

المدثر: ٢٧ - ٣٠

[27] And what will make you know what hell is?
[28] It leaves nothing nor does it spare anything.
[29] It scorches the humans.
[30] Over it are nineteen [angels].

Always beware of Jahannam and avoid behaviour and actions that lead to it.

Angels also do whatever Allah wants them to do. They obey him without question and execute his orders in a split second. Here are some of the jobs angels do. Let's start with the highest ranking angels of Allah.

Serving Around the Universe

Angels also obey Allah's commands in issues related to the vast universe. They execute the Lord's orders concerning the planets and the weather. They inspire the believers to do whatever is good for them and they protect the Heavens from the trespassings of the evil jinn. Most important of all they conveyed Allah's messages to His Prophets and messengers.

Mika'eel: The Power Behind the Weather

How many times have you listened to a weather forecast that turned out to be incorrect? Recently, American meteorologist predicted that Hurricane Rita would hit Houston. People were very scared because this came in the aftermath of the deadly Hurricane Katrina, so the majority of the city's population evacuated.

However, the hurricane made landfall somewhere else, sparing the city of Houston. Meteorologists know the science of meteorology and weather forecasting, but ultimately Allah is the final decision maker on weather and everything else in the universe.

Allah gives orders to Angel Mika'eel in regards to the weather. He moves the clouds and winds according to Allah's will. It is unfortunate that today it is more acceptable to heavily rely on the science of meterology rather than to openly accept that God is the controller of the weather. Meteorologists and news anchors never refer to God in such matters, they just talk about "mother nature." On one occasion, a news anchor in a Muslim country described to viewers how the weather would look in the days to come. At the end of his report he correctly said, InshaAllah, or God willing. This believing news anchor ended up being fired. In fact he was right, and all anchors should follow his conduct.

Jibreel جبريل : The Greatest Angel

We conclude this chapter with the angel who handles the most important task among angels: Angel Jibreel, or Gabriel. Jibreel جبريل is the greatest angel of all. He is responsible for revealing God's messages and books to His prophets. He was the angel who revealed the Qur'an to Prophet Muhammad ﷺ . In the next chapter, you will learn more details about this great angel, inshaAllah.

FAITH IN ACTION

- Always ask Allah's protection from Hellfire

Du'aa'

اللهم إني أسْألُكَ الجَنَّةَ وأَعوذُ بكَ من النار

Oh Allah, I ask you for Paradise and seek your protection from Hellfire

Reported in Ahmad

Angels And Men

Allah made the angels out of heavenly light
created for His service, to do what's right.
Whatever Allah commands, they must obey
and from these duties they never stray.

Unlike Humans, they cannot choose
so when Allah commands, they cannot refuse.
They are the dedicated servants of our Lord.
They won't do anything on their own accord.

Some angels are told to worship and pray
and they follow these commands night and day.
Some performing Sajdah and others in Rukoo'
From the moment of creation this is all they do.

Every angel has tasks that Allah has assigned.
Some are commanded to serve mankind.
Some provide sustenance from hunger and thirst.
Others are with us from the moment of birth.

Two angels are assigned to record our deeds,
whilst some take care of our other needs.
Like bringing us sunshine and also the rain.
Like protecting us from harm and also from pain.

There is another creation - it is called man.
They live on Earth for a very short span.
After their time expires they are returned
and through their deeds, paradise is earned.

Adam was first and he was made from mud
which was then turned into flesh and blood.
Unlike the angels, he has a choice to obey
- to go for guidance or to go astray.

So humans have choices to be the best
as freewill can raise them above the rest.
The ability to choose between wrong and right.
To return from darkness to knowledge and light.

Through choice we can follow Allah's command
and refrain from everything Allah has banned.
We can follow Islam, becoming pious and just
so both learning and practice become a must.

If we ignore Islam and follow our desire
and lose ourselves in building our empires.
Our purpose in life becomes obeying our lust
- chasing the Dunya we become spiritually bust.

When our whims and desires is all we select.
Our real purpose in life we tend to neglect.
When Islam isn't the centre of our lives,
our heart becomes empty where nothing survives.

Our Creator's wishes we no longer observe
when our nafs and ego is all we serve.
We forget the reality that life is a test
and the path of righteousness is the best.

If the Path we tread is of virtue and merit
then the gardens of paradise we will inherit.
Many hardships and trials we will ultimately face
When the pious and righteous we emulate.

The amount of wealth is a test from above.
Do we love to share or is it hoarding we love?
Are we grateful to Allah for whatever he has sent?
Or do we complain of poverty and show resent?

If Allah has given us power over others
Do we treat them as equals and as brothers?
or do we feel superior and are filled with pride?
Do we practice fairness or are their rights denied?

Allah has blessed us with youth and good health,
both these qualities are our greatest wealth!
Do we pick on others demonstrating our brawn?
Or are we up for Fajr at the crack of dawn?

Are we careful to use our precious time?
Or is it devoted to TV, music and rhyme?
Do we try to create a better place
and improve the conditions that Muslims face?

Do we obey our parents and give them respect?
Are we good role models are our morals correct?
Do we help other people and are we always fair?
Do we earn halal income or don't we care?

Do we follow the guidance from the Qur'an?
By shunning all evil and following Islam?
Do we read the Qur'an and heed its advice?
Or have we sold Jannah for a meagre price?

For all Allah's blessings we show gratitude
with generosity, kindness and the right attitude.
So in doing good deeds we should not delay
and our commitment to Islam should start today.

On the last day all souls will be raised
and we will face Allah – the most praised.
Standing before Allah what face will we show?
When the truth of our actions will freely flow.

By Zahid bin Ghulam

CHAPTER REVIEW

Projects and Activities

1. Write a real story that is related to angels and share it with your classmates and friends.
2. Develop a table in which you list all the angels you learned about in this chapter and what roles they play in this life and in the Hereafter.

Stretch Your Mind

1. Using a table, compare and contrast angels with humans in terms of:
   - _ What they are made of
   - _ Their roles in this life
   - _ Their deeds (good or bad)
2. People sometimes say, "you are just like an angel." What do they mean by that?
3. "The belief in angels improves people's behavior." Is this statement correct? Explain why or why not.

Study Questions

1. What are angels made of?
2. Define: a. Malak b. Mala'ikah c. The Hafathah d. Al-Katabah e. Ard-ul-Mahshar f. Hamalat-ul-Arsh
3. What are the three main functions of angels?
4. Describe the role of Malak-ul-Mawt?
5. Who are Ridwan and Malik?
6. Describe the dialogue that will take place between the people of Jahannam and Malik.
7. Describe the role of Israfeel.
8. Who is the angel that you may remember when you watch a report about the weather on TV? Describe the function of that angel.
9. Who is the greatest angel?

Jibreel عليه السلام , the Holy Spirit

CHAPTER OUTLINE

1. Who is Jibreel?
2. What is the significance of Angel Jibreel?
3. What is the main role of Angel Jibreel?
4. Is Angel Jibreel the Holy Spirit?
5. How is the Holy Spirit viewed in Christianity?
6. How does the Qur'an describe the 'Holy Spirit?'

VOCABULARY

Jibreel	جبْريل
Ar-Rooh-ul-Qudus	الرُّوحُ القـُدُس
Al-Isra' and Al-Mi'raj	الإسْراءُ وَالمِعْراج
Al-Buraq	البُراق
Bayt-ul-Maqdis	بيْتُ المَقـْدِس
Sidrat-ul-Muntaha	سِـدْرَةُ المُنْتهى
Al-bayt-ul-ma`moor	البَيْتُ المَعْمور

Significance of Angel Jibreel

The Angel Jibreel جبريل , or Gabriel, holds a very important place in Islam. Allah described this great angel in the Qur'an as الروح القُدس Ar-Rooh-ul-Qudus, or the Holy Spirit. He is the greatest of all angels who connected Allah's message to mankind. In obedience to the orders of Allah, Jibreel had supported Prophet Muhammad ﷺ and the Muslims every step of the way. He protected Muhammad ﷺ from the pagans of Makkah when they tried to hurt him. He led the angels in securing the migration of the Muslims, the Hijrah, from Makkah to Madinah. He also lead the angels again in helping the Muslims in their fight against the pagans in the battles of Badr, Al-Khandaq, Hunayn.

According to 'A'ishah رضي الله عنها and others, the Prophet ﷺ saw Angel Jibreel in his true form only twice, as it is indicated in the Qur'an:

The first sighting of Jibreel took place at the cave of Hira', on the occasion of the revelation of the first verses of the Qur'an, and the second time was during the Al-Mi'raj in the Seventh Heaven. Allah said in Surat-un-Najm,

"This is not but a revelation revealed, taught by the one mighty in power (Jibreel), who is very strong who appeared in complete manner, on the higher horizon... He saw him another time by the Lote Tree of the Far Boundary." (53, 4-14)

In the Hira' Cave

Angel Jibreel is mentioned several times in the Holy Qur'an along with other special angels. Each one of them has a special role. Angel Jibreel is known as the messenger angel because he was responsible for bringing Allah's words to Prophet Muhammad ﷺ.

Jibreel appeared in the cave of Hira' to the Prophet ﷺ while he was meditating. Then Jibreel communicated

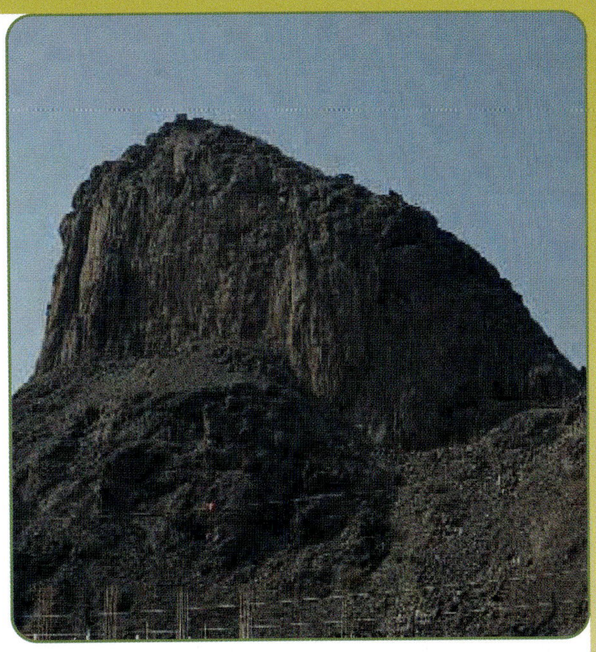

Allah's first message to him. As you learned in your elementary years, Angel Jibreel commanded Muhammad ﷺ to "read" By saying "iqra." The Prophet ﷺ replied, "I cannot read", as he was illiterate. The angel seized him and again commanded him, "Read!" The words of the Angel Jibreel to Prophet Muhammad ﷺ were:

﴿ اقْرَأْ بِاسْمِ رَبِّكَ الَّذِي خَلَقَ ﴿١﴾ خَلَقَ الْإِنسَانَ مِنْ عَلَقٍ ﴿٢﴾
اقْرَأْ وَرَبُّكَ الْأَكْرَمُ ﴿٣﴾ الَّذِي عَلَّمَ بِالْقَلَمِ ﴿٤﴾ عَلَّمَ الْإِنسَانَ مَا
لَمْ يَعْلَمْ ﴿٥﴾ ﴾
العلق: ١ - ٥

Read in the name of your Lord Who created (1).
He created man from a clot. (2)
Read and your Lord is Most Honorable,(3)
Who taught (to write) with the pen (4)
Taught man what he knew not. (5)

This was the first revelation the Prophet Muhammad ﷺ received from Allah. He was forty years old. Jibreel continued to communicate Al-Qur'an to Prophet Muhammad ﷺ over the next twenty three years.

Angel Jibreel would visit Prophet Muhammad to deliver a few ayaat at a time on a continuous basis. Every year during the month of Ramadan, Jibreel would review the verses of the Qur'an that he had delivered that year. In the 11th year after Hijrah, the year that the Prophet ﷺ passed way, Jibreel reviewed the whole Qur'an twice with him. The Qur'an was now complete and Prophet Muhammad ﷺ soon passed away. He was sixty three years old.

Jibreel is very well known for other important tasks here on earth.

The Journey of Al-Isra' and Al-Mi'raj

Another important task of Angel Jibreel was the Journey of Al-Isra and Al-Mi'raj الإسراء والمعراج.

One night Prophet Muhammad ﷺ was sleeping near thc Ka'bah in Makkah when the Angel Jibreel came to him and woke him up. The Angel Jibreel took his arm and led him to the Sacred Mosque in Makkah. Waiting for him nearby was a white creature that looked like a horse. It was called Al-Buraq البراق . Prophet Muhammad ﷺ and Angel Jibreel rode the Buraq towards Jerusalem. Within a blink of an eye they were at the old city and were met there by a group of prophets: Adam, Nooh, Ibraheem, Musa, Isa, and many others (AS). Led by the Angel Jibreel,

Prophet Muhammad ﷺ began ascending toward the seven heavens. Throughout the journey up to the

Heavens, the Prophet ﷺ was astounded. For the first time he had the opportunity to observe the magnificent unseen world. He saw the beautiful angels, the great prophets and messenHers, the sublime heavens and many other amazing wonders. When he arrived there, he communicated with Allah and received divine guidance on prayer for Muslims and other important matters. Let's learn from Rasoolullah ﷺ some details of his great journey to Heaven with Angel Jibreel.

To the Heavens with Jibreel:

The Hadeeth about the Journey of Al-Isra' wal-Mi'raj

Hadeeth Shareef

Anas ibn Malik narrated that the Messenger of Allah, peace and blessings be upon him, said:

I was brought al-buraq who is an animal, white and long, larger than a donkey but smaller than a mule. He would place its hoof at a distance equal to the range of his vision. I mounted it and came to بيت المقدس Bayt-ul-Maqdis (Jerusalem). I then tethered it to the ring used by the prophets. I entered the area of the mosque and prayed two rak'aat in it. I then came out and Gabriel brought me a vessel of wine and a vessel of milk. I chose the milk, and Gabriel said, "You have chosen al-fitra, the natural way."

He then ascended with me into the lower heavens and requested that they be opened. It was said: 'Who are you?' He responded: "Gabriel." It was then said, "Who is with you?" He responded: "Muhammad." It was then said: "Has revelation been sent to him?" He responded: "Revelation has been sent to him." (This exchange between Jibreel and the guards of Heavens happened at the entry of all the seven heavens.) It was then opened for us and there I was with Adam. He welcomed me and prayed for my well-being.

Then we ascended to the second Heaven... and when I entered Jesus and John welcomed me and prayed for my well-being.

Gabriel then ascended with me to the third Heaven ... and there I was with Joseph, who was given a great portion of beauty. He welcomed me and prayed for my well-being.

Gabriel then ascended with me to the fourth Heaven ... and there I was with Enoch. He welcomed me and prayed for my well-being.

Hadeeth Shareef

Gabriel then ascended with me to the fifth Heaven... and there I was with Aaron. He welcomed me and prayed for my well-being.

Gabriel then ascended with me to the sixth Heaven ... and there I was with Musa. He welcomed me and prayed for my well-being.

Gabriel then ascended with me to the seventh Heaven ... and there I was with Abraham who was leaning against البيت المعمور Al-Bayt-ul-Ma`moor into which enter seventy thousand angels each day never to return.

Then I was brought to سدرة المنتهى Sidrat-ul-Muntaha, the Lote Tree of the Furthest Limit. Its leaves were like the ears of an elephant and whose fruits at first appeared insignificant. But when Allah spread His command over them they transformed to the point where no one in creation could describe their beauty. Then Allah revealed what He revealed to me. He then made obligatory for me fifty prayers every night and day.

I began my descent until I reached Musa, who asked me: "What has your Lord made obligatory for your community?" I said to him, "Fifty prayers." He then said, "Return to your Lord and ask Him to reduce them. Your community will not be able to bear that. I know the people of Isra'eel from long experience and I have tested them." I then returned to my Lord and said, 'O Lord, make things lighter for my people'. He then reduced it by five prayers for me. I then returned to Musa and he said to me, "Your community will not be able to stand that. So return and ask Him to make things lighter." I kept going between my Lord and Musa until Allah said, "O Muhammad, there are five prayers every night and day. Each prayer is equal to ten prayers making them equal to fifty prayers. Whoever intends a good deed and does not do it, there will be written for him a single good deed. If he does it then there will be written for him ten good deeds. Whoever intends an evil deed and does not do it then there is nothing written against him. If he does it then there is written for him one evil deed."

I then descended until I reached Musa and informed him of what had occurred. He then said to me, "Return to your Lord and ask Him to make things lighter." The Messenger of Allah ﷺ then said, "I have returned to my Lord until I felt ashamed before Him."

Reported in Saheeh Muslim

He was There with Mary and Jesus

One of the most famous stories in the Qur'an is the incident in which Angel Jibreel (as) came to Maryam the mother of Isa (as) to inform her that she would miraculously give birth to Isa (as). Allah says:

﴿ وَاذْكُرْ فِي الْكِتَابِ مَرْيَمَ إِذِ انتَبَذَتْ مِنْ أَهْلِهَا مَكَانًا
شَرْقِيًّا ﴿١٦﴾ فَاتَّخَذَتْ مِن دُونِهِمْ حِجَابًا فَأَرْسَلْنَا إِلَيْهَا
رُوحَنَا فَتَمَثَّلَ لَهَا بَشَرًا سَوِيًّا ﴿١٧﴾ قَالَتْ إِنِّي أَعُوذُ
بِالرَّحْمَٰنِ مِنكَ إِن كُنتَ تَقِيًّا ﴿١٨﴾ قَالَ إِنَّمَا أَنَا رَسُولُ
رَبِّكِ لِأَهَبَ لَكِ غُلَامًا زَكِيًّا ﴿١٩﴾ ﴾

مريم: ١٦ - ١٩

And mention Maryam in the Book when she drew aside from her family to an eastern place;

So she took a veil (to screen herself) from them; then We sent to her Our spirit, and there appeared to her a well-made man.

She said: Surely I seek refuge from you to the Merciful Allah, if you are one guarding (against evil).

He said: I am only a messenger of your Lord: That I will give you a pure boy. [Surat-un-Nahl 19:16-19]

Is Angel Jibreel the Holy Spirit?

The term "Holy Spirit" is mentioned in the Qur'an four times. Many are not aware that it is an Islamic term and actually used in the Qur'an. This term refers to Angel Jibreel who communicates Allah's books to His prophets and messengers and faithfully executes Allah's commands in the world. For example, Allah says to Prophet Muhammad ﷺ:

﴿ قُلْ نَزَّلَهُ رُوحُ الْقُدُسِ مِن رَّبِّكَ بِالْحَقِّ
لِيُثَبِّتَ الَّذِينَ آمَنُوا وَهُدًى وَبُشْرَىٰ
لِلْمُسْلِمِينَ ﴿١٠٢﴾ ﴾

النحل: ١٠٢

Say: The Holy spirit has revealed it from your Lord with the truth, that it may support those who believe and as a guidance and good news for those who are Muslims. [Surat-un-Nahl 16:102]

﴿ وَلَقَدْ آتَيْنَا مُوسَى الْكِتَابَ وَقَفَّيْنَا مِن بَعْدِهِ
بِالرُّسُلِ ۖ وَآتَيْنَا عِيسَى ابْنَ مَرْيَمَ الْبَيِّنَاتِ وَأَيَّدْنَاهُ بِرُوحِ
الْقُدُسِ ۗ ﴾

البقرة: ٨٧

And We gave Musa the Book and We sent messengers after him one after another; and We gave Isa, the son of Maryam, clear signs and supported him with the Holy Spirit. [Surat-ul-Baqarah 2:87]

Prophet Muhammad ﷺ sometimes called Angel Jibreel Ar-Rooh-ul-Qudus, or the "Holy Spirit."

Holy Spirit in Christianity

The Holy Spirit is a very popular term in Christianity. However, this term has a different meaning than that in Islam. To understand what the Holy Spirit means in Christianity, we should first be familiar with the concept of "Trinity." According to Webster's Dictionary, "trinity" is:

"The union of three divine [Godly] persons, the Father, the Son, and the Holy Spirit, in one divinity (Godhood), so that all the three are one God as to substance, but three persons."

Based on the above definition, God has three different persons:

1. The Father who is God in Heaven
2. The Son, who is Jesus Christ
3. The Holy Spirit who is the Godly power in the world.

The concept of the trinity claims the union of three divine persons, the Father, the Son, and the Holy Spirit, in one God. The Qur'an is very clear in rejecting the trinity. It calls for the concept of Tawheed, or the belief in One True God. As for the son, Islam teaches that Jesus Christ is a great Prophet but not God. Also, the "Holy Spirit" in the Qur'an refers to the Angel Jibreel. He only executes God's commands. He is not a god.

Conclusion

The belief in angels is very important in Islam. Its' rejection is considered to be kufr, or disbelief. The most important of these angels is Angel Jibreel as he undertook important tasks that contributed to Islam and the Muslim Ummah.

It is quite clear from the above that Allah ﷻ and Prophet Muhammad ﷺ called Angel Jibreel عليه السلام by the name, Jibreel, in some instances, and by the "Holy Spirit" in other instances.

Holy Spirit is the English term for the Arabic Ar-Rooh-ul-Qudus. The "Holy Spirit" in the Qur'an refers to the Angel Gabriel and has nothing to do with trinity. The trinity is absolutely rejected by the strongest language in the Qur'an.

Fast Facts

Some Muslim historians say the Al-Israa' and Al-Mi'raj happened on 27th of Rajab, one year before Hijrah. Other Muslim historians give other dates.

سورة النجم

Surat-un-Najm 1-18

﴿ وَٱلنَّجۡمِ إِذَا هَوَىٰ ١ مَا ضَلَّ صَاحِبُكُمۡ وَمَا غَوَىٰ ٢ وَمَا يَنطِقُ عَنِ ٱلۡهَوَىٰٓ ٣ إِنۡ
هُوَ إِلَّا وَحۡيٞ يُوحَىٰ ٤ عَلَّمَهُۥ شَدِيدُ ٱلۡقُوَىٰ ٥ ذُو مِرَّةٖ فَٱسۡتَوَىٰ ٦ وَهُوَ بِٱلۡأُفُقِ ٱلۡأَعۡلَىٰ
٧ ثُمَّ دَنَا فَتَدَلَّىٰ ٨ فَكَانَ قَابَ قَوۡسَيۡنِ أَوۡ أَدۡنَىٰ ٩ فَأَوۡحَىٰٓ إِلَىٰ عَبۡدِهِۦ مَآ أَوۡحَىٰ ١٠
مَا كَذَبَ ٱلۡفُؤَادُ مَا رَأَىٰٓ ١١ أَفَتُمَٰرُونَهُۥ عَلَىٰ مَا يَرَىٰ ١٢ وَلَقَدۡ رَءَاهُ نَزۡلَةً أُخۡرَىٰ ١٣ عِندَ
سِدۡرَةِ ٱلۡمُنتَهَىٰ ١٤ عِندَهَا جَنَّةُ ٱلۡمَأۡوَىٰٓ ١٥ إِذۡ يَغۡشَى ٱلسِّدۡرَةَ مَا يَغۡشَىٰ ١٦ مَا زَاغَ ٱلۡبَصَرُ وَمَا
طَغَىٰ ١٧ لَقَدۡ رَأَىٰ مِنۡ ءَايَٰتِ رَبِّهِ ٱلۡكُبۡرَىٰٓ ١٨ ﴾

Understood Meaning

[53:1] I swear by the star when it goes down.

[53:2] Your companion [Muhammad] does not err, nor does he go astray;

[53:3] Nor does he speak out of desire.

[53:4] It is nothing but revelation that is revealed,

[53:5] The Mighty Jibreel has taught him,

[53:6] He looked powerful and handsome up high,

[53:7] When he was in the highest part of the horizon.

[53:8] Then he drew near, hanging [above Muhammad]

[53:9] So he was two bows far or even closer .

[53:10] And He revealed to Allah's servant what He revealed.

[53:11] The heart was not mistaken in what he saw.

[53:12] What! do you then dispute with him about what he saw?

[53:13] And certainly he saw him in another descent,

[53:14] At the farthest lote-tree;

[53:15] Near which is the Paradise.

[53:16] When the lote-tree was covered with greatness;

[53:17] The eye did not blur, nor did it miss.

[53:18] Certainly he saw the greatest signs of his Lord.

CHAPTER REVIEW

Projects and Activities

1. Read a brief book about Al-Isra' and Al-Mi'raj and write a 700-word book review on it.
2. Watch a documentary about Al-Quds and Al-Masjid-ul-Aqsa, and then write a 700 word report about what you learned.
3. Develop a list of at least three jobs Jibreel does serving Allah.

Stretch Your Mind

1. The Holy Spirit means a different thing for Muslims and Christians. What is the main difference in the definition of the Holy Spirit in Islam and Christianity?
2. Why did the Qur'an describe Jibreel as "very powerful?" Include in your answer at least three reasons for that.

Study Questions

1. Who is Jibreel? Include in your answer at least one ayah that mentions Jibreel in name.
2. What other names does Jibreel have?
3. What did Jibreel do in Ghar Hira'? Include in your answer the ayaat that describes this event.
4. What did Jibreel do during the night of Al-Isra' and Al-Mi'raj?
5. How did Jibreel protect and supported the Muslims at the time of Prophet Muhammad?
6. When and where were prayers prescribed to Muslims? Describe that event.
7. When did Prophet Muhammad see Jibreel in his real form?
8. What is the main job of Jibreel?
9. What other jobs does Jibreel have?
10. Define: Sidrat-ul-Muntaha, Al-Bayt-ul-Ma'moor, Al-Buraq, Baytul-Maqdis, Trinity.

The Great Hadeeth of Jibreel
Jibreel Teaches Sahabah about Islam

CHAPTER OUTLINE

1. The great Hadeeth of Jibreel.
2. What are the ethics of seeking knowledge?
3. What is Islam?
4. What are the pillars of Iman?
5. What is Ihsan?
6. What are some of the signs of the Day of Judgment?

VOCABULARY

- Islam إسْلام
- Salam سَلام
- Iman إيمان
- Ihsan إحْسان
- Hadeeth Jibreel حَديثُ جِبْريل
- The Pillars of Islam أرْكانُ الإسْلام
- Shahadah شَهادة
- Salah صلاة
- Zakah زكاة
- Siyam صِيام
- Hajj حَج

In this chapter you will learn one of the greatest ahadeeth of Prophet Muhammad. It is known as حديث جبريل Hadeeth of Jibreel. It was the only hadeeth that Prophet Muhammad said while Angel Jibreel was sitting with him in the form of a man. Jibreel asked the Prophet many important questions and received the Prophet's answers to them. Jibreel demonstrated how a serious student behaves in a learning setting. Let's learn what happened.

حَديثُ جِبْريل

عن عمر بن الخطاب رضي الله عنه قال : بينما نحنُ عندَ رَسولِ الله صَلى الله عليه وسلمَ ذاتَ يَوْم ، إذ طلعَ علينا رَجُلٌ شَديدُ بياض الثيابِ ، شَديدُ سَوادِ الشَّعر ، لا يُرى عليه أثَرُ السَّفر، ولا يعْرفُهُ منّا أحدٌ ، حتّى جلس إلى النبيِّ صَلى اللهُ عليهِ وَسلمَ ، فأسْندَ رُكْبتيْهِ إلى رُكْبتيْهِ ، ووضعَ كَفَّيْهِ على فخذيْهِ ، وقال : يا مُحَمَّدُ ، أخبِرْني عن الإسْلام ؟ فقالَ رَسولُ اللهِ صلى اللهُ عَليْهِ وَسلَّمِ : (الإسلامُ أنْ تَشْهدَ أنْ لا إلهَ إلا اللهُ وأنَّ مُحَمَّداً رَسُولُ اللهِ ، وتقيمَ الصَّلاةَ ، وتُؤْتي الزَّكاةَ ، وتَصومَ رمَضانَ ، وتَحُجَّ البَيْتَ إن اسْتطعْتَ إليْهِ سَبيلا) . قالَ : صَدقْتَ ، قالَ : فَعجِبْنا لهُ يَسْألهُ ويُصَدِّقهُ .

قالَ : فأخْبرْني عن الإيمان ؟ قال : (أنْ تُؤمنَ بالله وملائكتهِ وكُتبهِ ورُسُلهِ واليوْمِ الآخرِ ، وتؤْمنَ بالقدَرِ خيره وشره) . قال : صَدقْتَ .

قالَ فأخْبرني عن الإحْسان؟ قال: (أنْ تعْبُدَ اللهَ كأنكَ تراهُ ، فإنْ لمْ تكُنْ تراهُ فإنّه يراك).

قالَ : فأخْبرني عن السّاعة ؟ قال : (ما المَسْئولُ عَنْها بأعْلَمَ منَ السّائل) .

قالَ : فأخْبرني عن أماراتِها ؟ قال : (أنْ تلِدَ الأمَةُ رَبَّتَها ، وَأنْ تَرى الحُفاةَ العُراةَ العالَةَ رِعاءَ الشاءِ يَتطاولون في البُنْيان) .

قالَ : ثمَّ انطَلَقَ ، فَلبثْتُ مَليًّا ، ثمَّ قالَ لي : (يا عُمَر ، أتدْري مَن السّائل ؟) .

قلتُ : اللهُ ورَسولُهُ أعْلَمُ .

قالَ : (فإنَّهُ جِبْريلُ أتاكُم يُعلِّمُكُمْ دِينَكُمْ) رواه مسلم

The Hadeeth of Jibreel

Omar Ibn-ul-Khattab, (R) said:" While we were sitting one day with Rasoolullah ﷺ , there appeared to us a man dressed in extremely white clothes and with very black hair. No traces of traveling were visible on him, and none of us knew him.

He sat by the Prophet ﷺ , rested his knees to those of the Prophet, put his hands on the Prophet's thighs, and said, "O Muhammad! Tell me about Islam."

Rasoolullah ﷺ said, "Islam is to testify that there is no god but Allah and that Muhammad is His Messenger, to perform salah (prayer), pay the zakah (charity), fast during Ramadan, and perform Hajj (pilgrimage) to the House (Al-Ka'bah at Makkah), if you can travel to it."

The man said, "You have spoken the truth."

We were astonished; he asks him and approves what he said [as if he knew the answer before]. Then he went on to say, "Tell me about iman (faith)."

Rasoolullah ﷺ answered, "It is to believe in Allah, His angels, His Books, His Messengers and in the Last Day, and to believe in Qadar (fate),both in its good and in its evil aspects." The man said, "You have spoken the truth."

Then he (the man) said, "Tell me about ihsan." Rasoolullah ﷺ answered, "To worship and serve Allah as though you could see Him, although you cannot see Him, yet He sees you."

He said, "Inform me about the Hour."

Rasoolullah ﷺ said, "I don't know more about it than you."

So he said, "Well, tell me about its signs thereof (i.e. of its coming).

Said he, "The slave woman will give birth to her mistress, that you will see the barefooted ones, the naked, the poor, the herdsmen of the sheep (competing with each other to build) high rise buildings." Thereupon the man went off.

I waited a while, and then he (Rasoolullah ﷺ) said, "Oh Omar, do you know who that questioner was?"

I replied, "Allah and His messenger know better."

He said, "That was Jibreel. He came to teach you your religion."

[Muslim]

Main Lessons

1. Etiquettes of Learning

This hadeeth teaches the importance of learning and searching for knowledge. It also shows the adab (ethics) of seeking knowledge. Here are some of ethics of seeking knowledge that we can find in the hadeeth :

* We should have clear intention; to learn the knowledge for the sake of Allah alone.

* We should be clean and wear clean and tidy clothes.

* We should sit properly and close to the speaker. It is narrated that Jibreel first sat a little far apart, but the Prophet ﷺ invited him to come nearer to him.

* We should ask short and good questions to gain better understanding.

* We should seek knowledge from the right source and authority.

* We should maintain good listening skills. Jibreel asked his questions and listened carefully to what the Prophet ﷺ had to say.

2. Asking Good Questions is Half of Knowledge.

A well-known Arabic proverb says "A question is half of knowledge." This is true, because a question encourages teachers to impart their knowledge. Allah says in Surat-ul-Anbiyaa':

﴿فَسْـَٔلُوٓاْ أَهْلَ ٱلذِّكْرِ إِن كُنتُمْ لَا تَعْلَمُونَ ۝٧﴾

الأنبياء: ٧

So ask the knowledgeable people if you do not know. [21:7]

In the Qur'an , there are more than 1,200 questions.

Questions serve different educational purposes. Most importantly, they provoke the mind of the reader or listener to think about what he/she reads or hears.

In many ahadeeth of the Prophet ﷺ, he started by asking questions before he taught a lesson. Asking questions prepares the learners' minds and hearts, so the learners will be ready for answers and the knowledge in them.

When Ibn Abbas, one of the greatest scholars among the sahabah, was asked how he obtained all his knowledge, he replied: "with a questioning tongue and a reflecting heart.."

The type of questions we ask should be short and meaningful questions that will lead to valuable knowledge and good action. We should think about our question before asking it, to make sure that an answer to it will help us learn. Asking good questions will result in better learning as well as teaching. Those who are present when the questions are asked will also learn from the answers - thus, the questioner is teaching the others.

Angel Jibreel (AA) only asked questions and he didn't give any answers. In spite of that, the Prophet ﷺ described his action as "teaching Islam," when he said, "That was Jibreel. He came to teach you religion." Therefore, the good questions of Jibreel caused the Sahabah to learn from Rasoolullah ﷺ good knowledge. Similarly, your good questions and those of your classmates may help your class to learn important things in life.

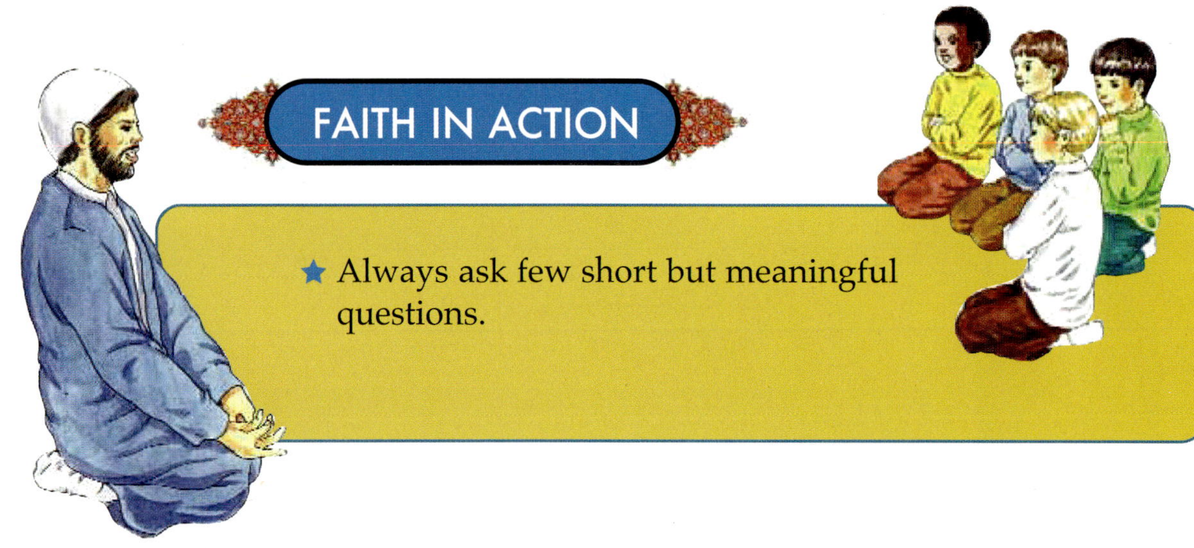

FAITH IN ACTION

- Always ask few short but meaningful questions.

3. The Pillars of Islam أركان الإسلام :

We know that you learned about the Five Pillars of Islam many years ago. Also, Jibreel asked the Prophet ﷺ about the Five Pillars in the presence of the Sahabah, who had learned the pillars many years before. Why? Allah wanted to remind the Sahabah and show them the importance of the Five Pillars of Islam.

The word Islam means "submission to God." The word Islam is derived from سَلام salam, which means "peace." Therefore, submitting to God brings peace and serenity to mankind. If you feel worried or afraid of someone or something that may harm you, you run to safety. There you attain peace of heart and stop worrying. In this life, there are many evil and harmful things and powers. Therefore, when you submit yourself to God, the most powerful of all, you will be safe and at peace.

Islam requires that you do five major acts of faith and worship:

a. To declare Shahadah الشهادة , or to believe and bear witness that there is no God but Allah and that Muhammad ﷺ is His final messenger.

Muslims repeat these words again and again during the course of their daily prayers. This declaration also marks the entry of a new Muslim into Islam, whereby he or she enjoys the brotherhood and fellowship of other Muslims.

Muslims pray in Al-Masjid-ul-Aqsa in Jerusalem.

b. To perform salah صلاة, or pray five times a day.

To maintain a strong spiritual relationship with your Creator, the five daily prayers are prescribed for Muslims during specified times of the day:

1. Dawn فَجْر
2. Noon ظُهْر
3. Mid-afternoon عَصْر
4. Sunset مَغْرب
5. Nightfall عِشاء

Although it is much preferable and more rewarding to pray in the masjid, we may pray in a clean place, virtually anywhere. The Islamic prayer involves standing, bowing, prostrating, and sitting in postures of humility before Allah. While in these postures, we recite verses of the Holy Qur'an and supplications in Arabic. During prayer, Muslims throughout the world face the holy city of Makkah, where the prophets Ibraheem and Isma'eel built the first house of worship of God on Earth. Al-Ka'bah, means "cubic building."

c. To give out zakah زكاة , or required charity -

Since all things belong to God, our wealth and possessions are only loaned to us by Allah. Accordingly, a 2.5% portion of a Muslim's wealth is a trust given to him on behalf of the poor, and every year must be given to help the poor. Muslims are encouraged to give additional optional charity to satisfy the needs of the poor and the disadvantaged.

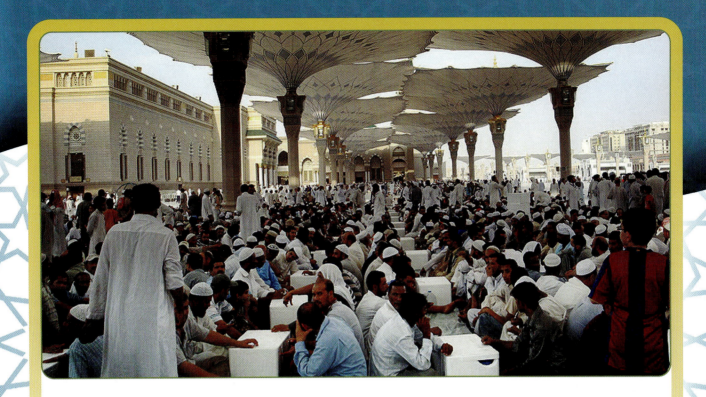

d. To observe siyam صيام , or fast the whole month of Ramadan.

Each year, during the month of Ramadan (the ninth month in the Muslim lunar calendar), Muslims must fast from dawn to sunset. They abstain from food and drink. Fasting teaches Muslims self-discipline and control of their desires. It trains them to develop strong will. Also the fasting person develops greater compassion for the plight of those who are hungry. Zakat-ul-Fitr, or charity of breaking the fast at the end of Ramadan, is a practical expression of this compassion.

e. To perform Hajj حج , or pilgrimage to Makkah at least once in a lifetime.

All Muslims who are physically fit and financially able are required to make a pilgrimage to Makkah at least once in their lives. More than two million pilgrims visit the holy city in the month of Thul-Hijjah; the last lunar month of each Islamic year. Many of the Hajj rites commemorate the remarkable obedience, submission, and sacrifices of Prophet Ibraheem and his older son, Prophet Isma'eel. Muslim pilgrims usually return to their homelands spiritually charged and more attached to Islamic values and the Muslim community. The refreshing experience of meeting great numbers of Muslim brothers and sisters of various races, colors, backgrounds and nationalities in one place is difficult to describe in words. Performing the same worship in similar humble garments leaves an unforgettable impression of brotherhood and unity.

Muslims perform Hajj in Al-Masjid-ul-Haram in Makkah.

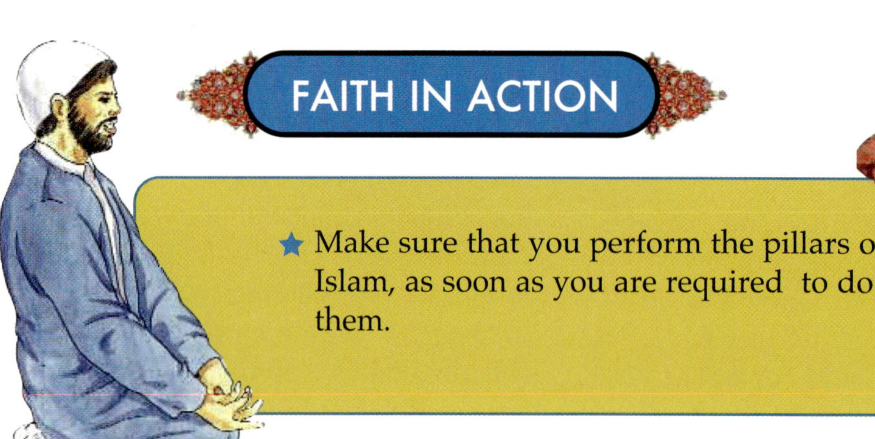

FAITH IN ACTION

- Make sure that you perform the pillars of Islam, as soon as you are required to do them.

These duties are called pillars to liken them to the pillars of a building. If the pillars are removed, the building will crumble. Even if one pillar falls, a part of the building, if not all, will fall too. Similarly, if a Muslim disbelieves in the pillars of Islam or some of them, he or she will not be a Muslim anymore.

4. The Articles of Faith

Angel Jibreel also asked Prophet Muhammad ﷺ about iman, which means strong belief or faith in the unseen. Rasoolullah , in his answer, explained the six articles of faith in Islam. Every Muslim is required to believe in and live by the six major articles of faith. These articles have deep, positive, and practical effects on the Muslim's daily life. They are as follows:

Jerusalem; many prophets and messengers passed through here

a. Belief in one God, Supreme and Eternal, Endlessly Merciful.

Allah reaches out to all His creations with compassion, mercy and care. He is ever available to His servants when they need to call upon Him for help, support or repentance. Allah cannot be seen in this life. He does not physically merge with His creatures or descend into them like people of some other faiths believe. He is unique, singular, and has neither partners nor associates.

b. Belief in all Prophets and messengers of God.

Allah sent a messenger or more to every nation of the ancient world. Allah says in Surat Fatir:

﴿ وَإِن مِّنْ أُمَّةٍ إِلَّا خَلَا فِيهَا نَذِيرٌ ﴿٢٤﴾ ﴾

فاطر: ٢٤

...and there was not a people but a messenger has been sent to them. [35:24]

Twenty-five prophets and messengers are named in the Qur'an. Among them are Adam, Nooh (Noah), Ibraheem (Abraham), Musa (Musa), Isa (Jesus) and Muhammad. There are thousands of other prophets and messengers that are not mentioned in the Holy Qur'an. Allah said in Surat An-Nisaa':

﴿ وَرُسُلًا قَدْ قَصَصْنَٰهُمْ عَلَيْكَ مِن قَبْلُ وَرُسُلًا لَّمْ نَقْصُصْهُمْ عَلَيْكَ ﴿١٦٤﴾ ﴾

النساء: ١٦٤

And (We sent) messengers We have mentioned to you before and messengers we have not mentioned to you. [4:164]

Muslims must believe that all these prophets brought the message of Islam, which teaches the oneness of God and submission to His will. Some messengers brought holy books from Allah.

c. Belief in the Books Revealed to Previous Prophets. Holy books revealed to Ibraheem, Musa, Dawood, Isa and Muhammad are mentioned in the Qur'an. However, due to lack of proper documentation, all holy books other than the Qur'an were neglected, changed, concealed or lost over time. The Qur'an is the only true, authentic and complete book of God in existence. It is also the only scripture that was recorded in its entirety during the lifetime of the prophet to whom it was revealed. It is the only book that remained in the original language of revelation. Therefore, it is the final message of Allah that must be followed by all mankind.

d. Belief in angels, spiritual beings whose function is to worship and serve God.

As you learned earlier, angels are one of the highly specialized creations of Allah. They are created from light and they only worship Allah and do good deeds. The most distinguished angel is Jibreel (Gabriel), who communicated God's revelations to His messengers. Jibreel is referred to in the Qur'an as "the Holy Spirit."

e. Belief in the Day of Judgment and the Eternal Life.

Every action, every word, and every intention of man in this life is recorded. Those with good records will go on to endless bliss in Jannah (Heaven), while those with bad records will suffer in Jahannam (Hell). Because these consequences will be absolutely real, the life-to-come is far more important than the present life. This belief causes the devout Muslim to be always mindful of God and heedful.

f. Belief in Al-Qadar.

Al-Qadar is God's commands and will concerning this world before it was created. The word Qadar comes from the Qur'an and the Sunnah. Allah says in Surat-ul-Qamar:Surely We have created everything according to a qadar (command and measure). [54:49]

﴿ إِنَّا كُلَّ شَيْءٍ خَلَقْنَٰهُ بِقَدَرٍ ٤٩ ﴾

القمر: ٤٩

And Allah calls upon Muslims to accept their Lord's will on them. He says in Surat-ut-Tawbah:

﴿ قُل لَّن يُصِيبَنَآ إِلَّا مَا كَتَبَ ٱللَّهُ لَنَا هُوَ مَوْلَىٰنَا ۚ وَعَلَى ٱللَّهِ فَلْيَتَوَكَّلِ ٱلْمُؤْمِنُونَ ٥١ ﴾

التوبة: ٥١

Say: "Nothing shall ever happen to us except what Allah has willed for us. He is our Lord and Protector. And in Allah let the believers put their trust." [Surat-ut-tawbah 9:51]

Also Prophet Muhammad ﷺ mentioned the belief in Al-Qadar, its good and evil, in the Hadeeth of Jibreel. He said that a part of iman is

وتؤمن بالقدر خيره وشره

"...to believe in qadar, both in its good and in its evil aspects."

This belief helps people to accept what happens to them in this life. However, people think that everything they do, like sin, is meant to be by God's qadar. That is incorrect understanding of Al-Qadar. Some people confuse the "actions upon people" with the "actions taken by people." The actions you take out of your free will are your own actions. You are responsible for them. Allah has given you the freedom to act and choose to do good deeds or bad ones. Allah encourages you to do good deeds, but He will not stop you if you insist on doing bad things because He gave you the brain and the freedom of choice with it.

However, actions which occur to you like weather, attacks, accidents, or diseases are acts of God and types of qadar, and they are meant for wisdom. Allah either wants to:

* test your faith,
* strengthen your will,
* wipe off some of your sins,
* grant you great rewards
* make you appreciate the gifts He

gave you like health, wealth and happiness,

* protect you against problems that are worse than the ones you have,

He has wisdom which we may never understand.

Finally, God is aware of all actions (good or bad), before, as, and after they occur. However, human beings are given the choice of doing what is good or what is evil. Hence, they enjoy or suffer the consequences of their actions in this life or in the Hereafter.

5. Al-Ihsan, Doing Good Things to Yourself and Others

Jibreel also asked the Prophet ﷺ about Al-Ihsan. Ihsan in Arabic is perfection or excellence. That is showing excellent worship, service and behavior. In this hadeeth, the Prophet teaches us about what would help us maintain excellent behavior toward Allah and His creation. The Prophet's ﷺ advice is:

1. to worship Allah as if we see Him, and,
2. to worship with the thought that He is seeing us.

If we always behave as if we see Allah, and be mindful that He is watching what we do, then our behavior will be excellent. The problem is that we tend to forget or become unaware that Allah is truly watching upon us.

﴿ وَأَحْسِن كَمَا أَحْسَنَ ٱللَّهُ إِلَيْكَ ﴿٧٧﴾ ﴾

القصص: ٧٧

"... and do good as Allah has done good to you." [28:77]

﴿ وَأَحْسِنُوٓا۟ إِنَّ ٱللَّهَ يُحِبُّ ٱلْمُحْسِنِينَ ﴿١٩٥﴾ ﴾

البقرة: ١٩٥

And spend in the way of Allah and cast not yourselves to perdition with your own hands, and do good (to others); surely Allah loves the doers of good. [2:195]

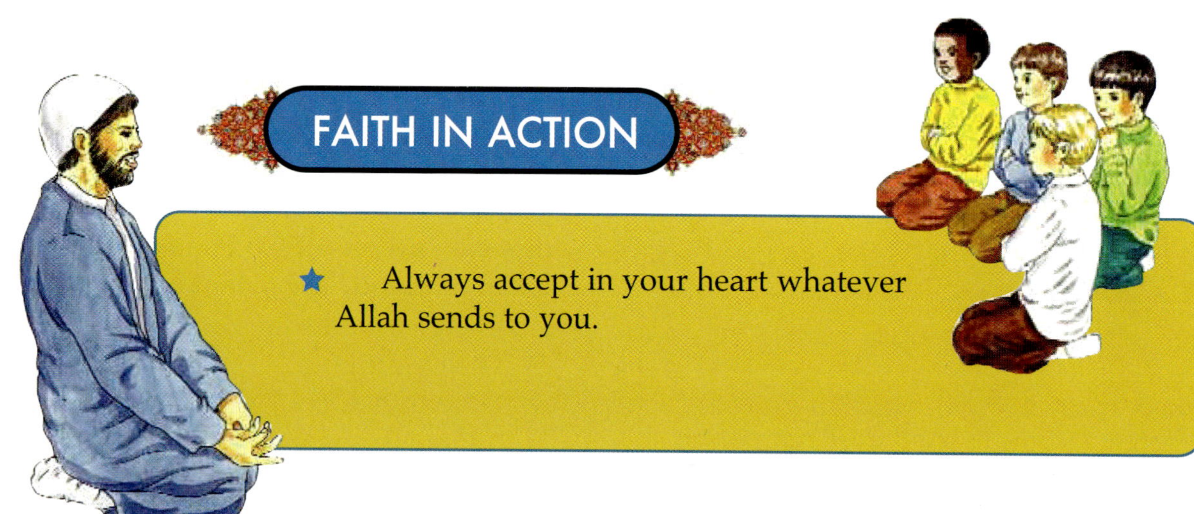

FAITH IN ACTION
★ Always accept in your heart whatever Allah sends to you.

Hadeeth Shareef

عن أبي يعلى شداد بن أوس رضي الله عنه ، عن رسول الله صلى الله عليه وسلم قال :

(إِنَّ اللهَ كَتبَ الإحْسانَ عَلى كُلِّ شَيْءٍ...) رواه مسلم

Abu Ya'la Shaddad Ibn Aws said that the Messenger of Allah ﷺ said:

"Surely Allah has required goodness in all things."

Reported by Muslim.

Try always to show ihsan, or excellent deeds toward Allah and His creation, as He has granted you excellent gifts.

6. The Signs of the "Hour"

Jibreel (P) finally asked the Prophet about the time of the Day of Judgment. The Prophet didn't know when that day will happen. Therefore, he told Jibreel that he didn't know better than he. Rasoolullah, didn't feel embarrassed to say "I don't know!"

Yawm-ul-Qiyahmah, or the Day of Judgment, is also called "The Hour." Allah says in Surat-ul-Qamar:

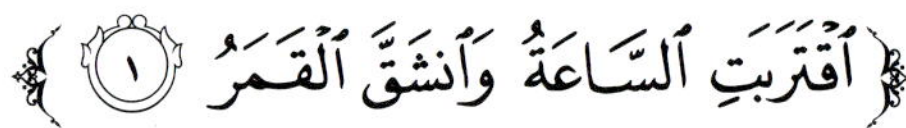

القمر: ١

The hour draws near and the moon did split. [54:1]

Only Allah knows when the Hour will take place. Allah says in Surat-ul-A'raf:

﴿ يَسْـَٔلُونَكَ عَنِ ٱلسَّاعَةِ أَيَّانَ مُرْسَىٰهَا ۖ قُلْ إِنَّمَا عِلْمُهَا عِندَ رَبِّى ۖ لَا يُجَلِّيهَا لِوَقْتِهَآ إِلَّا هُوَ ﴿١٨٧﴾ ﴾

الأعراف: ١٨٧

They ask you about the Hour, when will it take place? Say: The knowledge of it is only with my Lord; only He shall make its time known. [7:187]

So, when the Prophet couldn't answer the question. Jibreel asked the Prophet about the signs of the Day of Judgment. These signs tell that Yawm-ul-Qiyamah is near. There are major and minor signs of the Hour. Among the major signs are the sun rising from the west, the appearance of the false messiah, and the return of Jesus Christ to Earth. The Prophet in this hadeeth only mentioned two of the minor signs. He mentioned that desert people will gain wealth and compete in building high rises, and slave women will give birth to their mistresses. There are many other minor signs like people getting killed in large numbers, the appearance of Al-Mahdi (a great imam who will help Muslims at the end of time) and other minor signs.

CHAPTER REVIEW

Projects and Activities

1. Write a profile about Omar Ibn-ul-Khattab, the Sahabi who narrated the Hadeeth of Jibreel. Write about the first five points of Omar's life story below and only one of the remaining subjects there after:

1. Name
2. Place of Birth
3. Tribe and family
4. Life before Islam
5. How did he become a Muslim?
6. His Hijrah to Madinah
7. Battles and important events he participated in
8. Omar as a khaleefah
9. Omar's death

Stretch Your Mind

1. There are thousands of ahadeeth and stories of the Prophet and the Sahabah. However, this is the only time when Jibreel (P) appeared to the Sahabah. Why do you think this was the only time?
2. What is the difference between Islam and Iman?
3. Why do you think Allah kept the time of Yawm-ul-Qiyamah secret?

Study Questions

1. Describe Jibreel as he appeared to the Prophet and the Sahabah.
2. What are the ethics of learning from a teacher as Jibreel (P) showed in this hadeeth?
3. "A good question is half of knowledge." Explain this proverb.
4. What made Angel Jibreel's questions very effective?
5. What are the Pillars of Islam? Explain two of these pillars.
6. What are the Articles of Iman? Explain two of these articles.
7. Explain ihsan.
8. When is the Day of Judgment?
9. What does the "Signs of the Hour" mean?

LESSON ONE

Surat-ul-Jinn Verses (1-7) سورة الجن
A group of jinn believe in the Qur'an

CHAPTER OUTLINE

1. What are the jinn?
2. What are the different types of jinn?
3. How are the jinn different to us?

VOCABULARY

Jinn جن

Introduction

This surah was revealed in Makkah and has twenty-eight ayaat. The surah speaks about unseen beings created by Allah. It describes the behavior of a group of the jinn who chose to become Muslims. They obeyed Allah and His messenger Muhammad and disobeyed Iblees the leader of the evil jinn.

سورة الجن

Surat-ul-Jinn 1-7

﴿ قُلْ أُوحِيَ إِلَيَّ أَنَّهُ ٱسْتَمَعَ نَفَرٌ مِّنَ ٱلْجِنِّ فَقَالُوٓا۟ إِنَّا سَمِعْنَا قُرْءَانًا عَجَبًا ﴿١﴾ يَهْدِىٓ إِلَى
ٱلرُّشْدِ فَـَٔامَنَّا بِهِۦ ۖ وَلَن نُّشْرِكَ بِرَبِّنَآ أَحَدًا ﴿٢﴾ وَأَنَّهُۥ تَعَٰلَىٰ جَدُّ رَبِّنَا مَا ٱتَّخَذَ صَٰحِبَةً وَلَا وَلَدًا ﴿٣﴾
وَأَنَّهُۥ كَانَ يَقُولُ سَفِيهُنَا عَلَى ٱللَّهِ شَطَطًا ﴿٤﴾ وَأَنَّا ظَنَنَّآ أَن لَّن تَقُولَ ٱلْإِنسُ وَٱلْجِنُّ عَلَى ٱللَّهِ
كَذِبًا ﴿٥﴾ وَأَنَّهُۥ كَانَ رِجَالٌ مِّنَ ٱلْإِنسِ يَعُوذُونَ بِرِجَالٍ مِّنَ ٱلْجِنِّ فَزَادُوهُمْ رَهَقًا ﴿٦﴾ وَأَنَّهُمْ ظَنُّوا۟
كَمَا ظَنَنتُمْ أَن لَّن يَبْعَثَ ٱللَّهُ أَحَدًا ﴿٧﴾ ﴾

Understood Meaning

(72:1) Say: It has been revealed to me, that a group of jinn heard me reciting the Qur'an and they went and told their people, "We have just heard an amazing recitation."
(72:2) It guides you to true understanding, so we believed in it and we will not worship anyone other than our Lord.
(72:3) And we believe He is high over everything and He is our Lord, who never had a wife or a child,
(72:4) And the foolish among us (Iblees and his followers) used to say about Allah terrible lies.
(72:5) And we used to think that no human or jinn would ever tell a lie against Allah.
(72:6) And some men from mankind used to call on jinn for help, but they (jinn) added to their troubles.
(72:7) And they thought, like you used to think, that Allah would not bring anyone back from the grave.

Story of the Surah

Abdullah Ibn Mas'ood narrated, "We were with the Messenger of Allah one night and then suddenly we couldn't find him. We searched everywhere in the valley and surrounding passages and then we said, 'The jinn have taken him or he was secretly killed.' So then we had the worst night possible. The next morning he came from the direction of Hira' (the mountain with the cave in it where revelation first came down). We said, 'Oh Messenger of Allah, we lost you and we kept looking but we couldn't find you. So we just had the worst night possible.' He said, A jinn came to me calling me to a group of jinn. So I went with him and read to them the Qur'an. So then he took us to show us their traces and the traces of their fire."

Abdullah Ibn Abbas said, "The Messenger of Allah didn't read to the jinn or see them before. Rasoolullah had taken off with some of his companions to the Ukkath market (a place to about 50 miles the east of Makkah). At this time the shayateen were unable to approach Heaven and listen to what was going on. If they did, comets were thrown against them (there was an unusually high amount of shooting stars). So the devils went back to their people and it was said to them, "What happened to you?" They said, "We were prevented from approaching Heaven and listening to what is going on in the upper heavens; comets were thrown against us." Their people said, "Something has happened, so go search the land in the east and west and find out what happened that has prevented us from listening to the Heavens." So they left searching in the directions of east and west. A group of them passed by Prophet Muhammad ﷺ as he was leading his companions in Fajr prayer (When they were on their way to Ukkath market). When they heard the Qur'an they stopped and listened to it. Then they said, "This is what has come between us and listening to the Heavens." Then they returned to their people and said, "We have just heard an amazing recitation…" Then Allah revealed to His Messenger, "Say: It has been revealed to me, that a group of jinn heard me reciting the Qur'an and they went and told their people, 'We have just heard an amazing recitation.'

It is also related that the jinn asked him about food, and he said, "You can have every bone that Allah's name was mentioned over. When it is in your hands it will be covered with meat. And dung is food for your animals. *(All of the above narrations are reported in Saheeh Muslim)*

Lessons Learned

1. Who are the jinn?

The jinn are part of the unseen world. They are creatures of Allah that live and think independently. The jinn are made from a fire that was very hot and had no smoke. Jinn have abilities that seem magical to humans like becoming invisible, traveling fast, having many different forms and going into and through objects.

Each jinn can be good or evil. The evil jinn are called shayateen, or devils. They have gone away from the straight path. Shayateen, or devils, are under the leadership of Iblees, the one who refused to obey Allah and bow to Adam. Iblees is the father of all jinn as Adam is the father of all humans.

Like humans, those among the jinn who believe and obey Allah will go to Heaven. On the contrary, those who disbelieve and disobey Allah will go to Hell. To the best of our knowledge Allah has not sent a messenger from among the jinn to them. All messengers have come from the Children of Adam. Some of the previous prophets had been sent to the jinn. For example, Prophet Sulayman, or Solomon, had extensive involvement with the jinn. Prophet Muhammad ﷺ was specifically sent as a messenger to humans and jinn.

Good Muslim jinn, like good Muslim humans, do not usually hurt other Muslims. Evil jinn, however, may harm other jinn or humans. Sometimes, they may harm people by possessing them and controlling them mentally and physically. Allah and Prophet Muhammad ﷺ taught Muslims how to protect themselves from the harm of evil jinn.

1. Keep a close relationship with Allah
2. Read Al-Qur'an on daily basis
3. Practice thikr, or remembrance of Allah, every day

The above good deeds will help you

Evil jinn are called Shaytan

keep the evil jinn far away inshaAllah. Shayateen get hurt when a Muslim performs these kinds of Ibadah. So, a household busy with salah, Qur'an, thikr, isti'aathah, good deeds and other forms of obedience will be protected and sealed against shayateen and their evil powers, inshaAllah.

2. Muslim Jinn Believe in Allah and Reject Iblees

This surah shows that even jinn reject the claims of Iblees, who tries his best to confuse people. He causes people and jinn to disbelieve in Allah and to worship false gods or idols. The shayateen encourage others to commit terrible kufr and shirk and to believe blatant lies. These lies include the following:

- There is no God for the universe;
- There are many gods and goddesses for the world;
- God has partners, like a wife, a son and others;
- This life is the only life we will live and there is no Day of Judgment and eternal life;
- Prophets are liars and they committed lots of different major sins.

Even the jinn who are the children of Iblees rejected his lies when they listened to the truth. They loved the Qur'an and followed Allah's true guidance. They never expected that any person or jinn would dare to spread lies and falsehood about Allah. When they heard the truth of Islam, they figured out that Iblees was spreading evil and deceitful lies. When people and jinn believe these lies, they deserve the punishment of Hellfire. This is exactly what Iblees and his followers wish for us.

3. Fortune-Telling, Magic and Witchcraft

The Arabs and other nations before Islam used to call on jinn for help in their travels and other affairs. For example, if one wanted to stay somewhere for the night he would call out: "I ask for the support of the jinn who is in charge." So Allah revealed this verse to inform us that this habit was harmful to both them and the jinn.

Many people also used to seek the help of jinn to learn about the unseen and about God. They realized that jinn have abilities that humans do not have, so they would ask them for help. This is how black magic, witchcraft and fortune-telling started. Jinn can bring news from far away places in seconds. They can make things pop up or disappear in front of your eyes. They also can do many other extraordinary things.

As Allah tells us in these ayaat, some people seek the help of jinn to do unusual things and to impress other people. People like fortune-tellers, magicians and witches appear to perform magic and make people believe that this is their work. In fact it is the invisible jinn who enable them to do their "magic." The jinn carry things around for them and they can also impersonate the "magician" and fly around, go through walls or cut themselves into pieces.

Of course, some "magicians" do not use jinn. They perform illusions using high-level skills to entertain their audiences. This is not really magic but skillful performance and is not prohibited.

Some fortune-tellers claim that they can communicate with the spirits of dead people and pass messages to their relatives and loved ones who are still alive. This is impossible because the dead person's soul cannot be released after they are taken by the angel of death. What happens is that the jinn imitates the voice of the dead person. Today in America many people are beginning to realize that the so-called "mediums," who charge large amounts of money for their services and make dramatic appearances on T.V are indeed frauds. They take advantage of bereaved relatives who deeply miss their loved ones and cannot accept that they are gone. The deeds of the mediums are evil and they are only seeking money, power and television fame. Those who seek the help of mediums have also gone astray, as they should seek the help of Allah alone in their time of grief. This is why in Islam it is absolutely prohibited to take part in witchcraft and black magic. As a matter of fact, it is the worst sin after shirk and disbelief. It is clear then that those people who seek the help of jinn will cause themselves much trouble in this life and in the next. This is what Allah says in ayaat 6 and 7 of this surah.

A magician

Note: It is very possible that good Muslim jinn may approach pious, knowledgeable people seeking guidance and knowledge about Islam in their efforts to become better Muslims.

Hadeeth Shareef

عن أبي هريرة رضي الله عنه قال : قال رسول الله صلى الله عليه وسلم :
" اجتنبوا السبع الموبيقات. قالوا: يا رسول الله وما هن؟
قال: الشرك بالله والسحر " رواه البخاري

Once Rasoolullah said:
"Abandon the destructive sins; worshipping others beside Allah and magic."

Reported in Al-Bukhari

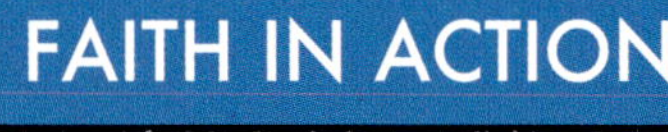

FAITH IN ACTION

- Always ask Allah for help before each class or anything else you do.
- Always ask for the help of Allah first before seeking the help of anyone or anything else.
- Avoid seeking the help of fortune-tellers, evil people, or anyone who deals with devils.

LESSON REVIEW

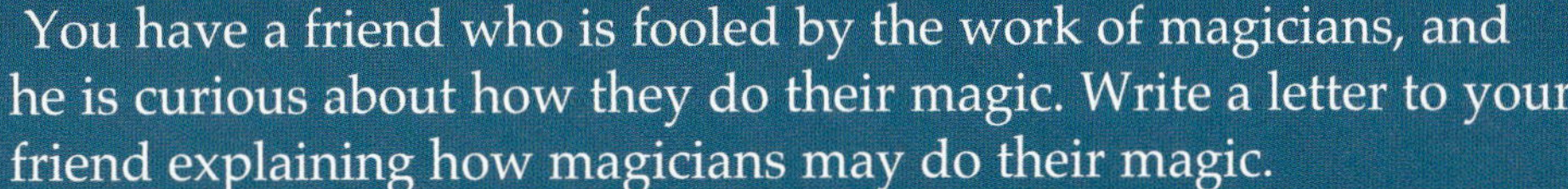

Projects and Activities

You have a friend who is fooled by the work of magicians, and he is curious about how they do their magic. Write a letter to your friend explaining how magicians may do their magic.

Stretch Your Mind

1. Compare and contrast: what are the similarities and differences between the jinn and the angels?

2. Compare and contrast: what are the similarities and differences between the jinn and the humans?

Study Questions

1. What are the jinn?
2. What are they made of?
3. What can evil jinn do to Muslims?
4. Do evil jinn lie? If the answer is yes, what lies do they spread in the world?
5. Do people have dealings with the jinn? In what way?
6. How can a Muslim protect himself and his family from the evil jinn?

LESSON TWO

Surat-ul-Jinn Verses (8-17) سورة الجن
Muslim Jinn and Evil Jinn

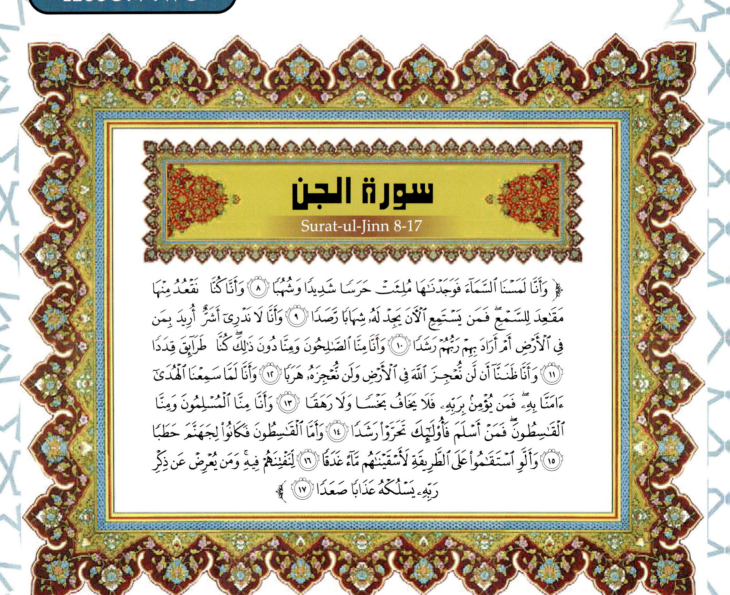

سورة الجن
Surat-ul-Jinn 8-17

﴿ وَأَنَّا لَمَسْنَا ٱلسَّمَآءَ فَوَجَدْنَٰهَا مُلِئَتْ حَرَسًا شَدِيدًا وَشُهُبًا ﴿٨﴾ وَأَنَّا كُنَّا نَقْعُدُ مِنْهَا
مَقَٰعِدَ لِلسَّمْعِ ۖ فَمَن يَسْتَمِعِ ٱلْـَٔانَ يَجِدْ لَهُۥ شِهَابًا رَّصَدًا ﴿٩﴾ وَأَنَّا لَا نَدْرِىٓ أَشَرٌّ أُرِيدَ بِمَن
فِى ٱلْأَرْضِ أَمْ أَرَادَ بِهِمْ رَبُّهُمْ رَشَدًا ﴿١٠﴾ وَأَنَّا مِنَّا ٱلصَّٰلِحُونَ وَمِنَّا دُونَ ذَٰلِكَ ۖ كُنَّا طَرَآئِقَ قِدَدًا
﴿١١﴾ وَأَنَّا ظَنَنَّآ أَن لَّن نُّعْجِزَ ٱللَّهَ فِى ٱلْأَرْضِ وَلَن نُّعْجِزَهُۥ هَرَبًا ﴿١٢﴾ وَأَنَّا لَمَّا سَمِعْنَا ٱلْهُدَىٰٓ
ءَامَنَّا بِهِۦ ۖ فَمَن يُؤْمِنۢ بِرَبِّهِۦ فَلَا يَخَافُ بَخْسًا وَلَا رَهَقًا ﴿١٣﴾ وَأَنَّا مِنَّا ٱلْمُسْلِمُونَ وَمِنَّا
ٱلْقَٰسِطُونَ ۖ فَمَنْ أَسْلَمَ فَأُو۟لَٰٓئِكَ تَحَرَّوْا۟ رَشَدًا ﴿١٤﴾ وَأَمَّا ٱلْقَٰسِطُونَ فَكَانُوا۟ لِجَهَنَّمَ حَطَبًا
﴿١٥﴾ وَأَلَّوِ ٱسْتَقَٰمُوا۟ عَلَى ٱلطَّرِيقَةِ لَأَسْقَيْنَٰهُم مَّآءً غَدَقًا ﴿١٦﴾ لِّنَفْتِنَهُمْ فِيهِ ۚ وَمَن يُعْرِضْ عَن ذِكْرِ
رَبِّهِۦ يَسْلُكْهُ عَذَابًا صَعَدًا ﴿١٧﴾ ﴾

Understood Meaning

(72:8) And when we go up to the sky to listen [to what is happening] we find it filled with powerful guards with flaming comets.

(72:9) And we used to sit in the sky in places we could listen to what was going on in the upper Heavens. Whoever goes to listen now will find a flaming comet waiting to hit him.

(72:10) And we don't know, is this happening because harm is going to be sent against the people on Earth or does their Lord want to send them guidance?

(72:11) Before we heard the Qur'an, some of us were good and some were less than good (this also means that some were believers and some were not). We were divided groups following different religions.

(72:12) And we knew that we cannot stop Allah from doing something in the Earth and we cannot stop him from punishing us by running away.

(72:13) And when we heard the guidance of the Qur'an and we believed in it. Whoever believes in his Lord will not be afraid of missing the reward for his good deeds and will not be afraid of being punished.

(72:14) Some of us are now Muslims and some of us are going away from the straight path. But whoever becomes a Muslim is on the right path.

(72:15) Those who go away from the right path, they will be like wood for Hell.

(72:16) (And Allah says) If they (the Jinn and people) stayed straight on the path, I would send to them lots of rain,

(72:17) As a test to show them who will be thankful and whoever refuses to make remembrance of Allah (by turning away from the Qur'an, or refusing to be thankful), they will enter into a very difficult punishment that will be too hard for them to take.

1. Iblees, the Arrogant Father of Jinn

When Allah created Iblees, a prominent jinn, he hosted him with the angels in Heaven. However, when Iblees disobeyed Allah and refused to prostrate to Adam, Allah expelled him from Heaven. Adam was also expelled from Jannah for his disobedience, but there was a major difference between Adam and Iblees. Prophet Adam recognized his mistake and repented. So, Allah accepted his repentance and will allow him back to Jannah in the Hereafter. Iblees, on the other hand, refused to admit his guilt. So, Allah cursed him and expelled him from Jannah forever. This has placed a great pressure on the offspring of Iblees, as they are born from an evil father. He has made it his mission to guide people and jinn on an evil path, away from the guidance of Allah. Jinn do, however, have the chance to accept Islam and follow the right path as do humans.

2. Jinn Cannot Sneak into Heaven

After Iblees was expelled from the Heavens, he and his followers would try to sneak into Heaven to learn about what was going on there. They would eavesdrop on the conversations of the angels about upcoming events in the world, ordered by Allah.

Abdullah Ibn Abbas رضي الله عنه said: "The shayateen used to go up to the sky to peek and listen. If they heard one true thing, they would mix it with nine false things. (Reported in Tirmithi)

The jinn would take the news and tell their fellow jinn and some humans about it. Humans would find the news interesting. In return for this interesting information the humans would be required to disbelieve in Allah and disobey him. Shayateen would get their human "friends" to disobey Allah by committing major sins. And some humans are foolish enough to even take Shaytan as their lord. Unfortunately, there are many "Satan worshippers" around the world now.

From the time that Muhammad ﷺ became His last Messenger, Allah prevented the jinn from sneaking into the Heavens. The angels boldly guarded the Heavens and would shoot every intruder jinn with a fiery object. The jinn at the time of Prophet Muhammad ﷺ couldn't understand why this was happening. But the reason why Allah سبحانه وتعالى did this was to protect the Qur'an. If the jinn had relayed even a few words of the Qur'an to the fortunetellers before it was revealed to Muhammad ﷺ they could have falsely claimed that the Messenger of Allah ﷺ received the Qur'an from them.

3. Muslim Jinn and Evil Jinn

These ayaat tell the story of the group of jinn who met with Prophet Muhammad ﷺ. They explain that they liked the message of the Qur'an and accepted Islam. They said that there are good and bad among the jinn. They understand that those who become Muslims would follow the straight path. On the other hand, the followers of Iblees will go astray and get punished in Jahannam. They acknowledge that in order for anyone to be on the straight path, one should look for the truth and exert enough effort to follow it. Getting the right guidance requires some work. We have to do our part to study and learn and ask Allah for guidance. If you do your part, Allah will bless you with performing the right actions that will lead you to Paradise insha Allah.

LESSON REVIEW

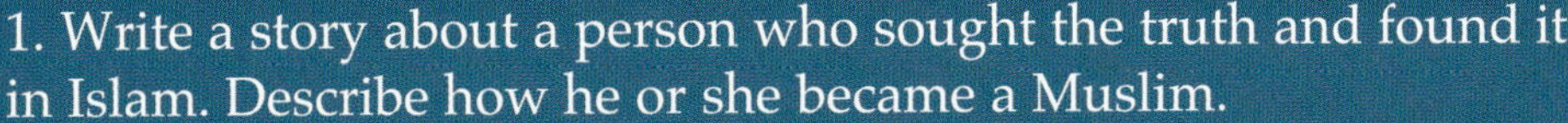

Projects and Activities

1. Write a story about a person who sought the truth and found it in Islam. Describe how he or she became a Muslim.

2. If a community is very good they will be tested in the end with many blessings to see if they will be thankful. If a community is very bad and they refuse warning Allah gives them a lot in this world because they will have nothing in the next. Think about these scenarios and try to find real world examples of each.

Study Questions

1. Who is the father of all jinn?
2. How, in the past, would the jinn get their news about what was going on in Heaven?
3. Why did Allah stop the jinn from sneaking into the Heavens?
4. What are the two types of jinn?
5. What is the name we use for evil jinn?
6. Are there Muslim jinn? If the answer is yes, describe how they became Muslims?

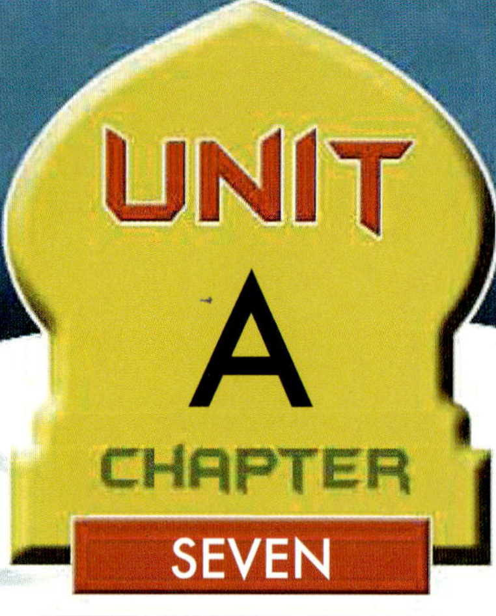

سورة الجن

Surat-ul-Jinn Verses (18-24) The Messenger of Allah Calls People to Islam

UNIT A

CHAPTER SEVEN

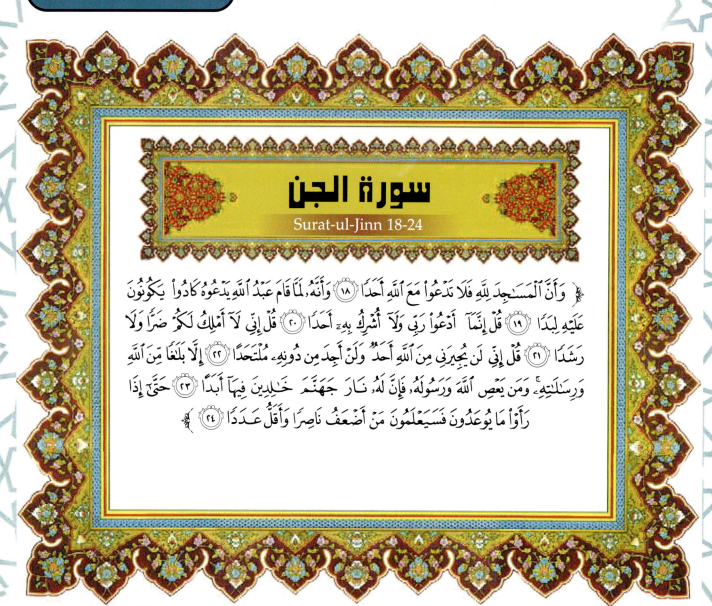

LESSON THREE

سورة الجن

Surat-ul-Jinn 18-24

﴿ وَأَنَّ ٱلْمَسَـٰجِدَ لِلَّهِ فَلَا تَدْعُوا۟ مَعَ ٱللَّهِ أَحَدًا ﴿١٨﴾ وَأَنَّهُۥ لَمَّا قَامَ عَبْدُ ٱللَّهِ يَدْعُوهُ كَادُوا۟ يَكُونُونَ
عَلَيْهِ لِبَدًا ﴿١٩﴾ قُلْ إِنَّمَآ أَدْعُوا۟ رَبِّى وَلَآ أُشْرِكُ بِهِۦٓ أَحَدًا ﴿٢٠﴾ قُلْ إِنِّى لَآ أَمْلِكُ لَكُمْ ضَرًّا وَلَا
رَشَدًا ﴿٢١﴾ قُلْ إِنِّى لَن يُجِيرَنِى مِنَ ٱللَّهِ أَحَدٌ وَلَنْ أَجِدَ مِن دُونِهِۦ مُلْتَحَدًا ﴿٢٢﴾ إِلَّا بَلَـٰغًا مِّنَ ٱللَّهِ
وَرِسَـٰلَـٰتِهِۦ ۚ وَمَن يَعْصِ ٱللَّهَ وَرَسُولَهُۥ فَإِنَّ لَهُۥ نَارَ جَهَنَّمَ خَـٰلِدِينَ فِيهَآ أَبَدًا ﴿٢٣﴾ حَتَّىٰٓ إِذَا
رَأَوْا۟ مَا يُوعَدُونَ فَسَيَعْلَمُونَ مَنْ أَضْعَفُ نَاصِرًا وَأَقَلُّ عَدَدًا ﴿٢٤﴾ ﴾

Understood Meaning

(72:18) (And it has been revealed to me) that all masajid (houses built for worship) are for Allah, so do not worship anyone other than Allah alone.

(72:19) And when the servant of Allah (Prophet Muhammad, peace be upon him) got up to call upon Allah in prayer, the jinn were crowding around almost on top of each other to hear the message.

(72:20) [Oh Muhammad] Say: I only call upon my Lord [and worship Him] and I do not associate other gods with him.

(72:21) [Oh Muhammad] Say: I myself cannot hurt you or guide you.

(72:22) [Oh Muhammad] Say: No one can protect me from Allah if Allah wanted to punish me, and I will not find anyone other than Allah to turn to.

(72:23) [My only protection] is to tell you about Allah and to convey and follow His message. And whoever disobeys Allah and His messenger will get the punishment of Hell forever, and they will never get out.

(72:24) When they see the punishment that they are being promised, they will know who really has the weaker support and who really is fewer in number.

Lessons Learned

1. Masajid are Houses of Allah

The masajid are called "houses of Allah." They belong to Allah and they must be respected. They are strictly built for worship, education and serious community affairs. There we should worship Allah alone, praise Him, recite and learn Al-Qur'an and do the things that make him pleased with us. We should not say or do anything disrespectful in the masajid. There are many Islamic community centers that have a masjid with additional facilities like multipurpose halls and even gymnasiums and playgrounds.

They are designed this way so that after peacefully worshipping in the Masjid brothers and sisters can play, chat or enjoy some sport or entertainment. This ensures that the prayer halls are kept peaceful and pure.

2. Worshipping Allah Alone

At the time of the Prophet (P), the pagans used to worship idols in Al-Masjid-ul-Haram. At one point, there were more than three hundred idols around Al-Ka'bah. When Prophet Muhammad ﷺ called his people to worship the one True God alone, Allah, they crowded together against him. They slandered him, threatened him and almost killed him. In these ayaat, Allah orders the people to worship Allah alone especially in the masajid, or houses of worship. He told His Messenger to continue calling for tawheed, the belief in and worship of the One True Creator.

Allah also guides people to avoid all actions of shirk. As you learned earlier, shirk means believing in and worshipping something other than Allah. The Qur'an teaches us to believe in Allah alone and worship Him, because He is the One who has created and sustained us. He is the only true God ever.

In many houses of worship, people glorify beings or things other than Allah. They even draw pictures and erect statues of their gods in their temples. We are instructed to worship Allah alone and to avoid displaying statues and drawings of living things in our masajid.

LESSON FOUR

Surat-ul-Jinn Verses (25-28) سورة الجن

Only Allah Knows When the Day of Judgment Is

سورة الجن

Surat-ul-Jinn 25-28

﴿ قُلْ إِنْ أَدْرِىٓ أَقَرِيبٌ مَّا تُوعَدُونَ أَمْ يَجْعَلُ لَهُۥ رَبِّىٓ أَمَدًا ﴿٢٥﴾ عَٰلِمُ ٱلْغَيْبِ فَلَا
يُظْهِرُ عَلَىٰ غَيْبِهِۦٓ أَحَدًا ﴿٢٦﴾ إِلَّا مَنِ ٱرْتَضَىٰ مِن رَّسُولٍ فَإِنَّهُۥ يَسْلُكُ مِنۢ بَيْنِ يَدَيْهِ وَمِنْ
خَلْفِهِۦ رَصَدًا ﴿٢٧﴾ لِّيَعْلَمَ أَن قَدْ أَبْلَغُوا۟ رِسَٰلَٰتِ رَبِّهِمْ وَأَحَاطَ بِمَا لَدَيْهِمْ وَأَحْصَىٰ كُلَّ شَىْءٍ
عَدَدًۢا ﴿٢٨﴾ ﴾

Understood Meaning

(72:25) Say: [Oh, disbelievers] I don't know if the punishment you are being promised is coming soon or if it will come upon you after a long time.

(72:26) Allah knows the unseen and Allah shows it to no one

(72:27) Except those who Allah picks as messengers then He sends to them guards to go in front of them and behind them.

(72:28) So that it is known that they delivered the message of their Lord and Allah controls everything they do and Allah knows everything and takes it all into account.

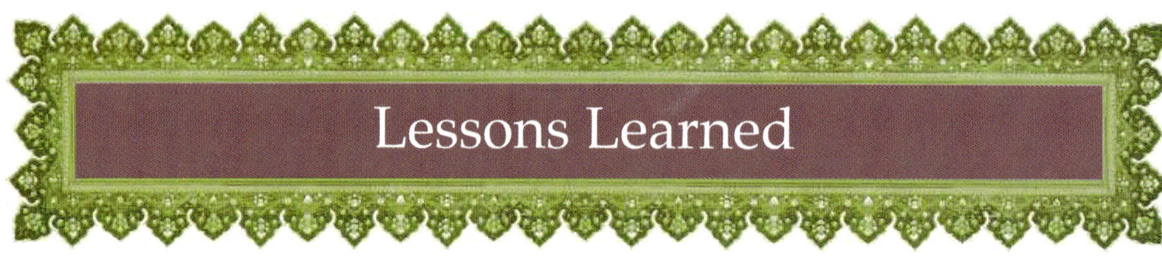

Lessons Learned

1. Only Allah Knows when Punishment is Due

Allah punishes the disbelievers for their evil deeds. He is the only one who decides when and how they should be punished. He might punish them in this life, like he did to the peoples of Nooh, Aad, Thamood, Phir'oun and others. However, He may delay their punishment to the Hereafter. Only God knows when the Day of Judgment will take place, as you learned earlier. However, He may guide them to Islam and forgive them like He did to most of the people of Makkah and Arabia.

2. Only Allah has Full Knowledge of the Unseen and the Future

Allah is the only one who has full knowledge of the unseen and what will happen in the future. He may inform some messengers and angels, like Jibreel, about the future. For example, Allah informed Prophet Muhammad ﷺ about some future developments including the signs of the Day of Judgment. These included the conquest of Constantinople, that Arabia will be filled with high-rise buildings, the return of Prophet Isa, or Jesus, the sun rising from the west and a few other future developments.

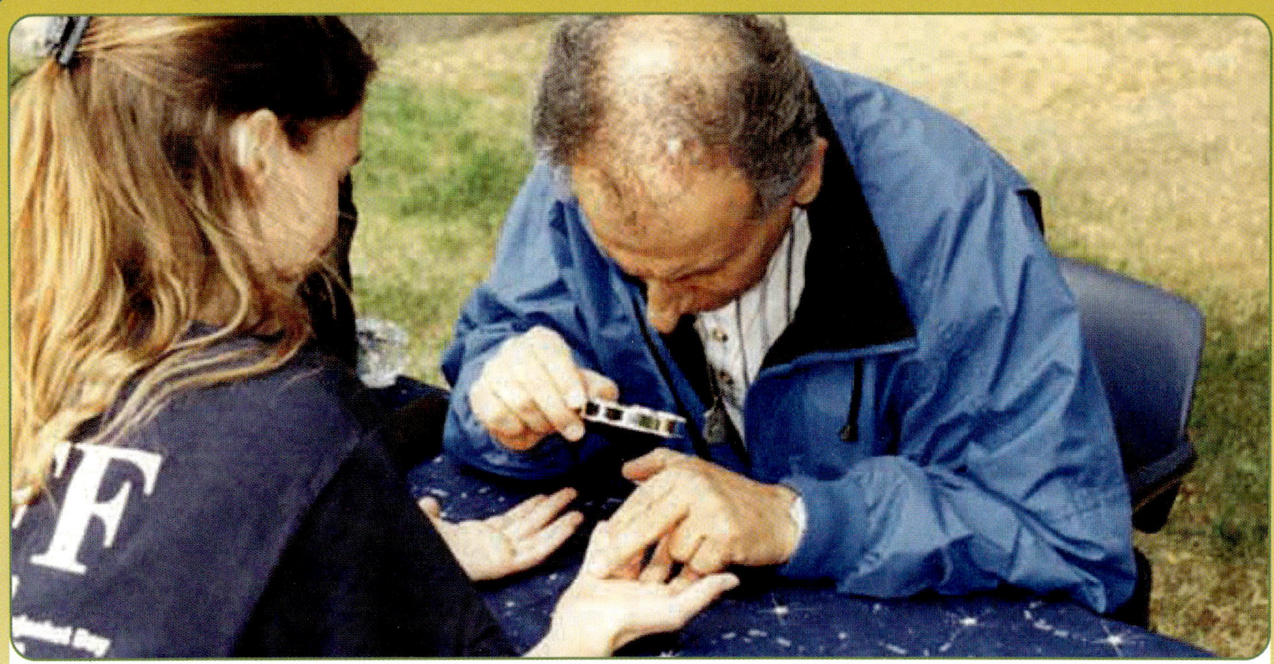

A fortune-teller reads the palm of this lady to determine her future!!

3. It is Haram to Deal with Fortune-Tellers

Some people make predictions about the future. Their predictions might be correct or prove to be wrong. Even when they are right, we should not believe that they knew for sure what would happen next. Political analysts, economic experts, weather experts and others usually issue many predictions. They predict that certain developments are likely to happen in the future, but they cannot claim with 100% confidence that their predictions will be correct.

Fortune-tellers and astrologists, on the other hand, claim that they see the future. Their sick motive is to manipulate vulnerable people for money, fame and power. It is prohibited in Islam to work as a fortune-teller or to even seek their services. No one may claim that he or she knows about the future for sure. Even prophets and messengers don't know everything about the future and the unseen, except for what Allah tells them.

FAITH IN ACTION

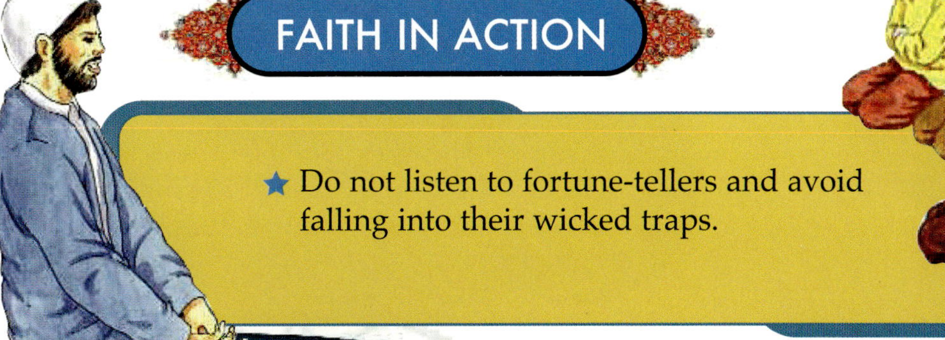

- Do not listen to fortune-tellers and avoid falling into their wicked traps.

4. Allah Protected the Qur'an from Change

When Allah conveyed the Qur'an to Prophet Muhammad ﷺ, He would send Jibreel and other guardian angels each time some ayaat of the Qur'an were revealed. The angels would keep away the jinn from Jibreel and the Prophet ﷺ while the Qur'an was being transmitted. This approach meant that no jinn could pick up the ayaat, distort them, and give humans the wrong version of the Qur'an. So, Allah made sure that Prophet Muhammad ﷺ would be the first to teach people the authentic Qur'an.

Hadeeth Shareef

عن صفية رضيَ اللهُ عنها أنَّ رَسولَ اللهِ ﷺ قال:
" مَنْ أتَى عَرّافاً فسألَهُ عَنْ شيْءٍ لَمْ تُقبَلْ لهُ صَلاةُ أرْبَعينَ لَيلَةً "

رواه مسلم وأحمد

Safiyyah, the wife of the Prophet ﷺ, narrated that Rasoolullah said:

"Whoever, goes to a fortune-teller and asks him about anything, Allah will reject his prayers for forty days." Reported in Muslim and Ahmad

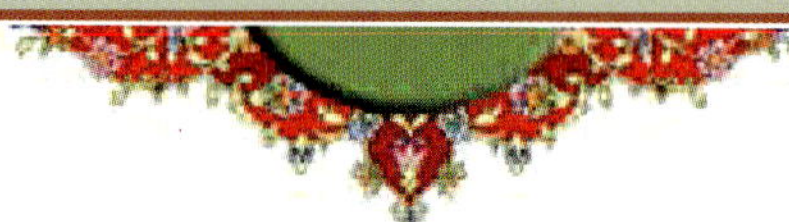

Prophet Muhammad ﷺ told early Muslims that Constantinople, now known as Istanbul, would become a Muslim city. Sure enough, Muslims under the Ottoman leader Muhammad II opened the city eight centuries after the passing of Prophet Muhammad ﷺ.

LESSON REVIEW

Projects and Activities

1. Visit a masjid and observe the Muslims there. Write a 500 word essay describing what you saw happening inside the masjid.

2. One time the Prophet ﷺ was praying next to Al-Ka'bah in the proper way, when Abu Jahl and some other evil leaders of Quraysh plotted to attack him. Read that story and share it with your class or friends.

Stretch Your Mind

Imagine you saw three of your friends playing and laughing in the masjid. Describe what you would say to them.

Study Questions

1. What are the masajid?
2. What did Allah order people to do in the masajid?
3. Can the Prophet ﷺ benefit or harm himself or anyone against Allah's will? Support your answer with ayaat from this surah.
4. Do fortune-tellers see the unseen? Do they know what will definitely happen in the future? Why, or why not?
5. Is it allowed in Islam to be a fortune-teller or to deal with one? Support your answer with a hadeeth.
6. Did Allah tell some people about the future? Who were they and give some examples of what He told them about.

Faith and Miracles: The Story of Prophet Musa

In the Palace of Phir'oun

Phir'oun was a wicked ruler who mistreated the Bani Isra'eel. In this lesson you will learn about the birth of Prophet Musa and how Allah protected him.

VOCABULARY

Bani Isra'eel	بني إسـرائيل
Tawakkul	توكـّل
Thiqah	ثِقـة

PEOPLE TO REMMEMBER

Musa	موسى
Loha (Musa's Mother)	لوحا
Maryam (Musa's sister)	مريم
Haroon (Musa's brother)	هارون
Phir'oun	فِـرْعَون
Asiah (Wife of Phir'oun)	آسـيَة

The Birth of Musa

You have probably studied Ancient Egyptian history in your history class. What do you think of when you hear the word Egypt? Do you think about the huge pyramids and the Nile River? Or do you remember the story of Prophet Musa and the Bani Isra'eel, or the children of Isra'eel in Egypt? For Muslims, Egypt is important not because of its huge pyramids and sphinx, it is important because Egypt is the birthplace of Prophet Musa.

Prophet Musa was born at the time of Phir'oun. Phir'oun was a ruler who hated the Bani Isra'eel, the descendants of Prophet Ya'qoub or Jacob. Phir'oun humiliated and disrespected the Bani Isra'eel. He made the women and men of Bani Isra'eel into slaves, working for very little or no pay at all. Phir'oun thought of himself as a god and he wanted his people to obey him and worship him alone.

The Strange Prophecy

One day Phir'oun was told that a boy from the Bani Isra'eel would be born and this boy would destroy his kingdom. When Phir'oun heard this prophecy, he became very worried and couldn't overcome his fear. So, a very evil idea jumped to his wicked head. He ordered that every male child born to the Bani Isra'eel should be killed. Phir'oun could not stand the thought of someone else having more power than him. Some historians said that Phir'oun killed thousands of children.

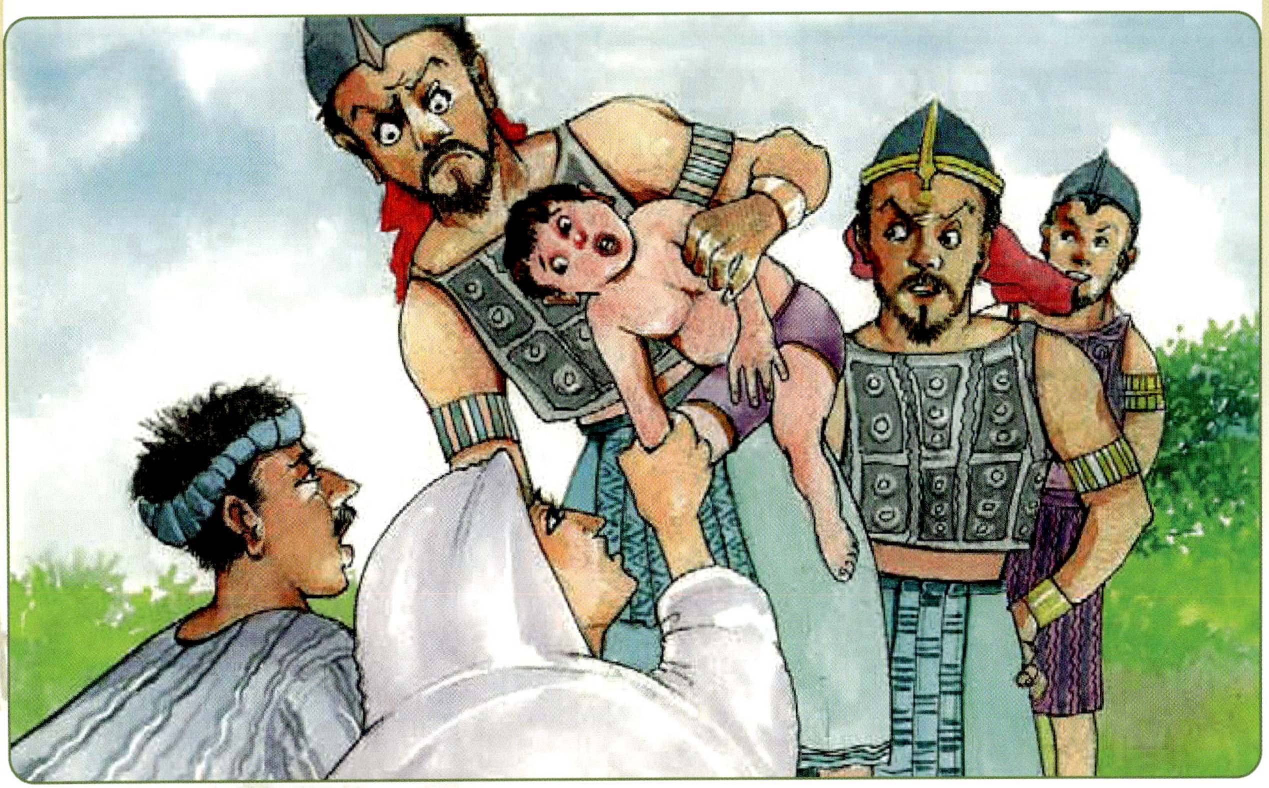

The Worried Mother

Loha, Musa's mother, feared for her unborn baby. She did not want her new child to be killed. She had two other kids, a girl, Maryam and a boy, Haroon. Musa's mother was a very pious and obedient servant of Allah, so she received an inspiration from Allah. Allah said in Al-Qur'an:

﴿ وَأَوْحَيْنَآ إِلَىٰٓ أُمِّ مُوسَىٰٓ أَنْ أَرْضِعِيهِ ۖ فَإِذَا خِفْتِ عَلَيْهِ فَأَلْقِيهِ فِى ٱلْيَمِّ وَلَا تَخَافِى وَلَا تَحْزَنِىٓ ۖ إِنَّا رَآدُّوهُ إِلَيْكِ وَجَاعِلُوهُ مِنَ ٱلْمُرْسَلِينَ ﴿٧﴾ ﴾

القصص: ٧

So We sent this inspiration to the mother of Musa: "Feed (your child), but when you fear about him, cast him into the river, but do not fear nor grieve: for We shall return him to you, and We shall make him one of Our messengers." [Surat-ul-Qasas

Allah ordered Musa's mother to put him into a chest and send it floating down the Nile River. Musa's mother did what Allah commanded her to do. She put Musa into a box and gently slid it onto the waters of the Nile. Then she asked her daughter Maryam to follow the box. She was very sad to let her son go, but she knew for sure that one day he would return back to her and become a prophet as Allah had promised her. She believed truly in her heart that Allah is the best protector of her child and family.

Musa in the Palace of Phir'oun

The box floated down the river and stopped at a riverbank near Phir'oun's palace. The guards of the palace found the baby and swiftly took it to Phir'oun and his wife. Phir'oun's wife, Asiah, instantly fell in love with baby Musa because Allah put in her heart strong love for this baby. Phir'oun's wife was very different from Phir'oun. He was a disbeliever; she was a believer. He was cruel; she was merciful. She was also very sad because Allah had not blessed her with a child of her own. When she saw baby Musa, she picked him up and she cried tears of joy. Phir'oun was amazed because he had never seen his wife this happy. She asked him if she could adopt the baby and Phir'oun agreed.

Musa Goes Back to his Mother

Phir'oun's wife could not breastfeed the baby so she ordered for nurses to suckle baby Musa. Many nurses were found, but Musa refused to drink from their breasts and kept crying. As you learned earlier, Musa's sister had followed the box floating down the river until it reached Phir'oun's palace. Musa's sister kept roaming around the palace until she learned that Phir'oun's wife and servants were looking for someone Musa could breast feed from. Musa's sister told them about a person who could feed the baby. They quickly ordered his sister to find the woman she was talking about. When Musa's sister Maryam arrived home, she saw how worried her mother had become. She wanted to know anxiously what had happened to her baby Musa. Maryam told her mom the good news. As soon as she learned what had happened, her worries subsided and she quickly went to the palace.

As baby Musa was put to his mother's breast, he instantly started drinking from her milk. SubhanAllah! Once again mother and son were reunited by a miracle from Allah. Musa's mother was appointed by Phir'oun as Musa's nurse. She was now paid good money for breast feeding her own son. Of course, Phir'oun and his wife did not know that the new nurse was none other than the baby's mother.

When Musa grew up his mother was allowed the privilege of visiting him in the palace. Allah had granted Musa good health, strength, knowledge and

سورة القصص

Surat Al-Qasas 28:5-14

﴿ وَنُرِيدُ أَن نَّمُنَّ عَلَى ٱلَّذِينَ ٱسۡتُضۡعِفُواْ فِي ٱلۡأَرۡضِ وَنَجۡعَلَهُمۡ أَئِمَّةٗ وَنَجۡعَلَهُمُ
ٱلۡوَٰرِثِينَ ٥ وَنُمَكِّنَ لَهُمۡ فِي ٱلۡأَرۡضِ وَنُرِيَ فِرۡعَوۡنَ وَهَٰمَٰنَ وَجُنُودَهُمَا مِنۡهُم مَّا
كَانُواْ يَحۡذَرُونَ ٦ وَأَوۡحَيۡنَآ إِلَىٰٓ أُمِّ مُوسَىٰٓ أَنۡ أَرۡضِعِيهِۖ فَإِذَا خِفۡتِ عَلَيۡهِ فَأَلۡقِيهِ
فِي ٱلۡيَمِّ وَلَا تَخَافِي وَلَا تَحۡزَنِيٓۖ إِنَّا رَآدُّوهُ إِلَيۡكِ وَجَاعِلُوهُ مِنَ ٱلۡمُرۡسَلِينَ ٧
فَٱلۡتَقَطَهُۥٓ ءَالُ فِرۡعَوۡنَ لِيَكُونَ لَهُمۡ عَدُوّٗا وَحَزَنًاۗ إِنَّ فِرۡعَوۡنَ وَهَٰمَٰنَ وَجُنُودَهُمَا
كَانُواْ خَٰطِـِٔينَ ٨ وَقَالَتِ ٱمۡرَأَتُ فِرۡعَوۡنَ قُرَّتُ عَيۡنٖ لِّي وَلَكَۖ لَا تَقۡتُلُوهُ عَسَىٰٓ
أَن يَنفَعَنَآ أَوۡ نَتَّخِذَهُۥ وَلَدٗا وَهُمۡ لَا يَشۡعُرُونَ ٩ وَأَصۡبَحَ فُؤَادُ أُمِّ مُوسَىٰ فَٰرِغًاۖ إِن
كَادَتۡ لَتُبۡدِي بِهِۦ لَوۡلَآ أَن رَّبَطۡنَا عَلَىٰ قَلۡبِهَا لِتَكُونَ مِنَ ٱلۡمُؤۡمِنِينَ ١٠
وَقَالَتۡ لِأُخۡتِهِۦ قُصِّيهِۖ فَبَصُرَتۡ بِهِۦ عَن جُنُبٖ وَهُمۡ لَا يَشۡعُرُونَ ١١ ۞ وَحَرَّمۡنَا
عَلَيۡهِ ٱلۡمَرَاضِعَ مِن قَبۡلُ فَقَالَتۡ هَلۡ أَدُلُّكُمۡ عَلَىٰٓ أَهۡلِ بَيۡتٖ يَكۡفُلُونَهُۥ لَكُمۡ وَهُمۡ لَهُۥ
نَٰصِحُونَ ١٢ فَرَدَدۡنَٰهُ إِلَىٰٓ أُمِّهِۦ كَيۡ تَقَرَّ عَيۡنُهَا وَلَا تَحۡزَنَ وَلِتَعۡلَمَ أَنَّ
وَعۡدَ ٱللَّهِ حَقّٞ وَلَٰكِنَّ أَكۡثَرَهُمۡ لَا يَعۡلَمُونَ ١٣ وَلَمَّا بَلَغَ أَشُدَّهُۥ وَٱسۡتَوَىٰٓ ءَاتَيۡنَٰهُ
حُكۡمٗا وَعِلۡمٗاۚ وَكَذَٰلِكَ نَجۡزِي ٱلۡمُحۡسِنِينَ ١٤ ﴾

28:5 And We wished to be gracious to those who were being oppressed in the land, to make them leaders (in Faith) and make them heirs,

28:6 To establish a firm place for them in the land, and to show Phir'oun, Haman, and their hosts, at their hands, what they were taking precautions against.

28:7 So We sent this inspiration to the mother of Musa: "Feed (your child), but when you fear about him, cast him into the river, but do not fear nor grieve: for We shall return him to you, and We shall make him one of Our messengers."

28:8 Then the people of Phir'oun picked him up (from the river): (It was intended) that (Musa) should be to them an adversary and a cause of sorrow: for Phir'oun and Haman and (all) their hosts were men of sin.

28:9 The wife of Phir'oun said: "(Here is) joy of the eye, for me and for you: Do not kill him. He may become of use to us, or we may adopt him as a son." And they perceived not (what they were doing)!

28:10 And there came a void in the heart of the mother of Musa: She almost disclosed his (case), had We not strengthened her heart (with faith), so that she would stay a (firm) believer.

28:11 And she said to the sister of (Musa), "Follow him." Then she (the sister) watched him from a distance and they did not notice. And they knew not.

28:12 And We decided that he refused suck at first, until (his sister came up and) said: "Shall I point out to you about the people of a house that will feed and raise him up for you and truly care about him?"...

28:13 Thus did We return him to his mother, that her eye might be comforted, that she might not grieve, and that she would know that the promise of Allah is true: but most of them do not understand.

28:14 When he reached full age, and became a man, We granted him wisdom and knowledge: and that is how We reward those who do good.

Lessons Learned

Destiny:

By the time Musa was born, his destiny of prophethood was already determined. All the events that lead Musa to Phir'oun's palace could only have happened through Allah's command. When we look at our lives we should also realize that we live according to Allah's plan, or destiny. So whatever happens in our lives, whether it is good or bad, we should embrace it and recognize that it is part of our destiny.

Obedience and Trust in Allah Pays off:

Imagine how Musa's mother felt when she had to separate from her newborn child. She was an obedient servant of Allah; therefore, she put all her trust, or Thiqah ثقة ,in Allah. With the guidance of Allah, mother and son were soon reunited and she was able to see her baby everyday. She took care of him and she even got paid for that by Phir'oun. We should be like Musa's mother who was obedient to Allah even in times of difficulty. She put her full trust in Allah that he was going to protect Baby Musa. If we completely submit to Allah and have a hundred percent trust in Him, then we will be under His great protection.

True Tawakkul:

Tawakkul تَوَكُّل ,or true reliance on Allah, is the attitude of a true believer. It reflects a strong trust in Allah almighty. However, true tawakkul requires that the Muslim ask Allah for help and do his part as well. Musa's mother trusted Allah, but at the same time, she put Musa in the box to save his life. She also sent his sister after him to find out his whereabouts.

Allah Controls Hearts:

Allah filled the heart of Phir'oun's wife with love and affection for Musa. This is a divine power. No one can control the emotions of people like Allah does. If you want people to love and respect you, then please Allah and make Him love you first, He will do the rest.

99 Names of Allah

الملك

Al-Malik

Allah is Al- Malik, meaning the King and The Sovereign Lord. He is the Lord of the whole universe. Leaders of different countries now and in the past call themselves kings and lords; something God does not like, since He is alone the King and the Lord of people. Early Muslim leaders were called khaleefah or ameer.

Du'aa'

عن البراء بن عازبٍ رضيَ الله عنه قال: قالَ رسولُ اللهِ صلى اللهُ عَليْهِ وسَلَّم: "إذا أتيْتَ مَضْجَعَكَ فتَوَضَّأ وُضوءَك للصَّلاة ثُمَّ اضْطَّجعْ على شِقِكَ الأيْمن وقُلْ:

اللهم أسلمتُ نفسي إليكَ، وفَوَّضْتُ أمْري إليك، وألجأتُ ظَهْري إليْك، آمَنْتُ بكِتابِكَ الذي أنْزَلت، وبِنَبِيِّكَ الذي أرْسَلت."

رواه البخاري ومسلم

Al-Baraa' Ibn Azib رضي الله عنه said, "Once Rasoolullah said, to me, 'When you go to bed, make wudoo' first, then lay on your right side and say:

"Oh Allah, I submit myself to You, and refer my affairs to You, and support myself by You. (I do that because I fear and love You.) (There is no refuge nor safety except with You.) I believe in your revealed book and the Messenger you sent."

This du'aa' is very important. It makes us renew our trust and reliance on Allah every night before we sleep. Don't miss saying this du'aa' every night.

FAITH IN ACTION

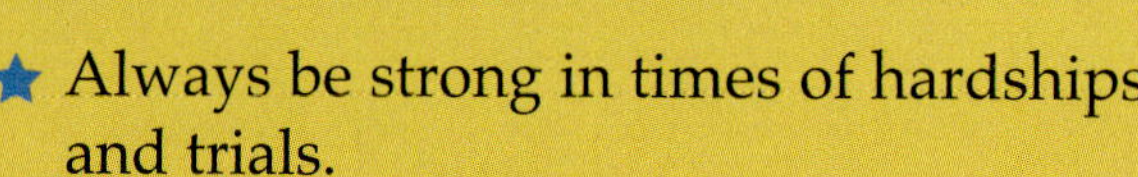

- Always be strong in times of hardships and trials.
- Always demonstrate full and heartily tawakkul, or reliance on Allah.
- Do your part, don't ask Allah to do things for you and you just sit there. Do your best and ask Allah to do the things that you cannot do.

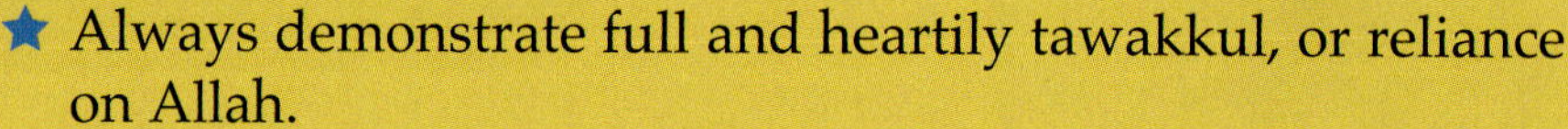

Fast Facts

The story of Musa and his people is repeated in the Qur'an more than eighty times. In some chapters of the Qur'an, the story was presented in a detailed manner, like in Surat-ul-Qasas. Most of the times, it was mentioned briefly like in Surat-us-Saff.

CHAPTER REVIEW

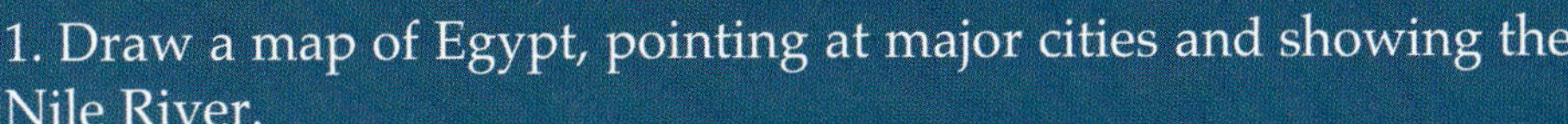

Projects and Activities

1. Draw a map of Egypt, pointing at major cities and showing the Nile River.

2. Write a poem or an essay about the birth of Musa. Explain how do you feel about that story.

Stretch Your Mind

1. Musa's sister's name was Maryam, was she the same person who became Prophet Isa's mother? Explain your answer.
2. Why was Phir'oun angry at the children of Isra'eel?
3. Why were the children of Isra'eel living in Egypt while their great grandfather Ya'qoub, whose name was also Isra'eel, lived in Palestine?

Study Questions

1. How did Phir'oun treat the Bani Isra'eel? List three examples.
2. Why did Musa's mother put her new baby in the box to float in the river?
3. How was Musa received in Phir'oun's palace?
4. How did Musa's mother become reunited with her son?
5. Why did Phir'oun easily accept to spare baby Musa's life, although he was afraid that a Jewish child would destroy his kingdom in the future?
6. Write three important lessons you learned from the story.

Musa Leaves Egypt

SUMMARY

When he grew up, Prophet Musa unintentionally killed an Egyptian man while he was trying to help his fellow Israeli man. This caused Musa to flee Egypt to settle in a town called Madyan, where he established a new family.

PLACES TO REMMEMBER

Sinai	سَـيـْـناء
Madyan	مَدْيَن

PEOPLE TO REMMEMBER

As-Samiriy	السَّــامِريّ
Shu'ayb	شُـعَيْب
Yi'ron	يثْرون
Saffoura	صفّـورا
Liya	لِيا
Sam'ana	سَـمعان

Unintentional Killing

One day while Musa was in the city, he saw two men fighting. One man was an Israelite and the other was an Egyptian. When the Israelite saw Musa, he begged him for help. Musa sided with the Israelite, because the Egyptians used to oppress and humiliate the Israelites. Musa punched the Egyptian with his fist on the chest. Musa did not intend to the kill man, but the man died from the blow. When the man died, Musa realized he had done something wrong and his heart was filled with deep sadness and regret. He begged Allah for forgiveness, and promised Him that he would never side with criminals and evil people in the future.

LEARNING MORE

According to some history books, the name of the Israelite man was Samaritan or As-Samiriy in Arabic. You will learn more about him in an upcoming chapter.

Musa in Danger

Meanwhile, the family of the victim went to Phir'oun and complained that an Israelite had just killed their relative. Phir'oun ordered his police to investigate the crime and find the killer.

The next day Musa saw the same Israelite he had helped the day before. He was involved in a fight with another Egyptian. Musa realized that the Israelite seemed to be a man who liked fighting with others a lot. Musa then became angry at the Israelite and shouted at him "you are truly such a trouble maker," and he attempted to push away the Egyptian man. The Israelite saw Musa angry at him, so he thought that Musa was about to attack him. In panic, the Israelite shouted at Musa, "are you going to kill me just as you killed the other man yesterday?" The Egyptian man and those standing by heard the Israelite say this and quickly went and reported it to the authorities. Shortly after, as Musa was walking in the city, a man approached him and said ,"O Musa the chiefs have taken counsel against you, they plotted to get you killed. Just leave town, this is my advice to you."

Musa Leaves Egypt

Musa knew that he was in great danger because the punishment for killing an Egyptian was death. Musa left Egypt in a hurry without going to Phir'oun's palace or changing his clothes to prepare for traveling. He trav-

eled east toward Palestine. While traveling in the hot desert, his only companion was Allah. His shoes were worn out from walking so much and he did not have money to buy a new pair of shoes.

Musa in Madyan

After crossing the Sinai desert, Musa saw a watering hole where shepherds water their sheep near the city of Madyan, which was in the northwestern part of Arabia, near Tabouk in Saudi Arabia now. Madyan was the city of an ancient prophet called Shu'ayb. Musa sat down near a tree and then he noticed two young women who were trying to care for their sheep. Musa felt that the women needed help, so he went and asked them if he could help in some way.

The older sister said: "We are waiting until the shepherds finish watering their sheep and then we will water ours."

Musa asked: "Why are you waiting?"

The younger sister said: "We cannot intermingle with men and push them away."

Musa was surprised to see that young women were herding because usually only men were supposed to do such hard and tiresome work. So Musa asked, "Why are you shepherding?"

The younger sister said: "Our father is an old man; his health is too poor to take care of the sheep."

Musa said: "I will water the sheep for you."

After watering their sheep, Musa returned to sit under the shade of the tree. Musa had no money, no food and

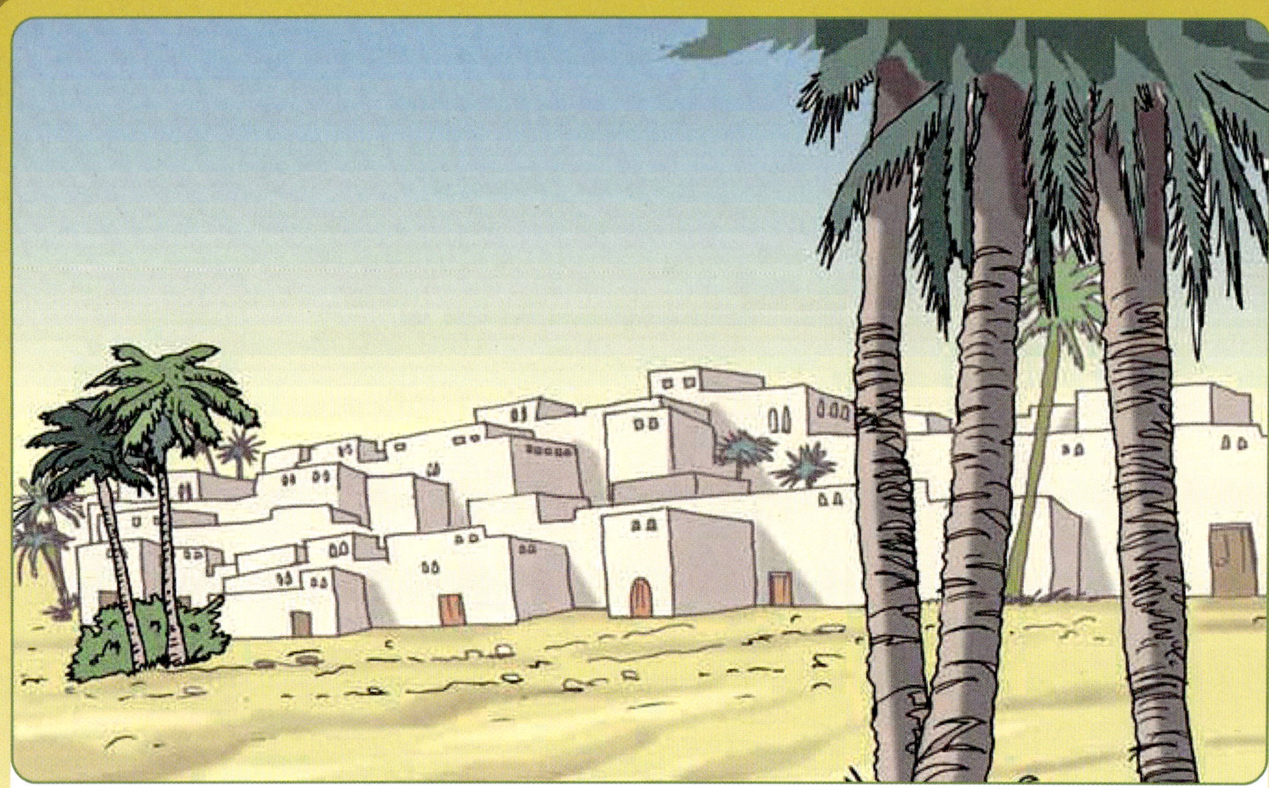

no home to go to. He prayed to Allah, "O my Lord! Truly, I need any good that you would send me."

Musa Meets A Pious Man

The young women returned home earlier than usual, which surprised their old father. The young women explained to their father that they received some help from a stranger, which was the reason they returned early. The father asked his daughters to invite the stranger to their home. Some scholars believe the girls' father was Prophet Shu'ayb. Others, however, think the old man was a different pious person whose name was Yi'roun. They say Prophet Shu'ayb lived around three hundred years before Musa's time. The historians say that the names of the two daughters were Saffoura and Liya.

One of the daughters went to Musa and shyly told him: "My father is grateful for what you have done for us. He invites you to our home so he may thank you personally."

Musa accepted the invitation. He was a very polite person. Therefore, he asked the girl if he could walk ahead of her so he would not look at her as they walked to her home. Musa arrived at the family's home and was kindly received by the girls' father.

Musa could sense that they lived comfortably as a happy and peaceful household. Musa introduced himself and he told them about what happened to him and why he had to flee from Egypt. The man comforted him and said, "Fear not, you have escaped from the wrong doers."

The New Family

One of the daughters suggested to her father that he employ Musa to take care of the sheep because he was very trustworthy. The old man agreed and told Musa: "I wish to marry you one of my daughters on condition that you agree to work for me for a period of eight or ten years." Musa agreed to the father's request. He married one of the daughters, Saffoura according to some historians, and he looked after the old man for ten years.

Time passed and Musa lived in seclusion far away from his family and people in Egypt. This period was very important in his life because it was major preparation toward becoming a prophet of Allah. Musa would contemplate about the world around him, such as the stars at night and the sunrise in the morning.

The religion of Musa was the same as the religion of Prophet Ya'coub, which was Islamic monotheism. Monotheism is the belief in one God. The forefather of Musa was Prophet Yacoub who was the grandson of Prophet Ibraheem. Therefore Musa was one of the descendants of Ibraheem and every prophet that came after Ibraheem was one of Prophet Ibraheem's descendants.

Back To Egypt

One day Musa really missed his family and people in Egypt. He went to his wife and told her, "Tomorrow we leave for Egypt." His wife said to herself, "There are a thousand dangers in the way to Egypt," but she put her trust in Allah and obeyed her husband.

Musa himself did not know the secret of the quick and sudden decision to return to a place of great danger for him. Did he want to visit his mother and siblings? Did he think of visiting Phir'oun's wife whom he loved and who loved him as if she was his mother?

No one knows what went through Musa's mind when he returned to Egypt. All we know is that Allah's destiny drove him to make a decision and he did. Destiny indeed guided him towards a matter of great importance.

Lessons Learned

Siding with the Righteous:

In the story of the Israeli man fighting with the Egyptian, Musa sided with the Israeli because he was from his own tribe. Musa unintentionally killed the Egyptian man and he begged Allah for forgiveness. That happened in order to emphasize the wrongfulness of siding unconditionally with our family, tribe, or nation. What makes a man superior to another man is not his family, tribe, or nation, but his righteousness.

Extending and taking sincere advice:

The good man, someone named Sam'aan or Shimon, gave Musa life saving advice. This is the attitude of good believers. So is the acceptance of sincere advice, as well. In this case, this advice worked out very well and saved Musa's life. Prophet Muhammad said that "Religion [guides] to giving and accepting sincere advice." He also considered extending good advice as the right of a Muslim on the other. Good and sincere advice is the one you extend to others for the sake of Allah and to help them be successful in this life and the next life.

Extending Help and Generosity to Others:

When Musa came near the young women, he saw that they were struggling to do their job. Out of kindness and sincerity, Musa decided to help them. In the end Musa was rewarded for his help by being welcomed to the home of the pious family. Furthermore, he was also offered to marry one of the young women. Whenever we see someone in need of our assistance, we should never hesitate to extend a hand. Whether the charity is through action, prayer, or money, Allah will reward us just as he rewarded Prophet Musa, inshaAllah.

Modesty الحَياءْ

The girls in this story showed us how modest and polite they were in the presence of men. They didn't want to mix with men at the well to water their sheep; rather, they kept a distance. Musa also was very modest, polite and gracious when he helped them. When he walked to their home, he didn't want to look at the girl that came to guide him to her home. He preferred to walk ahead of her for that reason. Islam teaches us to lower our gaze when we see people of the opposite gender and act modestly at all times.

Hadeeth Shareef

Prophet Muhammad ﷺ on Modesty:

١. عن عبد الله بن عمر قال : قال رسول الله ﷺ :
"الحياء من الإيمان" رواه البخاري

1. "Modesty is part of iman"

Reported in Al-Bukhari

٢. عن عمران بن حُصَين قال : قال رسول الله ﷺ :
"الحياءُ لا يأتي إلا بخَير" رواه البخاري

2. "Modesty would only bring goodness to people"

Reported in Al-Bukhari

٣. عن زيد بن طلحة قال : قال رسول الله ﷺ :
"لِكُلِّ دِينٍ خُلُق، وخُلُقُ الإسْلامِ الحَيَاء" رواه مالك

3. "Every religion has a special ethic, and the ethic of Islam is Modesty"

Reported in Malik

سورة القصص

Surat Al-Qasas 28:15-28

﴿ وَدَخَلَ ٱلْمَدِينَةَ عَلَىٰ حِينِ غَفْلَةٍ مِّنْ أَهْلِهَا فَوَجَدَ فِيهَا رَجُلَيْنِ يَقْتَتِلَانِ هَٰذَا مِن
شِيعَتِهِۦ وَهَٰذَا مِنْ عَدُوِّهِۦ ۖ فَٱسْتَغَٰثَهُ ٱلَّذِى مِن شِيعَتِهِۦ عَلَى ٱلَّذِى مِنْ عَدُوِّهِۦ فَوَكَزَهُۥ مُوسَىٰ
فَقَضَىٰ عَلَيْهِ ۖ قَالَ هَٰذَا مِنْ عَمَلِ ٱلشَّيْطَٰنِ ۖ إِنَّهُۥ عَدُوٌّ مُّضِلٌّ مُّبِينٌ ﴿١٥﴾ قَالَ رَبِّ إِنِّى ظَلَمْتُ
نَفْسِى فَٱغْفِرْ لِى فَغَفَرَ لَهُۥٓ ۚ إِنَّهُۥ هُوَ ٱلْغَفُورُ ٱلرَّحِيمُ ﴿١٦﴾ قَالَ رَبِّ بِمَآ أَنْعَمْتَ عَلَىَّ
فَلَنْ أَكُونَ ظَهِيرًا لِّلْمُجْرِمِينَ ﴿١٧﴾ فَأَصْبَحَ فِى ٱلْمَدِينَةِ خَآئِفًا يَتَرَقَّبُ فَإِذَا ٱلَّذِى ٱسْتَنصَرَهُۥ
بِٱلْأَمْسِ يَسْتَصْرِخُهُۥ ۚ قَالَ لَهُۥ مُوسَىٰٓ إِنَّكَ لَغَوِىٌّ مُّبِينٌ ﴿١٨﴾ فَلَمَّآ أَنْ أَرَادَ أَن يَبْطِشَ بِٱلَّذِى هُوَ
عَدُوٌّ لَّهُمَا قَالَ يَٰمُوسَىٰٓ أَتُرِيدُ أَن تَقْتُلَنِى كَمَا قَتَلْتَ نَفْسًۢا بِٱلْأَمْسِ ۖ إِن تُرِيدُ إِلَّآ أَن تَكُونَ
جَبَّارًا فِى ٱلْأَرْضِ وَمَا تُرِيدُ أَن تَكُونَ مِنَ ٱلْمُصْلِحِينَ ﴿١٩﴾ وَجَآءَ رَجُلٌ مِّنْ أَقْصَا ٱلْمَدِينَةِ يَسْعَىٰ
قَالَ يَٰمُوسَىٰٓ إِنَّ ٱلْمَلَأَ يَأْتَمِرُونَ بِكَ لِيَقْتُلُوكَ فَٱخْرُجْ إِنِّى لَكَ مِنَ ٱلنَّٰصِحِينَ ﴿٢٠﴾
فَخَرَجَ مِنْهَا خَآئِفًا يَتَرَقَّبُ ۖ قَالَ رَبِّ نَجِّنِى مِنَ ٱلْقَوْمِ ٱلظَّٰلِمِينَ ﴿٢١﴾ وَلَمَّا تَوَجَّهَ تِلْقَآءَ مَدْيَنَ قَالَ
عَسَىٰ رَبِّىٓ أَن يَهْدِيَنِى سَوَآءَ ٱلسَّبِيلِ ﴿٢٢﴾ وَلَمَّا وَرَدَ مَآءَ مَدْيَنَ وَجَدَ عَلَيْهِ أُمَّةً مِّنَ
ٱلنَّاسِ يَسْقُونَ وَوَجَدَ مِن دُونِهِمُ ٱمْرَأَتَيْنِ تَذُودَانِ ۖ قَالَ مَا خَطْبُكُمَا ۖ قَالَتَا لَا نَسْقِى
حَتَّىٰ يُصْدِرَ ٱلرِّعَآءُ ۖ وَأَبُونَا شَيْخٌ كَبِيرٌ ﴿٢٣﴾ فَسَقَىٰ لَهُمَا ثُمَّ تَوَلَّىٰٓ إِلَى ٱلظِّلِّ فَقَالَ
رَبِّ إِنِّى لِمَآ أَنزَلْتَ إِلَىَّ مِنْ خَيْرٍ فَقِيرٌ ﴿٢٤﴾ فَجَآءَتْهُ إِحْدَىٰهُمَا تَمْشِى عَلَى ٱسْتِحْيَآءٍ قَالَتْ
إِنَّ أَبِى يَدْعُوكَ لِيَجْزِيَكَ أَجْرَ مَا سَقَيْتَ لَنَا ۚ فَلَمَّا جَآءَهُۥ وَقَصَّ عَلَيْهِ ٱلْقَصَصَ
قَالَ لَا تَخَفْ ۖ نَجَوْتَ مِنَ ٱلْقَوْمِ ٱلظَّٰلِمِينَ ﴿٢٥﴾ قَالَتْ إِحْدَىٰهُمَا يَٰٓأَبَتِ ٱسْتَـْٔجِرْهُ ۖ إِنَّ
خَيْرَ مَنِ ٱسْتَـْٔجَرْتَ ٱلْقَوِىُّ ٱلْأَمِينُ ﴿٢٦﴾ قَالَ إِنِّىٓ أُرِيدُ أَنْ أُنكِحَكَ إِحْدَى ٱبْنَتَىَّ هَٰتَيْنِ
عَلَىٰٓ أَن تَأْجُرَنِى ثَمَٰنِىَ حِجَجٍ ۖ فَإِنْ أَتْمَمْتَ عَشْرًا فَمِنْ عِندِكَ ۖ وَمَآ أُرِيدُ أَنْ أَشُقَّ
عَلَيْكَ ۚ سَتَجِدُنِىٓ إِن شَآءَ ٱللَّهُ مِنَ ٱلصَّٰلِحِينَ ﴿٢٧﴾ قَالَ ذَٰلِكَ بَيْنِى وَبَيْنَكَ ۖ أَيَّمَا
ٱلْأَجَلَيْنِ قَضَيْتُ فَلَا عُدْوَٰنَ عَلَىَّ ۖ وَٱللَّهُ عَلَىٰ مَا نَقُولُ وَكِيلٌ ﴿٢٨﴾ ﴾

Understood Meaning

28:15 And he entered the city at a time when its people were resting and not watching: and he found there two men fighting, - one of his own people, and the other, of his foes. Now the man of his own people appealed to him against his foe, and Musa struck him with his fist and killed him [by mistake] He said: "This is a work of Evil (Satan): for he is an enemy that clearly misleads!"

28:16 He prayed: "O my Lord! I have indeed wronged my soul! So forgive me!" Then ((Allah)) forgave him: for He is the ever-Forgiving, Most Merciful.

28:17 He said: "O my Lord! For your Grace that you granted me, never shall I be a help to those who sin!"

28:18 So he saw the morning in the city, looking about, in fear, when behold, the man who had, the day before, sought his help called aloud for his help (again). Musa said to him: you are truly such a trouble maker!"

28:19 Then, when he decided to lay hold of the man who was an enemy to both of them, that [Israelite] man said: "O Musa! Do you want to kill me as you killed a person yesterday? Thy intention is none other than to become a powerful violent man in the land, and not to be one who sets things right!"

28:20 And there came a man, running, from the furthest end of the City. He said: "O Musa! The Chiefs are plotting to kill you: so get away, for I do give you a sincere advice."

28:21 He therefore got away from the city, looking about, in fear. He prayed "O my Lord! Save me from oppressive people."

28:22 Then, when he turned his face towards (the land of) Madyan, he said: "I do hope that my Lord will guide me to the straight path."

28:23 And when he arrived at the watering (place) in Madyan, he found there a group of men watering (their flocks), and beside them he found two women who were keeping back (their flocks). He said: "What is the matter with you?" They said: "We cannot water (our flocks) until the shepherds take back (their flocks): And our father is a very old man."

28:24 So he watered (their flocks) for them; then he turned back to the shade, and said: “O my Lord! Truly, I need any good that you would send me.”

28:25 Afterwards one of the two women came (back) to him, walking bashfully. She said: "My father invites you that he may reward you for having watered (our flocks) for us." So when he came to him and told him his story, he said: "Do not worry, you will be safe here from unjust people."

28:26 One of the women said: "O my (dear) father! Employ him: truly the best of men for you to employ is the (man) who is strong and trusty.”

28:27 He said: "I intend to wed one of my daughters to you, on condition that you serve me for eight years; but if you complete ten years, it will be (grace) from you. And I would not make the work hard on you: you will find me, if Allah wills, one of the righteous people."

28:28 He said: "Be that (the agreement) between me and you: whichever of the two terms I fulfill, let there be no ill-will to me. And Allah is a witness to what we say."

FAITH IN ACTION

- Always avoid unnecessary fights. They may lead you to bad results. Real strength and power is in patience and controlling one’s anger.
- Ask Allah for help when you need it before asking people. Sometimes it is enough to solve your problem, other times you need du’aa’ and some effort on your part.
- Always bemodest when you deal with people of the other gender.
- When you get into an agreement with others, fulfill your obligation to the best of your ability.

CHAPTER REVIEW

Projects and Activities

Draw a map of Egypt and Northern Arabia. Then trace the trip Musa took from Egypt to Madyan.

Stretch Your Mind

Why did Phir'oun agree to punish Musa and kill him for his mistake although he had treated him as his son for years?

Study Questions

1. Why did Prophet Musa side with the Israeli man when he saw the two men fighting?
2. How did Prophet Musa feel after he had unintentionally killed the Egyptian man?
3. Why did the Israeli man tell of Musa's mistake?
4. Why did Prophet Musa flee from Egypt? Where did he go to?
5. Whom did Prophet Musa meet in the new place ?
6. Describe what happened to Prophet Musa in the new city he moved to?
7. Why do some scholars think that the old man was not Prophet Shu'ayb?
8. Why did Prophet Musa decide to return to Egypt after many years?

Musa The Prophet

SUMMARY

Musa and his family left Madyan to head towards Egypt. As they journeyed through mountains and sand, Musa received this first revelation from Allah. Allah ordered him to go to Phir'oun and call him to believe in One God.

VOCABULARY

Mount Sinai جبل سيناء

Sinai desert

Musa Heads to Egypt

Musa left Madyan with his family and traveled back to Egypt. As Musa went through the Sinai desert, he discovered that he had lost his way. He asked Allah for help and he was guided in the right direction. At nightfall they reached Mount Sinai, or Jabal-ut-Tour. There he noticed a fire in the distance.

Musa Becomes a Messenger

As he got closer to the fire, he decided to go by it and get some for his family to warm up. Here is what Allah says about this in Surat-ul-Qasas 28: 29-30:

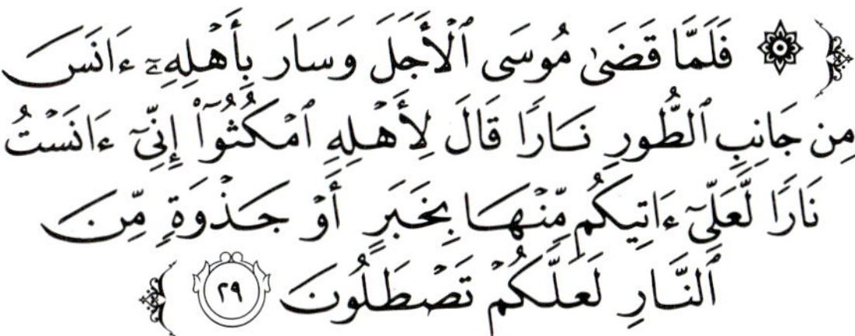
﴿ فَلَمَّا قَضَىٰ مُوسَى ٱلْأَجَلَ وَسَارَ بِأَهْلِهِۦٓ ءَانَسَ
مِن جَانِبِ ٱلطُّورِ نَارًا قَالَ لِأَهْلِهِ ٱمْكُثُوٓا۟ إِنِّىٓ ءَانَسْتُ
نَارًا لَّعَلِّىٓ ءَاتِيكُم مِّنْهَا بِخَبَرٍ أَوْ جَذْوَةٍ مِّنَ
ٱلنَّارِ لَعَلَّكُمْ تَصْطَلُونَ ﴿٢٩﴾ ﴾

القصص: ٢٩

"Now when Musa had fulfilled the term, and was traveling with his family, he noticed a fire in the direction of Mount Toor. He said to his family: "Stay right here; I saw a fire; I hope to bring you from there some information, or a burning firebrand, that you may warm yourselves."

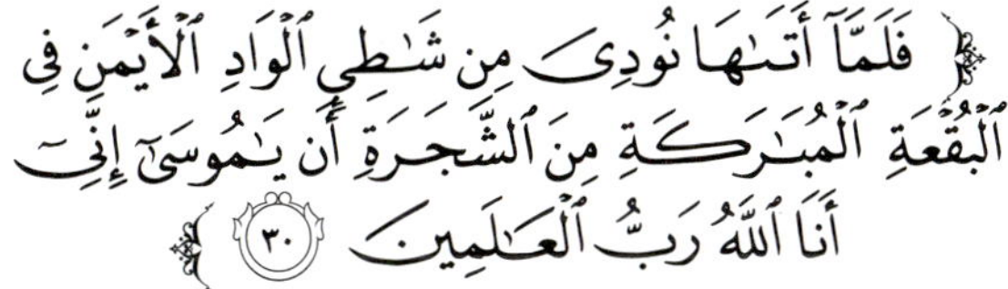
﴿ فَلَمَّآ أَتَىٰهَا نُودِىَ مِن شَٰطِئِ ٱلْوَادِ ٱلْأَيْمَنِ فِى
ٱلْبُقْعَةِ ٱلْمُبَٰرَكَةِ مِنَ ٱلشَّجَرَةِ أَن يَٰمُوسَىٰٓ إِنِّىٓ
أَنَا ٱللَّهُ رَبُّ ٱلْعَٰلَمِينَ ﴿٣٠﴾ ﴾

القصص: ٣٠

But when he came to the (fire), a voice was heard from the right bank of the valley, from a tree in the holy ground: "Oh Musa! Verily I am Allah, the Lord of the Worlds."

Musa was confused and he looked around. Allah then told Musa that there is no God but Allah, the true creator of

mankind, and that Musa should pray and worship Him alone. Then Allah surprised Musa, He chose him as a messenger of Allah to the children of Isra'eel. Furthermore, Allah ordered Musa to go to Egypt and call Phir'oun to believe in Allah and worship Him alone. Allah also wanted Musa to move the children of Isra'eel to Palestine if Phir'oun refused to follow the true faith.

Prophet Musa was in a complete shock, he never expected that, even in his dreams. Then suddenly, Allah asked him about the staff he was carrying, "What is that in your right hand, Musa?" He said, "It is my staff. I lean on it and beat down leaves for my sheep and I have other uses for it." There is no doubt that Allah knew what Musa was holding. He just wanted to prepare Musa for the miracle that his staff could perform.

A Time for Miracles

Allah commanded Musa: "Throw down your staff." He did so and at once it turned into a wriggling snake. Musa turned away so he could run, but Allah told him, "Grasp it and fear not. We shall return it to its former state." The snake changed back into his staff. Musa's fear was replaced by peace, because he realized that he was witnessing the truth.

Allah commanded him also to put his hands into his robe at the armpit. When he took out his hand it had a brilliant shine. Allah then told Musa, "These are two miracles from your Lord to Phir'oun and his chiefs." However, Musa feared that he would be arrested and killed by Phir'oun, so he turned to Allah and said, "My Lord I have killed a man among them, and I fear that they will kill me." Allah assured him of his safety and set his heart at rest. Musa asked Allah one more thing; to have his brother Haroon or Aaron help him in this difficult mission. Allah agreed.

Prophet Musa Faces Phir'oun

When Musa arrived in Egypt he went to Phir'oun along with his brother Haroon. They delivered their message to Phir'oun about Allah, His mercy, His paradise and about the duty of worshipping one God. The meeting with Phir'oun and his generals was not an easy matter. Phir'oun was furious at Musa and worried that he might be the one who would destroy his kingdom. After all, this is what the old prophecy

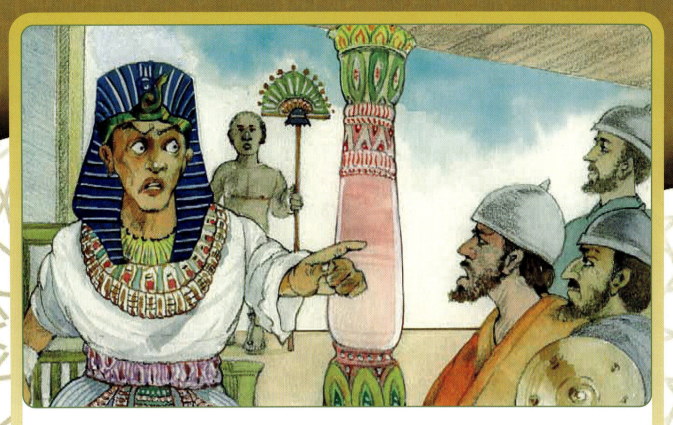

tells. Phir'oun listened to Musa's speech with arrogance and refused to believe in Allah and worship Him. Phir'oun claimed that he was God. He thought that Musa was crazy to challenge him like that. Phir'oun raised his hand and said, "What do you want from me?"

Musa answered: "I want you to send the children of Isra'eel with us."

Phir'oun asked: "Why should I send them when they are all my slaves?"

Musa replied: "They are the slaves of Allah, Lord of the Worlds."

Phir'oun then sarcastically asked him if his name was Musa. Musa answered, "Yes."

"Aren't you the Musa whom we picked up from the Nile as a helpless baby? Aren't you the one we raised in this palace? You ate and drank with us, and we provided you with so much wealth. Aren't you the Musa who is a fugitive, the killer of an Egyptian man, if memory does not betray me? It is said that killing is an act of disbelief. Therefore, you were a disbeliever when you killed. You are a fugitive from justice and you come to speak to me! What were you talking about Musa, I forget?"

Musa knew that Phir'oun was trying to threaten him. He ignored his threats and explained that he was not a disbeliever when he killed the Egyptian. He only went astray, and Allah had not yet given him revelation at that time. He made Phir'oun understand that he fled from Egypt because he was afraid of their revenge, although the killing was an accident. He told Phir'oun that Allah had forgiven him and made him one of His messengers.

سورة طه

Surat Taha 20:11-24

﴿ فَلَمَّآ أَتَىٰهَا نُودِيَ يَٰمُوسَىٰٓ ١١ إِنِّيٓ أَنَا۠ رَبُّكَ فَٱخۡلَعۡ نَعۡلَيۡكَ إِنَّكَ بِٱلۡوَادِ ٱلۡمُقَدَّسِ
طُوٗى ١٢ وَأَنَا ٱخۡتَرۡتُكَ فَٱسۡتَمِعۡ لِمَا يُوحَىٰٓ ١٣ إِنَّنِيٓ أَنَا ٱللَّهُ لَآ إِلَٰهَ إِلَّآ أَنَا۠ فَٱعۡبُدۡنِي
وَأَقِمِ ٱلصَّلَوٰةَ لِذِكۡرِيٓ ١٤ إِنَّ ٱلسَّاعَةَ ءَاتِيَةٌ أَكَادُ أُخۡفِيهَا لِتُجۡزَىٰ كُلُّ نَفۡسِۭ بِمَا
تَسۡعَىٰ ١٥ فَلَا يَصُدَّنَّكَ عَنۡهَا مَن لَّا يُؤۡمِنُ بِهَا وَٱتَّبَعَ هَوَىٰهُ فَتَرۡدَىٰ ١٦ وَمَا تِلۡكَ
بِيَمِينِكَ يَٰمُوسَىٰ ١٧ قَالَ هِيَ عَصَايَ أَتَوَكَّؤُاْ عَلَيۡهَا وَأَهُشُّ بِهَا عَلَىٰ غَنَمِي وَلِيَ
فِيهَا مَـَٔارِبُ أُخۡرَىٰ ١٨ قَالَ أَلۡقِهَا يَٰمُوسَىٰ ١٩ فَأَلۡقَىٰهَا فَإِذَا هِيَ حَيَّةٞ تَسۡعَىٰ ٢٠ قَالَ
خُذۡهَا وَلَا تَخَفۡۖ سَنُعِيدُهَا سِيرَتَهَا ٱلۡأُولَىٰ ٢١ وَٱضۡمُمۡ يَدَكَ إِلَىٰ جَنَاحِكَ تَخۡرُجۡ
بَيۡضَآءَ مِنۡ غَيۡرِ سُوٓءٍ ءَايَةً أُخۡرَىٰ ٢٢ لِنُرِيَكَ مِنۡ ءَايَٰتِنَا ٱلۡكُبۡرَى ٢٣ ٱذۡهَبۡ إِلَىٰ فِرۡعَوۡنَ إِنَّهُۥ
طَغَىٰ ٢٤ ﴾

20:11 But when he came to the fire, a voice was heard: "O Musa!

20:12 "Verily I am thy Lord! therefore (in My presence) put off thy shoes: thou art in the sacred valley Tuwa.

20:13 "I have chosen thee: listen, then, to the inspiration (sent to thee).

20:14 "Verily, I am Allah. There is no god but I: So serve thou Me (only), and establish regular prayer for celebrating My praise.

20:15 "Verily the Hour is coming - My design is to keep it hidden - for every soul to receive its reward by the measure of its endeavour.

20:16 "Therefore let not such as believe not therein but follow their own lusts, divert thee therefrom, lest thou perish!"

20:17 "And what is that in the right hand, O Musa?"

20:18 He said, "It is my rod: on it I lean; with it I beat down fodder for my flocks; and in it I find other uses."

20:19 ((Allah)) said, "Throw it, O Musa!"

20:20 He threw it, and behold! It was a snake, active in motion.

20:21 ((Allah)) said, "Seize it, and fear not: We shall return it at once to its former condition."

20:22 "Now draw your hand close to your side: it shall come out white (and shining), without harm (or stain) - as another sign."

20:23 "In order that We may show thee (two) of Our greater signs. "

20:24 "Go thou to Phir'oun, for he has indeed transgressed all bounds."

Lessons Learned

Wealth is Not Everything:

Allah gives us many examples of men like Phir'oun in the Qur'an to warn us about their actions. As you have learned before, anything good comes from Allah and He can easily take it away. Phir'oun thought he was superior because he possessed so much wealth and riches, but he failed to recognize that what he possessed belongs to Allah. And wealth is worthless and not blessed when it is not used for the sake of Allah. One should never be boastful about one's possessions in this world. A devout poor man who obeys Allah is better in the sight of Allah than a rich man who disobeys Allah and disbelieves in Him.

Wealth and Power Can Make People Tyrants:

Allah says in surat-ul-Alaq 96:6-7:

العلق: ٦ - ٧

"Nay. Indeed man transgresses, as he sees himself rich and self sufficient".

When man lacks the belief in Allah, he will easily be fooled by Shaytan and by his own powers. Instead of thanking God for what he gave Him, he would deny Allah's gifts and think that he got what he has only because he is smart and strong. Some people become tyrants, like Phir'oun did. Even when they see what proves them wrong, they will deny the truth and reject it. They do that because they strive to keep their positions and remain "powerful."

CHAPTER REVIEW

Projects and Activities

1. Draw a map of the Sinai Peninsula.

2. Write an essay about the important places in Sinai.

Stretch Your Mind

1. Why did Allah want Musa to move his people from Egypt to Palestine?
2. What is the difference between the miracle Prophet Musa saw and what some magicians do in magic shows?

Study Questions

1. How did Musa become a prophet of Allah?
2. What did Allah order Musa to do in Egypt?
3. Why was Musa fearful of returning to Egypt?
4. How did Phir'oun receive Musa's message?

Musa And The Magicians

Phir'oun became fearful after Musa had performed his miracles. He called for the best magicians from all over Egypt to showcase their magic against Musa.

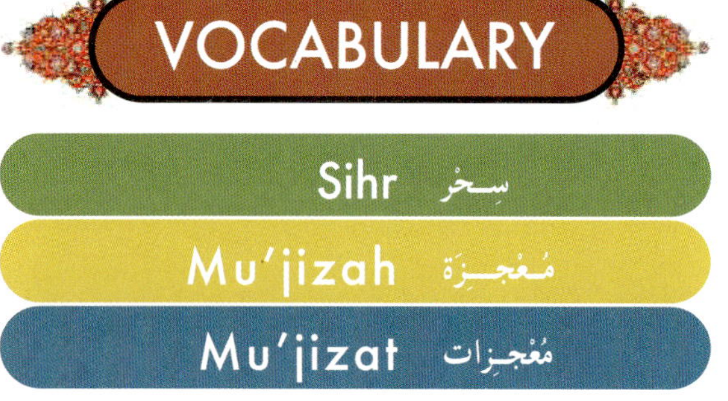

VOCABULARY
Sihr سِحْر
Mu'jizah مُعْجِزَة
Mu'jizat مُعْجِزات

Phir'oun Rejects Allah's Message

Musa met Phir'oun in his palace and conveyed Allah's message to him. He explained to him that this world has One Great Creator; Allah or God. And no one can claim that he or she is God. People should only worship the One True Creator. Musa's talk was simple and clear, but Phir'oun refused to believe. Even worse, he tried to threaten and humiliate Musa. He asked Musa how he dared to worship Allah and not him! Phir'oun claimed that he was a god. The punishment for not worshipping Phir'oun was prison.

Hadeeth Shareef

عن طارق بن شهاب رضي الله عنه قال : جاء رجل إلى النبي ﷺ فقال:
أي الجهاد أفضل؟
قال : "كلمة حق عند سلطان جائر"

رواه أحمد

Tariq ibn Shihab رضي الله عنه reported that a man came to the Prophet and asked:
"What is the best form of jihad?"
The Prophet said: "A word of truth in front of an unjust leader."

Narrated by Ahmad

Prophet Musa's Miracles

Musa said: "Even if I would bring you something obvious and very convincing." Phir'oun said, "Bring it forth, then, if you are truthful!"

So Musa "threw his stick, and behold, it was a serpent. And he drew out his hand, and behold, it was bright white to all!" (Surat-ush-Shu'araa' 26:30-33)

After Prophet Musa had performed the two miracles, Phir'oun was terrified. He feared that his rule was in danger. He remembered the old prophecy he learned many years before that a man from the children of Isra'eel would destroy his kingdom. So, he told his advisors: "These are two magicians who will strip you of your best traditions and drive you out of the country with their magic. What do you advise?" Phir'oun's advisors told him to detain Musa and his brother Haroon while they called for the cleverest magicians in the country. Then they too, could show their skills of magic and change sticks into serpents. This way, they thought, they could reduce the influence of Musa's miracles on the people.

Musa and Haroon were under arrest by Phir'oun's order. He sent messengers all over the land to recruit the best magicians. Phir'oun offered each successful magician a big reward. The event was scheduled to happen on the usual festival day, which attracted people from all over the Egyptian empire. Phir'oun arranged for a public contest between Musa and the magicians. Rumors were spread all over Egypt about Phir'oun's many magicians and a single man who claimed to be a prophet.

Everyone was excited about watching this great contest. Before the contest began, Musa stood up and the whole crowd was quiet. He addressed the magicians: "Woe unto you! Do not invent lies against Allah. He would destroy you completely by a punishment. And surely, he who invents a lie (against Allah) will fail miserably."

The Story of Qaroon

The Qur'an tells another story about a wealthy man called Qaroon قارون, who lived in the times of Prophet Musa عليه السلام. He was from among the children of Isra'eel. As Qaroon became richer, he became very arrogant. He had magnificent treasures. The key to these treasures could not even be carried by a group of strong men. He refused to thank Allah and follow Prophet Musa. Therefore Allah destroyed all of his wealth and punished him. Qaroon is an example to those who forget Allah's blessings and fail to remember that everything comes from Allah.

How can we avoid falling into similar traps such as the ones Qaroon and Phir'oun slipped into?

We need to totally obey Allah, thank Him for everything that happens in our lives, and be humble to Him.

Prophet Musa Prevails

Prophet Musa had spoken sincerely and made the magicians think and about what he said. But the magicians were fooled by greed and fame. They hoped to impress their people with their sihr, or magic, and expose Prophet Musa عليه السلام as a liar.

Prophet Musa asked the magicians to perform first. They threw their magical objects down on the ground. Their staffs and ropes took the shape of wriggling snakes. The crowd was amazed and Phir'oun and his men applauded loudly. Musaعليه السلام felt a little fear in his heart when he saw many snakes move and creep around him. "Don't be afraid, you will prevail. Throw your staff and it will swallow all of their snakes," Allah revealed to him. Then Musa threw his staff and it began to wriggle and it became a huge snake. The people stood up to witness the great miracle. Phir'oun and his men sat silently and watched as Musa's huge snake swallowed all the other snakes. Musa bent to pick it up and it became a staff again.

Phir'oun's Revenge

The crowd rose up like a great wave, shouting and screaming with excitement. They had never seen a wonder like this before! The magicians prostrated themselves to Allah, declaring, "We believe in the Lord of Musa and Haroon."

Phir'oun became very angry. He claimed that the magicians and Musa had secretly plotted together against Phir'oun. He demanded that the magicians confess to their plan, threatening them with death. The magicians refused to denounce Allah and stuck to their sincere belief. Phir'oun threatened to cut of their hands and feet and crucify them on the trunks of palm trees.

The magicians were the knowledgeable people and scholars of the Egyptian society. They understood that Prophet Musa spoke the truth so they prostrated to Allah. The people of Egypt were afraid of Phir'oun. Therefore they abandoned the magicians and left them to be killed. Allah had given the people of Egypt clear signs that Prophet Musa was a truthful messenger of God but they chose to ignore his message. The people did nothing but stand and watch as the magicians were killed, but Allah punished these people later for being cowards.

While Phir'oun returned to his palace, he was overcome with anger and rage. He argued with his ministers and generals, hated them for no reason, and commanded them to get out of his presence. When he was left alone, he tried to think more calmly. He drank several cups of wine, but his anger did not decrease.

Then he called all his ministers and generals for a serious meeting. Phir'oun entered the meeting with a harsh face. It was obvious that he was not going to give up so easily. He had established a kingdom with him being a god to be worshipped by all Egyptians. Now Musa came to destroy all that he built because he came with the message that there is no god but Allah. This meant that Phir'oun was a liar, not a god.

The False God

Phir'oun asked his ministers whether he was a liar. Hamaan, who was one of his top ministers fell to Phir'oun's knees and told him, "Who dared to accuse Phir'oun of lying?" Phir'oun turned to Hamaan and said: "O Hamaan build me a tower that I may arrive at the ways – the ways of the Heaven, and I may look upon the God of Musa but verily, I think him to be a liar."

Phir'oun issued his command to build a tower that would reach the Heavens. Phir'oun ignored the rules of architecture. Hamaan knew that such a building was impossible to build, but he foolishly issued a command to build it immediately. Hamaan said: "However your majesty let me object to Phir'oun for the first time. You will never find anyone in the Heavens. There is no God but you." Then Phir'oun said: "Oh Chiefs! I didn't know that you have an ilah (a god) other than me." Not only that, he also claimed that he was "the Highest God."

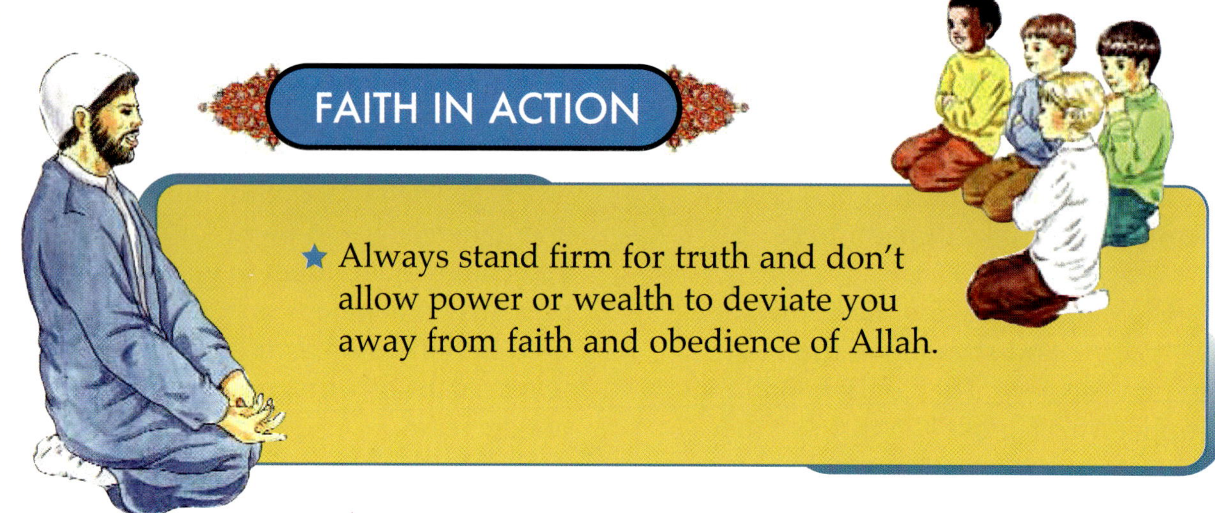

FAITH IN ACTION
★ Always stand firm for truth and don't allow power or wealth to deviate you away from faith and obedience of Allah.

سورة الأعراف

Surat-ul-A'raf 28:113-126

﴿ وَجَآءَ ٱلسَّحَرَةُ فِرۡعَوۡنَ قَالُوٓاْ إِنَّ لَنَا لَأَجۡرًا إِن كُنَّا نَحۡنُ ٱلۡغَٰلِبِينَ ١١٣ قَالَ
نَعَمۡ وَإِنَّكُمۡ لَمِنَ ٱلۡمُقَرَّبِينَ ١١٤ قَالُواْ يَٰمُوسَىٰٓ إِمَّآ أَن تُلۡقِيَ وَإِمَّآ أَن نَّكُونَ نَحۡنُ
ٱلۡمُلۡقِينَ ١١٥ قَالَ أَلۡقُواْۖ فَلَمَّآ أَلۡقَوۡاْ سَحَرُوٓاْ أَعۡيُنَ ٱلنَّاسِ وَٱسۡتَرۡهَبُوهُمۡ وَجَآءُو
بِسِحۡرٍ عَظِيمٖ ١١٦ وَأَوۡحَيۡنَآ إِلَىٰ مُوسَىٰٓ أَنۡ أَلۡقِ عَصَاكَۖ فَإِذَا هِيَ تَلۡقَفُ مَا يَأۡفِكُونَ
١١٧ فَوَقَعَ ٱلۡحَقُّ وَبَطَلَ مَا كَانُواْ يَعۡمَلُونَ ١١٨ فَغُلِبُواْ هُنَالِكَ وَٱنقَلَبُواْ صَٰغِرِينَ ١١٩
وَأُلۡقِيَ ٱلسَّحَرَةُ سَٰجِدِينَ ١٢٠ قَالُوٓاْ ءَامَنَّا بِرَبِّ ٱلۡعَٰلَمِينَ ١٢١ رَبِّ مُوسَىٰ وَهَٰرُونَ ١٢٢
قَالَ فِرۡعَوۡنُ ءَامَنتُم بِهِۦ قَبۡلَ أَنۡ ءَاذَنَ لَكُمۡۖ إِنَّ هَٰذَا لَمَكۡرٞ مَّكَرۡتُمُوهُ فِي ٱلۡمَدِينَةِ لِتُخۡرِجُواْ
مِنۡهَآ أَهۡلَهَاۖ فَسَوۡفَ تَعۡلَمُونَ ١٢٣ لَأُقَطِّعَنَّ أَيۡدِيَكُمۡ وَأَرۡجُلَكُم مِّنۡ خِلَٰفٖ ثُمَّ لَأُصَلِّبَنَّكُمۡ
أَجۡمَعِينَ ١٢٤ قَالُوٓاْ إِنَّآ إِلَىٰ رَبِّنَا مُنقَلِبُونَ ١٢٥ وَمَا تَنقِمُ مِنَّآ إِلَّآ أَنۡ ءَامَنَّا بِـَٔايَٰتِ
رَبِّنَا لَمَّا جَآءَتۡنَاۚ رَبَّنَآ أَفۡرِغۡ عَلَيۡنَا صَبۡرٗا وَتَوَفَّنَا مُسۡلِمِينَ ١٢٦ ﴾

Understood Meaning

28:113 So there came the sorcerers to Phir'oun: They said, "of course we shall have a (suitable) reward if we win!"

28:114 He said: "Yea, (and more),- for you shall in that case be (raised to posts) nearest (to my person)."

28:115 They said: "O Musa! will you throw (first), or shall we have the (first) throw?"

28:116 Musa said: "You throw [first]." So when they threw, they bewitched the eyes of the people, and struck terror into them: for they showed a great (feat of) magic.

28:117 We revealed to Musa: "Throw [now] your rod": and behold! it swallows up straight away all the falsehoods which they fake!

28:118 Thus truth was confirmed, and all that they made did fail.

28:119 So the (sorcerers) were defeated there and then, and were made to look small.

28:120 But the sorcerers fell down and prostrated in adoration.

28:121 They said: "We believe in the Lord of the Worlds,-

28:122 "The Lord of Musa and Aaron."

28:123 Phir'oun said [in anger]: "You Believed in Him before I give you permission? Surely this is a trick which you have planned in the city to drive out its people: but soon you shall know (the consequences).

28:124 "Be sure I will cut off your hands and your feet on apposite sides, and I will cause you all to die on the cross."

28:125 They said: "[Then] We will be sent back to our Lord:

28:126 "But you simply would punish us because we believed in the Signs of our Lord when they came to us [with Musa]! Our Lord! shower us with perseverance, and take our souls to you as Muslims!

Lessons Learned

Standing Up for Your Belief:

There is a great lesson to be learned from the magicians. They embraced Islam after they witnessed the sincerity of Musa and the clear signs from Allah. They knew the difference between سِحر magic and the mu'jizah مُعْجِزة miracle of Allah. Therefore, they sincerely believed that there was no God but Allah and that Musa was His messenger at that time. They insisted to stay as believers though Phir'oun had threatened them with death. We should have strong faith and belief just like those magicians. We should always remember that Allah protects His believers in the end.

Miracles vs. Witchcraft:

Miracles, or mu'jizat مُعجِزات ,are extraordinary actions that happen with Allah's help. They usually happen for a good cause like proving that prophets are true or to support the believers against evil people. The miracles that happened with Musa were to prove that Musa was a prophet and to support Musa against the evil of Phir'oun and his people.

Magic or witchcraft, on the other hand, is done by evil people to hurt or deceive others. However, those evil people cannot do witchcraft alone. They seek the help of unbeliever jinn. The jinn are created from fire, and most of them follow Shaytan as their leader. Jinn are invisible to mankind most of the time. Some jinn are Muslims but most of them are not. Prophet Muhammad spoke to groups of them and they followed him as Al-Qur'an confirmed in Surat Al-Jinn. They make things move, disappear, and change looks, among many other mysterious things.

Evil jinn help evil humans to do magic or witchcraft for bad purposes. The work of the magicians of Phir'oun was just an example. Shaytan and his evil jinn followers helped the magicians of Phir'oun to make their staffs and robes look as snakes, but they were not real snakes. Only Allah can make real snakes. When the magicians and their jinn helpers made people see their robes and staffs look as snakes, Allah enabled Musa to do the same, and the work of Allah then defeated the works of jinn and the magicians. This made the magicians of Phir'oun discover that their jinn helpers were defeated by Allah. Therefore, they submitted to Allah and followed Prophet Musa عليه السلام.

Not all magicians use the help of the jinn, some magic is done without their help. The art of producing illusions by the skillful hands is also called magic.

Some skillful professionals do such stunts and make believe moves on their own without the interference of jinn. Others, still, seek the help of jinn to do their sophisticated magic.

Doing magic with the help of the jinn is Haram or prohibited in Islam, especially if it is done for an evil purpose. The Prophet forbade Muslims to approach witchcraft and considered it next to shirk, or disbelief. However, seeking the help of Muslim jinn to help possessed people and counter the evil work of witch-crafters is permissible according to many Muslim scholars.

FAITH IN ACTION

- Always follow sincere Muslim scholars and leaders.
- Always avoid following arrogant people who disbelieve and disobey Allah.
- Always avoid dealing with magic or being fooled by it.

Hadeeth Shareef

عن أبي هـريرة رضي الله عنه قال : قال رسـول الله ﷺ :
" اجتنبوا الموبقات : الشرك بالله والسـحر"
رواه البخاري

Abu Hurayrah رضي الله عنه reported that Prophet Muhammad said:

"Abandon the destructive sins: shirk, claiming partners with Allah, and sihr, whichcraft."

Al-Bukhari

CHAPTER REVIEW

Projects and Activities

1. Prophet Musa was courageous by speaking the truth against Phir'oun. Write a story you learned about a man or a woman who stood for the truth against an arrogant and powerful leader.
2. Write a poem about the story you learned in this chapter.

Stretch Your Mind

1. Why did prophets need to perform miracles sometimes?
2. What is the difference between a miracle and magic?
3. Why do you think the magicians changed so fast from following Phir'oun to following Prophet Musa in worshipping Allah?
4. Why do you think the magicians chose death over obeying Phir'oun?

Study Questions

1. What miracles did Musa perform in front of Phir'oun?
2. What was Phir'oun's reaction to Musa's miracles?
3. Why did Phir'oun seek the greatest magicians from all over Egypt?
4. What happened at the event with Musa and the magicians?
5. How did the magicians react?
6. How did Phir'oun react to the magicians prostrating to Allah?
7. What does Islam say about magic and witchcraft? Support your answer with a Hadeeth.

God is With Me

Most of the people in Egypt refused to follow the message of Musa. The children of Isra'eel were still under the oppression of Phir'oun. Prophet Musa asked for the children of Isra'eel to leave with him but Phir'oun refused. Allah inflicted many punishments on the Egyptians but still they refused to allow the children of Isra'eel to leave with Musa.

Phir'oun Plans to Kill Prophet Musa

Phir'oun was afraid that Musa would mislead the Egyptian people. He suggested to his ministers that Musa be killed. All the ministers agreed except one whose name is not mentioned in the Qur'an. The Qur'an only says that the man was a believer.

This believer spoke in the assembly where the idea of killing Musa had been introduced. He proved that it was not a good idea:

"Musa did not say more than that Allah, the True Creator, is his Lord. Later, he came with clear evidence that he was a messenger. There are two possibilities; either Musa is righteous or a liar. If he lies, he will be responsible for his lie. If he is righteous and we slay him, who would protect us from God's punishment. Musa does not deserve to be killed," the man argued.

This angered Phir'oun and his ministers. As usual, they threatened to harm the man, but he stood fast on his belief. However, Allah protected His believer.

Musa asked Phir'oun to release the children of Isra'eel from slavery. The Prophet wanted to move them from Egypt to Palestine. Phir'oun refused and called the Egyptian people and the children of Isra'eel, to a huge gathering. He reminded the people that he was their highest lord, who provided them with all their needs. He told them that Musa was just a poor man.

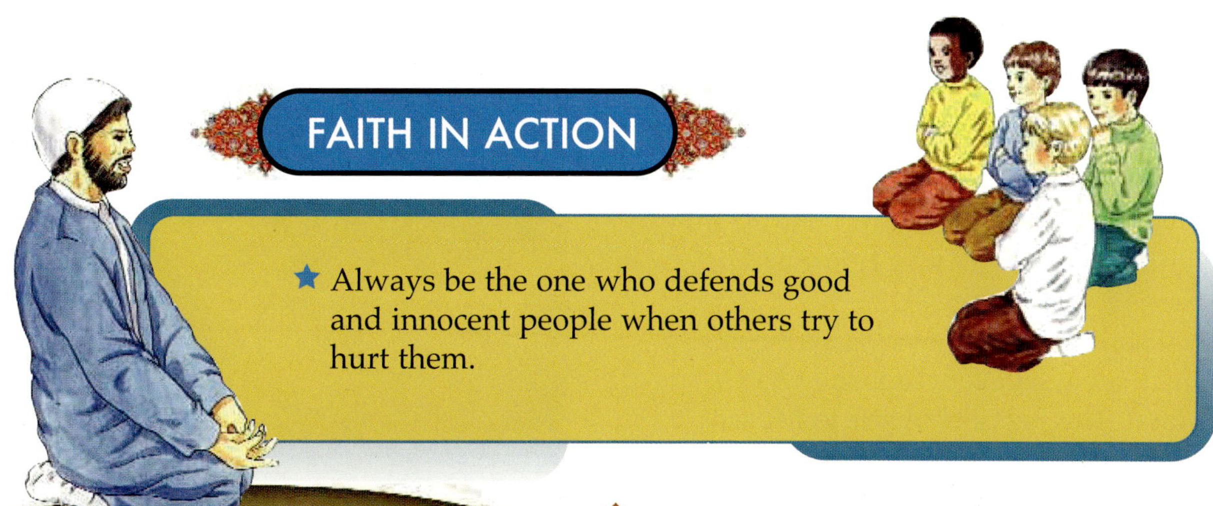

FAITH IN ACTION

- Always be the one who defends good and innocent people when others try to hurt them.

So the Egyptian people appealed to Musa and said,

"Oh Musa! Pray to your Lord for us because of His promise to You. If You will remove the punishment from us, we indeed shall believe in You, and we shall let the children of Isra'eel go with You." (Surat-ul-A'raf 7:134)

Prophet Musa prayed to Allah and Allah stopped the suffering caused by the flood. Once again the people were able to cultivate their land and grow their crops. But when Prophet Musa asked them to fulfill their promise to believe in the True God and release the children of Isra'eel, they refused.

Then Allah sent swarms of locusts, which ate whatever crops they had grown. The people hurried to Musa, asking him to pray to Allah to remove the locusts. They promised that they would send the children of Isra'eel with him this time. The locusts left, but they, again, did not fulfill their promise.

Then another sign of God's wrath came; the punishment of lice. It ate

Locusts

what they stored of wheat and other valuable crops. Again they sought Prophet Musa's help and they repeated their promise. He prayed again, but the Egyptians still refused to believe and release the children of Isra'eel.

Another punishment came to the Egyptians. The land suddenly was filled with frogs. They jumped on the food of the Egyptians, shared their beds, invaded their houses, and troubled them a lot. The Egyptians went to Musa again, promising him they would believe in Allah and release the children of Isra'eel. He prayed to Allah and Allah took away the problem of the frogs, but they again broke their promise.

Later, the Nile water was changed into blood. When Musa and his people drank the water, it was ordinary water. On the other hand, if any Egyptian filled his cup with water, he discovered his cup full of blood. They hurried to Musa as usual, but as soon as everything returned to normal, they turned their backs on Allah.

▲ *Frogs*

Prophet Musa and his People Leave Egypt

Allah decided to put an end to Phir'oun's crimes after He had given him so many chances. Allah commanded Prophet Musa to leave Egypt with the children of Isra'eel. So they prepared themselves to leave. This later became known as the "Exodus." At night, Musa led his people towards the Red Sea, and in the morning they reached the beach. By then Phir'oun discovered that Musa and the children of Isra'eel had fled, so he led a huge army to stop them.

The Greatest Miracle

The children of Isra'eel were impatient and nervous. Joshua (Yoosha' Ibn Noon), said: "In front of us is this impassable barrier, the sea, and behind us the enemy; surely death cannot be avoided!"

Musa replied,

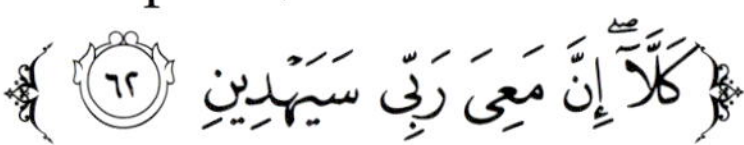

"Nay, verily my Lord is with me and He will guide me!"[26:62]

These words filled the Children of Isra'eel with hope. When they saw the army approaching quickly, some of them lost hope again and were willing to return back to slavery. At that moment Allah revealed to Prophet Musa:

"Strike the sea with your staff!"

Musa did as he was commanded. A violent wind blew, in a moment the sea parted, with the waves standing like mountains on each side. Allah had made a path for them through the sea. Everyone was overcome with awe.

Musa led his people across. This miracle proved Musa's claim that "Verily! My Lord is with me!" As they looked back, they saw Phir'oun and his army getting near, about to take the same path across the parted sea which the children of Isra'eel took. In great fear and panic, the children of Isra'eel asked Musa to ask Allah to close the sea. But, Allah commanded Musa not to strike the sea with his staff again, because Allah's command was already in action.

The End of Phir'oun

Phir'oun and his army had seen the miracle, how the sea had split, but being the pretender that he was, Phir'oun turned to his men and said: "Look! The sea has opened at my command so that I may follow those rebels and arrest them!" They rushed across the split sea, and when they reached the middle of the path, Allah commanded the sea to return to its original form.

Phir'oun realized his end had come so out of fear he declared:

"I believe that there is no god worthy of worship except Allah in Whom the children of Isra'eel believe, and I am of those who surrender to Him."

But Allah did not accept this declaration from the tyrant. The water closed over him, drowning him and his entire army. Later, the waves threw his corpse up to the seashore. The Egyptians saw him and knew that their false god whom they worshipped and obeyed for years was nothing but a wicked man. This false god could not keep death away from his own neck.

Hadeeth Shareef

عن عبد الله بن عمر رضي الله عنه قال: قال رسول الله ﷺ :

إن الله يقبل توبة العبد ما لم يغرغر

رواه الترمذي وأحمد

Abdullah ibn Omar رضي الله عنه narrated that Rasoolullah ﷺ said:

"Allah accepts the repentance of his servant as long as his soul is not about to come out."

Reported by At-Tirmithi and Ahmad

FAITH IN ACTION

- Do your best to avoid sins and disobedience. And when you commit a sin, do not wait long before you repent. Make it your habit to be restless whenever you sin and immediately repent and seek the forgiveness of Allah.

سورة الشعراء

Surat-ush-Shu'araa' 52-67

وَأَوْحَيْنَآ إِلَىٰ مُوسَىٰٓ أَنْ أَسْرِ بِعِبَادِىٓ إِنَّكُم مُّتَّبَعُونَ ﴿٥٢﴾ فَأَرْسَلَ فِرْعَوْنُ فِى ٱلْمَدَآئِنِ حَٰشِرِينَ
﴿٥٣﴾ إِنَّ هَٰٓؤُلَآءِ لَشِرْذِمَةٌ قَلِيلُونَ ﴿٥٤﴾ وَإِنَّهُمْ لَنَا لَغَآئِظُونَ ﴿٥٥﴾ وَإِنَّا لَجَمِيعٌ حَٰذِرُونَ ﴿٥٦﴾
فَأَخْرَجْنَٰهُم مِّن جَنَّٰتٍ وَعُيُونٍ ﴿٥٧﴾ وَكُنُوزٍ وَمَقَامٍ كَرِيمٍ ﴿٥٨﴾ كَذَٰلِكَ وَأَوْرَثْنَٰهَا بَنِىٓ إِسْرَٰٓءِيلَ
﴿٥٩﴾ فَأَتْبَعُوهُم مُّشْرِقِينَ ﴿٦٠﴾ فَلَمَّا تَرَٰٓءَا ٱلْجَمْعَانِ قَالَ أَصْحَٰبُ مُوسَىٰٓ إِنَّا لَمُدْرَكُونَ ﴿٦١﴾
قَالَ كَلَّآ ۖ إِنَّ مَعِىَ رَبِّى سَيَهْدِينِ ﴿٦٢﴾ فَأَوْحَيْنَآ إِلَىٰ مُوسَىٰٓ أَنِ ٱضْرِب بِّعَصَاكَ ٱلْبَحْرَ ۖ فَٱنفَلَقَ
فَكَانَ كُلُّ فِرْقٍ كَٱلطَّوْدِ ٱلْعَظِيمِ ﴿٦٣﴾ وَأَزْلَفْنَا ثَمَّ ٱلْءَاخَرِينَ ﴿٦٤﴾ وَأَنجَيْنَا مُوسَىٰ وَمَن مَّعَهُۥٓ
أَجْمَعِينَ ﴿٦٥﴾ ثُمَّ أَغْرَقْنَا ٱلْءَاخَرِينَ ﴿٦٦﴾ إِنَّ فِى ذَٰلِكَ لَءَايَةً ۖ وَمَا كَانَ أَكْثَرُهُم مُّؤْمِنِينَ ﴿٦٧﴾

Translation

26:52 We revealed to Musa: "Travel by night with my servants; definitely you will be followed."

26:53 Shortly after, Phir'oun sent heralds to (all) the cities.

26:54 [He said]: "These (Israelites) are but a small group,

26:55 "And they are making us furious;

26:56 "But we are all fore-warned."

26:57 So We expelled them from gardens, springs,

26:58 Treasures, and every kind of honorable position;

26:59 Thus it was, but We made the Children of Isra'eel inheritors of such things.

26:60 So they chased them at sunrise.

26:61 And when the two groups saw each other, the people of Musa said: "We will be overtaken."

26:62 (Musa) said: "Nay! Verily my Lord is with me! Soon He will guide me!"

26:63 Then We revealed: "Strike the sea with you rod." So it divided, and each separate part became like the huge, firm mass of a mountain.

26:64 And We made the other party [Phir'oun and his soldiers] approach nearer.

26:65 We rescued Musa and all who were with him;

26:66 But We drowned the others.

26:67 Verily there is a sign in this: but most of them do not believe.

سورة يونس

Surat Younus 90-92

﴿ وَجَٰوَزۡنَا بِبَنِيٓ إِسۡرَٰٓءِيلَ ٱلۡبَحۡرَ فَأَتۡبَعَهُمۡ فِرۡعَوۡنُ وَجُنُودُهُۥ بَغۡيٗا وَعَدۡوًاۖ حَتَّىٰٓ إِذَآ
أَدۡرَكَهُ ٱلۡغَرَقُ قَالَ ءَامَنتُ أَنَّهُۥ لَآ إِلَٰهَ إِلَّا ٱلَّذِيٓ ءَامَنَتۡ بِهِۦ بَنُوٓاْ إِسۡرَٰٓءِيلَ وَأَنَا۠ مِنَ ٱلۡمُسۡلِمِينَ
(٩٠) ءَآلۡـَٰٔنَ وَقَدۡ عَصَيۡتَ قَبۡلُ وَكُنتَ مِنَ ٱلۡمُفۡسِدِينَ (٩١) فَٱلۡيَوۡمَ نُنَجِّيكَ بِبَدَنِكَ
لِتَكُونَ لِمَنۡ خَلۡفَكَ ءَايَةٗۚ وَإِنَّ كَثِيرٗا مِّنَ ٱلنَّاسِ عَنۡ ءَايَٰتِنَا لَغَٰفِلُونَ (٩٢) ﴾

Translation

10:90 We took the Children of Isra'eel across the sea: Phir'oun and his hosts followed them in arrogance and aggression. And when we almost drowned him he said: "I believe that there is no god except Him Whom the Children of Isra'eel believe in: I am of those who submit (to Allah in Islam)."

10:91 [It was said to him]: "Ah now!- But a little while ago, you disobeyed! and you did mischief (and violence)!
10:92 "This day We will keep your [dead] body, that you may be a lesson to those who come after you! but verily, many among mankind are heedless of Our Signs!"

Lessons Learned

1. Complete Trust in Allah:

When everyone was afraid of Phir'oun, Musa was not. He put his full trust in Allah and found nothing to be feared but Him. The Children of Isra'eel thought that Phir'oun was going to capture and kill them on the beaches of the Red Sea. Only Musa had complete trust in Allah. He shouted, "Verily Allah is with me and He will guide me," and this was exactly what happened. Prophet Muhammad said a similar thing to Abu Bakr when they were hiding from the pagans of Makkah in the cave of Tawr. Abu Bakr whispered, "Oh Prophet of Allah, if one of them would look into this cave they will see us." Prophet Muhammad said with full confidence in Allah, "Do not worry, Allah is with us." Strong believers put their complete trust in Allah and their faith in God never wavers.

2. The Danger of Late Tawbah (Repentance):

There is a very important lesson to draw from Phir'oun's late repentance. He waited to the very last moment of his life and he was rejected by Allah. Allah grants plenty of time and opportunity to everybody to believe in him. There is enough time to consider Allah's messages and reminders, and finally, follow them. If a man wastes the time he has been allowed and attempts to ask forgiveness only at the moment of death, his repentance is worthless. At the moment of death, a person can clearly sense the reality and closeness of the Hereafter. This is an important warning to all those who believe in "living it up," until they are old. Those who wait until they are old may reach the last moment of death when faith and repentance no longer have value. So don't wait until you are old to wear hijab or start praying. Do it while you have your youth and health and Allah will grant you Paradise inshaAllah.

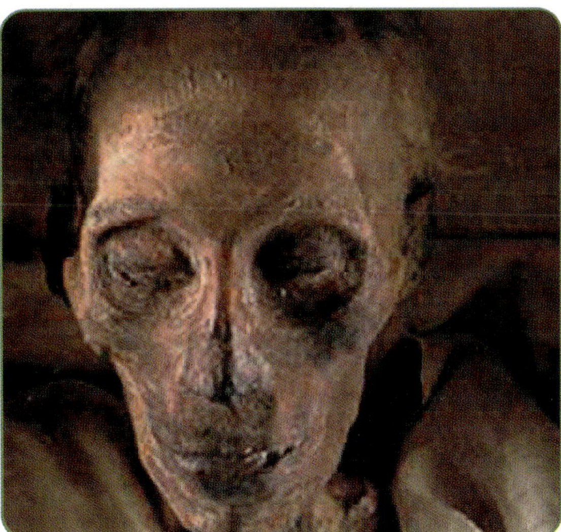

Ramses II is thought to be the Phir'oun whom Allah drowned. His body is still preserved, as Allah promised.

Locust

A locust is a large GRASSHOPPER. The Arabic name for locusts is jaraad. It is one of the jumping insects that you can see in parks, fields and even in your backyard. They are about 1 inch long and come in different colors, but the most common color for a locust is dark brown.

Locusts are known for their traveling. They travel thousands of miles looking for food. They travel in swarms of huge numbers. The Science News Magazine reported that "in July 1875, the Rocky Mountain locust swept across the Great Plains .... If calculations of that day are accurate, as they seem to be, then 3.5 trillion (3,500,000,000,000) locusts passed over an elongated area covering some 198,000 square miles. Witnesses reported the sky turning black; the sun eclipsed. Traveling at 15 miles per hour, the voracious swarm devastated crops and ate each other."

Locust Meals:

Believe it or not, locust can be a delicious meal for many people around the world. People cook it and eat it like they eat shrimp. People in Arabia used to eat locust. Once, Prophet Muhammad was asked about eating it and said: "I don't eat it, but I would not prohibit you from it."

▲ *Locust*

عن عبد الله بن عمر رضي الله عنه قال: قال رسول الله صلى الله عليه وسلم :
"أحلت لنا ميتتان ودمان ، فأما الميتتان فالحوت والجراد ، وأما الدمان فالكبد والطحال"
رواه أحمد وابن ماجه

Allah made halal for you two dead animals and two types of blood; The two dead are fish and locust; and the two bloods are liver and spleen. Reported in Ahmad and Ibn Majah

Meaning: By two dead animals, the prophet meant the animals that you can catch and leave them to die and you still can eat them without having to slaughter. On the other hand, livers and spleens of sheep, cows, camels and other halal animals are good to eat. The Prophet called them bloods, because there are great blood percentages in these organs. As for the Prophet himself, although he made it halal to eat locust, he did not like it, so he did not eat it.

CHAPTER REVIEW

Projects and Activities

Create with your classmates a model made of sand and other available materials which shows the split sea and the army of Phir'oun trying to apprehend Bani Isra'eel. At the end of the project you can demonstrate how the sea returned to its normal situation and made Phir'oun and his army drown in the Red Sea.

Stretch Your Mind

1. In what way are the stories of Musa and Prophet Muhammad with their enemies similar?

2. Why do you think Musa was not afraid of Phir'oun at the sea shore?

Study Questions

1. What punishments did Allah bring to Phir'oun and the Egyptians?
2. Did the Egyptians fulfill the promise of releasing the children of Isra'eel? Why.
3. What did Allah order Musa and the children of Isra'eel to do?
4. What kind of miracle happened when the children of Isra'eel reached the Red Sea?
5. What happened to Phir'oun and his men?
6. List three lessons that we can draw from the story you learned in this chapter.
7. Locust and blood were used as a punishment against Phir'oun and the Egyptians. Now-a-days they are used as food by many people around the world. Are they halal for Muslims to eat? Suppost your answer with a hadeeth.

Wavering Faith

In spite of Phir'oun's death, he left a bad influence on the souls of the children of Isra'eel. He had made them used to submitting to someone other than Allah. Phir'oun had oppressed their souls and spoiled their nature so much that they began to disobey Musa.

VOCABULARY

Al-Mann المَنّ

As-Salwa السَّلوى

PEOPLE TO REMEMBER

As-Samiriy: Samaritan السَّامريّ

PLACES TO REMEMBER

Sinai Peninsula سَـيْناء

Jabal-ut-Toor: جَبَلُ الطّور

Mount Sinai جَبَلُ سيناء

Prophet Musa Leads the Children of Isra'eel to Palestine

Allah had directed Prophet Musa عليه السلام to lead the Children of Isra'eel to the Promised Land (Palestine) through the Sinai Peninsula.

While they were traveling, the children of Isra'eel did not show complete obedience to their Lord. Despite all of Allah's favors, they could not stay away from evil and continued to reject Allah's laws. Although Phir'oun was dead, his influence upon their souls still remained. Their recovery needed a long period of time. Prophet Musa returned to his Lord, telling Him that he was responsible only for the actions of himself and his brother Haroon. He complained that he did not have enough control over his people's attitudes. He also prayed to his Lord to judge between his people and himself.

▲ *A picture of Sinai from the space.*

Allah issued His judgment against that generation of the children of Isra'eel who were corrupted by the Egyptians. They must wander in the wilderness of Sinai until that generation had produced another generation. The new generation could be more righteous and God-fearing.

The Wandering in Sinai Desert

▲ *Sinai Desert*

The days of restless wandering began. The Children of Isra'eel entered Sinai and could not find their way out of it to Palestine. They started walking to no destination, day and night, morning and evening. As they traveled, each day they would end at the point where they began. As they chose to be confused in terms of their faith in God, Allah punished them by making them get lost and confused in the Sinai Desert.

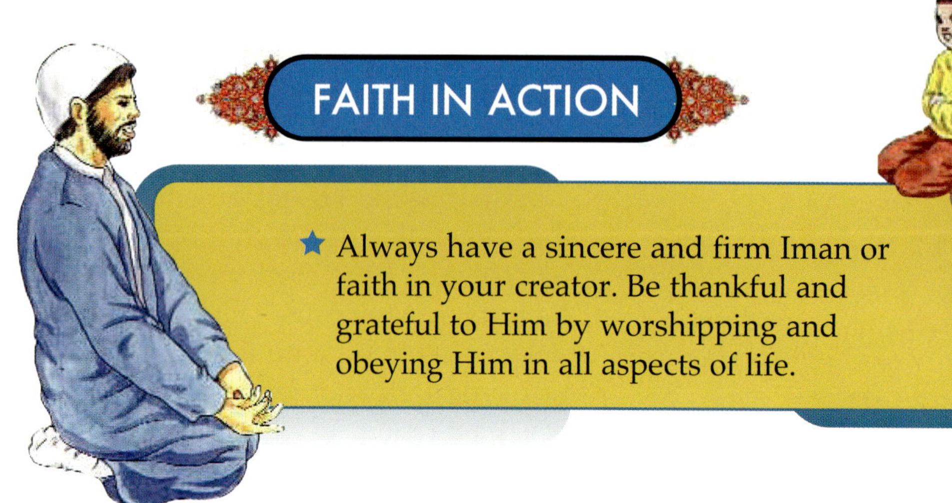

FAITH IN ACTION

★ Always have a sincere and firm Iman or faith in your creator. Be thankful and grateful to Him by worshipping and obeying Him in all aspects of life.

Prophet Musa Speaks to God

Musa came to the same place where he had spoke to Allah for the first time. Allah instructed him to purify himself by fasting for thirty days, after which he was to go to Mount Sinai, where he would be given the divine law.

Musa fasted thirty days. Due to fasting, the odor of his breath became unpleasant. He disliked speaking to his Lord while he had the unpleasant smell of his mouth. Therefore, he ate a plant of the Earth and then his Lord said to him: "Why did you break your fast?" Musa said: "O my Lord, I disliked to speak to You with my mouth not having a pleasant smell." Allah said: "Do you not know, Musa, the odor of the faster's mouth is better scented to Me than the rose. Go back and fast ten days; then come back to Me." Musa did what Allah commanded.

▲ *Mount Sinai*

Special Places

Mount Sinai

Mount Sinai is the mountain where God spoke to Prophet Musa. That is, at least, what people in that area believe. This belief itself has drawn visitors for over a thousand years. Although no archeological evidence of Musa' presence on the mountain exists, there are many relics of faith throughout the eons. Nearing the summit, one can see an amphitheater where, locals believe, the 70 wise men waited while God spoke with Musa, then finally a small chapel and mosque are located at the top. It takes about 3 hours to climb the 7,498-foot peak following the Path of Musa, a stairway of nearly 4,000 steps.

The Children of Isra'eel Turn to Idol Worshipping

Prophet Musa عليه السلام had been gone for forty days and his people were becoming restless. They did not know that Allah had added ten extra days to Musa's stay. As-Samiriy, or Samaritan, an evil man, suggested to the children of Isra'eel that they needed another guide. Musa, he claimed, had broken his promise. He said to them: "In order to find true guidance, you need a god, and I shall provide one for you."

So he collected all their gold jewelry, dug a hole in which he placed the gold in it, and lit a huge fire to melt it down. From the melted gold he made a golden calf. Some of Children of Isra' accepted the golden calf as their god. Prophet Haroon (P), Musa's brother, who acted as their leader in Musa' s absence, felt very sad and spoke up:

"O my people! You have been deceived. Your Lord is the Most Beneficent. Follow and obey me."

They replied: "We shall stop worshipping this god only if Musa returns."

Those who had remained steadfast in belief separated themselves from the idol worshippers.

The Return of Prophet Musa

After forty days, Musa returned to his people carrying tablets of Allah's revelations and guidance, the Tawrat. Upon his return, Musa saw his people worshipping the idol they made with their hands. They were also singing and dancing around that golden calf. Musa was shocked and angered by what he saw. He threw down the tablets of the law which he was carrying for them. He tugged Haroon's beard and his hair, crying: "What held you back when you saw them going astray? Why did you not stop this corruption?"

Haroon replied:

"O son of my mother, let go of my beard! The fold considered me weak and were about to kill me. So make not the enemies rejoice over me, nor put me among the people who are wrong-doers."

When Musa understood Haroon's helplessness, he began to handle the situation calmly and wisely. At least seventy people, along with Haroon, refused to worship the idol, but they did not support Haroon and nor did they exert enough effort to stop others from doing the awful act of idol worshipping.

Allah then ordered Musa to punish those who worshipped the idol. They were to line up and get killed by those who did not worship the idol. Then

Allah forgave them all. Some historians say that even those who did not worship the idol, but did nothing to stop it were to be killed too as a punishment for their passive attitudes.

Musa asked the Children of Isra' to pray to Allah for forgiveness and repent for their sins. He chose seventy elders, all of whom did not worship the idol, to accompany him on a trip to Mount Sinai to seek Allah's forgiveness on behalf of all the Children of Isra'. He ordered them:

"Rush towards Allah and repent for what you did and ask His forgiveness for your shortcomings."

Later, Prophet Musa ordered the Children of Isra' to obey God and practice the Tawrat that was revealed to him. They told Musa عليه السلام that they would do that only if the required worship and laws were easy to do.

The Elders Accompany Musa to Mount Sinai

Musa returned to Mount Sinai with the seventy elders and there he communicated with Allah. He hoped that they would become strong believers when they heard him speak with Allah. The elders heard Musa speaking with his Lord. This was probably the last miracle that they would see. However, the seventy elders who heard the miracles were not yet satisfied. They said to Musa:

"O Musa! We shall never believe in you until we see Allah plainly." [Surat-ul-Baqarah 2:350]

Their stubborn demand was rewarded with punishing lightning bolts and a violent quake which resulted in their deaths.

Musa knew what had happened to the seventy elite and was filled with sadness. He prayed to his Lord, asking Him to forgive them, because they were unwise and rude. Allah forgave the elders and brought them back to life. Additionally, Allah raised one of the mountains above their head causing the Earth to shake under their feet. They all became frightened that the mountain would fall on them. Allah then ordered them to follow the Tawrat "strongly" and fully obey their Lord. They fell in prostration and promised God to do just that.

Wavering Faith

Even after all of that, most of Bani Isra'eel kept on showing unacceptable behavior with God. Allah granted them great food like الـمَنْ "al-mann" and السّلْوى"as-salwa." "al-mann" was a sweet and nutritious food falling on them every morning like the falling of the snow in the winter time. "As-salwa," on the other hand was a kind of bird like the dove but was easy to catch. When the Children of Isra'eel became thirsty and lacked drinkable water, Allah ordered Musa to strike a rock with his staff. Miraculously, water gushed out from twelve places in the ground. Despite all these favors and blessings that Allah granted to the Children of Isra'eel, most of them refused to show gratitude and sincere obedience to their Lord.

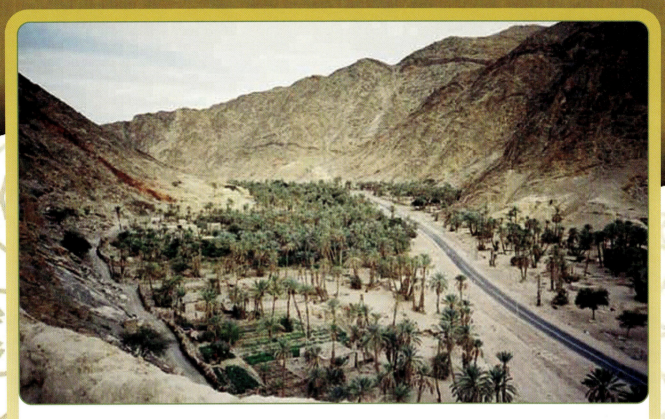

The Oasis of Feiran in Sinai is, according to locals, scholars, and legend, where Musa struck a rock with his staff, bringing forth a spring so his people could drink. Feiran is now the site of the largest oasis in all of Sinai. The heart of the oasis is a spectacular sprawl of palms that stretches over three miles in length. Maybe this is the reason why Feiran is called the "Pearl of Sinai."

Haroon and Musa Die

Prophet Haroon عليه السلام died shortly before Prophet Musa عليه السلام. His people were still wandering in the wilderness when he died.

Abu Hurayrah narrated: "The Angel of Death was sent to Prophet Musa عليه السلام. Prophet Musa did not want to die until he felt that he had done his job with Bani Isra'eel. The angel returned to his Lord and said: 'You have sent me to a slave who does not want to die.' Allah said: 'Return to him and tell him to put his hand on the back of an ox and for every hair that will come under it, he will be granted one extra year of life.' Prophet Musa عليه السلام said: 'O Lord! What will happen after that?' Allah replied: 'then death.' Musa said: 'Let it come now then!' Musa, however, requested Allah to let him die close to the Holy Land so that he would be at a distance of a stone's throw from it." Abu Hurayrah added: "Prophet Muhammad ﷺ said: 'If I were there, I would show you his grave below the red sand hill on the side of the road.'" This story is reported in Saheeh-ul-Bukhari.

Musa عليه السلام, prophet of Allah, and the one to whom Allah spoke to directly, met his death with a happy soul. His faithful heart looked forward to the final return to his Lord.

۞ وَوَٰعَدۡنَا مُوسَىٰ ثَلَٰثِينَ لَيۡلَةٗ وَأَتۡمَمۡنَٰهَا بِعَشۡرٖ فَتَمَّ مِيقَٰتُ رَبِّهِۦٓ أَرۡبَعِينَ لَيۡلَةٗۚ
وَقَالَ مُوسَىٰ لِأَخِيهِ هَٰرُونَ ٱخۡلُفۡنِي فِي قَوۡمِي وَأَصۡلِحۡ وَلَا تَتَّبِعۡ سَبِيلَ ٱلۡمُفۡسِدِينَ
﴿١٤٢﴾ وَلَمَّا جَآءَ مُوسَىٰ لِمِيقَٰتِنَا وَكَلَّمَهُۥ رَبُّهُۥ قَالَ رَبِّ أَرِنِيٓ أَنظُرۡ إِلَيۡكَۚ قَالَ لَن تَرَىٰنِي
وَلَٰكِنِ ٱنظُرۡ إِلَى ٱلۡجَبَلِ فَإِنِ ٱسۡتَقَرَّ مَكَانَهُۥ فَسَوۡفَ تَرَىٰنِيۚ فَلَمَّا تَجَلَّىٰ رَبُّهُۥ لِلۡجَبَلِ
جَعَلَهُۥ دَكّٗا وَخَرَّ مُوسَىٰ صَعِقٗاۚ فَلَمَّآ أَفَاقَ قَالَ سُبۡحَٰنَكَ تُبۡتُ إِلَيۡكَ وَأَنَا۠ أَوَّلُ
ٱلۡمُؤۡمِنِينَ ﴿١٤٣﴾ قَالَ يَٰمُوسَىٰٓ إِنِّي ٱصۡطَفَيۡتُكَ عَلَى ٱلنَّاسِ بِرِسَٰلَٰتِي وَبِكَلَٰمِي فَخُذۡ مَآ
ءَاتَيۡتُكَ وَكُن مِّنَ ٱلشَّٰكِرِينَ ﴿١٤٤﴾ وَكَتَبۡنَا لَهُۥ فِي ٱلۡأَلۡوَاحِ مِن كُلِّ شَيۡءٖ
مَّوۡعِظَةٗ وَتَفۡصِيلٗا لِّكُلِّ شَيۡءٖ فَخُذۡهَا بِقُوَّةٖ وَأۡمُرۡ قَوۡمَكَ يَأۡخُذُواْ بِأَحۡسَنِهَاۚ سَأُوْرِيكُمۡ دَارَ
ٱلۡفَٰسِقِينَ ﴿١٤٥﴾ سَأَصۡرِفُ عَنۡ ءَايَٰتِيَ ٱلَّذِينَ يَتَكَبَّرُونَ فِي ٱلۡأَرۡضِ بِغَيۡرِ ٱلۡحَقِّ وَإِن يَرَوۡاْ
كُلَّ ءَايَةٖ لَّا يُؤۡمِنُواْ بِهَا وَإِن يَرَوۡاْ سَبِيلَ ٱلرُّشۡدِ لَا يَتَّخِذُوهُ سَبِيلٗا وَإِن يَرَوۡاْ
سَبِيلَ ٱلۡغَيِّ يَتَّخِذُوهُ سَبِيلٗاۚ ذَٰلِكَ بِأَنَّهُمۡ كَذَّبُواْ بِـَٔايَٰتِنَا وَكَانُواْ عَنۡهَا غَٰفِلِينَ ﴿١٤٦﴾
وَٱلَّذِينَ كَذَّبُواْ بِـَٔايَٰتِنَا وَلِقَآءِ ٱلۡأٓخِرَةِ حَبِطَتۡ أَعۡمَٰلُهُمۡۚ هَلۡ يُجۡزَوۡنَ إِلَّا
مَا كَانُواْ يَعۡمَلُونَ ﴿١٤٧﴾ وَٱتَّخَذَ قَوۡمُ مُوسَىٰ مِنۢ بَعۡدِهِۦ مِنۡ حُلِيِّهِمۡ عِجۡلٗا جَسَدٗا
لَّهُۥ خُوَارٌۚ أَلَمۡ يَرَوۡاْ أَنَّهُۥ لَا يُكَلِّمُهُمۡ وَلَا يَهۡدِيهِمۡ سَبِيلًاۘ ٱتَّخَذُوهُ وَكَانُواْ ظَٰلِمِينَ
﴿١٤٨﴾ وَلَمَّا سُقِطَ فِيٓ أَيۡدِيهِمۡ وَرَأَوۡاْ أَنَّهُمۡ قَدۡ ضَلُّواْ قَالُواْ لَئِن لَّمۡ يَرۡحَمۡنَا رَبُّنَا
وَيَغۡفِرۡ لَنَا لَنَكُونَنَّ مِنَ ٱلۡخَٰسِرِينَ ﴿١٤٩﴾ وَلَمَّا رَجَعَ مُوسَىٰٓ إِلَىٰ قَوۡمِهِۦ غَضۡبَٰنَ
أَسِفٗا قَالَ بِئۡسَمَا خَلَفۡتُمُونِي مِنۢ بَعۡدِيٓۖ أَعَجِلۡتُمۡ أَمۡرَ رَبِّكُمۡۖ وَأَلۡقَى ٱلۡأَلۡوَاحَ وَأَخَذَ بِرَأۡسِ
أَخِيهِ يَجُرُّهُۥٓ إِلَيۡهِۚ قَالَ ٱبۡنَ أُمَّ إِنَّ ٱلۡقَوۡمَ ٱسۡتَضۡعَفُونِي وَكَادُواْ يَقۡتُلُونَنِي فَلَا تُشۡمِتۡ بِيَ
ٱلۡأَعۡدَآءَ وَلَا تَجۡعَلۡنِي مَعَ ٱلۡقَوۡمِ ٱلظَّٰلِمِينَ ﴿١٥٠﴾ قَالَ رَبِّ ٱغۡفِرۡ لِي وَلِأَخِي وَأَدۡخِلۡنَا
فِي رَحۡمَتِكَۖ وَأَنتَ أَرۡحَمُ ٱلرَّٰحِمِينَ ﴿١٥١﴾ إِنَّ ٱلَّذِينَ ٱتَّخَذُواْ ٱلۡعِجۡلَ سَيَنَالُهُمۡ
غَضَبٞ مِّن رَّبِّهِمۡ وَذِلَّةٞ فِي ٱلۡحَيَوٰةِ ٱلدُّنۡيَاۚ وَكَذَٰلِكَ نَجۡزِي ٱلۡمُفۡتَرِينَ ﴿١٥٢﴾ وَٱلَّذِينَ عَمِلُواْ
ٱلسَّيِّـَٔاتِ ثُمَّ تَابُواْ مِنۢ بَعۡدِهَا وَءَامَنُوٓاْ إِنَّ رَبَّكَ مِنۢ بَعۡدِهَا لَغَفُورٞ رَّحِيمٞ ﴿١٥٣﴾ وَلَمَّا
سَكَتَ عَن مُّوسَى ٱلۡغَضَبُ أَخَذَ ٱلۡأَلۡوَاحَۖ وَفِي نُسۡخَتِهَا هُدٗى وَرَحۡمَةٞ لِّلَّذِينَ هُمۡ لِرَبِّهِمۡ
يَرۡهَبُونَ ﴿١٥٤﴾ وَٱخۡتَارَ مُوسَىٰ قَوۡمَهُۥ سَبۡعِينَ رَجُلٗا لِّمِيقَٰتِنَاۖ فَلَمَّآ أَخَذَتۡهُمُ ٱلرَّجۡفَةُ قَالَ
رَبِّ لَوۡ شِئۡتَ أَهۡلَكۡتَهُم مِّن قَبۡلُ وَإِيَّٰيَۖ أَتُهۡلِكُنَا بِمَا فَعَلَ ٱلسُّفَهَآءُ مِنَّآۖ إِنۡ هِيَ إِلَّا فِتۡنَتُكَ
تُضِلُّ بِهَا مَن تَشَآءُ وَتَهۡدِي مَن تَشَآءُۖ أَنتَ وَلِيُّنَا فَٱغۡفِرۡ لَنَا وَٱرۡحَمۡنَاۖ وَأَنتَ خَيۡرُ ٱلۡغَٰفِرِينَ
﴿١٥٥﴾ ۞ وَٱكۡتُبۡ لَنَا فِي هَٰذِهِ ٱلدُّنۡيَا حَسَنَةٗ وَفِي ٱلۡأٓخِرَةِ إِنَّا هُدۡنَآ إِلَيۡكَۚ قَالَ عَذَابِيٓ
أُصِيبُ بِهِۦ مَنۡ أَشَآءُۖ وَرَحۡمَتِي وَسِعَتۡ كُلَّ شَيۡءٖۚ فَسَأَكۡتُبُهَا لِلَّذِينَ يَتَّقُونَ
وَيُؤۡتُونَ ٱلزَّكَوٰةَ وَٱلَّذِينَ هُم بِـَٔايَٰتِنَا يُؤۡمِنُونَ ﴿١٥٦﴾

Understood Meaning

7:142 We appointed for Musa thirty nights, and completed (the period) with ten (more): thus was completed the term with his Lord, forty nights. And Musa had charged his brother Aaron (before he went up): "Act for me among my people: Do right, and follow not the way of those who do mischief."

7:143 When Musa came to the place appointed by Us, and his Lord addressed him, He said: "O my Lord! show (yourself) to me, that I may look upon thee." Allah said: "By no means canst thou see Me (direct); But look upon the mount; if it abide in its place, then shalt thou see Me." When his Lord manifested His glory on the Mount, He made it as dust. And Musa fell down in a swoon. When he recovered his senses he said: "Glory be to Thee! To Thee I turn in repentance, and I am the first to believe."

7:144 ((Allah)) said: "O Musa! I have chosen thee above (other) men, by the mission I (have given thee) and the words I (have spoken to thee): take then the (revelation) which I give thee, and be of those who give thanks."

7:145 And We ordained laws for him in the tablets in all matters, both commanding and explaining all things, (and said): "Take and hold these with firmness, and enjoin thy people to hold fast by the best in the precepts: soon shall I show you the homes of the wicked,- (How they lie desolate)."

7:146 Those who behave arrogantly on the Earth in defiance of right - them will I turn away from My signs: Even if they see all the signs, they will not believe in them; and if they see the way of right conduct, they will not adopt it as the way; but if they see the way of error, that is the way they will adopt. For they have rejected our signs, and failed to take warning from them.

7:147 Those who reject Our signs and the meeting in the Hereafter,- vain are their deeds: Can they expect to be rewarded except as they have wrought?

7:148 The people of Musa made, in his absence, out of their ornaments, the image of calf that produced a cow voice, (for worship): did they not see that it could neither speak to them, nor show them the way? They took it for worship and they did wrong.

7:149 When they repented, and saw that they had erred, they said: "If our Lord have not mercy upon us and forgive us, we shall indeed be of those who perish."

7:150 When Musa came back to his people, angry and grieved, he said: "Evil it is that ye have done in my place in my absence: did ye make haste to bring on the judgment of your Lord?" He put down the tablets, seized his brother by (the hair of) his head, and dragged him to him. Aaron said: "Son of my mother! The people did indeed reckon me as naught, and went near to slaying me! Make not the enemies rejoice over my misfortune, nor count thou me amongst the people of sin."

7:151 Musa prayed: "O my Lord! Forgive me and my brother! Admit us in your mercy! You are the Most Merciful of those who show mercy!"

7:152 Those who took the calf (for worship) will indeed be overwhelmed with wrath from their Lord, and with shame in this life: thus do We recompense those who invent (falsehoods).

7:153 But those who do wrong but repent thereafter and (truly) believe,- verily thy Lord is thereafter Oft-Forgiving, Most Merciful.

7:154 When the anger of Musa was appeased, he took up the tablets: in the writing thereon was guidance and mercy for such as fear their Lord.

7:155 And Musa chose seventy of his people for Our place of meeting: when they were seized with violent quaking, he prayed: "O my Lord! If it had been Thy will Thou couldst have destroyed, long before, both them and me: wouldst Thou destroy us for the deeds of the foolish ones among us? This is no more than Thy trial: by it Thou causest whom Thou wilt to stray, and Thou leadest whom Thou wilt into the right path. Thou art our Protector: so forgive us and give us Thy mercy; for Thou art the best of those who forgive.

7:156 "And ordain for us that which is good, in this life and in the Hereafter: for we have turned unto Thee." He said: "With My punishment I visit whom I will; but My mercy extendeth to all things. That (mercy) I shall ordain for those who do right, and practise regular charity, and those who believe in Our signs;"

Lessons Learned

Gratefulness to Allah

Allah blessed Bani Isra'eel with many great favors and gifts. Yet, many of them failed to show their gratefulness to Allah. They listened to the bad people among them and disobeyed Prophets Musa and Haroon. They also followed their desires and committed the sins that Allah warned them about.

Sincere Muslims should obey Allah and thank Him for every blessing Allah grants them. They worship, remember and obey Allah everyday. This is a thankful attitude which leads to Jannah. This attitude blesses what we have in dunya too. Allah says: "Your Lord declares to you that if you thank [Allah], I will bless you more." [Surat Ibraheem 14:7]

Worshipping other than God

Rather than worshipping their creator alone, the Children of Isra'eel accepted the idea of worshipping a golden idol. This shows that many of them at that time glorified gold, jewelry and money. They elevated these worldly values and worshipped them as god. Many people now make the same mistake. Rather than obeying and glorifying Allah, who created them and gave them everything, they glorify, live and die for dunya and money. They also glorify rich and famous people and follow them even if they are evil. Some even call them idols. They worship gold, money, fancy homes and cars, and rich and famous people. They work hard to enjoy their lives and own more money. They follow the lifestyle of rich and famous people while they disobey Allah and refrain from worshipping Him. Their hearts are connected to dunya much more than to their creator. They love money, cars, actors, and actresses, more than masajid, Qur'an, prayers, prophets and righteous people. This is dangerous lifestyle and it leads to displeasure of Allah and punishment in this life and in Jahannam.

Protecting Ourselves from Hypocrites

Hypocrites can be found among believers. For example, Samiritan or As-Samiri was among the Children of Isra'eel. He was one of the reasons behind the deviation of the Children of Isra'eel. Hypocrites never openly express unbelief in their religion or in God. They usually pretend to be faithful, knowledgeable and smart. This way they keep their presence and positions in the society. This way they continue to influence people of weak faith and cause them to disobey Allah and lead a non-Muslim lifestyle. They are capable of affecting many naïve people. We should do our best to protect ourselves from insincere people and hypocrites, because their only mission is to lead people astray.

CHAPTER REVIEW

Projects and Activities

1. By now, you have learned the whole story of Prophet Musa. Write a poem about him.
2. Draw a painting showing one of these scenes:
   - The staff of Musa becoming a snake.
   - The staff of Musa causing, with the power of Allah, the split of the sea.
   - The staff of Musa causing, with the power of Allah, twelve springs to gush out of the rock.

Stretch Your Mind

1.Why do you think the Children of Isra' accepted the idea of worshipping the calf idol after all the miracles God did for them?
2.What are the similarities and differences between the Israelites' worship of the idol and the Arabs' worship of idols during the time of Prophet Muhammad?
3.Why do you think the Children of Isra' were reluctant to obey Prophet Musa despite all the help he extended to them and the miracles Allah supported him with?

Study Questions

1. How did the Children of Isra' respond to Prophet Musa?
2. Why did Allah command Musa to go and stay for thirty days?
3. Who made the children of Isra'eel worship the calf idol? Explain how this happened.
4. How did Musa react to his people worshipping the golden calf?
5. What happened to the seventy elders that Musa chose to listen to the Lord near Mount Sinai?
6. What lesson can you learn from the story of seventy elders and the raised mountain.
7. Where is the grave of Prophet Musa? Support you answer with a hadeeth.

Al-Qur'an-ul-Kareem: The Last Holy Book

Al-Qur'an-ul-Kareem: The Last Holy Book

CHAPTER OUTLINE

1. What is Al-Qur'an?
2. When was Al-Qur'an revealed?
3. What are the main elements of Al-Qur'an message?
4. What makes Al-Qur'an a special and great book?

VOCABULARY

- Al-Qur'an القرآن
- Al-Wahy الوحي
- Surah سُــورة
- suwar سُــوَر
- As-Sab'ut-Tiwal السَّــبْعُ الطِّوال

What is Al-Qur'an?

Al-Qur'an القرآن is the holy book for Muslims. It is the miraculous word of God revealed to Prophet Muhammad ﷺ through the Angel Jibreel, or Gabriel. Therefore, Al-Qur'an is a wahy وحي , or divine revelation, that has reached us through a holy connection starting from Allah ﷻ, to the Angel Jibreel, to the Prophet Muhammad ﷺ . The wahy, or Qur'anic revelation,s are regarded by Muslims as the exact words of Allah.

As you learned earlier, Allah revealed a few books to past prophets and messengers. Prophet Ibraheem received As-Suhuf (the Scrolls), Prophet Musa received At-Tawrah (Torah), Prophet Dawood received Az-Zaboor (the Psalms), and Prophet Isa received Al-Injeel (The Bible).

Many years later, Allah revealed Al-Qur'an to Prophet Muhammad ﷺ through the Angel Jibreel عليه السلام . The Prophet ﷺ was 40 years old when the Qur'an began to be revealed to him, and he was 63 when the revelation was completed. Prophet Muhammad ﷺ was the final messenger of Allah to humanity, and therefore the Qur'an is the last message which Allah has sent to mankind.

The Qur'an was originally revealed in the Arabic language, but it has been translated later by Muslim scholars into many other languages.

The Qurán is one of the two main divine sources of guidance which form the basis of Islam. The Sunnah is the authentic spoken words and actions of Prophet Muhammad ﷺ . What makes the Qur'an different from the Sunnah is primarily its form. The Qur'an is literally the word of Allah, whereas the Sunnah was inspired by Allah, but the wording and actions are the Prophet's. The Sunnah has important roles in relation to Al-Qur'an. It explains the meaning of Al-Qur'an, it details some of its guidance, and it describes how to implement it into real life.

Books of Allah

Book of Allah	Prophet Name
As-Suhuf (Scrolls)	Ibraheem (Abraham)
At-Tawrah (Torah)	Musa (Moses)
Az-Zaboor (Psalms)	Dawood (David)
Al-Injeel (Bible/Gospel)	Isa (Jesus)
Al-Qur'an	Muhammad ﷺ

Fast Facts

The word "Al-Qur'an" was repeated in the Qur'an 56 times.

The literal meaning of "Qur'an" in Arabic is "recitation."

The Greatness of Al-Qur'an

The Qur'an is a great book of God. To Muslims, it is the holiest book in the world. It is also the final message sent from God to mankind. Therefore, some describe it as "the Final Testament." Let us learn how great the Qur'an is by reading this beautiful hadeeth about it. Ali (R) narrated that Rasoolullah ﷺ once said,

"… It is [Al-Qur'an] the book of Allah, it has the tales of people who came before you, and it tells you what will happen after your time, and it helps making judgment on things that occur among you. It is the truth, not falsehood. Whoever rejects it will be destroyed, and whoever seeks guidance outside it will go astray. It is the strong robe of Allah, it is the book of wisdom and it is the straight path. Thoughts would not go astray with it, tongues would not err if they use it, and scholars will not get enough of it. You will not get bored, even when you read it again and again, and it will always surprise and inspire you. The jinn said when they heard it, "We heard an outstanding Qur'an." Whoever says its verses will say the truth, whoever used it in making judgments will be fair, and whoever called others to it will be guided to the straight path." Reported in Ad-Darimi.

Fast Facts

Al-Qur'an is the most sacred book in the history of mankind. It is the last revelation God sent to Earth and it is intended for all humanity.
It is the most read and memorized book in the entire world.

The Qur'an speaks in powerful and moving language. It talks about:

1. The reality and attributes of God
2. The spiritual world
3. God's purpose for creating mankind
4. God's rules for a righteous and happy life
5. Man's responsibility toward God and the world
6. The coming of the Day of Judgment
7. The Hereafter

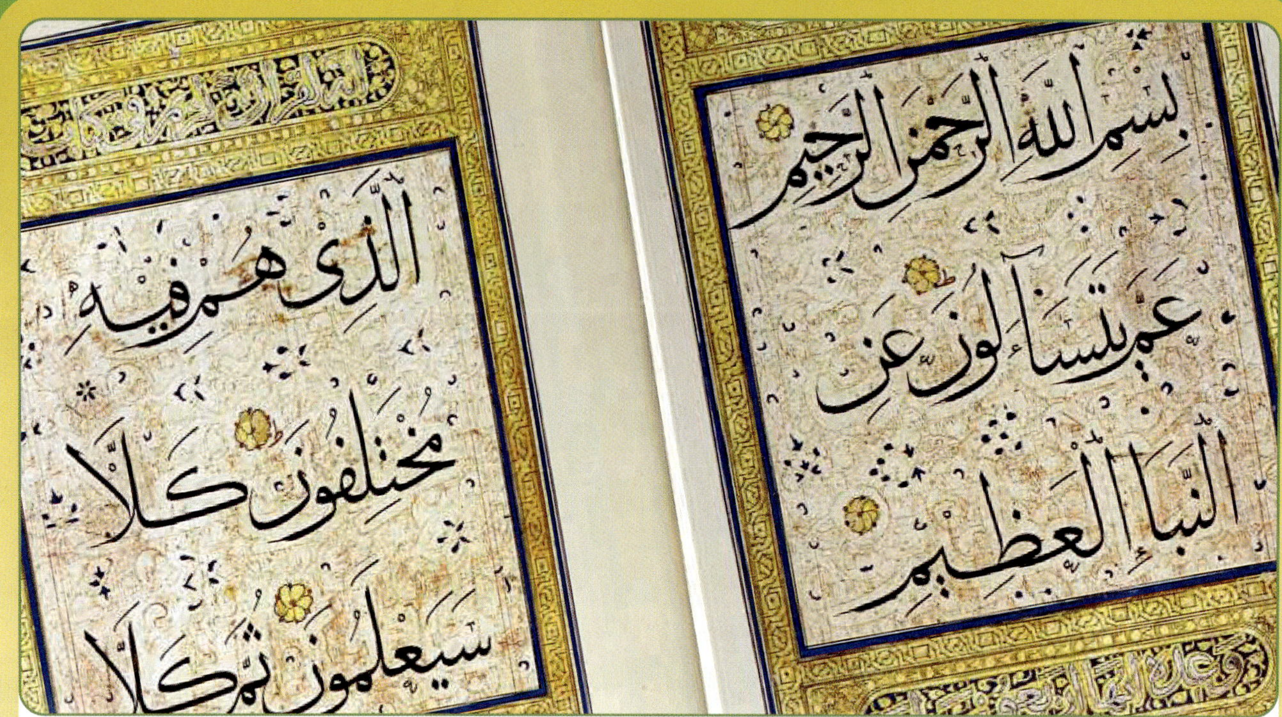

Names in the Qur'an

- Allah mentioned the names of twenty five prophets and messengers including Adam, Idrees, Nooh, Hood, Salih, Ibraheem, Isma'eel, Is-haq, Loot, Ayyoob, Ya'qoob, Yousuf, Shu'ayb, Musa, Haroon, Thu'l-kifl, Dawood, Sulayman, Ilyas, Al-Yasa', Younus, Zakariyya, Yahya, 'Isa and Muhammad.

- Maryam is the only woman whose name is explicitly mentioned in the Qur'an and her name is also the title of a surah; it is 19th surah in Al-Qur'an.

- Zaid Ibn Harithah was the only Sahabi who has his name mentioned explicitly in Al-Qur'an.

- Three mosques are referred to in the Qur'an: Masjid-ul-Haram (Makkah), Masjid-ul-Aqsa (Jerusalem), Masjid Qubaa (near Madinah). Also mentioned is Masjid-ud-Dirar, the "mosque" constructed by the hypocrites of Madinah for the purpose of causing trouble.

- The Qur'an mentions the following land and sea animals: camel, cow, ram, sheep, goat, horse, mule, donkey, wolf, elephant, dog, monkey, snake, pig, frog, fish.

- Al-Qur'an mentions the following birds: crow, hoopoe, swifts, hud hud, salwa.

- Al-Qur'an mentions the following insects: ant, bee, fly, mosquito, termites, flea, and locust.

- Al-Qur'an mentions the following plants: grain, garlic, onion, al-mann, date, olive, grape, pomegranate, and fig.

CHAPTER REVIEW

Projects and Activities

Write a letter to a non-Muslim friend in which you describe how great Al-Qur'an is.

Stretch Your Mind

If Al-Qur'an had a companion, what would be that companion? Explain your answer.

Study Questions

1. Define Al-Wahy, Al-Qur'an, As-Sunnah.
2. Name the books that Allah sent to humanity before Al-Qur'an.
3. Over how many years was the Qur'an revealed to Prophet Muhammad ﷺ until it was completed?
4. What are the main elements found in the message of Al-Qur'an?
5. What are the qualities mentioned in the hadeeth that describe Al-Qur'an that make it a truly special and great book?
6. What is the role of Sunnah in relation to Al-Qur'an?
7. Name: The masajid mentioned in Al-Qur'an
   The only Sahabi mentioned in Al-Qur'an by name
   The only woman named in Al-Qur'an
   The language of Al-Qur'an

Short History of Al-Qur'an

CHAPTER OUTLINE

1. When and where was Al-Qur'an revealed?
2. How was Al-Qur'an recorded and preserved?
3. Translations of Al-Qur'an.

VOCABULARY

- Kuttab-ul-Wahy كُتّابُ الوحْي
- Al-Mushaf Al-Uthmani المصْحَفُ العُثماني
- suwar Makkiyyah سُوَر مكية
- suwar Madaniyyah سُوَر مدنية

When was Al-Qur'an revealed?

The revelation of Al-Qur'an started in the month of Ramadan during the year 610 AD. At that time Prophet Muhammad ﷺ was in a cave called Ghar Hiraa'. It is located on the top of Jabal-un-Noor, or the Mount of Light near Makkah. Jibreel عليه السلام. continued to teach Prophet Muhammad ﷺ passages of Al-Qur'an every now and then. The revelation continued throughout the following 23 years of the life of Rasoolullah ﷺ until he passed away. At that point, revelation of Al-Qur'an was completed.

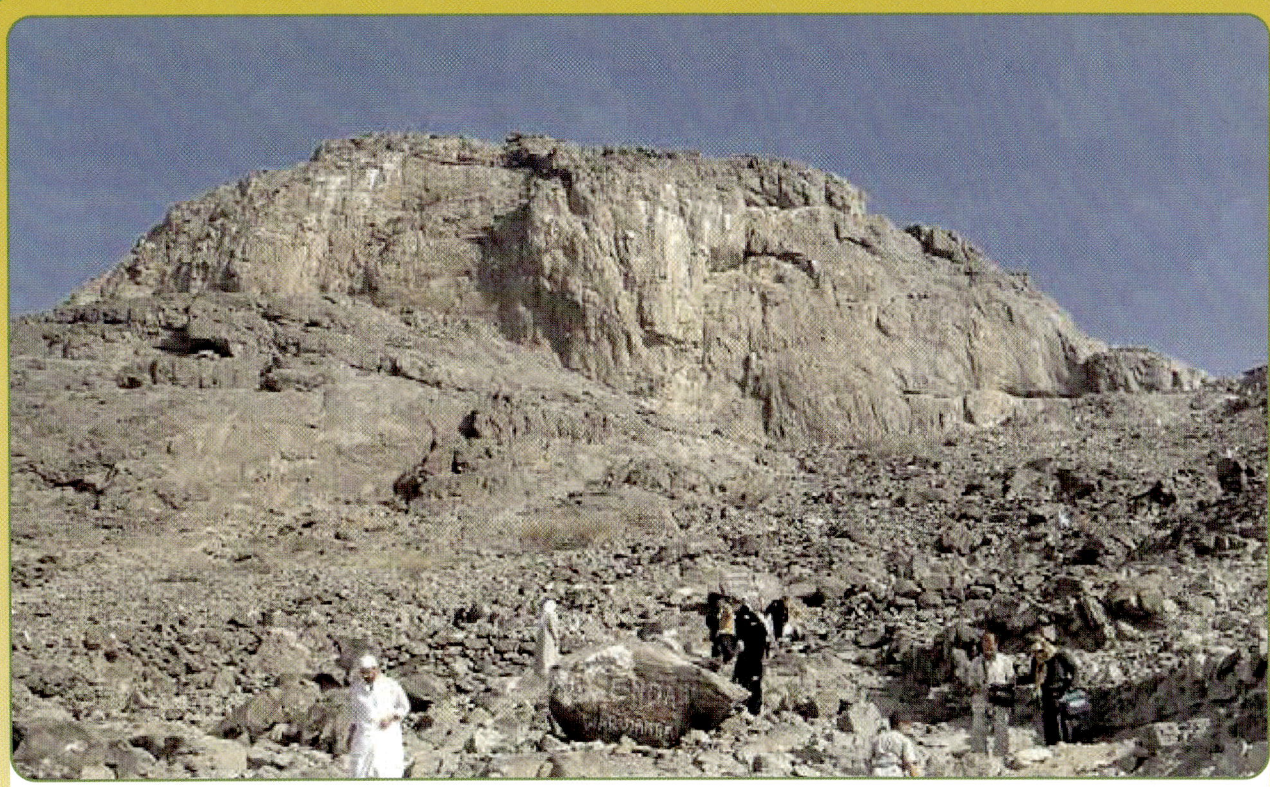

Jabal-un-Noor near Makkah, where the first passage of Al-Qur'an was revealed to Prophet Muhammad ﷺ

Where was Al-Qur'an revealed?

You learned earlier that the revelation of Al-Qur'an started in Ghar Hiraa' near Makkah. Angel Jibreel ordered the Prophet ﷺ saying "Iqra'," or read. "I can't read," the Prophet replied. Jibreel repeated his order two times and received the same answer from the Prophet ﷺ. Then, Jibreel revealed the first five ayaat of Surat-ul-Alaq. Later, the Prophet ﷺ received most of the suwar of Al-Qur'an in Makkah for 13 years. When Prophet Muhammad ﷺ migrated to Madinah, the Qur'an continued to be revealed to him in Madinah for ten years, until he passed away. However, some ayaat of Al-Qur'an were revealed in different places during the Prophet's travels in Arabia.

The scholars of Al-Qur'an described the suwar of Al-Qur'an that were revealed before Al-Hijrah as سور مكية suwar Makkiyyah or Makkan Chapters. Most of these where revealed while the Prophet ﷺ was in Makkah. On the other hand, they described the suwar revealed after Al-Hijrah as سور مدنية suwar Madaniyyah, or Madani Chapters. Most of these chapters were revealed while the Prophet was in Madinah. There are about 87 suwar Makkiyyah and 27 suwar Madaniyyah in Al-Qur'an. The word سوَر suwar is the plural of سورَة surah, which means a chapter of the Qur'an.

▲ *Makkah*

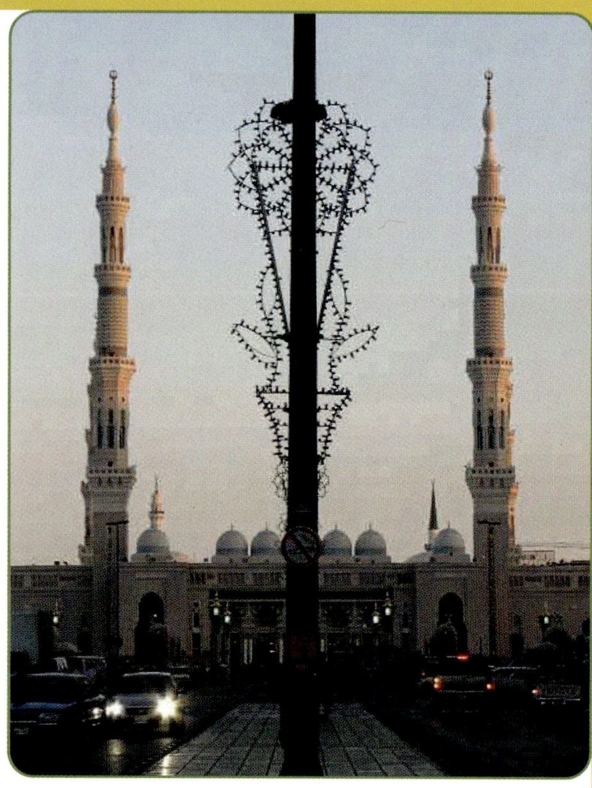

▲ *Madinah*

Teaching the Qur'an

As you learned earlier, the Qur'an was not all revealed at one time. Allah taught His Prophet the Qur'an a passage at a time. In turn, Rasoolullah ﷺ taught the people of his time the verses he received from Allah through Jibreel عليه السلام as soon as he learned them. Abdullah Ibn Mas'ood رضي الله عنه said: Rasoolullah used to teach us ten ayaat or so every time, then we would memorize them, learn them and apply in our daily life. Then Rasoolullah would teach us another revealed passage of Al-Qur'an.

Prophet Muhammad ﷺ used to explain the ayaat to the Sahabah through his beautiful words and great actions. That made it helpful for the Sahabah to live the Qur'an and put it into action. This teaches us a great lesson: the Qur'an was not sent to us for recitation or memorization only. Rather, we must apply it to our lives and live it every day.

Recording Al-Qur'an

Prophet Muhammad ﷺ used to ask some of the literate Sahabah to write the revealed verses on scrolls, wood, skin, flat rocks, or animal bones. Paper as we know it was not available at that time. These people were called كتاب الوحي Kuttab-ul-Wahy, or the Scribes of

Revelation. Zaid Ibn Thabet, Ubayy Ibn Ka'b, Sa'd Ibn Abi Waqqas and Mu'awiyah Ibn Abi Sufyan were some of the scribes who documented Al-Qur'an.

Prophet Muhammad ﷺ taught the verses, and told them the names of the suwar, or the chapters of the Qur'an, and where each ayah should be. Immediately after the death of Rasoolullah ﷺ, Abu Bakr As-Siddeeq became the first Khaleefah, or the leader of the Muslims, following the Prophet. He ordered Zaid Ibn Thabet رضي الله عنه to gather all the written ayaat of the Qur'an in one big collection. The Qur'an was written down as soon as the Prophet received it from Allah سبحانه وتعالى through Angel Jibreel عليه السلام. Then it was all collected and kept in a safe place, at the house of Hafsah Bint Omar Ibn-ul-Khattab رضي الله عنه, the wife of Rasoolullah and daughter of Omar Ibn-ul-Khattab رضي الله عنه, soon after the death of Prophet Muhammad ﷺ.

During the time of the third Khaleefah, Uthman Ibn Affan رضي الله عنه, Zaid Ibn Thabet and other Sahabah prepared seven identical copies of Al-Qur'an. It was called Al-Mushaf Al-Uthmani المصحف العثماني، since it was compiled by the direction of Khaleefah Uthman. He later sent these authentic manuscripts to major Muslim cities at that time. Khaleefah Uthman ordered all Muslims to make only authentic and accurate copies of these master manuscripts. Ancient Qur'anic manuscripts had been dated as far back the seventh century to the time of Khaleefah

▲ *A page from the copy of the ancient Holy Qur'an.*

Uthman.

In brief, the original text of Al-Qur'an we have today was collected shortly after the death of the Prophet during the time of Khaleefah Abu Bakr As-Siddeeq رضي الله عنه and later copied and distributed by the Khaleefah Uthman Ibn Affan رضي الله عنه. This important manuscript was the master of all the Qur'anic copies we have now.

Based on the above description of the recording process of Al-Qur'an, the Qur'an we have now is the same revelation Allah gave to Prophet Muhammad ﷺ through Angel Jibreel. It is the eternal words of God, letter by letter, that have never changed since the time of Prophet Muhammad ﷺ, and they will stay the same for eternity. Allah says in Surat-ul-Hijr,

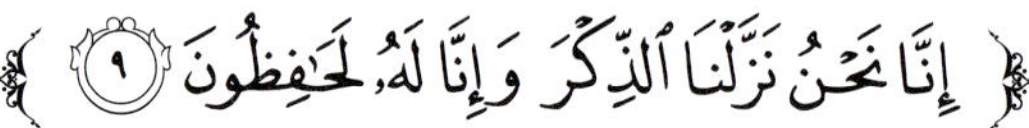
إِنَّا نَحْنُ نَزَّلْنَا ٱلذِّكْرَ وَإِنَّا لَهُۥ لَحَٰفِظُونَ ٩

"Surely We have revealed the Reminder and We will most surely be guarding it." [Surat-ul-Hijr 15:9]

Muslim scholars say that Allah entrusted the people of the book to guard their books from any loss or change. However, they were not up to that responsibility and as a result many parts of their holy books got changed or even disappeared. Therefore, Allah took upon Himself the responsibility of protecting Al-Qur'an against any change or loss.

Fast Facts

Al-Qur'an Includes:

- 323,760 huroof (letters).
- 105,685 nuqtat (dots) in the Qur'an.
- 86,430 words.
- 6236 ayaat (verses) in the Qur'an.
- 14 verses of prostration. ١٤ سجدة
- 87 suwar Makkiyyah ٨٧ سور مكية
- 27 suwar Madaniyyah ٢٧ سور مدنية

Who is Who?

زيد بن ثابت

ZAID IBN THABET THE QUR'AN COMPILER

You might ask yourself how was the Qur'an compiled in such a way: surah after surah and ayah after ayah? Well, you should be thankful to the efforts of a Great Sahabi, Zaid Ibn Thabet and other Sahabah.

Ansari from Madinah:

Zaid was eleven years old when the Prophet ﷺ came to Madinah. He embraced Islam with his family and was blessed by the Prophet's du'aa' for him.

When the pagans of Makkah came to attack the Muslims in Madinah in the time of the Battle of Uhud, Zaid Ibn Thabet came to Prophet Muhammad ﷺ. He accompanied a group of his peers to beg the Prophet to accept them in any position in the Mujahideen lines to defend Muslims in Madinah. The Prophet refused because of their young age, but he promised Zaid and Abdullah Ibn-Omar to accept them next time.

Zaid's Qualities.

Zaid Ibn Thabet's Islamic character was developing very fast. Not only did he succeed as a mujahid, but also as an educated person with various talents. He was following the revelation of the Qur'an, memorizing and scribing it.

When the Prophet ﷺ launched his message to the outside world and wanted to send letters to the kings and caesars of the world, he ordered Zaid to learn their languages, and Zaid learned in no time.

As time passed, Zaid became very knowledgeable in the Qur'an and was respected by all. All Sahabah who memorized Qur'an knew that Zaid was one of the most knowledgeable.

Over twenty-three years the Qur'an was revealed verse by verse, according to the necessity of the occasion. Some were able to memorize and write those verses like Ali Ibn Abu Talib, Ubai Ibn-Ka'b, Abdullah Ibn Masoud, Abdullah Ibn Abbas, and Zaid Ibn Thabet, who memorized the Qur'an. Therefore, the Prophet ﷺ assigned Zaid Ibn Thabet and others to document the suwar and the ayaat when they were revealed to him. So when Rasoolullah ﷺ used to receive some Qur'an from Jibreel, he would call Zaid and other literate Sahabah and order them to write down the ayaat he had just received. After the death of the Prophet ﷺ pages of Al-Qur'an were kept by few Sahabah in Madinah.

Important Work:

During the time of Abu Bakr As-Siddeeq in the battle of Yamama, a great number of the memorizers of Al-Qur'an were martyred. That made Omar Ibn-ul-Khattab رضي الله عنه panic, because he was afraid that Al-Qur'an may be lost. Therefore, he went to Khaleefah Abu Bakr رضي الله عنه insisting that Al-Qur'an should be compiled in one collection or book, before others were martyred.

Abu Bakr رضي الله عنه made istikharah prayer and consulted other Sahabah on this project. Later, Abu Bakr called upon Zaid, entrusting him with such an important matter. Zaid achieved the mission that was critical to the fate of Islam. He went on collecting the ayaat and suwar from the memorizers and the scrolls. He matched, compared and revised the templates until he collected all the Qur'an in one place. He was able to arrange all the scrolls in one copy of the Qur'an. The copy was approved by all the scholars and the scribes among the Sahabah رضي الله عنهم. These scribes were used to hearing and learning Al-Qur'an from the Prophet ﷺ, himself.

Zaid commented after that: "By Allah, had they asked me to move a mountain from its place, it would have been easier for me."

This was only the first stage. When Uthman Ibn-Affan became the Khaleefah رضي الله عنه, Islam was spreading in all directions. So, he ordered that the Qur'an be copied and distributed to major Muslim cities.

Again Zaid was called upon, together with Sa'eed Ibn Al-Aas, Abdullah Ibn Al-Zubair, and Abdur-Rahman Ibn Al-Harith Ibn Hisham to carry out this mission. He brought the scrolls of Al-Qur'an from Hafsah رضي الله عنها, the Prophet's widow and Umar's daughter, they were kept.

Zaid started his mission of 'Uthman's Mushaf by copying the scrolls that were available at Hafsah's home. Thus Zaid achieved two great missions in the history of Islam. He compiled the Qur'an in the time of Abu Bakr, then he made seven identical copies at the time of Uthman.

The Translations of the Qur'an

Years and centuries passed after Al-Qur'an was documented in Arabic. People throughout the world wanted to learn Al-Qur'an, but they could not understand the Arabic language. So Al-Qur'an was translated from Arabic into many other languages over the centuries. To date, translations of the Qur'an exist in at least forty languages. These include Amharic (Ethiopian), Dutch, English, Farsi, French, Hindi, Latin, Malay, Portuguese, Russian, Spanish, Turkish, Urdu, and many other languages. It is reported that the first known translation was made by Sahabi Salman Al-Farisi into his native Persian language, Farsi.

Muslims, however, are still ordered to learn and recite Al-Qur'an in Arabic, even if this is not their native language and they cannot speak it. They are also encouraged to learn Arabic so they can easily understand the words of God and be able to read the traditional Islamic books explaining Al-Qur'an, which are mostly written in Arabic.

It should be known, however, that translations of Al-Qur'an are regarded by Muslims as the understood meaning of the Holy Book. They are not considered other versions of the Qur'an. This means that the English translation, for example, is not the Qur'an in English; rather, it is the meaning of the Qur'an as the translator understood it.

Among the most well-known Qur'an translators into English are Abdullah Yusuf Ali, Muhammad Habib Shakir, Marmaduke Pickthall, Muhammad Asad and Dr. T. B. Irving. There are currently more than twenty English translations of the meaning of the Qur'an that are available in print.

CHAPTER REVIEW

Projects and Activities

See to the right a page from the original manuscript of Al-Qur'an which was copied and made available to all Muslims during the time of Khaleefah Uthman. The page includes ayaat 7 to 10 from surah 2, Al-Baqarah. Open your Qur'an and compare the text of these ayaat in this ancient piece with the Qur'an you have now. Remember, at that time, manuscripts did not include dots, vowels and other punctuations. Also, the old manuscript did not include numbers that separate the ayaat in the surah. Ayah 7 starts in the second line of the piece. Parts of the ayaat cannot be seen due to poor copying.

Stretch Your Mind

1. Why didn't Allah send the Qur'an to Prophet Muhammad ﷺ all at once?
2. What is the most important lesson you can infer from the story of collecting and recording Al-Qur'an?

Study Questions

1. When was Al-Qur'an first revealed and where?
2. Who was the angel who brought the Qur'an from Allah to Prophet Muhammad?
3. Describe his first visit to Rasoolullah ﷺ ?
4. Describe briefly how Al-Qur'an was collected in one collection after the passing
5. of Prophet Muhammad ﷺ .
6. Define: 1. Al-Mushaf Al-Uthmani 2. Kuttab-ul Wahy 3. Surah Makkiyyah 4. Surah Madaniyyah
7. Who was Zaid Ibn Thabet? What was his role in compiling the Qur'an?

suwar and ayaat

CHAPTER OUTLINE

1. The structure of Al-Qur'an.
2. What are the longest suwar of Al-Qur'an?
3. How is Al-Qur'an organized?

VOCABULARY

- Juzu' جُزْء
- Ajzaa' أَجْزاء
- Surah سُــورة
- suwar سُــوَر
- As-Sab'ut-Tiwal السَّــبْعُ الطِّوال

The Structure of Al-Qur'an

The Qur'an is made of 114 suwar (chapters). Each surah of Al-Qur'an is made of few or many ayaat, or verses. The longest Surah in Al-Qur'an has 286 ayaat while the shortest surah has only three ayaat; Surat-ul-Kawthar. The rest of the suwar has different numbers of ayaat that fall in between. Like the suwar have different lengths, the ayaat have different lengths too.

As you learned earlier, there are two main types of suwar in Al-Qur'an; As-suwar Al-Makkiyyah which were revealed in Makkah before the Hijrah,

and As-suwar Al-Madaniyyah, most of which were revealed in Madinah after the Hijrah. The Makki ayaat are generally short and succinct while the Madani ayaat are relatively long and elaborate.

The suwar of Al-Qur'an are not put in chronological order. Al-Qur'an starts with Surat-ul-Fatihah (Surah 1) and ends with Surat-un-Nas (Surah 114). Some of the suwar long, but others are very short. Among the long suwar are:

1. Al-Baqarah (The Cow)
2. Al-Imran (The Family of Imran)
3. An-Nisaa' (The Women)
4. Al-Ma'idah (The Food Table)
5. Al-An'aam (The Cattle)
6. Al-Araf (The Heights)
7. Al-Anfal (The Spoils of War).

The above suwar are called السَّبْعُ الطوال As-Sab-'ut-Tiwal or "The Long Seven." These long chapters come in the beginning of Al-Qur'an after Surat-ul-Fatihah and make up the first one third of Al-Qur'an. The short suwar of Al-Qur'an are mostly included in the thirtieth جُزْء juzu', or part, at the end of the Holy Book. Only one short Surah is outside the thirtieth juzu', which is Surat-ul-Fatihah, the first surah in Al-Qur'an, which is located in the first juzu'.

There are 30 أجْزاء ajzaa' (parts), each juzu' has a number of suwar. The great scholars of Islam divided the Qur'an into 30 equal parts. This way people can read the whole Qur'an during one month, as the Prophet recommended, if they read one part a day.

Fast Facts

- The longest surah is Surat-ul-Baqarah with 286 ayaat.

- The shortest is Surat-ul-Kawthar with 3 ayaat..

- The greatest and most revered verse is Ayat-ul-Kursiy, which is also called the "Chief of All Verses."

- The longest ayah is Ayat-ud-Dayn (The Loan Verse), which is ayah 282 in Surat-ul-Baqarah.

- In chronological order, Surat-ul-'Alaq was the first surah.

- The first word ever revealed is "Iqra'," or read, which is in ayah 1 of Surat-ul-Alaq.

- Surat-un-Nasr was the last full Surah to be revealed.

- Surat Ya-Sin is the "Heart of the Qur'an."

- Surat-ur-Rahman contains the most number of repeated ayat: 3. It is also called "Aroos-ul-Qur'an," the Beauty of Al-Qur'an.

- The names of 25 prophets are mentioned in the Qur'an, 6 of which are title of a surah: Younus, Ibraheem, Hud, Nuh, Yousuf, Muhammad ﷺ .

Who is Who?

عبد الله بن عمرو بن العاص

Abdullah Ibn Amr Ibn-ul-Aas

Abdullah Ibn Amr Ibn-ul-Aas رضي الله عنه was a very bright young student of Prophet Muhammad ﷺ. He was born in 606 A.D. to his father Amr Ibn-ul-Aas, another great companion of the Prophet. It is interesting to note that Abdullah embraced Islam before his father did. Abdullah used to love learning Qur'an and the hadeeth of Rasoolullah ﷺ.

One day, Abdullah came to Rasoolullah ﷺ and asked his permission to write his hadeeth. Prophet Muhammad ﷺ used to prevent anyone from writing what he said, except the Qur'an. The Prophet didn't want his talk to mix with the Qur'an. When Abdullah asked him for permission, surprisingly, the Prophet agreed. He knew that Abdullah was sharp and organized, so he would not mix the hadeeth with the Qur'an in his journal. He just asked him to keep it for himself. Abdullah recorded many ahadeeth of Rasoolullah ﷺ in a journal and it was later called "As-Saheefat-us-Sadiqah," or the "Truthful Journal."

One other time, Abdullah came to Rasoolullah ﷺ and asked him, "In how many days should I read the whole Qur'an?."

"Read the whole Qur'an in one month," the Prophet ﷺ answered.

"I can do better than that," Abdullah said.

"Then read it in twenty days," the Prophet added.

"But I can do better than that," Abdullah said again.

"Then read it in fifteen days," the Prophet said.

" but I can do better than that," Abdullah said again.

"Then read it in ten days," the Prophet said.

"But I can do better than that," Abdullah insisted.

"Then read it in seven days, and don't read it all in less than this period of time," the Prophet concluded.

Abdullah grew up to be one of the great scholars among the companions of Rasoolullah ﷺ. He narrated thousands of the ahadeeth of the Prophet.

Abdullah was so motivated to learn the Qur'an and the hadeeth of Prophet Muhammad ﷺ. Abu Hurayrah, the well-known Sahabi, once said, "No one used to memorize the hadeeth of the Prophet more than me, except Abdullah Ibn Amr."

Abdullah Ibn Amr died in 684 A.D.

hadeeth Shareef

عن عبد الله بن عمرو رضي الله عنه قال : قال لي رسول الله صلى الله عليه وسلم :

" ...إقرأ القرآن في شهر... "

رواه البخاري

Abdullah Ibn Amr narrated that Rasoolullah ﷺ said to him:

"Read the whole Qur'an in one month."

Reported in Al-Bukhari

CHAPTER REVIEW

Projects and Activities

Open the Qur'an and locate in it the suwar, ajzaa', As-Sab'ut-Tiwal, Qisar-us-suwar, Saktaat, the longest surah, the shortest surah, and the longest ayah of the Qur'an.

Stretch Your Mind

1. Why do you think the Qur'an was revealed in the Arabic language?
2. As you learned last year, ancient books of Allah were either changed by people or lost. Why do you think the Qur'an has never been changed nor lost?

Study Questions

1. In what period of time should we read the whole Qur'an? Support your answer with a hadeeth?
2. Briefly name the following:
   - a. The longest surah
   - b. The shortest surah
   - c. The first surah revealed
   - d. The last surah revealed in full
   - e. The greatest ayah
   - f. The Heart of the Qur'an
   - g. Aroos-ul-Qur'an
   - h. Kuttab-ul-Wahy
   - i. The only woman named in Al-Qur'an
   - j. The only Sahabi named in Al-Qur'an
3. What are the As-Sab'ut-Tiwal?

You Love it, Then Respect it!

CHAPTER OUTLINE

1. Al-Qur'an deserves our respect
2. How should we respect Al-Qur'an?

VOCABULARY

At-Taharah	الطَّهارَة
At-Tadabbur	التَدَبُّر
Al-Isti'aathah	الاسْتِعاذة
Al-Basmalah	البَسْملة
Khushoo'	خُشوع
Ahkam-ut-Tajweed	أحْكامُ التَّجويد

Al-Qur'an Deserves our Respect

We all know that Al-Qur'an is the most important book for Muslims. Since it is, then it should be treated with the utmost respect. You should realize that you are holding the words of Allah in your hands. So, how should we treat the Qur'an with the respect it deserves? Here are some helpful tips.

1) Taharah and Cleanliness:

It is recommended that you should have wudoo' when reading Al-Qur'an and touching it. Think about it for a moment; if you are going to visit a very important person, you will make sure that you are clean, neat and have the best clothes on. Reading Al-Qur'an means you are getting closer to Allah, so you have to be clean and well kept.

2) Facing Al-Qiblah:

It is also recommended that you should face the Qiblah when reading the Qur'an. The best direction for Muslims to face is towards the Al-Ka'bah. We face Al-Qiblah when we pray, make du'aa' and read Al-Qur'an. Even when we sleep, we try to lay on our right side and make our face and body toward Al-Qiblah.

3) Humble Heart and Khushoo':

When carrying Al-Qur'an, it is important to realize that you are holding Allah's words in your hands. Can you think of any words better than Allah's words? Surely not! So that means you should have a humble heart when reading the Qur'an. Last year you learned about khushoo' خُشوع , which is simply having your heart humbled and connected with Allah while worshipping Him. Reciting Al-Qur'an is one of the great forms of worship in Islam and it requires the observance of khushoo'. Reading Al-Qur'an without having our hearts effected is not the best way of recitation. This shows little respect

toward Al-Qur'an.

4) Al-Isti'aathah and Al-Basmalah:

Before reciting the Qur'an, the person should say Al-Isti'aathah, which is

أعوذ باللهِ من الشّـَيْطانِ الرَّجيم

"A'oothu billahi- min-ash-Shaytan-ir-rajeem"

I seek the protection of Allah against the cursed devil.

Then we recite Al-basmalah, which is:

بسم اللهِ الرَّحْمن الرَّحيم

Bismillah-ir-rahman-ir-raheem
In the name of Allah, the Beneficient the Merciful

Allah commanded us to seek refuge with Him against the Shaytan always and especially when we are about to recite Al-Qur'an. Allah doesn't like Shaytan to be around us when we recite Al-Qur'an. This way, Allah will protect us from Satan and make us focus on our recitation. Allah says,

﴿ فَإِذَا قَرَأْتَ ٱلْقُرْءَانَ فَٱسْتَعِذْ بِٱللَّهِ مِنَ ٱلشَّيْطَٰنِ ٱلرَّجِيمِ ﴿٩٨﴾ إِنَّهُۥ لَيْسَ لَهُۥ سُلْطَٰنٌ عَلَى ٱلَّذِينَ ءَامَنُوا۟ وَعَلَىٰ رَبِّهِمْ يَتَوَكَّلُونَ ﴿٩٩﴾ إِنَّمَا سُلْطَٰنُهُۥ عَلَى ٱلَّذِينَ يَتَوَلَّوْنَهُۥ وَٱلَّذِينَ هُم بِهِۦ مُشْرِكُونَ ﴿١٠٠﴾ ﴾

النحل: ٩٨ - ١٠٠

So when you recite the Qur'an, seek refuge with Allah from the accursed Shaytan. Surely he has no authority over those who believe and rely on their

Lord. His authority is only over those who befriend him and those who associate others with Him. [16:98-100]

We recite Al-Isti'aathah when we recite from the beginning of a surah. But if we start from the middle of a surah, there is no need then to recite Al-Basmalah.

This means "I seek Allah's protection from the rejected Shaytan." This will help keep the Shaytan from tempting and distracting you while you read Al-Qur'an.

We can recite Al-Isti'aathah, Al-Basmalah and the first ayah with pausing and breathing after reciting each one of them. We may also recite them altogether without pausing in between.

5) Observing Ahkam-ut-Tajweed أحكامُ التـجويد , or Rules of Recitation:

If you are reading the Arabic text of the Qur'an then it is important to pronounce the words correctly , as best as you can. But don't be afraid to read it just because you cannot recite it well. The blessed Prophet ﷺ said the person who recites the Qur'an with difficulty will get twice the reward of the person who says it easily and correctly. But that does not mean you should purposely pronounce the words incorrectly! Allah is merciful and He recognizes the effort we make to get closer to Him.

Additionally, you should learn to

read the Qur'an according to Ahkam-ut-Tajweed, or rules of recitation. This can only be learned with a Qur'an teacher. Only listening to someone who reads well, according to Ahkam-ut-Tajweed would help, but it is not enough. Learning the Qur'an recitation with a teacher is the best way to learn Ahkam-ut-Tajweed. The Prophet ﷺ learned it orally from Jibreel, and the Sahabah learned it orally from the Prophet ﷺ . Then it was passed down orally from the Sahabah to the next generations of the Ummah. If you perfect Ahkam-ut-Tajweed, then you will be reading Al-Qur'an like the Prophet ﷺ taught it. Allah said in the Qur'an:

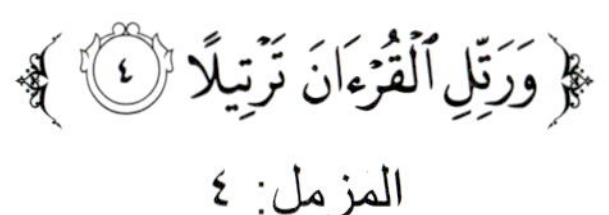

المزمل: ٤

Wa rattil-il-Qur'ana tarteela

This means, "Recite Al-Qur'an according to the rules of recitation."

hadeeth Shareef

عن عائشة رضيَ الله عنها قالت: قال رسولُ الله صلى الله عليهِ وسلَّم:

" الماهِرُ بـالقـرْآنِ مَعَ السَّفرة الكرام البررة، والذي يَقـرَأ القـرْآنَ ويتقطع فيه وهُوَ عليْهِ شـاقٌ لهُ أجْران "

رواه مسلم

A'ishah رضي الله عنه narrated that Rasoolullah ﷺ said, "The skillful reciter of Al-Qur'an will be joined with the Prophets, the honorable and the obedient servants of Allah, [in the hereafter]. And the reciter who finds difficulty reading it will be granted double rewards."

Reported in Saheeh Muslim

6) At-Tadabbur التدَبُّر :

At-Tadabbur means reflection and deep understanding of Al-Qur'an. It is focusing on its meanings and guidance. It is very important to pay attention to the meaning of the words you are reading. If you read the words without thinking about them, then all you will be doing is mouthing the words.

It is very important for Muslims to learn Arabic, the language of Al-Qur'an, to understand it first hand. This way you would not need a translation nor transliteration of Al-Qur'an. However, if you don't understand Arabi,c you should read a Qur'an which has both the Arabic text and the English translation. This way you read the translation to understand the meaning of the ayaat you read. Learning Arabic requires at least one year of your study and focus, and it is worth it.

Afterwards, you should reflect on the lessons you have learnt in the Qur'an. It is reported that the Blessed Prophet once said that a person's reward is increased if they understand the meaning of what they are doing. The word "tadabbur" means to reflect upon something, and Allah, Himself, advises us to do this when reading His book. There are many ways you can reflect about what you read. One good way is to read the Qur'an, and then write down the lessons you have learned and the actions you should take.

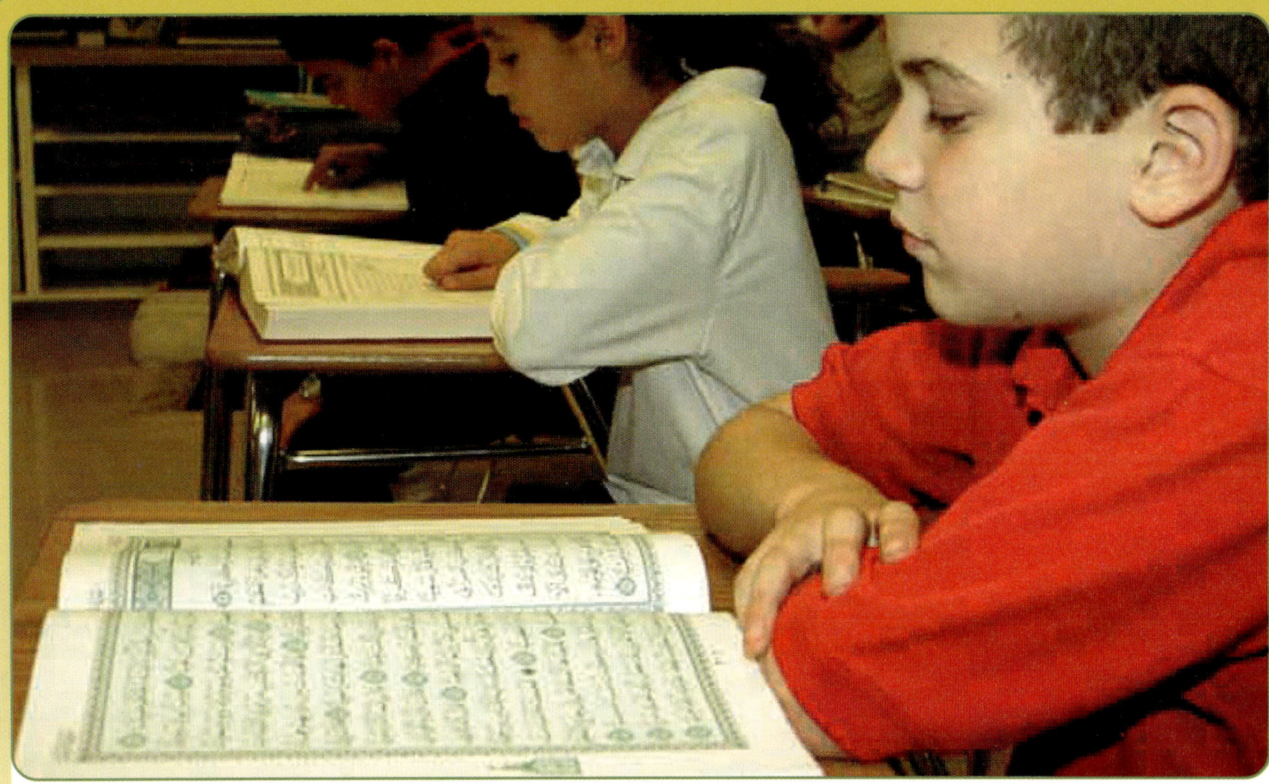

Many people rejected the message of Islam because they didn't read Al-Qur'an and understand it. Allah says about them,

﴿ أَفَلَا يَتَدَبَّرُونَ ٱلْقُرْءَانَ أَمْ عَلَىٰ قُلُوبٍ أَقْفَالُهَآ ﴾

محمد: ٢٤

Don't they reflect on the Qur'an? Nay, on the hearts there are locks. [47:24]

Finally, it is easier to experience tadabbur when you:

- Have good intention and mean to reflect on what you read.
- Recite in a calm place, like the masjid or a quiet room.
- Recite while you are comfortable and relaxed.

7) Interacting with Al-Qur'an:

Interacting with its meanings and guidance is one of the ways to give due respect to Al-Qur'an. For example, whenever the reader reads ayaat about the description of Jannah, the reader should feel hopeful and happy, and ask Allah to grant him or her Jannah. On the other hand, when the reader goes through ayaat on the Judgment Day or Hellfire, the reader should feel scared and recognize the importance of the event. Having a little fear is good because it discourages us from doing things that will lead us to hellfire.

8) Handle it with Care and Respect:

At all times, we should handle the Qur'an and carry it with the utmost respect. The Qur'an is not any object; it contains the words of Allah. Therefore, we should love and respect it.

There should be no eating or drinking while reading the Qur'an. Eating and drinking will only distract you from concentrating on the words you are reading. So, if you are hungry or thirsty, take a break from reading the Qur'an.

After you have finished reading, make sure you keep the Qur'an in a place where it will be safe. We should place it in secure places and away from the reach of children and those who do not understand the holiness of this great book.

But remember, the Qur'an is not a decoration and it should never go unread or unused! You should make it a habit to read the Qur'an every day.

9) Implementing the Qur'an:

This is the most important duty we need to fulfill toward the Qur'an. Allah sent His book to us so we would implement it and apply its guidance. Reading Al-Qur'an without acting upon it is unacceptable behavior. Allah says,

﴿ وَقُلِ ٱعْمَلُوا۟ فَسَيَرَى ٱللَّهُ عَمَلَكُمْ وَرَسُولُهُۥ وَٱلْمُؤْمِنُونَ ۖ وَسَتُرَدُّونَ إِلَىٰ عَـٰلِمِ ٱلْغَيْبِ وَٱلشَّهَـٰدَةِ فَيُنَبِّئُكُم بِمَا كُنتُمْ تَعْمَلُونَ ﴿١٠٥﴾ ﴾

التوبة: ١٠٥

"And say: Act; so Allah will see your action and (so will) His Messenger and the believers; and you shall be brought back to the Knower of the unseen and the seen, then He will inform you of what you did." [9:105]

FAITH IN ACTION

- Always recite Al-Qur'an when you have wudoo'
- Always say Al-Isti'aathah and Al-Basmalah when you start reciting Al-Qur'an
- Always recite Al-Qur'an according to Ahkam-ut-Tajweed
- Always carry and handle Al-Qur'an with great respect
- Always think about and interact with the Qur'an you recite
- Always act upon the lessons and meanings you learn in Al-Qur'an

Wise Poetry

Side By Side

They lie on the table side by side, the Holy Qur'an and the T.V. Guide.
One is well worn and cherished with pride.
Not the Qur'an, but the T.V. Guide.
One is used daily to help folks decide.
No, not the Qur'an, but the T.V. Guide.
As the pages are turned, what shall they see.
Oh, what does it matter, turn on the T.V.
So they open the book in which they confide.
No, not the Qur'an, but the T.V. Guide.
The Word of Allah is seldom read.
Maybe a verse before they fall into bed.
Exhausted and sleepy and tired as can be.
Not from reading the Qur'an, from watching T.V.
So then back to the table side by side, lie the Holy Qur'an and the T.V. Guide.
No time for prayer, no time for the Word, the book of Allah is seldom heard.
But forgiveness, knowledge, and spirituality are found in the Qur'an, not on T.V.

Anonymous

CHAPTER REVIEW

Projects and Activities

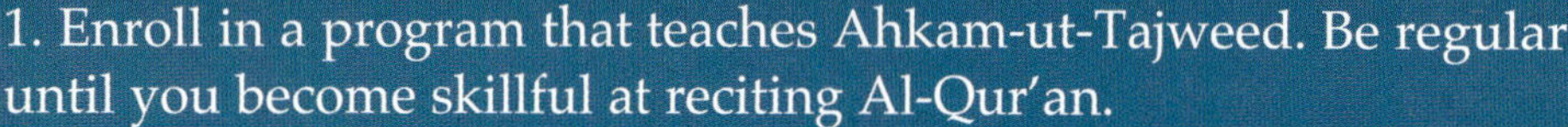

1. Enroll in a program that teaches Ahkam-ut-Tajweed. Be regular until you become skillful at reciting Al-Qur'an.

2. Research a story about a Sahabi or any good person who used to experience khushoo' and get spiritually effected when reading Al-Qur'an.

Stretch Your Mind

Why do you think that Al-Qur'an has special rules of recitation and the hadeeth does not?

Study Questions

1. Define:

At-Tadabbur	التَّدَبُّر
Al-Isti'aathah	الاسْتِعاذة
Al-Basmalah	البَسْملة
Khushoo'	خُشوع
Ahkam-ut-Tajweed	أحْكامُ التَّجويد

2. Why is it recommended to have Wudoo' when reading the Qur'an?

3. Why should we feel scared when reading a description of Hellfire and the day of Judgment? What should we say when we read that?
4. What is the benefit of learning the Arabic language?
5. What would help you to reflect and experience tadabbur when you recite the Qur'an?
6. What do you think are the 5 most important ways to show respect for Al-Qur'an?
7. Describe the following actions as respectful or disrespectful of Al-Qur'an:

a. Muhammad didn't read Al-Qur'an for a week.
b. Asmaa went into the bathroom wearing a necklace with Ayat-ul-Kursi engraved on it.
c. Sayed removed Al-Qur'an from the passenger seat in his dad's car and put it in the glove compartment.
d. Sulayman was reciting Al-Qur'an while peaking at the TV.
e. Sabeen liked an ayah she recited so she quickly wrote it down in her notebook.
f. Khadeejah figured out that her recitation of Al-Qur'an was not good, so she enrolled in tajweed class at the masjid.

Mission Possible: Becoming a Hafith

CHAPTER OUTLINE

1. Is it important to memorize the Qur'an?
2. What are the things that would help us memorize Al-Qur'an?

VOCABULARY

- Thikr ذِكْر
- Tafseer تفسير
- Hifth حِفظ
- Hafith حافِظ
- Ikhlas إخلاص

Becoming a hafith حافظ , or a person who memorizes the whole Qur'an, is one of the best aspirations that a Muslim can have. You might wonder how you can become a hafith. Is it possible that you would memorize the whole Al-Qur'an? Many people have done it, and with enough dedication and discipline, memorizing Al-Qur'an is mission possible.

The Importance of Learning Al-Qur'an by Heart

Becoming a hafith حافظ , or memorizing the whole Qur'an or large portions of it is one of the best things you can accomplish in your life. It will bless your heart, sharpen you mind, expand your knowledge and qualify you to win a high place in Jannah. Prophet Muhammad ﷺ once said: "The one who memorized Al-Qur'an will be asked to read it by heart during the Day of Judgment. He will be told: "Read and step up [the levels in Jannah], your elevation up the levels of Jannah will stop at the last ayah you could recite."

Things that Make Memorizing Al-Qur'an Possible

Memorizing the Al-Qur'an is very possible, but requires hard work and strong determination. Let's learn together what it takes to become a hafith.

1. Sincerity

To become a hafith, or a person who memorizes the whole Qur'an, it is important to have ikhlas إخلاص , or sincerity. You should learn Al-Qur'an for the sake of Allah alone to earn His pleasure and win Paradise inshaAllah. Allah says:

﴿تَنزِيلُ ٱلْكِتَٰبِ مِنَ ٱللَّهِ ٱلْعَزِيزِ ٱلْحَكِيمِ ۝١ إِنَّآ أَنزَلْنَآ إِلَيْكَ ٱلْكِتَٰبَ بِٱلْحَقِّ فَٱعْبُدِ ٱللَّهَ مُخْلِصًا لَّهُ ٱلدِّينَ ۝٢﴾

الزمر: ١ - ٢

The revelation of the Book is from Allah, the Mighty, the Wise.

Surely We have revealed to you the Book with the truth, therefore worship Allah, and be sincere to Him in obedience. [Surat-uz-Zumar 39:1-2].

According to a hadeeth Qudsi, Allah says: "I am so independent that I don't need an associate. Thus whoever worship for the sake of other than Allah as well as for My sake, I will reject that worship and the one whom he associated with Me." So there will be no reward for the one who reads and memorizes Al-Qur'an for the sake of showing off or gaining a good reputation.

2. Proper Recitation

After you have your intention in check you should learn to read Al-Qur'an with correct pronunciation and tajweed. Learning Al-Qur'an recitation with a teacher is the best way to learn Ahkam-ut-Tajweed. The Prophet learned it orally from Jibreel, and the Sahabah learned it orally from the Prophet. Then it was passed down orally from the Sahabah to the next generations of the Ummah. If you perfect Ahkam-ut-Tajweed, then you will be reading Al-Qur'an like the Prophet ﷺ taught it.

3. Quality Memorization from the First Time

You also have to focus your mind when you are reading. This will help you remember the verses and recite it fluently without having to try hard to recall it.

When you study for an important test in school, you usually study the material by dividing it into sections. The best way to memorize Al-Qur'an is by deciding how much to memorize each day. After you have set out this goal, you have to keep on repeating the portion you have memorized over and over until you memorize it very well. You should never move on to a new part until you have perfectly memorized the previous part, so that it will stick in your mind. Abdullah Ibn Mas'ood رضي الله عنه said: "We used to learn with Rasoolullah about ten ayaat of Al-Qur'an every time. We would learn, memorize, understand its meanings and lessons, and practice it. When

we were satisfied that we did all of that, we would then move to learn another set of ayaat."

After memorizing each part, it is important for you to repeat it night and day, by reciting it in your daily prayers. This way it will become easy for you to memorize Al-Qur'an. Everyone can do this, even if you are busy with other things.

Finally, you should recite what you have memorized to another hafith or someone who knows Al-Qur'an well. The person you recite it to should be someone who knows how to recite Al-Qur'an properly, so that he or she can point out any mistakes in pronunciation, tajweed or reading. So reciting to another person is an excellent way of correcting your mistakes and perfecting your memorization.

4. Understanding the Meaning of Al-Qur'an

Many students of Al-Qur'an memorize it without proper understanding. This goes counter to the wisdom behind memorizing Al-Qur'an. Understanding is the key to memorization. One of the helpful things in memorizing is understanding the meaning of the verses and knowing how they are connected to one another. This means that you have to read the tafseer, or the interpretation of some of the ayaat and suwar which you are memorizing.

5. Continuous Review

Memorizing Al-Qur'an is different from memorizing any other material. It is probably not a big deal to forget poems or songs that you know. However, it is bad to forget portions of Al-Qur'an that you had memorized. You should try your best to NEVER forget what you have memorized of Al-Qur'an. So you have to keep reviewing it and always work hard at remembering what you have memorized. The Prophet ﷺ said: "The one who has memorized Al-Qur'an is like the owner of a hobbled camel. If he pays attention to it and takes care of it, he will keep it, but if he lets it go, he will lose it." This means that the one who has memorized the Al-Qur'an has to recite it regularly as a part of daily thikr.

Some parts of Al-Qur'an resemble one another in their meanings and wording. Allah says,

﴿ ٱللَّهُ نَزَّلَ أَحْسَنَ ٱلْحَدِيثِ كِتَٰبًا مُّتَشَٰبِهًا مَّثَانِىَ تَقْشَعِرُّ مِنْهُ جُلُودُ ٱلَّذِينَ يَخْشَوْنَ رَبَّهُمْ ثُمَّ تَلِينُ جُلُودُهُمْ وَقُلُوبُهُمْ إِلَىٰ ذِكْرِ ٱللَّهِ ۚ ذَٰلِكَ هُدَى ٱللَّهِ يَهْدِى بِهِۦ مَن يَشَآءُ ۚ وَمَن يُضْلِلِ ٱللَّهُ فَمَا لَهُۥ مِنْ هَادٍ ﴿٢٣﴾ ﴾

الزمر: ٢٣

"Allah has sent down the Best Statement, a Book, its parts resembling each other (in goodness and truth) and oft-repeated. The skins of those who fear their Lord shiver from it (when they recite it or hear it). Then their skin and their heart soften to the remembrance of Allah." [Az-Zumar 39:23].

So as a good reader of Al-Qur'an you should pay attention to the parts of Al-Qur'an which resemble one another, as this will help you memorize it properly.

6. Memorizing Al-Qur'an at young Age

The one who is truly blessed is the one whom Allah allows to make the most of the best years for memorizing, which comes between the ages of five and twenty-three. During these years, a person is able to memorize things very well. Before the age of five, a person is normally not yet well prepared to do that, and after the age of twenty-three the ability to memorize decreases. Young people of your age should make the most of their youth years and memorize the Book of Allah. Now you are at the age which you will be able to memorize it quickly. A person once said that, "Learning by heart at young age is like carving something on stone; while learning something at old age is like writing something on sand." So learning something at a young age means it will stick in your mind, but when you learn something when you are old it will be easily forgotten. However, there are some people who memorized the whole Qur'an at old age. Despite the huge difficulty, their love of Al-Qur'an and strong discipline combined with Allah's help made them able to do it.

7. High Discipline:

Hifth, or memorizing the whole Qur'an, requires strong discipline. You have to be regular in memorizing Al-Qur'an. You should devote a set time every day for memorizing and review. Solid discipline means strong resolve, continuous work and completion of the task at hand. This is true in memorizing Al-Qur'an, and in all aspects of life, as well. This discipline is not required only to complete the memorizing of Al-Qur'an; it is required also for review to keep Al-Qur'an in the mind. This is a life time task. This might seem a difficult job, but if you develop the habit, it becomes a normal and easy routine in your daily schedule. It makes your life full of blessings, happiness and peace.

Strong discipline also entails dealing with distractions. Spending long hours watching TV, play time and other time wasters are examples of distractions. These distractions inhibit students from memorizing Al-Qur'an regularly and developing good study habits.

Conclusion

It is our duty towards the Book of Allah that we should memorize it properly, follow its guidance, and make it the center of our lives. Hopefully these rules will form a good foundation for those who sincerely want to memorize the Book of Allah properly and live by it.

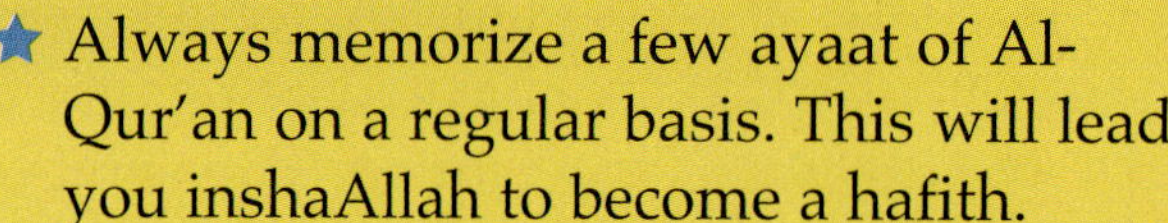

- Always memorize a few ayaat of Al-Qur'an on a regular basis. This will lead you inshaAllah to become a hafith.
- Whenever you memorize a few ayaat, try your best to implement them in your daily life, like the Sahabah used to do.

hadeeth Shareef

عن علي بن أبي طالب رضي الله عنه قال: قال رسول الله صلى الله عليه وسلم:

" من تعلم القرآن فاستظهره وحفظه أدخله الله الجنة وشفعه بعشرة من أهل بيته كلهم قد وجبت لهم النار "

رواه أحمد

Ali Ibn Abi Talib رضي الله عنه narrated that Rasoolullah ﷺ said:

"Whoever learns and memorizes Al-Qur'an, Allah would grant him Jannah and enable him to intercede [during the Day of Judgment] for ten of his relatives, who will be condemned to Hell-fire." *Reported in Musnad Ahmad*

This hadeeth:

- Encourages Muslims to memorize the whole Al-Qur'an by heart
- Encourages Muslims to understand Al-Qur'an and practice it
- Tells that those who memorize Al-Qur'an and practice it will be granted Jannah
- They will also help ten of their relatives to go to Jannah after they were about to go to Hellfire.

CHAPTER REVIEW

Projects and Activities

Conduct an interview with a hafith. Ask him at least ten open-ended questions and record his answers. Write one page about the lessons you learned from the interview.

Stretch Your Mind

List at least three differences between you as a future hafith and you without memorizing the whole Qur'an or large portion of it.

Study Questions

1. What is the most important thing one should have when he or she starts memorizing Al-Qur'an?
2. How did the Prophet and the Sahabah learn the Al-Qur'an?
3. Why is it important to learn Al-Qur'an from teachers?
4. List five of the methods that would help you memorize Al-Qur'an?
5. Why is understanding the meaning of Al-Qur'an important?
6. Why is it easier to memorize when you are young?

LESSON ONE

سورة المزمل

Surat-ul-Muzzammil [Verses 1-9]
Stand up and Pray at Night

VOCABULARY
Qiyam-ul-Layl قيام الليل
Al-Muzzammil المزمل
Tarteel ترتيل

Introduction

This surah has twenty ayaat. All of them were revealed in Makkah except for the last ayah, which was revealed in Madinah.

This surah starts with the command from Allah to the final messenger, Prophet Muhammad ﷺ, peace be upon him, to get up and prepare himself for his great mission. The work ahead requires a very strong connection with Allah, so he is told to stand at night in prayer. Night prayer was required on the Prophet to strengthen his heart for what was coming next.

Ibn Abbas said, "Once, the Messenger of Allah got up for prayers at night and prayed thirteen Rak'aat. I estimate his standing for each Rak'ah to be as long as Surat-ul-Muzzammil."

(Reported in Sunan Abu Dawood).

سورة المزمل
Surat-ul-Muzzammil 1-9

بِسْمِ يَٰٓأَيُّهَا ٱلْمُزَّمِّلُ ﴿١﴾ قُمِ ٱلَّيْلَ إِلَّا قَلِيلًا ﴿٢﴾ نِصْفَهُۥٓ أَوِ ٱنقُصْ مِنْهُ قَلِيلًا ﴿٣﴾ أَوْ زِدْ عَلَيْهِ وَرَتِّلِ ٱلْقُرْءَانَ تَرْتِيلًا ﴿٤﴾ إِنَّا سَنُلْقِى عَلَيْكَ قَوْلًا ثَقِيلًا ﴿٥﴾ إِنَّ نَاشِئَةَ ٱلَّيْلِ هِىَ أَشَدُّ وَطْـًٔا وَأَقْوَمُ قِيلًا ﴿٦﴾ إِنَّ لَكَ فِى ٱلنَّهَارِ سَبْحًا طَوِيلًا ﴿٧﴾ وَٱذْكُرِ ٱسْمَ رَبِّكَ وَتَبَتَّلْ إِلَيْهِ تَبْتِيلًا ﴿٨﴾ رَّبُّ ٱلْمَشْرِقِ وَٱلْمَغْرِبِ لَآ إِلَٰهَ إِلَّا هُوَ فَٱتَّخِذْهُ وَكِيلًا ﴿٩﴾

Understood Meaning

(73:1) O you who is covered [in garments].

(73:2) Stay up most of the night in prayer

(73:3) Half of the night or a little less

(73:4) Or add a little more and read Al-Qur'an in a nice proper way.

(73:5) I will be giving you some words of weight

(73:6) Definitely getting up in the night for worship is difficult, but it is also better for bringing your heart and mind together in prayer.

(73:7) During the day you have a long time to do your things and rest.

(73:8) And remember the name of your Lord and worship Him in a devout way.

(73:9) The Lord of the East and the West, there is no god deserving of worship except Him. So depend on Him for help and support.

The Story of the Revelation

It is narrated that the leaders of the kuffar got together to talk about the Messenger of Allah. Some said he was crazy, some said he was a fortuneteller, and some said he was a magician.

When the Messenger of Allah heard of this meeting, he felt very sad and covered himself. Then Jibreel came with the opening verses of this surah and the next.

Lessons Learned

1. Perfecting the Recitation of Al-Qur'an

Allah orders the Prophet and all Muslims to recite Al-Qur'an in a tarteel manner, which means in a clear, correct and beautiful way. It refers to making your voice sound nice and reciting according to the rules of Tajweed. The Messenger of Allah said, "The person who doesn't recite the Qur'an with rhythm is not one of us."

(Reported in Saheeh-ul-Bukhari)

The people before Islam used to sing and recite poems when they traveled on their camels. So the Messenger of Allah was encouraging people to replace that singing with recitation of Al-Qur'an in a nice way. The nice recitation helps in reflecting on the meaning of the verses so that you get emotionally affected as you recite the verses. Additionally, reciting the Qur'an according to the rules of tajweed imitates the recitation of Rasoolullah ﷺ and his companions. It doesn't mean we should sing the Qur'an by stretching and shortening the reading to match an artificial rhythm or music composition. Doing this would distract or change the meanings of the verses.

2. Words of Weight

This concept that came in ayah 4 of this surah has great meaning. Here are some of these meanings:

a. Receiving Al-Qur'an was truly heavy. When Prophet Muhammad ﷺ used to receive the Qur'an from Jibreel عليه السلام, he used to feel a great pressure. He would sweat and experience huge weight on his heart, mind and body. It is said that if the Messenger of Allah was on a camel when the revelation came, it would be forced to sit down.

b. Al-Qur'an is a heavy responsibility toward Allah. We must fulfill these obligations to please Him, live positively in this life, and win Jannah and stay away from Hell in the next life.

c. It is heavy against the kuffar and the hypocrites.

d. Heavy in the Arabic language can

also mean high in honor.

If we are to learn a lesson from all of the above possible meanings of ayah 4, it will be that Al-Qur'an is an extraordinary book. It is a great divine message that brings us a great honor and puts on our shoulders a great responsibility.

3- Qiyam-ul-Layl: قيام الليل

In this surah, Allah orders Prophet Muhammad ﷺ to perform long prayers at night. Therefore, Rasoolullah ﷺ used to pray at night about half of the night, a little more or less. As you learned earlier, this was a fard prayer for the Prophet only. In our case, Qiyam-ul-Layl is optional for us, but it is a very much recommended prayer. As a matter of fact, scholars say it is the most important optional prayer we can ever perform. It is the most rewarded optional prayer, because it is the hardest to do.

Qiyam-ul-Layl, or the night prayer, can be done anytime after Ishaa' and before Fajr. However, the best kind of Qiyam-ul-Layl is At-Tahajjud. This means waking up from sleep in the middle of the night or at the later part of it, before Fajr, and praying then. It should be noted though that we should conclude the night prayer with Salat-ul-Witr, which should always be the last prayer of the night.

A'ishah رضي الله عنه woke up once, late in the night, and found Rasoolullah ﷺ praying Qiyam-ul-Layl. He was so tired and his feet were swelling hard. "Why are you doing this although Allah has forgiven all your past and future sins?" A'ishah asked the Prophet. "Shouldn't I be a grateful servant?"

Rasoolullah answered.

This hadeeth teaches us a great lesson. As Muslims, we must try our best to worship Allah and show Him our gratefulness for all the gifts and blessings He gave us. Becoming a grateful servant of Allah cannot be through saying Al-hamdulillah alone. It requires great efforts, continuous good deeds and a lot of worship, and that is what Prophet Muhammad ﷺ used to do.

For Your Information

A'ishah, may Allah be pleased with her, was asked about how the Messenger of Allah would perform night prayers. She answered, "Don't you read Surat Al-Muzzammil?"... "Allah made night prayers an obligation at the beginning of this surah. So the Messenger of Allah stood at night in prayer with his companions for a year, until their feet became swollen. Allah held the end of the surah in the sky for twelve months. Then He made it easier for us by revealing the end of the surah. So night prayer has become a recommended ibadah after it was at first obligatory."

(Muslim)

Ibn Abbas said, "When the first part of Al-Muzzammil was revealed, they used to stand in prayer, almost as much as they stand in the month of Ramadan, until the end of the surah was revealed. Between the revelation of the beginning of the surah and the end of it was about a year."

(Reported in Mustadrak Al-Hakim)

FAITH IN ACTION

- Pray Qiyam-ul-Layl regularly, as much as you can.
- Learn Ahkam-ut-Tajweed and try your best to recite the Qur'an in the best manner possible.
- Remember Allah all the time and praise Him regularly, as much as you can.
- Start calling a non-Muslim friend to Islam and practice the concept of patience if they do not respond favorably to you.

LESSON REVIEW

Study Questions

1. What is the meaning of Al-Muzzammil?
2. What did Allah order Prophet Muhammad ﷺ to do in the beginning of this surah? Why?
3. Why did Rasoolullah ﷺ want to pray tahajjud so much?
4. What does the word "tarteel" mean?
5. Why did Allah describe Al-Qur'an as "words of weight?"

LESSON TWO

سورة المزمل
Surat-ul-Muzzammil Verses [10-19]
(Wrapped in clothing)
Be Patient

سورة المزمل
Surat-ul-Muzzammil 10-19

﴿ وَاصْبِرْ عَلَىٰ مَا يَقُولُونَ وَاهْجُرْهُمْ هَجْرًا جَمِيلًا ﴿١٠﴾ وَذَرْنِي وَالْمُكَذِّبِينَ أُولِي النَّعْمَةِ
وَمَهِّلْهُمْ قَلِيلًا ﴿١١﴾ إِنَّ لَدَيْنَا أَنكَالًا وَجَحِيمًا ﴿١٢﴾ وَطَعَامًا ذَا غُصَّةٍ وَعَذَابًا أَلِيمًا ﴿١٣﴾ يَوْمَ
تَرْجُفُ الْأَرْضُ وَالْجِبَالُ وَكَانَتِ الْجِبَالُ كَثِيبًا مَّهِيلًا ﴿١٤﴾ إِنَّا أَرْسَلْنَا إِلَيْكُمْ رَسُولًا شَاهِدًا
عَلَيْكُمْ كَمَا أَرْسَلْنَا إِلَىٰ فِرْعَوْنَ رَسُولًا ﴿١٥﴾ فَعَصَىٰ فِرْعَوْنُ الرَّسُولَ فَأَخَذْنَاهُ أَخْذًا وَبِيلًا ﴿١٦﴾
فَكَيْفَ تَتَّقُونَ إِن كَفَرْتُمْ يَوْمًا يَجْعَلُ الْوِلْدَانَ شِيبًا ﴿١٧﴾ السَّمَاءُ مُنفَطِرٌ بِهِ ۚ كَانَ وَعْدُهُ
مَفْعُولًا ﴿١٨﴾ إِنَّ هَٰذِهِ تَذْكِرَةٌ ۖ فَمَن شَاءَ اتَّخَذَ إِلَىٰ رَبِّهِ سَبِيلًا ﴿١٩﴾ ﴾

Understood Meaning

(73:10) And be patient when the disbelievers say hurtful things about you and wisely stay away from them (when they do this).

(73:11) And leave to Me those wealthy disbelievers, let them have little more time.

(73:12)We have chains to tie them and a raging Hell to punish them in,

(73:13) And food that sticks in the throat and lots of other painful punishment.

(73:14) [This punishment comes] on the day when the Earth and the mountains will shake and the mountains will be like a pile of fine sand.

(73:15) [You disbelievers] I have sent you a messenger to be a witness against you (on that day). He is sent to you like I sent to Pharaoh another messenger.

(73:16) Pharaoh disobeyed his messenger, [like you are disobeying your messenger], so I destroyed him in a severe way [by drowning him and his supporters].

(73:17) So how will you save yourselves from a scary day that would turn the hair of children white from terror?

(73:18) The sky will be torn during that day and Allah's promise [to bring you back from the dead for judgment] will happen.

(73:19) This is just a reminder and warning. So whoever wants should take the path to his Lord [by obeying Allah's Messengers].

Lessons Learned

1. Patience is a Great Virtue

The disbelievers of Makkah used to hurt the Prophet ﷺ so much. They called him a liar, a fortune teller, a magician among other very bad names. Rasoolullah ﷺ felt hurt and insulted. Immediately, Allah ordered the Prophet to show sabr, or patience. He also recommended that the Prophet should avoid contact with them. This teaches us that when evil people hurt or insult us we should not get depressed and lose our temper. Instead, we must focus on the good work we do and not get distracted. Sabr or patience is a great virtue that all Prophets had and Allah taught them to use it in times of distress.

2. Allah Punishes the Evil People

Allah likes all disbelievers to be guided to the straight path. He sent the people of the Quraysh the message of Al-Qur'an with Prophet Muhammad ﷺ. Rasoolullah ﷺ tried his best to make them believe in the message of Al-Qur'an and follow Allah's guidance. He wished them good and wanted them to have a happy life and win Paradise after death. But they rejected Islam and insisted on fighting the Prophet and hurting him. They even tried to kill him and his followers as you learned in past years. Therefore Allah told Prophet Muhammad ﷺ that He will punish evil people in Hellfire.

A few years after this warning, Muslims won the Battle of Badr and most of the evil leaders of the Quraysh were killed there. A'ishah (R) said, "After Allah revealed this verse 'leave to me those disbelievers…' it was only a short time until the Battle of Badr."

3. Al-Qur'an is a Great Reminder

In ayah 19, Allah describes Al-Qur'an as " a reminder." It reminds us time and time again to have strong faith, do good deeds and show pious character. The more we recite the Qur'an and act upon it, the more we become good people and develop noble personalities. Abandoning the Qur'an and not reciting it regularly will deprive us from its great reminders.

PUTTING QUR'AN INTO ACTION

- Always practice sabr with others.
- Whenever others insult you or hurt your feelings avoid doing the same evil things they did to you. Defend your self by avoiding them in a wise and honorable way.
- Always fear Allah and His punishment. Avoid actions that lead to Hellfire.

Study Questions

1. What did Allah order Prophet Muhammad to do with those who insulted him?
2. What did Allah prepare for the evil people in the next life? Describe the punishment they will suffer then.
3. Describe what will happen on the Day of Judgment.
4. What a special value did Allah mention about the Qur'an? And what does this help us in our daily lives?

LESSON THREE

سورة المزمل

Surat-ul-Muzzammil Verse [20]

(Wrapped in clothing)

Pray, Recite and Give Charity

سورة المزمل

Surat-ul-Muzzammil 20

﴿ إِنَّ رَبَّكَ يَعْلَمُ أَنَّكَ تَقُومُ أَدْنَىٰ مِن ثُلُثَيِ ٱلَّيْلِ وَنِصْفَهُۥ وَثُلُثَهُۥ وَطَآئِفَةٌ مِّنَ ٱلَّذِينَ مَعَكَ ۚ وَٱللَّهُ يُقَدِّرُ
ٱلَّيْلَ وَٱلنَّهَارَ ۚ عَلِمَ أَن لَّن تُحْصُوهُ فَتَابَ عَلَيْكُمْ ۖ فَٱقْرَءُوا۟ مَا تَيَسَّرَ مِنَ ٱلْقُرْءَانِ ۚ عَلِمَ أَن سَيَكُونُ
مِنكُم مَّرْضَىٰ ۙ وَءَاخَرُونَ يَضْرِبُونَ فِى ٱلْأَرْضِ يَبْتَغُونَ مِن فَضْلِ ٱللَّهِ ۙ وَءَاخَرُونَ يُقَٰتِلُونَ فِى سَبِيلِ
ٱللَّهِ ۖ فَٱقْرَءُوا۟ مَا تَيَسَّرَ مِنْهُ ۚ وَأَقِيمُوا۟ ٱلصَّلَوٰةَ وَءَاتُوا۟ ٱلزَّكَوٰةَ وَأَقْرِضُوا۟ ٱللَّهَ قَرْضًا حَسَنًا ۚ وَمَا تُقَدِّمُوا۟
لِأَنفُسِكُم مِّنْ خَيْرٍ تَجِدُوهُ عِندَ ٱللَّهِ هُوَ خَيْرًا وَأَعْظَمَ أَجْرًا ۚ وَٱسْتَغْفِرُوا۟ ٱللَّهَ ۖ إِنَّ ٱللَّهَ غَفُورٌ رَّحِيمٌۢ ﴿٢٠﴾ ﴾

Understood Meaning

(73:20) (O Muhammad,) Your Lord knows that you stay up less than two thirds of the night or half of the night or a third of the night, with a group of your companions. Allah sets the exact length of the night and day, so Allah knows how much of the night you stay up in prayer. Allah knew that you would not be able to completely meet this responsibility. So He eased things for you. Therefore, read what is easy for you to read from Al-Qur'an (in your night prayers and worship). Allah knows that some of you will be sick (and will be unable to get up for prayers). And Allah knows that others will travel in the land trying to make a living from Allah's blessing. And Allah knows that others will be out fighting for the sake of Allah, so they will have difficulty doing their night prayers.

So read what is easy for you to read from Al-Qur'an. And do your five daily prayers completely and give your Zakah. And give to Allah a nice loan by spending your money for the sake of Allah. Remember that whatever good you do now, you will find your reward with Allah. The good you find with Allah will be better for you than what you spent, and the reward will be more than what you expect.

And ask Allah for forgiveness. Allah is very forgiving and very merciful.

hadeeth Shareef

عن أبي هريرة رضي الله عنه قال : قال رسول الله ﷺ :

" أفضلُ الصَّلاةِ بعدَ الفريضة قيام الليل "

رواه النسائي والدارمي

Abu Hurayrah narrated that Rasoolullah ﷺ said:

"The best prayer after the obligatory ones is Qiyam-ul-Layl (Late Night Prayer)."

Reported in Sunan An-Nasa'ee and Sunan Ad-Darimi

Lessons Learned

1. Qiyam-ul-Layl: Optional but important.

As you learned earlier, Qiyam-ul-Layl was fard on everyone early on. Allah knew that it was hard on Muslims to pray Qiyam-ul-Layl every night, especially for those who travel, or those in the military fighting the enemies. Later, He instructed them to do whatever worship they could at night. And, Qiyam-ul-Layl became optional, but still favorable to Allah.

It is true that we only have to do five daily prayers to start with. Rasoolullah ﷺ was asked if there were any other obligatory prayers, other than the five daily prayers and he said, "No, but you can do extra." (Reported in Saheeh-ul-Bukhari) However, part of being thankful for the blessings of Allah is to pray at night, as Rasoolullah ﷺ used to do. So we must always do the best we can and never be happy to do just the minimum.

2. Salah and Zakah are the Best Good Deeds.

Allah orders the Muslims to perform their prayers properly and give out their zakah. Allah mentioned salah and zakah together in many ayaat in Al-Qur'an. These two types of ibadah are very important in Islam. Salah is the best ibadah you present to Allah, while zakah is the best good deed you do to your Muslim brothers and sisters and needy ones. Therefore, worship in Islam is not only good deeds you do to, Allah but also good favors you do to others.

The Messenger of Allah once said, *"Who of you loves his own money more than the money that will be left for his inheritors?"*

"Everyone loves the money he spends on himself more than the money he leaves for his inheritors," the companions replied.

Rasoolullah then said, *"Your money is what you keep with you for the Day of Judgment (by spending it for the sake of Allah) and what you save and do not spend is actually the money of your inheritors."*

Reported in Saheeh-ul-Bukhari)

3. Rewards are the Best Gain One Can Make in this Life.

Whatever good deeds a Muslim does will be great for him or her in the next life. Earning rewards for the next life is much more important than saving money for this life. Allah tells us that the good deeds we do for His sake are much better than the worldly things we gain in this life. Rewards bring us Jannah, while money buys us little of this humble life.

99 Names of Allah

Al-Qayyoom

﴿ ٱللَّهُ لَآ إِلَٰهَ إِلَّا هُوَ ٱلْحَىُّ ٱلْقَيُّومُ ۚ لَا تَأْخُذُهُۥ سِنَةٌ وَلَا نَوْمٌ ﴾ البقرة

Allah, no God but He, He is the Alive, the Controller, No slumber takes Him nor sleep.

Allah is controlling the world and taking full care of it. He never rests nor sleeps.

PUTTING QUR'AN INTO ACTION

- ★ Read Al-Qur'an whenever you can.
- ★ Do your prayers regularly without skipping any prayer.
- ★ Give charity to the needy whenever you can.
- ★ Always do good deeds and collect rewards. Rewards are so valuable for you in the next life; they will help you win Jannah, inshaAllah.

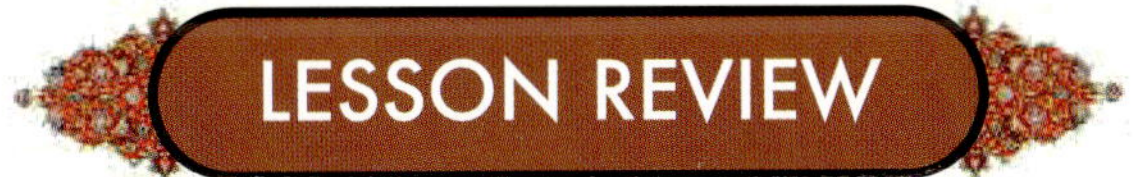

LESSON REVIEW

Study Questions

1. What did Allah change concerning Qiyam-ul-Layl for Muslims? Why did He make this change?
2. What good deeds did Allah tell Muslims to do in this ayah?
3. What did Allah say about good deeds?
4. What does Al-Qayoom mean? Support your answer with an ayah.

One of the gates of Al-Masjid An-Nabawi (The Prophet's Mosque) in Madinah.

Prophet Muhammad Calls for Peace

Unit Introduction

During your elementary school years you have learned parts of the Seerah, or life story of Prophet Muhammad. You probably studied that in the "I love Islam" textbooks. In this series, "Learning Islam," we are going to continue learning the beautiful story of Prophet Muhammad. However, before we do that let's remind you of what you learned during the past years.

Arabs before Islam

Islam calls for peace to all mankind. Without Islam, people will suffer hatred, racism, and wars. This was the situation in Arabia before the time of Prophet Muhammad. Tribes used to fight and kill each other for money, power and honor. They were in continuous fighting and lengthy wars.

Other nations around Arabia were not more peaceful than the Arabs. The Romans and the Persians used to fight all the time. They had huge armies, thus when they fought, tens of thousands would lose their lives. The Persians and the Romans also used to pay some Arab tribes to fight for them. The Ghassanid, for example, used to fight for the Romans while the Manathirah were agents for the Persians. Often times these two tribes would fight each other while the Persian and Roman armies were resting.

Muhammad Becomes the Last Messenger to Mankind

Prophet Muhammad lived in this pitiful environment when Allah chose him as a messenger. God wanted Muhammad to guide the peoples in Arabia and around the world to faith, ethics, brotherhood and peace. The message of Islam called for all these virtues.

When Prophet Muhammad called his people in Makkah and other tribes to Islam, the leaders of Makkah feared for their positions. They thought that he would become their new leader and their privileges will go away. It was also hard for them to change their evil life-styles. Worshipping idols, drinking, gambling, infanticide, raiding, stealing, and murder were daily actions in Arabia and the surrounding nations.

Prophet Muhammad insisted on changing this situation. Therefore, the Makkans and other Arab tribes took him as their enemy.

Prophet Muhammad Migrates to Madinah

Quraysh, the tribe of the Prophet, tried to kill him and persecuted his followers. This made Prophet Muhammad and the Muslims migrate to Madinah and establish the first Muslim society in Madinah. Quraysh stole all the wealth and the properties of the hundreds of Muslims that left Makkah, and invested their belongings in their trades. When the Prophet and his followers tried to capture some of the Quraysh caravans running from Makkah to Syria, Quraysh declared an all-out war against him.

The Battle of Badr

As you learned in your elementary years, the first serious military encounter between Muslims and the Quraysh was during Ramadan in the second year after Hijrah. The fight took place near the village of Badr between Makkah and Madinah and this event was later called "The Battle of Badr." The Quraysh army was one thousand fighters strong, charging against a small unprepared Muslim army of little over three hundred fighters. Amazingly, the Muslims defeated the pagan army that was three times bigger than theirs. This defeat was very painful for Quraysh, which lost seventy of their leaders and fighters. Angels participated in the fight and supported the Muslims against their enemies. The pagans of Makkah decided to avenge their loss.

The Battle of Uhud

In the third year after Hijrah, the pagans came to Madinah with a two-thousand- fighter-army. They wanted to finish the Muslims and destroy them forever. The two armies met near the mountain of Uhud, few miles north of Madinah, and this battle later became known as "The Battle of Uhud." The Muslim army was about seven hundred fighters who could overcome the Quraysh army in the beginning. Some Muslim fighters made a serious mistake and disobeyed strict orders of the Prophet, a matter that made the Muslims lose the battle in the end. The Muslims lost about seventy martyrs, including Hamzah, the uncle of Prophet Muhammad. But Quraysh could not destroy the Muslims as they were hoping to do.

The Battle of the Trench

During the fifth year of Al-Hijrah, the Quraysh again tried to finish the Muslims in Madinah. This time, they gathered ten thousand pagan fighters from Quraysh and other hostile tribes around Arabia. Their mission was to invade Madinah, capture or kill Prophet Muhammad and main leaders of Muslims and rid Arabia from Islam. Surprised by the news, theMuslims looked for a creative way to deter this huge and hostile army. Salman Al-Farisi (R) suggested to the Prophet to dig a long trench to stop the pagan army from entering Madinah. Everyone, including the Prophet worked on the trench until it was complete. This plan worked and the enemies could not come into the city. Later, Allah made the weather bad on the pagans and strong winds scattered their tents and belongings. Angels also helped making the enemies feel insecure, until they withdrew to their lands, and the pagans failed to achieve their evil goal. This event was called "The Battle of the Trench."

Prophet Muhammad Responds with Peaceful Initiative

After this important event, the Prophet made a surprise move toward Quraysh. He decided to respond to Quraysh's offense, but in a peaceful way. This is what you will learn over the next few chapters.

THE PEACEFUL MARCH TO MAKKAH

CHAPTER OUTLINE

1. What are Al-Ash-hur-ul-Hurum?
2. The Prophet decides to go to Makkah for Umrah
3. Why did Rasoolullah travel toward Makkah?
4. The events that led to the Pledge of Ar-Ridwan
5. What is Bay'at-ur-Ridwan?

VOCABULARY

- Al-Ash-hur-ul-Hurum الأشهُرُ الحُرُم
- Al-Masjid-ul-Haram المَسجِدُ الحَرام
- Hadiy هَدْي
- Al-Hudaybiyah الحُدَيْبِيَة
- Bay'at-ur-Ridwan بَيعَةُ الرِّضوان

Longing for Makkah

Six years had passed since the Prophet ﷺ had left his beloved Makkah. The city had been in the hands of the pagan tribe of Quraysh, but Islam had still grown during this time. The pagans had tried to attack the Muslims at various times and had suffered some defeat, like in the Battle of Uhud.

According to Arab custom every Arab was entitled to visit Al-Masjid-ul-Haram المَسجِدُ الحَرام, or the sacred mosque in Makkah, unarmed. Fighting of any kind was prohibited during الأشهُرُ الحُرُم

Al-Masjid-ul-Haram in Makkah.

Al-Ash-hur-ul-Hurum, or the Sacred Months. These months are four: Thul-Qi'dah; Thul-Hijjah; Muharram; and Rajab. These months were named sacred so that people could visit Makkah during these times without fearing being killed or attacked.

Table: Al-Ash-hur-ul-Hurum

1	Muharram (1)*	مُحرَّم
2	Rajab (7)*	رَجب
3	Thul-Qi'dah (11)*	ذو القِعدة
4	Thul-Hijjah (12)*	ذو الحجة

* The number of the month in the Hijri Calendar (9)

The Prophet's Vision

During the month of شـوّال Shawwal, six years after Hijrah, Prophet Muhammad ﷺ received a beautiful vision. In his dream, he saw himself entering Makkah, performing Hajj, then shaving his head. He also saw that he sacrificed some animals in the name of Allah upon his entry into Makkah without fighting. The Prophet ﷺ naturally thought that his dream was from God and must be fulfilled, because prophets' dreams usually come true.

Prophet Muhammad ﷺ made immediate preparations to make pilgrimage to Makkah. When asked

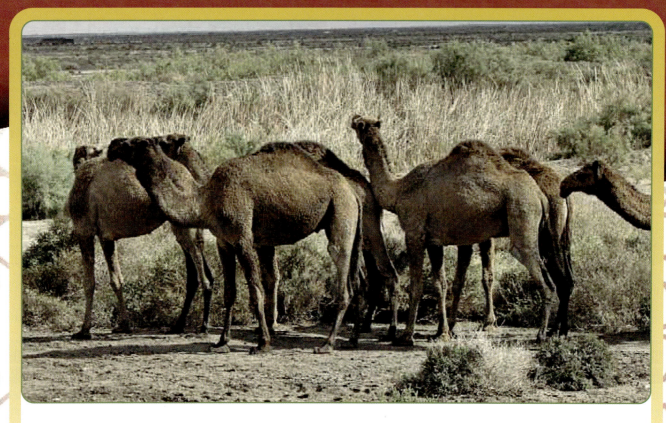

whether the Quraysh would let him enter Makkah peacefully, he replied: "Certainly not by fighting and most surely in peace." The Prophet ﷺ encouraged his companions to join him in this special trip. Almost all of them wanted to accompany him in such a peaceful expedition. The people wondered if they were to take their spears, bows and arrows with them. "No, nothing," said the Prophet ﷺ, "except the travelers' swords," - to use as protection against pirates and wild animals.

The Prophet ﷺ sent word to all neighboring tribes, asking them to accompany him to Makkah. He informed them that he was going on Umrah, the lesser pilgrimage, in the month of Thul-Qi'dah, one of the sacred months. Hence, there would be no fighting. He also sent messages to the Quraysh that he was bound to Makkah on a peaceful Umrah trip.

The Real Objective

It seems that the real objective of the Messenger of Allah ﷺ was to find a peaceful way to resolve the conflict between the Muslims and the pagans. All along, the Prophet ﷺ was hoping that the pagans of Quraysh and in Arabia would accept the message of Islam peacefully. He also wanted to counter the Quraysh's war mongering attitude with a spirit of peace.

The Muslims' hearts were filled with joy at the prospect of being able to visit Makkah after six years of painful separation. Additionally, this journey was meant to satisfy their human need to reunite with their relatives and friends in their hometown.

The Way to Makkah

In the month of Thul-Qi'dah in the 6th year after Hijrah, the Prophet ﷺ set off with the intention of performing Umrah. His intention was not war, but he suspected that the Quraysh would wage war against him. So, he took about 1,400 of the Muhajireen and Al-Ansar. The Prophet ﷺ took about seventy camels with him as هدْي hadiy. The hadiy is the sacrificial animal like a sheep, cow or camel, that a pilgrim slaughters in Makkah as part of the Hajj or Umrah rituals. The Prophet ﷺ took the hadiy with him, so people would be aware that he intended to pay a visit to Al-Masjid Al-Haram in Makkah.

The Prophet's ﷺ plans were not to the liking of the pagan Quraysh. In breach of all Arab traditions, they prepared to prevent the peaceful party from performing the rites of Umrah. They marched to oppose and fight the peaceful expedition.

When the Prophet ﷺ and his men reached 'Asfan, near Makkah, Bishr Ibn Sufiyan Al-Ka'bi met him and said:" Oh Messenger of Allah, the Quraysh has heard of your coming. They all set off with their camels to Thee-Tuwa in preparation for a long and arduous war with you. They swear that you will never enter Makkah in spite of them, And Khalid Ibn-ul-Walid is leading the cavalry.

The Prophet ﷺ angrily said: "Woe unto Quraysh! The war had eaten them up. What harm would there be if they let me and the Arabs meet freely? What do the Quraysh think? By God, I will continue to struggle for the sake of Allah on the path He set me for, until He gives me the victory or this advance goes on."

The Prophet Avoids War

When the Prophet ﷺ heard about Quraysh's fighters coming his way, he asked about an alternative route to avoid them. A man from Bani Aslam suggested they take a rugged rocky road to the west along the shore of the Red Sea. After a hard journey, they reached a plain and the Prophet ﷺ ordered them to take a road that led to Al-Hudaybiyah at the lower side of Makkah. When the Quraysh forces saw the dust of the caravan change route, they returned to Makkah. The Prophet ﷺ continued his ride until he reached a place called الحدَيْبِيَة Al-Hudaybiyah, fifteen miles northwest of Makkah. His camel halted there near a well. His men wondered why in the world the camel would do that.

The Prophet ﷺ said: "Some Power has prevented it like the One that prevented the elephant of Abrahah." The

Prophet ﷺ was referring to Abrahah's attack on the Ka'bah, which was thwarted by Allah in the year of the Prophet's birth. He then swore: "If the Quraysh ask me today for peace, I will grant them peace and the joining of peaceful relations." He also swore that if the Quraysh offered him any opportunity to mend family relations, he would accept it no matter what.

The Prophet ﷺ ordered his companions to set up a camp there, but they complained that there was no water in the valley. He ﷺ responded by taking an arrow and handing it to one of his companions. He asked him to pierce one of the dried wells with it. The companion did as he was asked, and to their amazement, water miraculously gushed out profusely from the well.

Negotiations Started

The tribes around Makkah noticed the unusual movement going on around the city. They knew about the state of war between the Quraysh and the Muslims. Therefore, some of these tribes considered mediating to avert a possible clash between the two groups.

Budayl Ibn Warqa', a tribal leader, came to the Prophet ﷺ to inquire about the Prophet's intentions. He wanted to act as a mediator and told the Prophet ﷺ that the Quraysh will fight him and the Muslims and would prevent them from entering Makkah. Prophet Muhammad ﷺ acknowledged the peaceful purpose of Budayl's visit.

Khuza'ah was a friendly tribe to both the Muslims and the Quraysh. In fact some of the Khuza'ah people were Muslims. Khurash Ibn Umayyah, a leader of the tribe, went to the Makkans. He told them that Prophet Muhammad ﷺ had come only for a visit to Makkah for worship during the sacred months. He told the Quraysh that they had been too quick to judge Muhammad's ﷺ reason for coming to Makkah.

The Quraysh scolded Khurash, then insulted and almost killed him. They refused to allow Muslims into Makkah and said: "Even if Muhammad did not intend war, he will never enter without our permission. We will not let the Arabs think that we were caught off guard by Muhammad ﷺ." The Quraysh didn't want the Arabs to believe that they did not have the power to stop the Muslims from entering Makkah, and thus be perceived as weak. They wanted to prove to Arabia that the tribe of Quraysh was in full control of Makkah. Khuza'ah conveyed to the Prophet ﷺ what they had learned from the Quraysh, not withholding any information about the situation from him.

The Quraysh really wanted a solution to the awkward situation in which they found themselves. According to Arabian custom, the Quraysh was obligated to allow all Arabs to visit Al-Ka'bah, the Sacred House, especially during sacred months. So they sent

Urwah Ibn Masoud Al-Thaqafy as an emissary to Prophet Muhammad ﷺ . He came to the Prophet ﷺ and sat by him and said: "Oh Muhammad! You collected the mob of the Arabs and came to destroy your tribe!"

"The Quraysh now came out with their camels and wore their leopard skins, swearing: "You'll never enter Makkah without our permission. And your people will flee and leave you alone," Urwah said.

Abu Bakr angrily said: "Are we the ones who would flee and leave him alone?"

While talking Urwah kept reaching to the Prophet's ﷺ beard, Al-Mughirah Ibn Shu'bah was standing by the Prophet's ﷺ head wearing mail armor with nothing showing except his eyes. Each time Urwah tried to grab at the Prophet's ﷺ beard, Al-Mughirah kept hitting his hand saying: "Keep your hand off the Prophet's ﷺ face before it never returns to you." Urwah asked: "Who is this rough and tough man?" The Prophet ﷺ smiled and told him he was his nephew. Then the Prophet ﷺ told him that he did not come for war and that he was only there to pay homage to the House of Allah.

Urwah went back to Makkah and told the Quraysh how the companions loved, revered, and protected Prophet Muhammad ﷺ. He told them: "Oh Quraysh! I have seen Kisra in his throne, and Caesar in his palace, and An-Najashi in his kingdom, and by Allah, I have never seen such a kingdom like Muhammad's. His companions will never give him up to you."

The Prophet's Emissary to the Quraysh

The Prophet ﷺ later asked Uthman Ibn Affan to go as his emissary to the Quraysh as he was determined to perform his Umrah before returning to Madinah. Uthman immediately set off towards Makkah. At the city's outskirts, he was met by Aban Ibn Saeed Ibn-ul-'Aas who took him into his protection until he could convey the message of the Prophet ﷺ. Uthman hurried to Abu Sufyan and the leaders of the Quraysh to pass on the message. After he had finished they said to him: "If you wish to make tawaf around the House, you can do that by yourself only." Uthman said: "I will certainly not perform Tawaf until the Prophet ﷺ had done so." So, the Quraysh held him hostage. When Uthman was delayed, the Muslims feared that he had been killed or hurt.

Bay'at-ur- Ridwan

بَيْعَةُ الرِّضْوان

Uthman was very dear to Prophet Muhammad ﷺ. He was one of the first people to embrace Islam. He was blessed with a noble personality and would serve as a role model for future generations. He was the most generous contributor to the Muslim state in Madinah. In addition to that, Uthman was a cousin of the Prophet ﷺ and son-in-law. He was married to the Prophet's daughter Ruqayyah, and then to another of his daughters, Ummu Kulthoom, after Ruqayyah's death.

When the Prophet ﷺ heard that Uthman had been captured, and that he may have been killed, he said: "We will not leave this place until we have accomplished our objective, even if we have to fight these people."

The Prophet called his men and stood under a tree to take their pledge. All of the fourteen hundred Muslims offered their sincere pledge to obey Allah and his Prophet ﷺ, even in matters of life and death. This pledge is called in Arabic بيْعَةُ الرِّضْوان Bay'at-ur-Ridwan. It was given that name because Allah was pleased with all of those who were part of this Bay'ah. Rasoolullah ﷺ struck his hand above theirs and each man took the pledge. They were filled with faith and resolved to die to avenge the death of Uthman. History affords no better example of "all for one and one for all."

When all his followers had finished taking the oath, the Prophet ﷺ struck his own right hand on his left (representing Uthman) and repeated the formula of the oath as if Uthman was present in person. Their swords were now unsheathed and war was almost certain, whether victory or martyrdom. And lo! There was Uthman returning from Makkah.

Allah says with regard to this pledge:

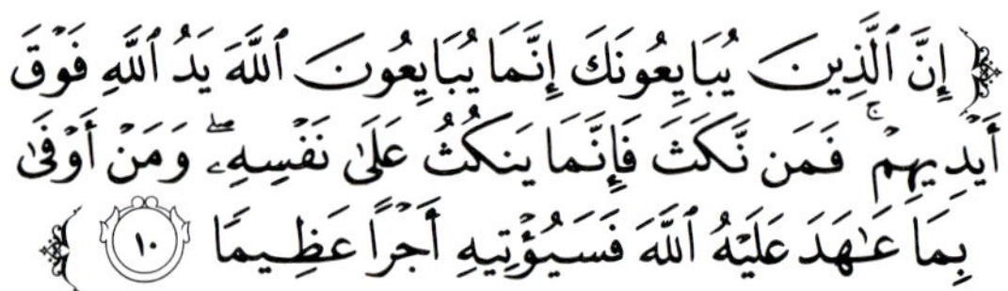

الفتح: ١٠

Surely those who swear allegiance to you do but swear allegiance to Allah; the hand of Allah is above their hands. Therefore whoever breaks the oath, he breaks it only to the injury of his own soul, and whoever fulfills what he has pledged to Allah, He will grant him a great reward. [48:10]

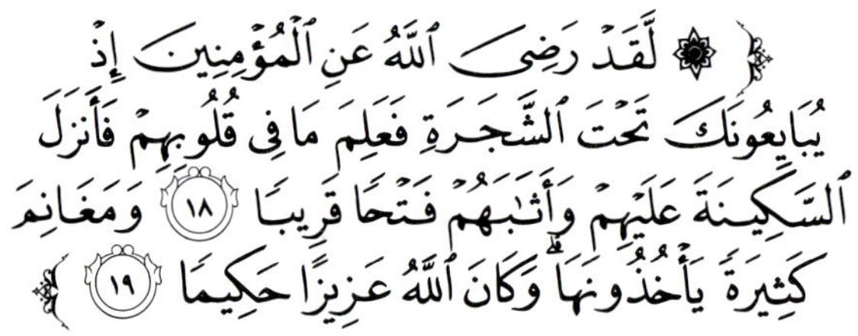

الفتح: ١٨ - ١٩

Certainly Allah was well pleased with the believers when they swore allegiance to you under the tree, and He knew what was in their hearts, so He sent down tranquility on them and rewarded them with a near victory. [48:18]

And many other gains which they will take; and Allah is Almighty, All-Wise. [48:19]

CHAPTER REVIEW

Projects and Activities

1. Create a poster of all the Islamic lunar months. Highlight Al-Ash-hur-ul-Hurum with red.

2. Write an essay explaining the ayaat 10, 18 and 19 of Surat-ul-Fateh.

3. Write a one-page profile about Uthman Ibn Affan (R).

Scratch Your Mind

What was the difference between the trip which the Prophet ﷺ took to Makkah and the expedition the Quraysh made a year earlier to Madinah at the time of the Battle of Al-Khandaq.

Study Questions

1. When did the Prophet ﷺ head to Makkah and why?
2. Why did he choose the month of Thul-Qi'dah to perform his visit to Makkah?
3. What was the Prophet's ﷺ main motive for visiting Makkah, additional to worshipping in Al-Masjid Al-Haram?
4. What was the Quraysh's reaction to Prophet Muhammad's ﷺ initiative?
5. Who was Prophet Muhammad's ﷺ Muslim emissary to the Makkans? What happened to him?
6. What is Bay'at-ur-Ridwan? Why did the Prophet ﷺ call for it? And where did it happen?

Sulh-ul-Hudaybiyah: The Peace Treaty with Quraysh

CHAPTER OUTLINE

1. What was Sulh-ul-Hudaybiyah?
2. What did the Treaty of Hudaybiyah call for?
3. What were the benefits of Sulh-ul-Hudaybiyah?
4. What were the main events that followed the treaty?

VOCABULARY

Sulh-ul-Hudaybiyah صلح الحديبية

Treaty of Hudaybiyah

Shortly after the Quraysh released 'Uthman رضي الله عنه, they sent Suhayl Ibn Amr to the Prophet ﷺ to make a settlement with him. The moment the Prophet ﷺ saw Suhayl coming, he predicted that the Quraysh wanted to resolve the stand-off peacefully.

Suhayl approached the Prophet ﷺ and talked diplomatically. The two spent time in lengthy negotiations before coming to an agreement.

The Quraysh offered a deal to Prophet Muhammad ﷺ. The terms included the following:

1. Prophet Muhammad ﷺ and the Muslims would withdraw that year but they would come back the following year. Muslims would be permitted to visit Makkah next year and perform their Umrah and stay in Makkah for three days.

2. The Quraysh and Muslims would commit to a truce for ten years. During this period the Muslims and the Quraysh would refrain from fighting and avoid provocation.

3. The Muslims and the Quraysh would be free to sign alliance treaties with any tribes around Arabia. (As a result of this item Banu Bakr made an alliance with the Quraysh; and Banu Khuza'ah made an alliance with the Prophet ﷺ).

4. The Muslims would reject any person from the Quraysh defecting to Madinah to become a Muslim. But the Quraysh would be free to receive any Muslim wishing to change his religion and join the Makkans.

After some discussion Prophet Muhammad ﷺ accepted the proposal. When the agreement was to be committed to writing, the Prophet ﷺ called Ali Ibn Abi Talib رضي الله عنه and started dictating the words: "In the name of Allah, Ar-Rahman Ar-Raheem", but Suhayl, the ambassador of the Quraysh, declared that he knew nothing about Ar-Rahman Ar-Raheem, and insisted to write instead 'Bismik-Allaumma, or in your name, oh Allah!' The Muslims murmured, but Prophet Muhammad ﷺ yielded. He then went on to dictate: "This is the treaty of peace between Muhammad Rasoolullah ﷺ, meaning the Messenger of Allah…' Suhayl protested again and refused to acknowledge Muhammad ﷺ as the Messenger of Allah. He said, "Had we agreed that you are a messenger of Allah, we would not be fighting!" He simply asked to write "Muhammad Ibn 'Abdullah." The Muslims murmured louder than before, and refused to consent to the change.

The heads of the two tribes of Madinah, Osayd Ibn Hodayr and Sa'd Ibn Ubadah, held the hand of the scribe and declared that "Muhammad the apostle of God" must be written, or the sword must decide. The Makkan representatives whispered to one another as they were amazed by the strong faith Muslims had in Muhammad. The Prophet ﷺ said: "I swear by Allah that I am His Messenger even though you do not believe." But Prophet Muhammad ﷺ made a sign to his companions to hold their peace and again gave way.

The Statement of the Treaty

"In your name, O God!

This is the treaty of peace concluded by Muhammad Ibn Abdullah and Suhayl Ibn Amr. They have agreed to allow their arms to rest for ten years. During this time each party shall be secure, and neither shall injure the other; no secret damage shall be inflicted, but honesty and honor shall prevail between them. Whoever in Arabia wishes to enter into a treaty and covenant with Muhammad can do so, and whoever wishes to enter into a treaty or covenant with the Quraysh can do so. And if a Qurayshite comes without permission of his guardian (Wali) to Muhammad, he shall be delivered up to the Quraysh; but if, on the other hand, one of Muhammad's people comes to the Quraysh he shall not be delivered up to Muhammad. This year Muhammad, with his companions, must withdraw from us, but next year he may come amongst us and remain for three days, yet without their weapons except those of a traveler, the swords remaining in their sheaths."

Witnesses

When they had completed writing the statement of the treaty, they had both Muslim men and disbelieving men stand as witnesses: Omar Ibn Al-Khattab, Abdul Rahman Ibn 'Awuf, Abdullah Ibn Suhayl Ibn Amr, Sa'ad Ibn Abi Waqass, Mahmoud Ibn Maslamah, Mikraz Ibn Hafs (a disbeliever at the time), and Ali Ibn Abi Talib, who wrote the scroll.

The Story of Abu Jandal

The ink of the treaty had hardly dried when Abu Jandal, son of Suhayl Ibn Amr, came and joined the Muslims. When Suhayl saw him, he became furious and caught hold of him, beat him, and dragged him back. Abu Jandal cried: "Oh Muslims! Will you drive me back to the pagans and let them persecute me and put my faith on trial?"

The Prophet ﷺ asked Suhayl to allow his son to join the Muslims, but he refused. Rasoolullah then said: "Oh Abu Jandal! Be patient and control yourself, surely God will make some way out for you and for the oppressed (in Makkah). We have bound ourselves to make peace between ourselves and the people (Quraysh) and we have given them and they have given us the covenant of God, and we will not break that."

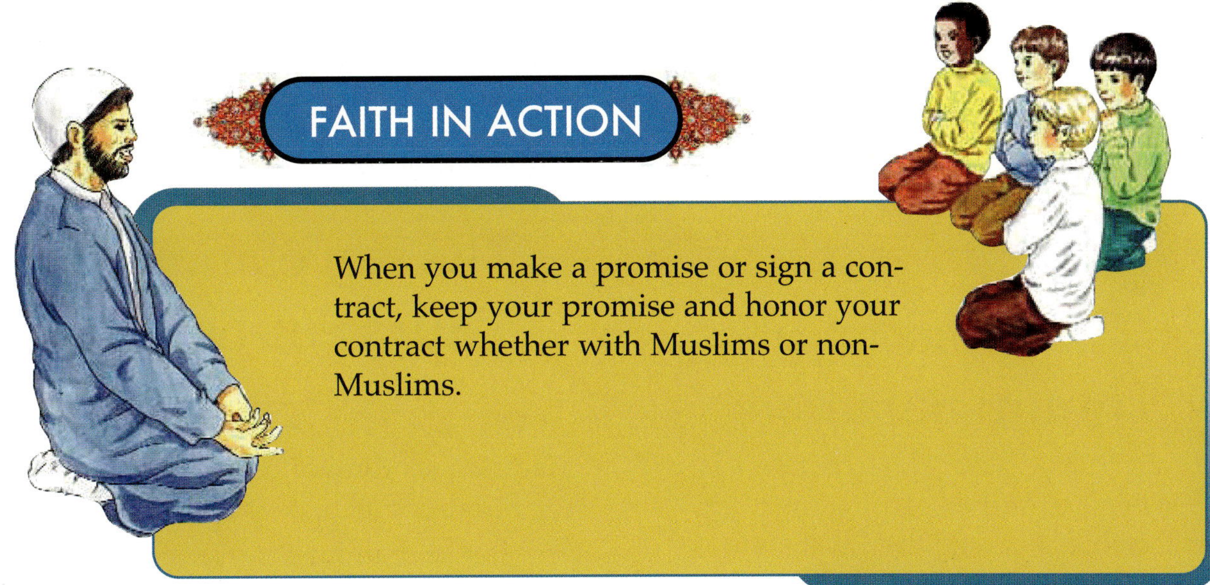

FAITH IN ACTION
When you make a promise or sign a contract, keep your promise and honor your contract whether with Muslims or non-Muslims.

Internal Unrest

When the Sahabah left Madinah, they had no doubt that they would open Makkah, as shown in the dream that the Prophet ﷺ had received. But when they saw what the Prophet ﷺ had to endure during the negotiations, many of them felt that this was a humiliation to the Prophet ﷺ and to Islam. The Abu Jandal scene compounded the negativity that they were feeling.

Omar Ibn-ul-Khattab jumped with fury and walked beside Abu Jandal telling him to be patient. Omar even went so close to him hoping that Abu Jandal would snatch his sword and kill his oppressors and flea. Then he came to the Prophet ﷺ ,exploding with anger, and said: "Aren't you indeed the Prophet of Allah?"

The Prophet ﷺ said: "I sure am."

Omar asked: "Aren't we right and they are wrong?" The Prophet said: "Yes we are."

Omar said: "Then why should we give the lowly a say in our religion?"

The Prophet ﷺ said: "I am the servant and Messenger of Allah; and I am not going to disobey Him and He will grant me victory."

Omar said: "Didn't you tell us that we will perform tawaf around the Sacred House?" He said: "Yes, but did I say this year?"

Omar said: "No." He said: "Then you will come and perform tawaf."

After that conversation Omar went to Abu Bakr and said: "Oh Abu Bakr! Isn't he the Messenger of Allah? "Abu Bakr said:" Certainly."

Abu Bakr advised him to stick with the Prophet no matter what.

Omar later used to say: "Since that day, I have been giving charity, fasting, praying and freeing slaves for fear of what I uttered that day."

The Wisdom of Ummu Salamah

When he finished signing the treaty, the Prophet ﷺ asked the Sahabah to slaughter their sacrifice and shave their heads. This was the ritual signifying the completion of their Umrah. No one moved. He repeated his request three times, but most of the Muslims didn't obey. The Prophet ﷺ entered the tent of his wife Ummu Salamah and complained to her. It was the custom of Rasoolullah to accompany his wives in turns whenever he left Madinah, and this was the turn of Ummu Salamah. So, the Prophet ﷺ related to her what happened between him and his companions. She asked: "Oh Prophet of Allah! Do you want them to listen to you?" "Yes," he replied. "Then, go out and don't speak to any one until you slaughter and get shaved yourself."

He got out and did exactly that. When they witnessed him ﷺ doing so they got up and slaughtered and fought each other to get shaved first.

This incident demonstrates how Rasoolullah ﷺ would consult with and value the opinions of his wives. Additionally, it shows that leaders should take the initiative of acting and doing the right thing, and then their followers are more likely follow through.

The Revelation of Surat-ul-Fateh

Half way between Makkah and Madinah, God revealed to Muhammad ﷺ Surat-ul-Fateh, or the Victory (48). Prophet Muhammad ﷺ was extremely happy, for God told him clearly in this surah that the Treaty of Al-Hudaybiyah was a victory. Furthermore, he was promised a series of victories in the future. He also received Allah's approval of everything he had done. These ayaat brought peace to the hearts of the Muslims.

Translation

1. Surely We have given to you a clear victory

2. That Allah may forgive your community their past faults and those to follow and complete His favor to you and keep you on a right way,

3. And that Allah might help you with a mighty help.

4. He it is Who sent down tranquility into the hearts of the believers that they might have more of faith added to their faith-- and Allah's are the hosts of the Heavens and the Earth, and Allah is Knowing, Wise--

5. That He may cause the believing men and the believing women to enter gardens beneath which rivers flow to abide therein and remove from them their evil; and that is a grand achievement with Allah.

Benefits of the Treaty

Although some Muslims at the time thought that the treaty included unfavorable clauses, it was a great victory for Muslims, as Allah mentioned in Surat-ul-Fateh. There follows a list of some of the benefits of the Treaty of Al-Hudaybiyah:

1. Spreading Islam in Arabia.

Allah and his Prophet ﷺ wanted the opportunity to communicate with the Arabian tribes and to introduce Islam to them. The treaty allowed this to happen. During the two years following the signing of the treaty, more people embraced Islam than ever before.

2. Saving the Lives of the Quraysh People.

Allah and His Prophet ﷺ didn't want to lose any additional life from among the non-Muslims of the Quraysh. Allah wanted to guide the hearts of the Makkans to Islam peacefully. Muhammad ﷺ was sent as a mercy to mankind, and that is why he showed patience and agreed to some unfair terms in the contract. He did this hoping that Quraysh would accept Islam without bloodshed during the period of the truce.

3. Protecting Muslim Lives in Makkah.

Not all Makkans were idol worshippers. There were already many Muslim men and women in Makkah who were hiding their faith. Had armed conflict taken place in Makkah and the Muslims had been successful in opening the city by force, some Makkan Muslims would likely have been killed or hurt by the fighting. The Treaty of Al-Hudaybiyah prevented that from happening.

4. Recognizing the Power of Islam in Arabia.

The treaty was a landmark in that, for the first time, the Quraysh recognized the Muslims as a legitimate and major power in Arabia. They conceded in writing that Islam was an equal power to them.

The only thing Muslims lost was the opportunity to perform their Umrah and see their friends and families in Makkah. The Prophet ﷺ made sure not to commit to any long term loss. For example, he did not relinquish his and the Muslims' right to return and settle in Makkah if they ever wished to do so. He didn't accept that worshipping idols would continue forever in his home city of Makkah. He was confident in his knowledge that sooner or later, Islam would prevail among his people in Makkah.

CHAPTER REVIEW

Projects and Activities

1. Write a "Who's Who" journal about 10 personalities who played roles in the events of Sulh-ul-Hudaybiyah.

2. Write a play that portrays the events of the Hudaybiyah Treaty.

Stretch Your Mind

1. Why do you think Allah called the Treaty of Al-Hudaybiyah a "victory?"
2. Why didn't Omar Ibn-ul-Khattab and many other companions think favorably about the treaty in the beginning?
3. What did the Prophet ﷺ do based on Ummu Salamah's advice, and what was the reaction of his companions? What lesson may we learn from that story?

Study Questions

1. What were the main terms of the Treaty of Al-Hudaybiyah?
2. Who were the people that signed the treaty on behalf of the Muslims and the Quraysh?
3. What were the things that the Quraysh's representatives objected to while writing the document of the treaty? How did the Prophet ﷺ resolve the disagreement?
4. Which of the treaty terms caused some problems in the minds of the sahabah?
5. Who was Abu Jandal and what did he do during the time of signing the treaty?
6. Why didn't the Prophet help Abu Jandal? What lesson do you learn from that?
7. What did Omar رضي الله عنه say to Abu Bakr رضي الله عنه, and what was his answer?
8. Which tribes made alliances with the Muslims and with the Quraysh?
9. What were the benefits of Sulh-ul-Hudaybiyah?
10. Which surah was revealed after the Treaty of Al-Hudaybiyah?

Ummu Salamah: A Role Model in Patience and Wisdom

CHAPTER OUTLINE

1. Who was Ummu Salamah?
2. Ummu Salamah embraces Islam
3. The Hijrah to Abyssinia
4. Ummu Salamah's heartbreaking story of her Hijrah to Madinah
5. The death of Abu Salamah
6. Ummu Salamah marries Rasoolullah

Who was Ummu Salamah?

Her real name was Hind Bint Abi Umayyah Al-Makhzoomy. Her father was known for his generosity and kind heart. Her mother was 'Aatikah Bint Abdul-Muttalib, and she was a cousin of Prophet Muhammad ﷺ Ummu Salamah's husband was Abdullah ibn Abdulasad, who is known by his nick-name, Abu Salamah – father of Salamah, their son.

Becoming a Muslim

Both Abu Salamah and Ummu Salamah were among the first persons to accept Islam. As soon as the news of their becoming Muslims spread, the Quraysh reacted with frenzied anger. They began hounding and persecuting Ummu Salamah and her husband, but the couple did not waver and remained steadfast in their new faith.

The Migration to Abyssinia

Life in Makkah became unbearable for many of the new Muslims. The Prophet ﷺ recognized the oppression that they were enduring and gave permission for them to emigrate to Abyssinia. For Ummu Salamah, it meant abandoning her spacious home and giving up the traditional ties of lineage and honor for something new, hoping for the pleasure and reward of Allah.

Ummu Salamah and her companions received great hospitality and protection from the Abyssinian ruler, King Negus. However, their desire to return to Makkah, to be near their beloved Prophet ﷺ, and the source of revelation and guidance, persisted.

News eventually reached that the number of Muslims in Makkah had increased. Among them were Hamzah ibn Abdulmuttalib and Omar ibn-ul-Khattab. Their faith had greatly strengthened the community and they heard that the Quraysh had eased the persecution somewhat. Thus a group of the immigrants, including Abu Salamah and Ummu Salamah, decided to return to Makkah.

Heartbreaking Story

However, contrary to what they had hoped for, the situation had not really improved in Makkah. There was still a great deal of oppression towards the Muslims. Therefore, the Prophet ﷺ gave permission to his companions to emigrate to Madinah. Ummu Salamah and her husband were among the first to leave.

Let us allow Ummu Salamah to tell us her story of immigration:

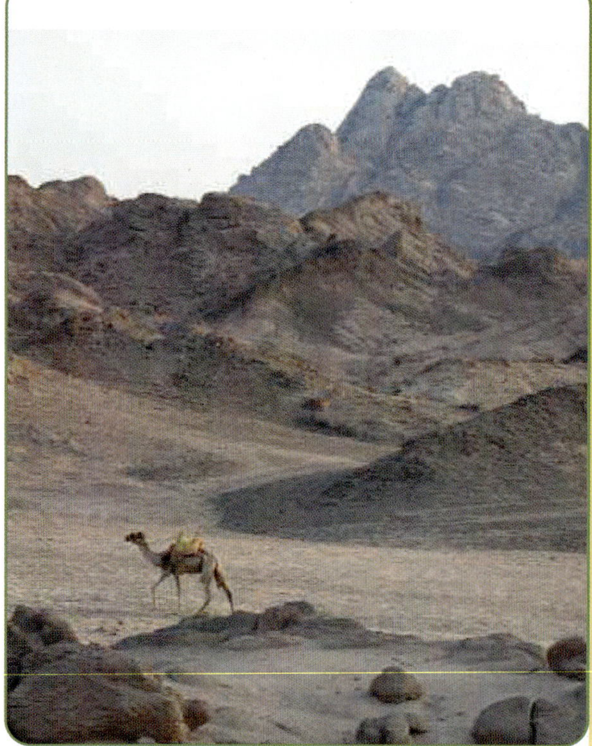

"When Abu Salamah (my husband) decided to leave for Madinah, he prepared a camel for me, hoisted me on it and placed our son Salamah on my lap. My husband then took the lead and went on without stopping or waiting for anything. Before we were out of Makkah, however, some men from my clan stopped us and said to my husband:

"Though you are free to do what you like with yourself, you have no power over your wife. She is our daughter. Do you expect us to allow you to take her away from us?"

They then pounced on him and snatched me away from him. My husband's clan, Banu Abdulasad, saw them taking both me and my child. They became hot with rage.

"No! By Allah," they shouted, "we shall not abandon the boy. He is our son and we have a first claim over him."

They took him by the hand and pulled him away from me. Suddenly in the space of a few moments, I found myself alone and lonely. My husband headed for Madinah by himself and his clan had snatched my son away from me. My own clan, Banu Makhzoom, overpowered me and forced me to stay with them.

From the day when my husband and my son were separated from me, I went out at noon every day to that valley and sat at the spot where this tragedy occurred. I would recall those terrible moments and weep until night fell on me.

I continued like this for a year or so until one day, a man from the Banu Umayyah passed by and saw my condition. He went back to my clan and said:

"Why don't you free this poor woman? You have caused her husband and her son to be taken away from her."

He went on trying to soften their hearts and play on their emotions. At last they said to me, "Go and join your husband if you wish."

But how could I join my husband in

Madinah and leave my son, a piece of my own flesh and blood, in Makkah among the Banu Abdulasad? How could I be free from anguish and my eyes be free from tears, were I to reach the place of Hijrah, not knowing anything of my little son left behind in Makkah?

Some realized what I was going through and their hearts went out to me. They petitioned the Banu Abdulasad on my behalf and moved them to return my son.

I did not want to linger in Makkah until I found someone to travel with me. I was afraid something might happen that would delay or prevent me from reaching my husband. So I promptly got my camel ready, placed my son on my lap and left in the direction of Madinah.

I had just about reached Tan'eem (about three miles from Makkah) when I met Uthman ibn Talhah. (He was a keeper of the Ka'bah in pre-Islamic times and was not yet a Muslim.)

"Where are you going, Bint Zad ar-Rakib?" he asked.

"I am going to my husband in Madinah."

"And there isn't anyone with you?"

"No, by Allah. Except Allah and my little boy here."

"By Allah, I shall never abandon you until you reach Madinah," he vowed.

He then took the reins of my camel and led us on. I have, by Allah, never met an Arab more generous and noble than he. When we reached a resting place, he would make my camel kneel down, wait until I dismounted, lead the camel to a tree and tether it. He would then go to the shade of another tree. When we had rested, he would get the camel ready and lead us on.

This he did every day until we reached Madinah. When we got to a village near Quba (about two miles from Madinah), he said, "Your husband is in this village. Enter it with the blessings of God." He turned back and headed for Makkah".

Du'aa'

"حَسْبِيَ اللهُ وَنِعْمَ الوَكِيل"

Whenever you are in trouble say:

"Allah is enough for me. He is the best to rely on."

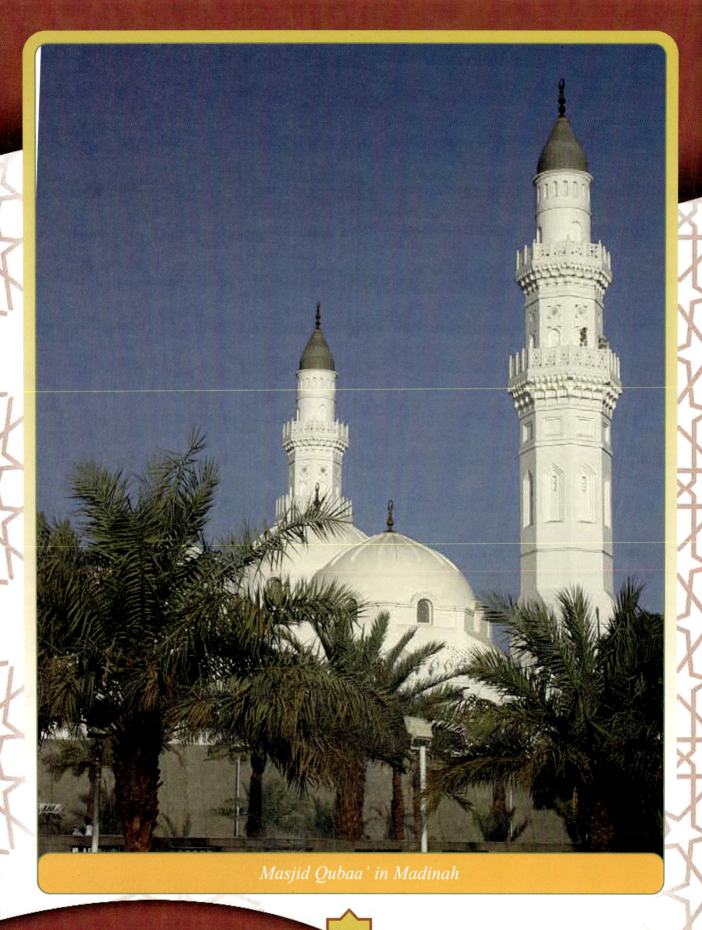

Masjid Qubaa' in Madinah

The New Life in Madinah

Their roads finally met after the long separation. Ummu Salamah was overjoyed to see her husband, and he was delighted to see his wife and son.

Great and momentous events followed, one after the other. There was the Battle of Badr, in which Abu Salamah fought. The Muslims returned victorious and strengthened. Then there was the Battle of Uhud, in which the Muslims were sorely tested. Abu Salamah came out of this wounded very badly. He appeared at first to respond well to treatment, but his wounds never healed completely and he remained bedridden.

Abu Salamah Passes Away

Once while Ummu Salamah was nursing her husband, he said to her:

"I heard the Messenger of God saying, 'Whenever a calamity hits anyone, he should say,

إنا لله وإنا إليهِ راجِعون ، اللهُمَّ أجِرْني في مصيبتي
وأخْلِفْ لي خيراً منْها

'Surely from Allah we are, and to Him we shall certainly return.' And he would pray, 'Oh Allah, reward me for my plight and give me in return something better than what I lost."

Abu Salamah remained sick in bed for several days. One morning the Prophet ﷺ came to see him. The visit was longer than usual. While the Prophet ﷺ was still at his bedside, Abu Salamah passed away. With his blessed hands, the Prophet ﷺ closed the eyes of his dead companion. He then raised these hands to the Heavens and prayed:

"O Lord, grant forgiveness to Abu Salamah. Elevate him among those who are near to You. Take charge of his family at all times. Forgive us and him, O Lord of the Worlds. Widen his grave and make it light for him."

Ummu Salamah remembered the prayer her husband had quoted on his deathbed from the Prophet and began repeating it, "O Lord, reward me for my plight . . ." But she could not bring herself to continue . . . "O Lord give me something better than what I lost," because she kept asking herself, "Who could be better than Abu Salamah?" But it did not take long before she completed the supplication.

The New Umm-ul-Mu'mineen

Both the Muhajiroon and Ansar felt they had a duty to Ummu Salamah. When she had completed the iddah (four months and ten days after the passing of the husband), Abu Bakr proposed marriage to her, but she declined. Then Omar asked to marry her, but she also declined his proposal. The Prophet ﷺ then approached her, and she agreed:

"O Messenger of Allah, I have three

characteristics. I am a woman who is extremely jealous, and I am afraid that you will see in me something that will anger you and cause Allah to punish me. I am a woman who is already advanced in age and I am a woman who has a young family."

The Prophet ﷺ replied:

"Regarding the jealousy you mentioned, I pray to Allah, the Almighty, to let it go away from you. Regarding the question of age you have mentioned, I am afflicted with the same problem as you. Regarding the dependent family you have mentioned, your family is my family."

They were married, and so it was that Allah answered the prayer of Ummu Salamah and gave her better than Abu Salamah. From that day on, Hind al Makhzumiyah was no longer the mother of Salamah alone, but became the Mother of all Believers; "Ummu al-Mu'mineen."

This story is full of lessons, but one that stands out is that it shows the great sacrifices the early Muslims like 'Ummu Salamah made for Islam. Although these sacrifices were heavy and painful at the time, they would bring them great success, blessings, the pleasure of Allah, a sense of achievement and, eventually, a high level in Jannah inshaAllah.

Source: "Companions of the Prophet", Vol. 1, By: Abdul Wahid Hamid. A few modifications applied.

FAITH IN ACTION

- Always remain steadfast in your faith no matter what difficulties you may face.
- Always trust that Allah will help you out when you face tragedies, sooner or later.
- Whenever you are tested with a tragedy or difficulty say the du'aa':

إنا لله وإنا إليهِ راجِعون ، اللهُمَّ أجِرْني في مصِيبَتي وأخْلِفْ لي خيراً منْها

"Surely from Allah we are and to Him we shall certainly return. Oh Allah, reward me for my plight and give me in return something better than what I lost."

CHAPTER REVIEW

Projects and Activities

1. Write an essay about facing tragedies. Use the story of Ummu Salamah to give your essay a human dimension.
2. Create a poster for the du'aa' to say when a calamity hits. Artistically display the du'aa' in Arabic and English.
3. 'Uthman Ibn Talhah, who helped Ummu Salamah reunite with her husband in Madinah, was not a Muslim. Research his story and figure out what happened to him afterward.

Stretch Your Mind

1. What makes the pagans of Makkah treat Ummu Salamah in that harsh way? Relate that to what happens to Muslims in some prejudiced communities around the world.

2. If you are to choose one word as a title for the story of Ummu Salamah, what would that word be?

Study Questions

1. What was the real name of Ummu Salamah? And who was her mother?
2. Who was Ummu Salamah's husband? Indicate his real name.
3. Where was the first trip of Ummu Salamah to? Why did she travel?
4. What lessons can one learn from the story of Ummu Salamah's hijrah to Madinah?
5. Describe the efforts Abu Salamah did for Islam in Madinah.
6. What was the du'aa' Ummu Salamah learned when her husband was about to die?
7. What did Ummu Salamah say to the Prophet ﷺ when he wanted to marry her? And what was his response?

Ja'far and the King of Abyssinia

CHAPTER OUTLINE

1. Who was Ja'far Ibn Abi Talib?
2. How did he embrace Islam?
3. Where did he migrate to from Makkah?
4. What did Ja'far say to the King of Abyssinia?
5. What were the King's questions to Jafar?
6. What did the King do to Muslims in Abyssinia?
7. What religion did the King choose before he died?

VOCABULARY

Al-Habashah الحَبَشة

Negus 

Early Childhood in Makkah

Abu Talib, uncle of the Prophet ﷺ, was a noble figure in Makkah, but poor. Before becoming a prophet, Muhammad ﷺ said to his other uncle, Al-Abbas:

"Your brother, Abu Talib, has a large family. Let us go to Abu Talib and take over responsibility for some of his children. I will take one of his sons and you can take another and we will look after them."

"What you suggest is certainly good," replied Al-Abbas.

Together they went to Abu Talib and said to him: "We want to ease some of your financial burden until things become better for you."

Abu Talib agreed, but said, "Keep Aqeel with me, then you may do whatever you like." So, Prophet Muhammad ﷺ took Ali into his household and Al-Abbas took Ja'far into his.

Did You Know?

There were five men from the Hashim clan who looked so like the Prophet ﷺ that they were often mistaken for him ﷺ. Ja'far was one of them. The others were Abu Sufyan ibn al-Harith and Qutham ibn Al-Abbas, both of whom were cousins of the Prophet ﷺ, As-Saib ibn Ubayd, who was the grandfather of the great Imam Ash Shafi'ee, and Al-Hasan ibn Ali, the grandson of the Prophet, who resembled him most of all.

Ja'far Embraces Islam

Ja'far lived with his uncle, Al-Abbas, until he married as a young man. His wife was Asmaa' bint Omays, a sister of Maymounah, who later became a wife of the Prophet ﷺ. Ja'far and Asmaa' were among the first people to accept, Islam and they did so under the guidance of Abu Bakr as-Siddeeq رضي الله عنه.

The Immigration to Abyssinia

The Quraysh made life intolerable for Ja'far, Asmaa' and other Muslims in Makkah. They tried to obstruct them from observing their acts of worship and other duties. So Ja'far sought the

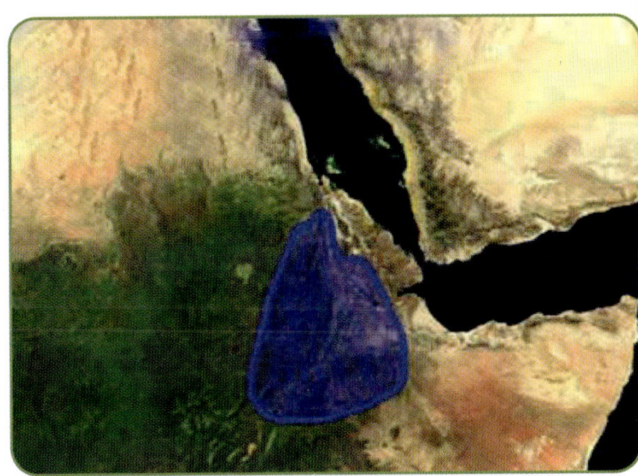

▲ *Skyview of Ethiopia location*

Prophet's ﷺ permission to make hijrah to the land of Abyssinia, now present day Ethiopia. With great sadness, the Prophet granted his permission for them and a group of Sahabah to make hijrah. It pained him that these pure

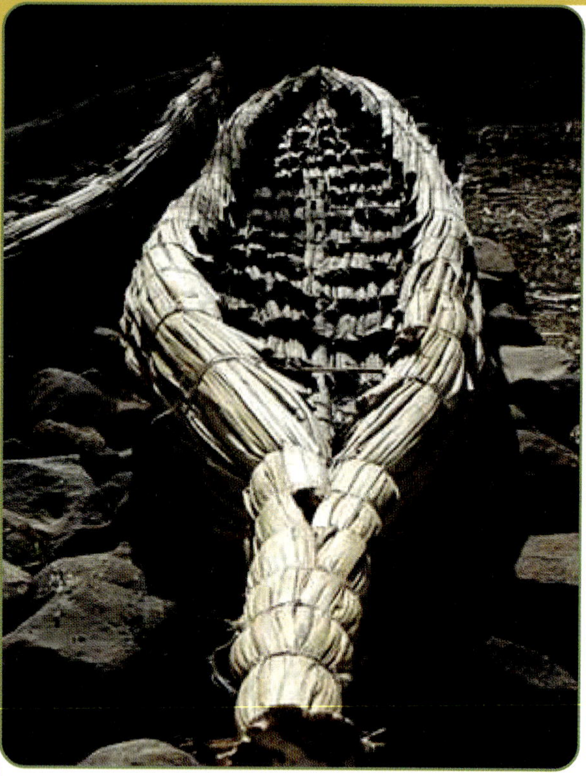

A boat from Ethiopia.

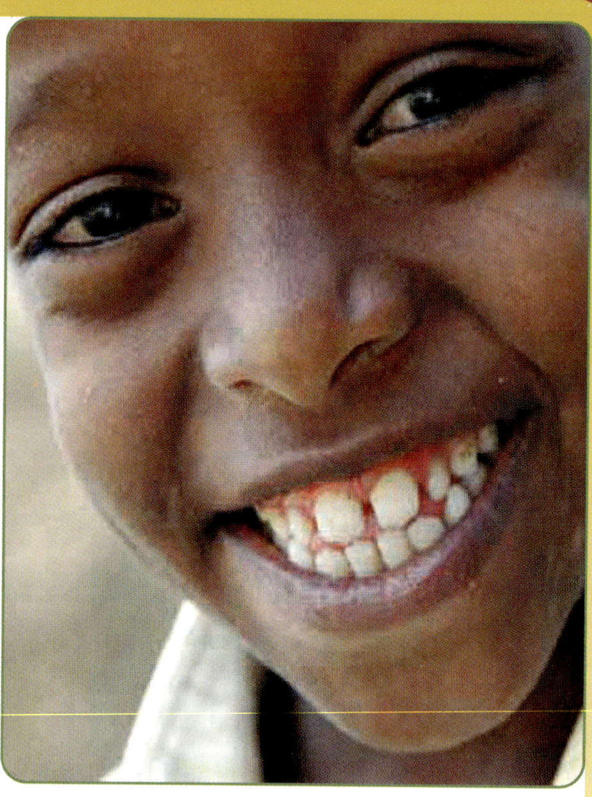

An Ethiopian boy.

and righteous people should be forced to leave their homes and families and abandon their cherished scenes and memories of their childhood, not for any crime, but simply because they said, "Our Lord is One. Allah is our Lord." Muhammad is the messenger.

The group of Muhajireen, led by Ja'far ibn Abi Talib, left Makkah bound for the land of Abyssinia, looking forward to enjoying freedom of religion there. Soon they settled down in this new land under the care and protection of Negus, the King of Abyssinia. Negus was a just and righteous ruler, just as Prophet Muhammad ﷺ described him. Now Abyssinya became the first land outside Arabia to experience Islam.

Fast Facts

Abyssinia is the old name for the East African horn that includes the present countries of Ethiopia, Somalia, Eritrea and parts of Sudan. The Arabic name of Abyssinia is Al-Habashah الحَبَشَة .

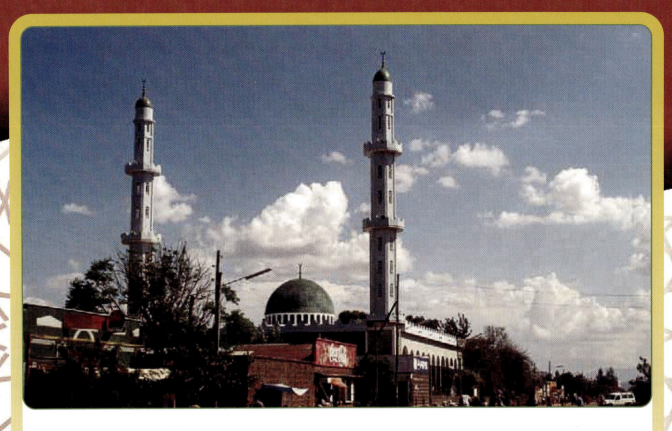

A mosque in Ethiopia

The Quraysh Chase Muslim Immigrants to Abyssinia

The Quraysh promptly found out about the Muslims' migration to Abyssinia and the situation became a popular topic of discussion among the people of Makkah. The leaders of the Quraysh planned to drag the Muslim defectors back to Makkah using two of their most formidable men to, Amr ibn al-Aas and Abdullah ibn Abi Rabiah. They dispatched them on their mission with valuable and highly sought after presents for Negus and his bishops, in order to buy their favor.

On their arrival in Abyssinia, the two Quraysh emissaries first presented their gifts to the bishops, and to each of them they said: "There are some wicked young people in the king's land. They have attacked our religion and caused disunity among our people. When we speak to the king about them, advise him to surrender them to us." The bishops agreed.

Amr and Abdullah then went to the Negus himself and presented him with gifts which he greatly admired. They said to him:

"O King, there is a group of evil persons from among our youth who have escaped to your kingdom as defectors. They practice a religion which neither

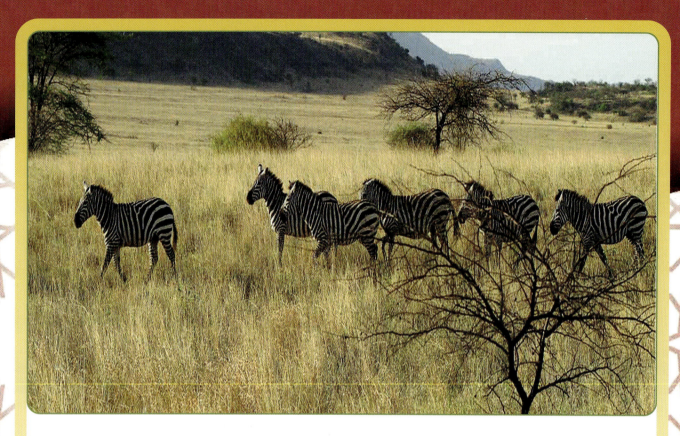

▲ *Scenery from Ethiopia*

we nor you know. They have left their fathers' religion and have not entered into your religion. Our respected leaders, who are their own parents and uncles, have sent us to you to request you to return them. They know best what trouble they have caused."

Negus looked towards his bishops, who said: "They speak the truth, Our Lord. Their own people know them better. Send them back."

The Negus wisely said: "No. By God, I won't surrender them to anyone until I myself hear their side of the story. If what these two men have said is true, then I will hand them over to you. If however it is not so, then I shall protect them so long as they desire to remain under my protection."

Amr and Abdullah became very worried. They were afraid that the king would be influenced by the Muslims' account of their story. They tried to prevent the king from hearing the Muslim version of events, but none could change the king's decree.

Fast Facts

The king's title in Abyssinia was Negus. The Arabic word for Negus is An-Najashi النَجاشي .

Da'wah, in the Royal Court of Abyssinia

Negus then summoned the Muslims to meet him, so that they could put forward their case. They knew that this was probably their only chance to maintain their asylum in Abyssinia. So before the meeting, they consulted with one another within the group and together they came up with a good plan. They agreed that Ja'far ibn Abi Talib should be their spokesperson, so he prepared a beautiful and sincere address to the king and his advisors.

In the court of Negus, the bishops, and the Qurayshite emissaries were seated when the Muslims entered and took their seats. Negus turned to them and asked:

"What is this religion you follow which divided you from the religion of your people? You also did not enter my religion nor the religion of any other community that we know of."

Ja'far ibn Abi Talib then approached and made a speech that was moving and eloquent and which is still one of the most compelling descriptions of Islam. He said:

"Oh king, we were a people in a state of ignorance and immorality. We were worshipping idols and eating the flesh of dead animals. We were committing all sorts of sins and shameful deeds. We were also breaking the ties of kinship, treating guests badly, and the strong among us oppressed the weak.

We remained in this state until Allah sent from among us a prophet. His lineage, truthfulness, trustworthiness and integrity were well-known to us. He called us to worship God alone and to renounce the idols which we and our ancestors used to worship besides Allah.

He commanded us to speak the truth, to honor our promises, to be kind to our relatives and to be helpful to our neighbors. He ordered us to avoid all forbidden acts. He prevented us from bloodshed, obscenities, lying and false witness, stealing orphan's property and slandering chaste women.

He ordered us to worship Allah alone and not to worship anything with Him. He ordered us to pray, to give charity and fast in the month of Ramadan.

We believed in him and what he brought to us from Allah. We follow him in what he has asked us to do and we keep away from what he forbade us from doing.

Thereupon, oh king, our people attacked and tortured us. They put the harshest punishment on us to make us renounce our religion and take us back to immorality and the worship of idols.

They oppressed us, made life intolerable for us and obstructed us from observing our religion. So we left for your country, choosing you over anyone else, desiring your protection and hoping to live in justice and in peace in your midst."

The Negus was impressed and was eager to hear more. He asked Ja'far: "Do you have with you something of what your Prophet brought from God?"

"Yes," replied Ja'far.

"Then read it to me," requested Negus. Ja'far, in his rich, beautiful voice recited for him the first portion of Surat Maryam, which deals with the story of Jesus and his mother Mary.

The King's Soft Heart

Upon hearing the Qur'an, Negus and his bishops were moved to tears. The king then said to the Muslims: "The message of your Prophet and that of Jesus came from the same light..." To Amr and his companion, he said: "Go, I will never surrender them to you." That, however, was not the end of the matter. The wily Amr said to his companion, "I will go to the king tomorrow. I will mention something which will certainly destroy them." The next day, Amr went to Negus and said:

"O King, these people say something terrible about Jesus the son of Mary, that he is a slave. Send for them and ask them what they say about him."

The king summoned the Muslims once more and Ja'far spoke on their behalf once more. Negus put the question: "What do you say about Jesus, the son of Mary?"

"We only say what has been revealed to our Prophet," replied Ja'far.

"And what is that?" enquired the Negus.

"Our Prophet says that Jesus is the servant of God and His Prophet. He is God's spirit and His word which He cast into Mary the Virgin."

Negus was obviously excited by this reply of Ja'far and exclaimed: *"By God,*

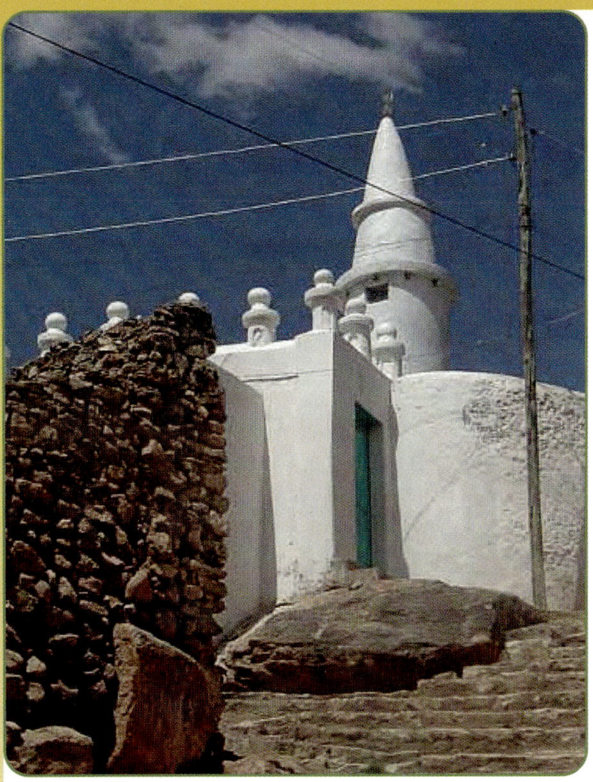

A mosque in Harar, Ethiopia

Jesus the son of Mary was exactly as your Prophet has described him."

The bishops around Negus grunted in disgust at what they had heard and were reprimanded by Negus. He turned to the Muslims and said:

"Go, you are safe and secure in my land. Whoever hurts you will be punished. Whoever hurts you will be punished. Whoever hurts you will be punished. I don't like to gain a mountain of gold for hurting a single one of you."

Quraysh's Mission to Abyssinia Fails

The king then instructed his bishops: *"Return their gifts to these two men. I have no need of them."*

Amr and his companion left broken and frustrated.

The Muslims stayed in the land of Negus, who proved to be most generous and kind to his guests.

Muslims Live Safely in Abyssinia

Ja'far and his wife Asmaa' spent about ten years in Abyssinia, which became a second home for them. There, Asmaa' gave birth to three children whom they named Abdullah, Muhammad and Awn. Their second child was possibly the first child in the history of Islam to be given the name Muhammad, after the Prophet ﷺ.

Ja'far Returns to Arabia

In the seventh year of the Hijrah, Ja'far and his family left Abyssinia with a group of Muslims and headed for Madinah. When they arrived the Prophet ﷺ was just returning from the successful conquest of Khaybar. He was so overjoyed at meeting Ja'far that he said: "I do not know what fills me with more happiness, the conquest of Khaybar or the coming of Ja'far."

Father of the Poor

Muslims, in general, and the poor among them, especially, were just as happy with the return of Ja'far as the Prophet ﷺ was. Ja'far quickly became known as a person who was much concerned for the welfare of the poor and needy. For this, he was nicknamed, the "Father of the Poor." Abu Hurayrah said of him: "The best of men towards us needy folk was Ja'far ibn Abi Talib. He would pass by us on his way home and give us whatever food he had. Even if his own food had run out, he would send us a pot in which he had placed some butterfat and nothing more. We would open it and lick it clean..."

King of Abyssinia Embraces Islam

Prophet Muhammad ﷺ told the Muslims later that King Negus had embraced Islam. When he died, the Prophet ﷺ and the Muslims in Madinah made Salat-ul-Janazah, the funeral prayer, in his absence.

From that point in history onwards, Islam started to find acceptance in Ethiopia and the continent of Africa. Nearly half of the population of Ethiopia profess Islam as their faith, as is the case with Africa as a whole.

Projects and Activities

1. Write a profile about Asmaa' Bint Omays, the wife of Ja'far.

2. Imagine that you are invited to a church to talk for ten minutes about Islam. Prepare a short speech for that occasion and present it to your class or family.

3. Read about Islam in Ethiopia now and write a 700 word essay about it.

Stretch Your Mind

1. The address Ja'far made to the king was described by historians as one of the most eloquent speeches about Islam. Point out three aspects of the speech which make it special and effective.

2. Ja'far, his family and other Muslims stayed for many years in Abyssinia. Why do you think they did not move to Madinah right after the Hijrah of the Prophet ﷺ and the Muhajireen?

Study Questions

1. Who were Ja'far's father, uncle, brothers and cousin according to the story?
2. Who was the person who encouraged Ja'far to embrace Islam?
3. Why did Ja'far migrate from Makkah to Abyssinia?
4. What did the Quraysh do when they learned about the migration of Muslims to Abyssinia? Who executed their plan?
5. What was the strategy of the Quraysh's delegation to get the Muslims back to Makkah?
6. Who was the King of Abyssinia? Was he fair? Why or why not?
7. List ten points that describe Prophet Muhammad ﷺ and his message which Ja'far mentioned in his speech.
8. What was Amr's trick to cause the king to change his positive opinion of the Muslims?
9. What was the most important point that caught the attention of the king? And how did Ja'far handle the king's question?
10. When did Ja'far return to Prophet Muhammad ﷺ in Madinah?
11. What was Ja'far famous for in Madinah?
12. What was the king's religion when he died? And what did Rasoolullah ﷺ do after his death?

A Threat From The North: The Battle Of Mu'tah

CHAPTER OUTLINE

1. What nations and tribes used to live to the north of Arabia?
2. Where is Mu'tah?
3. What were the events that led to the Battle of Mu'tah?
4. Who where the commanders of the Muslim army?
5. How did the battle come about?
6. Which commander became well-known after this battle?
7. What lessons do we learn from the events of this battle?

VOCABULARY

- Shaheed شهيد
- Shuhadaa' شُـــهداء
- Ash- Shahadah الشَـــهادة
- An-Nasr النـصْر

PLACES TO REMMEMBER

- Mu'tah مؤتة

PEOPLE TO REMMEMBER

- Zaid Ibn Harithah زيد بن حارثة
- Ja'far Ibn Abi Talib جعفر بن أبي طالِب
- Abdullah ibn Rawahah عبد الله بن رواحة
- Khalid Ibn-ul-Waleed خالِد بن الوليد
- Saifullah سَيْفُ الله
- Asmaa' Bint Omays أسماء بنت عُميَس

Hostile Enemies to the North

The Quraysh was not the only tribe which was hostile towards Muslims in Arabia. Some tribes in the north of Arabia were also enemies of Islam and Muslims. Also, the Romans in Syria and Palestine were considering waging war against the Muslims.

In the month of Jumada Al-Oula of the eighth year after Hijrah, just three months after the Prophet ﷺ had returned from his Umrah to Makkah, the Prophet ﷺ sent fifteen men as peaceful messengers of Islam to one of the tribes at the border with Syria. The Muslims' friendly greetings were met by aggression.

Another set back occurred when the Prophet had sent Dihyah Al-Kalbi to the governor of Bosra, in Syria, with his letter to Caesar, the ruler of the Roman Empire. The letter had remained unanswered so a second messenger was sent to Bosra again. Before the message reached Bosra, a chief of the Ghassanid tribe captured the messenger and put him to death. Arabs and the people of the surrounding nations always used to exercise respect towards message carriers, even if they were dispatched from a nation they happened to be at war with at the time. So the act of killing a Muslim messenger was extreme and unconventional and could not go unpunished. However, there was a risk of retaliation because the Ghassanids were close allies of Caesar.

▲ *Bosra, an ancient city in Syria.*

The Muslim Army Heads North

The Prophet ﷺ decided to raise an army of three thousand men and appointed Zaid Ibn Harithah their commander. Rasoolullah ﷺ instructed that if Zaid should be killed, Ja'far Ibn Abi Talib should take his place. The Prophet ﷺ also named Abdullah ibn Rawahah as the third commander if Ja'far were to be killed. If the three men were all to die, then the men in the army would be at liberty to choose their own commander.

The Muslim army proceeded to march to battle and when they reached Ma'an, a city in the south of present day Jordan, they heard disturbing news. They learned that the northern tribes were very strong and had gathered one hundred thousand fighters. Also, the

Roman army had joined them with an additional one hundred thousand soldiers. Thus the enemy soldiers were two hundred thousand men strong.

Zaid ibn Harithah, the leader of the small Muslim army, decided to stop and hold a war council. Most of the men wanted to send the Prophet ﷺ a message of what they heard about the enemy's huge army. The Prophet ﷺ would either order the men to return home or provide them with more men and weapons. Abdullah Ibn Rawahah rose up and reminded the war council that what they were about to do is jihad, or struggle (in this case a military struggle), for the sake of God. He also said: "We have before us one of the two good things; either An-Nasr النَّصْر (victory) or Ash- Shahadah الشَّهادَة (martyrdom). Then we will join our brothers who were martyrs before us and be their companions in the gardens of Paradise."

The Muslim army was moved by the message of Abdullah Ibn Rawahah's statement, so they continued marching on towards the enemy. As they came towards the Dead Sea, they could see the enemy army. The Muslims could see that they were greatly outnumbered by a huge army of a size which they had never before been confronted.

During the Battle of Badr in the second year after Hijrah, the Muslims were three hundred and fourteen, while Quraysh's army was about one thousand fighters. In the Battle of Uhud in third year after Hijrah, Muslims were

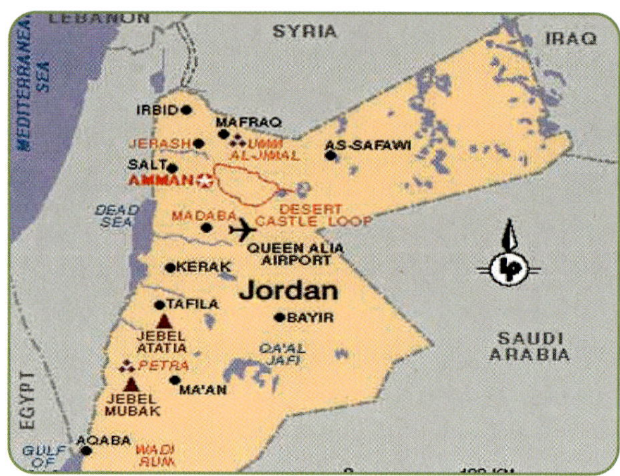

Jordan map locating Ma'an and Mu'tah

around one thousand while the enemies were about two thousand. The largest army ever to attack Muslims was eight thousand strong at the Battle of the Trench. Now the enemy's army was a massive two hundred thousand fighters.

The two Armies Meet in Mu'tah

When Zaid Ibn Harithah saw the many enemy soldiers, he gave orders for the Muslims to withdraw to Mu'tah, a village south of Jordan. Here they organized themselves and prepared for the battle. The enemy army followed the Muslim army towards Mu'tah and shortly after, as they were getting closer, Zaid gave the order to attack. Zaid, with the battle standard in his hand, led his men into combat. He fought the enemy courageously and fiercely and was wounded many times until he fell as a great shaheed شهيد , or martyr.

Muslim Commanders are Martyred

When Zaid was martyred, Ja'far ibn abi Talib became the commander of the army. He mounted his horse, spurred it on, then called out:

"How wonderful is Paradise as it draws near! How pleasant and cool is its drink! Punishment for the Byzantines is not far away!"

Ja'far carried the flag, charged against the enemies, and penetrated deep into the Byzantine ranks. After a tremendous fight, Ja'far lost his right hand so he carried the flag with his left hand, which he later lost as well. He refused to give up and managed to keep the standard raised with what remained of his arms. He nobly fell as another great shaheed. Rasoolullah ﷺ said that Allah gave Ja'far two wings with which he will fly everywhere in Jannah. After the death of Ja'far, Abdullah Ibn Rawahah assumed the leadership of the Muslim army. At first Abdullah hesitated when he saw the waves of the enemy fighters. However, he promptly regained his courage and started to chant,

My soul, I swear you will get in
You will get in, or I'll force you, then
The enemies came to cause our demise
Why then I see you hate the Paradise
****
Oh my soul, if you are not killed here, you will later die
The time of death is now, it just came by
Whatever you wished for is now given to you
You will be on the straight path like the other two*

Tomb of Zaid ibn Harithah رضي الله عنه *in the village of Mu'tah in Jordan*

* *Referring to Zaid and Ja'far*

He then led the army until he was killed as another great martyr. Now, the three main leaders of the Muslim army were martyred. The tombs of the three commanders and other shuhadaa' شُهَداء or martyrs who fell in this battle are now in the township of Mu'tah in Jordan.

The Two Armies Stop the Fight

After the death of Abdullah, the Muslim army chose Khalid ibn-ul-Waleed as their commander. Khalid had great military skills and experience. During the fight, he succeeded in killing many of the enemy fighters and he broke nine swords during combat. He knew that his small Muslim army could not achieve victory in this battle against the huge enemy army, so he decided to withdraw in order to avoid losing many more Muslim warriors.

Khalid, however, realized that he needed to secure a safe and honorable retreat for his small army. During the night he altered the formations of the different brigades. He switched the right wing with the left wing and the front with the rear. This made the Muslim army appear different from the enemy's view. The generals of the enemy army actually thought that the Muslims had received backup overnight. That made the Romans and their Arab allies consider retreating.

The Muslim army was able to withdraw without suffering any greater loss. The Roman army also decided to stop fighting to avoid more casualties. Although the enemy had a great power edge over the Muslims they gained no advantage from it.

In a way the battle was a victory for Khalid because he was able to withdraw the Muslims without suffering too much causality. According to historical accounts, the Muslims had only twelve martyrs whilst the enemy sustained many more casualties than that.

The Prophet ﷺ received the news about the battle as it happened from Allah through Angel Jibreel. He learned about the loss of the three courageous commanders and how Khalid ibn-ul-Waleed led the Muslim army after them. When the Prophet ﷺ told his companions about the battle and the deaths of Zaid, Ja'far and Abdullah he said: "Then one of God's Swords took the standard, and God opened up the way for them." Khalid ibn-ul-Waleed then came to be called " سَيْفُ الله Saifullah" or "the Sword of God."

Condolences to the Martyrs' Families

The Prophet ﷺ went to the house of Ja'far to meet with his wife Asmaa' bint Omays and her children. "Oh Asmaa'," he said, "bring me Ja'far's sons." Asmaa' duly brought her sons to him and the Prophet ﷺ kissed them, and tears began to flow from his eyes. Asmaa' became concerned, "Oh Messenger of God," she said, "you are dearer to me than my father and my mother. What makes you cry? Has news reached you about Ja'far and his companions?" "They were all martyred today," said the Prophet ﷺ. Asmaa' was overcome with sadness and she began crying. When the Prophet returned to his house, he ordered food to be prepared for the family of Ja'far. He also consoled the families of Zaid, Abdullah and other martyrs.

The Prophet ﷺ was so moved by the deaths of the three leaders that tears would flow from his eyes whenever he described the battle.

That same night the Prophet ﷺ had a vision of Paradise. He saw that Zaid, Ja'far, Abdullah, and other martyrs were there. He saw Ja'far flying with wings, like an angel. When he went to the mosque in the morning to offer fajr prayer, he did not feel much sorrow and sadness. His vision showed that the martyrs were all in Paradise.

سورة آل عمران
Surat-ul-Iman 169-171
﴿ وَلَا تَحْسَبَنَّ ٱلَّذِينَ قُتِلُوا۟ فِى سَبِيلِ ٱللَّهِ أَمْوَٰتًۢا ۚ بَلْ أَحْيَآءٌ عِندَ رَبِّهِمْ يُرْزَقُونَ ﴿١٦٩﴾
فَرِحِينَ بِمَآ ءَاتَىٰهُمُ ٱللَّهُ مِن فَضْلِهِۦ وَيَسْتَبْشِرُونَ بِٱلَّذِينَ لَمْ يَلْحَقُوا۟ بِهِم مِّنْ خَلْفِهِمْ أَلَّا
خَوْفٌ عَلَيْهِمْ وَلَا هُمْ يَحْزَنُونَ ﴿١٧٠﴾ يَسْتَبْشِرُونَ بِنِعْمَةٍ مِّنَ ٱللَّهِ وَفَضْلٍ وَأَنَّ ٱللَّهَ لَا
يُضِيعُ أَجْرَ ٱلْمُؤْمِنِينَ ﴿١٧١﴾ ﴾

Translation

[3:169] And do not think of those who were killed in Allah's way as dead; nay, they are alive (and) are provided with sustenance from their Lord;

[3:170] They are happy with what Allah has given them out of His grace and they rejoice for the sake of those who are behind them who have not yet joined them, that they shall have no fear, nor shall they grieve.

[3:171] They rejoice on account of favor from Allah and (His) grace, and that Allah will not waste the reward of the believers.

FAITH IN ACTION

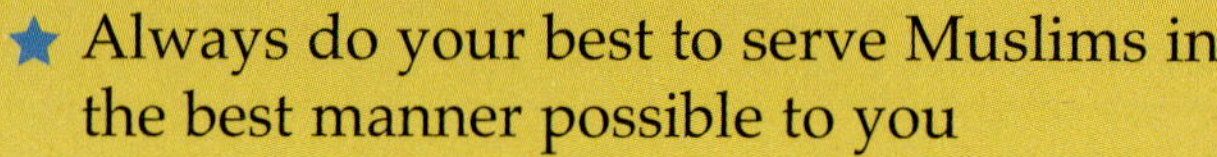

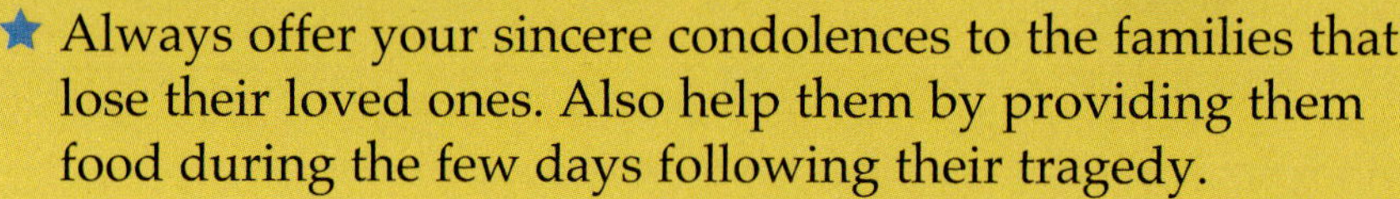

- Always do your best to serve Muslims in the best manner possible to you
- Always offer your sincere condolences to the families that lose their loved ones. Also help them by providing them food during the few days following their tragedy.

hadeeth Shareef

عن أبي هريرة رضي اللهُ عنه قال: قال رسولُ اللهِ صلى اللهُ عليهِ وسلم:

" مَنْ قُتِلَ في سَبيل اللهِ فهو شَهيد ، ومَنْ ماتَ في سَبيل اللهِ فهو شَهيد ..."

رواه مسلم

Abu Hurayrah رضي الله عنه narrated that Rasoolullah ﷺ said:

"Whoever is killed for the sake of Allah is a martyr, and whoever dies for the sake of Allah is a martyr."

Reported in Muslim

CHAPTER REVIEW

Projects and Activities

1. Type a one-page life story of one of the following Sahabah:
   - Zaid Ibn Harithah
   - Asmaa' Bint Omays
   - Abdullah Ibn Rawahah
2. The town of Mu'tah is located in Jordan, one of the Muslim countries. Prepare a country profile on this country that includes pictures of the Islamic landmarks there.

Stretch Your Mind

1. Khalid Ibn-ul-Waleed ordered the withdrawal of the Muslim army from the battle. Was that an act of cowardice or wisdom? Explain your answer?

2. Imagine you were a neighbor of a person who lost his father during jihad against a hostile enemy. How would you console that boy?

Study Questions

1. What caused the Battle of Mu'tah?
2. When did the Battle of Mu'tah happen and where?
3. Who were the enemies of Muslims in Mu'tah?
4. Who were the commanders in this battle?
5. Who was Saifullah? What role did he play in the battle?
6. How did the Muslims end the war?
7. What is martyrdom?

سورة الصف

Surat-us-Saff

This surah was revealed in Madinah and it is 14 verses long. The title of the surah means "The Row." In the past, armies used to arrange themselves in rows prior to fighting. If there was a gap or a weakness in the line, the enemy could smash through and defeat the army. So Allah commanded the Muslims in this surah to fight their hostile enemy together in strong solid rows like a brick wall.

The surah also talks about the mistakes of ancient peoples who disbelieved in their prophets. It confirms that Prophet Isa, or Jesus, told his people about the future coming of Prophet Muhammad.

The lessons of this Surah are not limited to matters of fighting the evil enemies. It stresses the importance of unity and working together. Allah wants every Muslim to be strong and to support other Muslims so that the "Muslim wall" becomes strong. This is symbolic today for all of the projects we do together. We need to spend as much time trying to improve our working relationships with those around us as we spend on trying to improve ourselves individually.

سورة الصف

Surat-us-Saff: Verses (1-4)
Struggling on Allah's Path

UNIT D

CHAPTER SIX

LESSON ONE

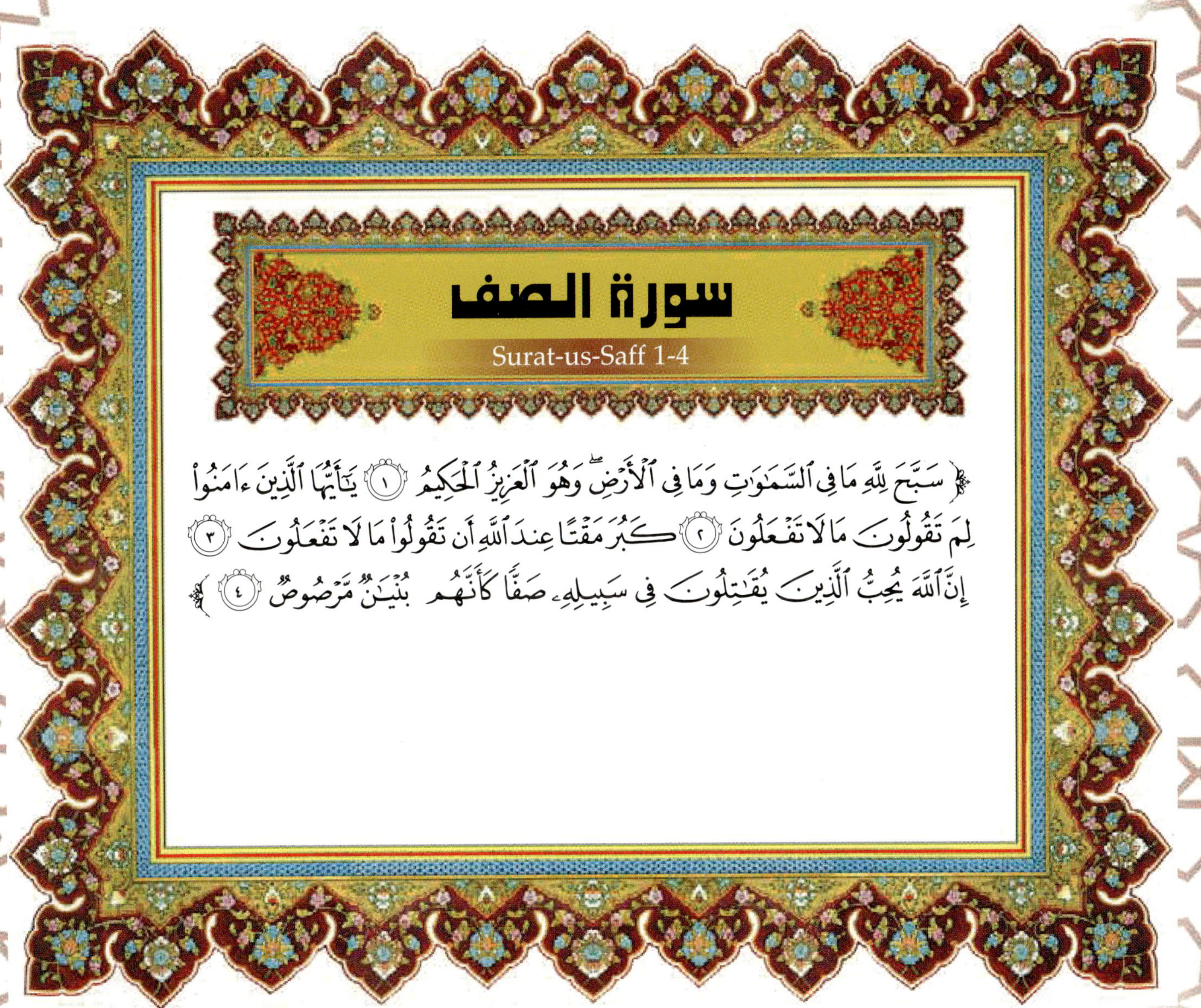

سورة الصف

Surat-us-Saff 1-4

﴿ سَبَّحَ لِلَّهِ مَا فِي السَّمَٰوَٰتِ وَمَا فِي الْأَرْضِ ۖ وَهُوَ الْعَزِيزُ الْحَكِيمُ ﴿١﴾ يَٰٓأَيُّهَا الَّذِينَ ءَامَنُوا
لِمَ تَقُولُونَ مَا لَا تَفْعَلُونَ ﴿٢﴾ كَبُرَ مَقْتًا عِندَ اللَّهِ أَن تَقُولُوا مَا لَا تَفْعَلُونَ ﴿٣﴾
إِنَّ اللَّهَ يُحِبُّ الَّذِينَ يُقَٰتِلُونَ فِي سَبِيلِهِۦ صَفًّا كَأَنَّهُم بُنْيَٰنٌ مَّرْصُوصٌ ﴿٤﴾ ﴾

(61:1) Everything in the Heavens and the Earth has always glorified Allah, and Allah is the Almighty and All-Wise.

(61:2) Oh Believers, why do you say what you do not do?

(61:3) It is a very hateful act for Allah that you say what you don't do.

(61:4) Allah loves those who fight in His cause in organized ranks like well-built walls.

Reason for Revelation

Prophet Muhammad was a prophet for twenty three years; thirteen in Makkah and another ten in Madinah. Allah had ordered the Muslims to be peaceful in Makkah and not fight the hostile disbelievers for thirteen years. Many of the Muslims were killed, hurt and humiliated by the evil leaders of the Quraysh. Despite all of the suffering, the Prophet insisted on remaining peaceful with the Makkans. When Muslims migrated to Madinah and the disbelievers continued to threaten them, Allah ordered them to go on jihad and fight their evil enemies.

Before jihad was mandated on Muslims at that time, a number of companions kept saying, "If we knew what was the most beloved thing to Allah we would do it." Then Allah revealed to His messenger that the most beloved things to Him at that time were: true belief in Allah and jihad against the hostile enemies of Muslims. When the command for jihad became known, a number of companions backed down. They started to backtrack because they were afraid of making jihad and getting killed. So Allah revealed these verses. This narration is reported in At-Tabari & Tirmithi.

Main Lessons

1. Tasbeeh and Glorifying Allah

All creations praise Allah and glorify Him. Planets, stars, animals, plants, humans and all other creations praise their creator in their own ways and languages. Allah says in Surat-ul-Israa':

﴿ تُسَبِّحُ لَهُ ٱلسَّمَٰوَٰتُ ٱلسَّبْعُ وَٱلْأَرْضُ وَمَن فِيهِنَّ ۚ وَإِن مِّن شَىْءٍ إِلَّا يُسَبِّحُ بِحَمْدِهِۦ وَلَٰكِن لَّا تَفْقَهُونَ تَسْبِيحَهُمْ ۗ إِنَّهُۥ كَانَ حَلِيمًا غَفُورًا ﴿٤٤﴾ ﴾

الإسراء: ٤٤

The seven Heavens and the Earth, and all beings therein, declare His glory: there is not a thing but celebrates His praise; And yet you don't understand how they glorify [Him]! Verily He is Forbearing, Most Forgiving! [17:44]

We should make tasbeeh and glorify Allah as often as possible. Tasbeeh starts in the heart. Our hearts must love Allah, glorify Him and be grateful for His endless favors and blessings. Then we praise and thank God by our tongues.

2. Double Personality

Allah dislikes it when we show double personalities. Saying one thing and doing the opposite is the first step

toward hypocrisy. It weakens the character of the Muslim and spreads distrust in the society. This, in fact, is a very common problem today. Many Muslims promise their parents and teachers to perform certain duties, but they don't. They behave well among family and turn bad among friends. They often promise they will study harder, respect authority, and behave according to Islamic and school rules. Unfortunately, many of these promises go unfulfilled.

ayaat two and three stress that Allah detests it when Muslims say something and do another. We must always do what we say, as long as what we say is good.

hadeeth Shareef

عن أبي هريرة رضي الله عنه قال : قال رسول الله صلى الله عليه وسلم:

" آيَـةُ المُنافِق ثَـلاث: إذا حَدَّثَ كَـذَب وإذا وَعَدَ أخْـلَف وإذا اؤتُـمِن خان "

رواه البخاري ومسلم

Abu Hurayrah رضي الله عنه narrated that Rasoolullah ﷺ said, "The signs of a hypocrite are three; he lies when he speaks, he breaks his promise, and he betrays the trust."

Reported in Al-Bukhari and Muslim

hadeeth Shareef

عن أبي هريرة رضي الله عنه قال : قال رسول الله صلى الله عليه وسلم:

" إن شَـرَّ الناسِ ذو الوجْهَيْن ، الذي يَأتي هؤلاء بوجه وهؤلاء بوجه "

رواه البخاري ومسلم

Abu Hurayrah رضي الله عنه narrated that Rasoolullah ﷺ said, "The worst of people is the one who has double personalities. He appears to people in one personality and to others in an opposite personality."

Reported in Al-Bukhari and Muslim

3. Jihad: Struggling on Allah's Path

The Arabic term "Al-Jihad fee sabeelillah الجِهادُ في سَبيل الله " is usually translated, "Fighting for the sake of Allah." A more accurate translation is "The Struggle on Allah's Path." Allah's path is Islam, and Islam is the total submission to God and following His guidance. If we live our life following this path, we will reach Paradise at its end, inshaAllah.

Not all people follow God's path, which is also called in the Qur'an "As-Sirat-ul-Mustaqeem الصِراط المستقيم ," or the Straight Path. Some follow Shaytan and refuse to obey Allah and submit to Him. They even hurt Muslims and try to force them to do evil things, exactly as Shaytan did to Prophet Adam عليه السلام . Allah orders us to defend ourselves and our society against those who fight us and threaten our good way of life. Therefore, sometimes we have to struggle against evil people to protect ourselves and society. This also keeps us on the straight path, away from the evil path of Shaytan and his followers.

Sometimes, struggling on God's path requires fighting hostile and evil enemies. This military jihad, or struggle, must be always done under the official leadership of the Muslim Ummah. Jihad, or struggle, on Allah's path must only be done to keep peace and justice on Earth.

Success in any kind of jihad, whether military or otherwise, is dependent on strong teamwork ,as ayah 4 stresses. No social effort is ever accomplished properly by an individual, no matter how talented and strong he or she is. As Muslims, we must always develop and strengthen our brotherly relationships with the Muslims around us. This is particularly true on the battlefield. If even a small group of soldiers do not do their part, they can put the whole army at risk. This is what happened at the Battle of Uhud, as you learned in your elementary years.

LESSON REVIEW

Projects and Activities

1. Create artwork on a poster or as sculpture that includes the phrase "SubhanAllah wa bihamdihi, SubhanAllah Al-Atheem."

2. Write a 500 word essay on the negative effects of "double personalities" behavior on the Muslim society.

3. As a class or a family, discuss the problem of people saying something and then not doing it. As a group discuss the most common occurrences of this problem for the class. Agree as a group on a set of goals to gradually reduce this problem. After a week reopen this issue and measure the progress towards achieving the goals.

Stretch Your Mind

Describe the behavior of a person who has a "double personality." List five examples of his or her dual personality actions.

Study Questions

1. What do the creations of Allah do all the time?
2. What is the behavior that Allah dislikes as mentioned in the beginning of this Surah?
3. What are the signs of a hypocrite's behavior? Support your answer with a hadeeth.
4. What is the proper meaning of jihad?
5. What did Allah order the Muslims to do when facing the enemies?

LESSON TWO

سورة الصف

Surat-us-Saff: Verses (5-9)

God's True Religion will Prevail

سورة الصف

Surat-us-Saff 5-9

﴿ وَإِذْ قَالَ مُوسَىٰ لِقَوْمِهِۦ يَـٰقَوْمِ لِمَ تُؤْذُونَنِى وَقَد تَّعْلَمُونَ أَنِّى رَسُولُ ٱللَّهِ
إِلَيْكُمْ ۖ فَلَمَّا زَاغُوٓا۟ أَزَاغَ ٱللَّهُ قُلُوبَهُمْ ۚ وَٱللَّهُ لَا يَهْدِى ٱلْقَوْمَ ٱلْفَـٰسِقِينَ ﴿٥﴾ وَإِذْ قَالَ عِيسَى
ٱبْنُ مَرْيَمَ يَـٰبَنِىٓ إِسْرَٰٓءِيلَ إِنِّى رَسُولُ ٱللَّهِ إِلَيْكُم مُّصَدِّقًا لِّمَا بَيْنَ يَدَىَّ مِنَ ٱلتَّوْرَىٰةِ وَمُبَشِّرًۢا بِرَسُولٍ يَأْتِى مِنۢ
بَعْدِى ٱسْمُهُۥٓ أَحْمَدُ ۖ فَلَمَّا جَآءَهُم بِٱلْبَيِّنَـٰتِ قَالُوا۟ هَـٰذَا سِحْرٌ مُّبِينٌ ﴿٦﴾ وَمَنْ أَظْلَمُ مِمَّنِ ٱفْتَرَىٰ عَلَى ٱللَّهِ
ٱلْكَذِبَ وَهُوَ يُدْعَىٰٓ إِلَى ٱلْإِسْلَـٰمِ ۚ وَٱللَّهُ لَا يَهْدِى ٱلْقَوْمَ ٱلظَّـٰلِمِينَ ﴿٧﴾ يُرِيدُونَ لِيُطْفِـُٔوا۟ نُورَ ٱللَّهِ بِأَفْوَٰهِهِمْ
وَٱللَّهُ مُتِمُّ نُورِهِۦ وَلَوْ كَرِهَ ٱلْكَـٰفِرُونَ ﴿٨﴾ هُوَ ٱلَّذِىٓ أَرْسَلَ رَسُولَهُۥ بِٱلْهُدَىٰ وَدِينِ ٱلْحَقِّ لِيُظْهِرَهُۥ
عَلَى ٱلدِّينِ كُلِّهِۦ وَلَوْ كَرِهَ ٱلْمُشْرِكُونَ ﴿٩﴾ ﴾

Translation

(61:5) Remember that Musa said to his people, "Why do you mistreat me (by disobeying me) when you know that I am the Messenger of Allah to you (by all the miracles that happened)?!!" But when they deviated Allah turned their hearts away. And Allah does not guide the disobedient people.

(61:6) And when Isa, the son of Maryam said, "Oh Children of Israel, I am the Messenger of Allah to you. I confirm the truth of what came before me of the Tawrah and I give the good news of a messenger who is coming after me, whose name is Ahmad. Then when he presented them with evidence and miracles, they said, "This is clearly magic."

(61:7) Who is more unjust than the one who makes up lies against Allah, when they are being called to Islam. Allah will not guide those who are unjust.

(61:8) They want to blow out the light of Allah with their mouths, and Allah will complete the spreading of His light, even if the disbelievers hate it.

(61:9) Allah sent His messenger with the true guidance and the religion of truth to make it overcome all religions, even if the polytheists hate it.

Reason for Revelation

Allah mentioned Prophets Musa and Isa, peace be upon them both, in this surah because the Muslims were having a hard time with some leaders of the Jews of Madinah. They refused to believe in Prophet Mhammad and broke an important agreement he signed with them upon his coming to Madinah. Some of them even tried to hurt him and the Muslims. However, not all Jews were evil, some Jewish leaders and scholars were friendly to the Muslims, and a few even became Muslim.

Main Lessons

1- Learning from the Mistakes of People before us:

We should learn lessons form people before us. The Jews disobeyed Prophets Musa and Isa عليه السلام.. Their disobedience led them to go astray more. Allah is fair and He doesn't misguide people until they insist on disobedience and rejection of the truth. And Allah doesn't punish people until they receive a clear warning and a message which they insist on disobeying.

The Israelites disobeyed Allah's Ten Commandments to them. They disobeyed Prophet Musa's commands to fight their hostile pagan enemies and liberate the promise land: Palestine. Instead, they told Musa, "Go with your lord to fight, we are waiting right here." So the Muslims should be warned not to fall into this trap of thinking that Allah will give them victory even if they do nothing. As Muslims, if we want Allah to bless us with his favors and guidance, we need to obey Him and avoid sin and disobedience.

They later disbelieved in Prophet Isa and rejected his message. Islam teaches us to believe in all prophets of God and their original and authentic messages.

2. Prophet Isa Told about the Coming of Prophet Muhammad.

All the messengers from Allah confirmed and supported the one truth that they all brought. The original Bible told about previous prophets like Adam, Noah, Ibraheem and others. It also told about the coming of Prophet Muhammad ﷺ. Ayah 6 tells how Prophet Isa told the Israelites about the future coming of the Prophet. The name given in this ayah is "Ahmad."

Ahmad and Muhammad are both names for the Prophet Muhammad ﷺ. He was called "Ahmad," because this word means "the one who praises Allah the most." Then when he was born, he was given the name "Muhammad" which means "the one who is praised."

Prophet Muhammad ﷺ, deserving of both of the above names, because no one praised Allah more than him, and no person gets as much praise as him. He used to glorify and praise Allah most of the day and pray almost half of the night, praising his Lord. On the other hand, there are 1.2 billion Muslims today who pray for him and his family in every prayer that they do every day.

3. Rejecting the Truth is Great Injustice

According to ayah 7, there is no one who is more unjust than those who reject the truth about God, prophets and faith when they are called to believe. Some disbelievers of Madinah, Makkah and Arabia were being called to Islam. Although they knew Muhammad was a true Prophet, they rejected him.

4. Spreading Lies about Islam Won't Work

The disbelievers thought that by simply fabricating lies about the Prophet and his message, they would cover up the truth. They thought by doing this they would deceive people and stop Islam from spreading in Arabia. The disbelievers thought Islam was weak and that they could blow it out like you blow out a candle. Unfortunately, many people now think the same way. They describe Islam and the Prophet in a negative way. They fabricate lies and false tales about the Qur'an and Prophet Muhammad in their books, magazines, websites and elsewhere to scare people away from Islam. The infamous Danish cartoons that depicted Prophet Muhammad ﷺ as a terrorist were just one horrible example of that. However, in ayah 8, Allah promised the Prophet and the Muslims, that the message of Islam will prevail.

Despite all the untruth spread about our religion, Islam is the fastest growing religion in the world - Subhana Allah!

Fast Facts

The word kafiroon, or kuffar, comes from the root "kafar," which means "cover." This refers to the action of covering up the truth.

5. Islam will be the Choice of People

The globetrotting coach of Morocco's national football team, Frenchman Phillipe Troussier, has converted to Islam.

In ayah 9, Allah confirms that He sent His messenger with the true guidance and religion. He said that He will make Islam prevail in the world. This had led people in Arabia and its surroundings to follow Islam and leave their polytheist beliefs. This happened at the time of Prophet Muhammad and continues to happen tnow.

People around the world discover that Islam is God's true and original faith that He wants them to follow. Islam now is the fastest growing religion in the world. We must always try our best to live Islam and maintain our Islamic character. The more we live our Islam properly, the more our actions will attract others to Islam in the way our beloved Prophet Muhammad did.

We should also expect to face hatred and severe opposition from some disbelieving people. This is to be expected because people were raised in a certain way and have difficulty accepting change. We should counter their negative behavior with our positive attitudes. This will help us win their hearts and minds and cause them to see the truth and follow it.

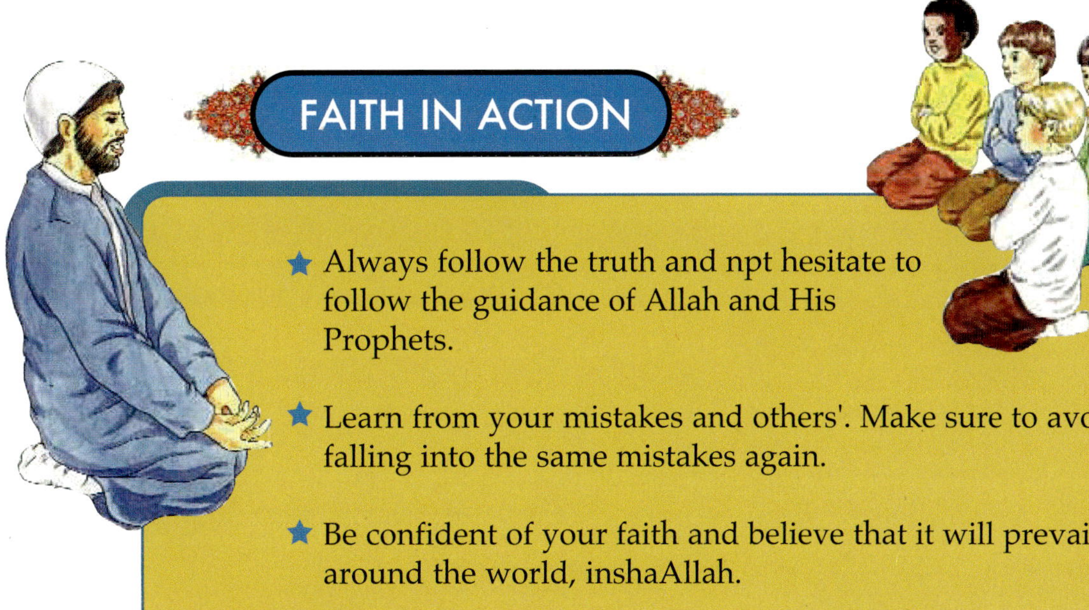

FAITH IN ACTION

- Always follow the truth and npt hesitate to follow the guidance of Allah and His Prophets.
- Learn from your mistakes and others'. Make sure to avoid falling into the same mistakes again.
- Be confident of your faith and believe that it will prevail around the world, inshaAllah.

LESSON REVIEW

Projects and Activities

1. Read a short book about the story of Prophet Musa (P).
2. Read a short book about the story of Prophet Isa (P).

Stretch Your Mind

Why did Allah mention the stories of Prophets Musa and Isa in this surah?

Study Questions

1. What did Prophet Musa say to his people as described in this surah?
2. What happened to the disbelievers among Prophet Musa's people when they deviated?
3. What did Prophet Isa say to his people, as described in this surah?
4. What good news did Prophet Isa bring to the Children of Isra'eel?
5. What is the greatest injustice one can do, according to this surah?
6. What do the disbelievers try to do against the prophets, as described in ayah 8?
7. What promise did Allah give in ayah 9 of this surah?

UNIT D CHAPTER SIX

LESSON THREE

Surat-us-Saff: Verses (10-14) سورة الصف
The Successful Business

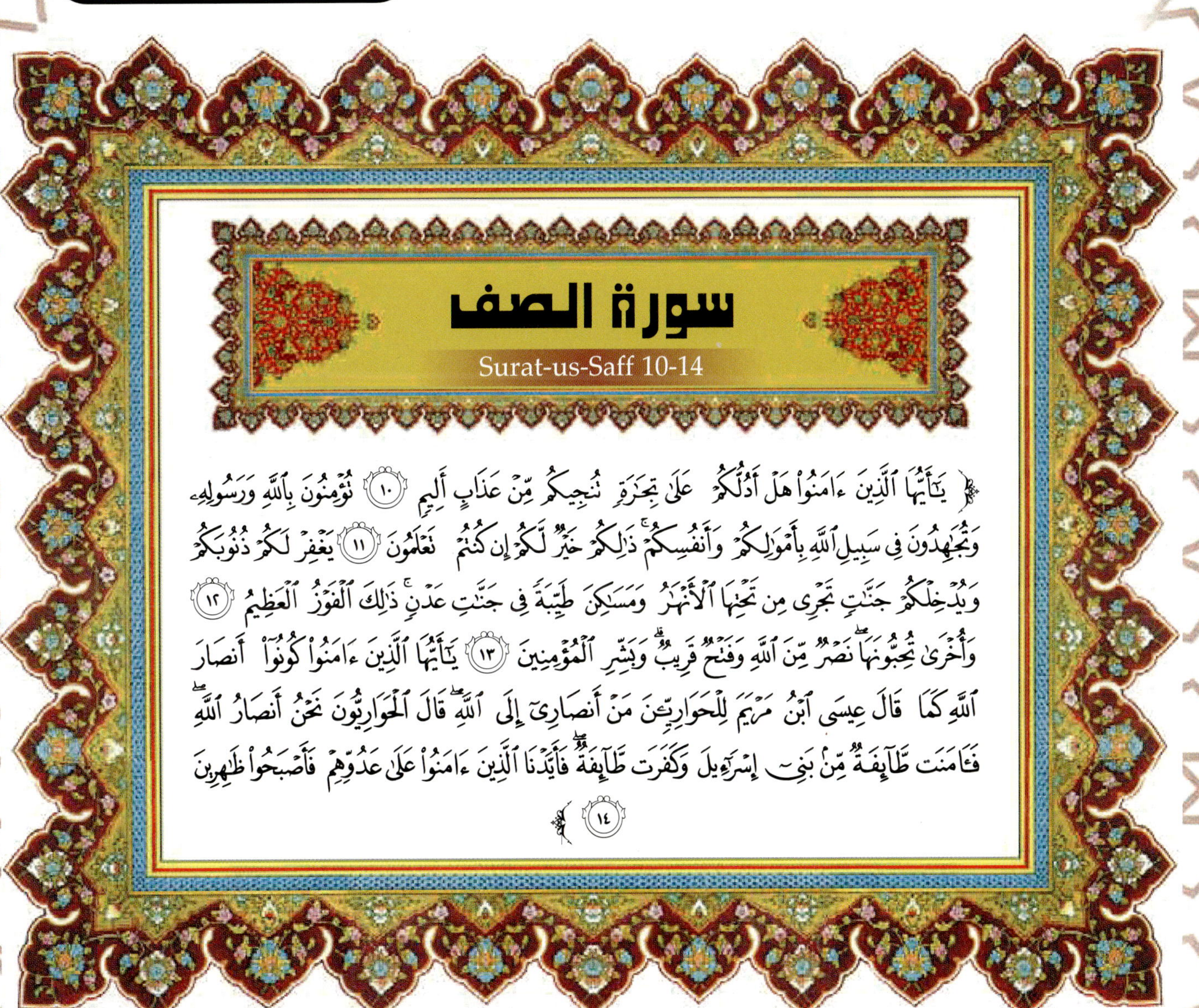

سورة الصف

Surat-us-Saff 10-14

﴿ يَٰٓأَيُّهَا ٱلَّذِينَ ءَامَنُواْ هَلۡ أَدُلُّكُمۡ عَلَىٰ تِجَٰرَةٖ تُنجِيكُم مِّنۡ عَذَابٍ أَلِيمٖ ١٠ تُؤۡمِنُونَ بِٱللَّهِ وَرَسُولِهِۦ
وَتُجَٰهِدُونَ فِي سَبِيلِ ٱللَّهِ بِأَمۡوَٰلِكُمۡ وَأَنفُسِكُمۡۚ ذَٰلِكُمۡ خَيۡرٞ لَّكُمۡ إِن كُنتُمۡ تَعۡلَمُونَ ١١ يَغۡفِرۡ لَكُمۡ ذُنُوبَكُمۡ
وَيُدۡخِلۡكُمۡ جَنَّٰتٖ تَجۡرِي مِن تَحۡتِهَا ٱلۡأَنۡهَٰرُ وَمَسَٰكِنَ طَيِّبَةٗ فِي جَنَّٰتِ عَدۡنٖۚ ذَٰلِكَ ٱلۡفَوۡزُ ٱلۡعَظِيمُ ١٢
وَأُخۡرَىٰ تُحِبُّونَهَاۖ نَصۡرٞ مِّنَ ٱللَّهِ وَفَتۡحٞ قَرِيبٞۗ وَبَشِّرِ ٱلۡمُؤۡمِنِينَ ١٣ يَٰٓأَيُّهَا ٱلَّذِينَ ءَامَنُواْ كُونُوٓاْ أَنصَارَ
ٱللَّهِ كَمَا قَالَ عِيسَى ٱبۡنُ مَرۡيَمَ لِلۡحَوَارِيِّـۧنَ مَنۡ أَنصَارِيٓ إِلَى ٱللَّهِۖ قَالَ ٱلۡحَوَارِيُّونَ نَحۡنُ أَنصَارُ ٱللَّهِۖ
فَـَٔامَنَت طَّآئِفَةٞ مِّنۢ بَنِيٓ إِسۡرَٰٓءِيلَ وَكَفَرَت طَّآئِفَةٞۖ فَأَيَّدۡنَا ٱلَّذِينَ ءَامَنُواْ عَلَىٰ عَدُوِّهِمۡ فَأَصۡبَحُواْ ظَٰهِرِينَ
١٤ ﴾

(61:10) Oh believers, should I guide you to a business that will save you from a painful punishment?

(61:11) You must believe in Allah and His Messenger and to struggle on Allah's path with your money and lives. This is the best thing for you, if you only knew.

(61:12) Allah will forgive the bad deeds you did and will have you enter gardens in Paradise with rivers flowing through them. You will also get very nice homes in your eternal gardens. This is the great win.

(61:13) You will also get another thing that you love. You will get the support from Allah to give you victory and the opening (of Makkah) soon and give the good news to the believers.

(61:14) Oh believers, be supporters of Allah's religion like the disciples were. Isa the son of Maryam said to the disciples, "Who will be my supporters for Allah's cause?" The disciples said, "We are the supporters of Allah's religion." Then a group from the Children of Israel believed and another group disbelieved. So I helped those who believed against those who were their enemies, and they overcame them.

Reason for Revelation

It is said that these verses of the surah were revealed first. Then when some Muslims started to hesitate about fighting ,the verses which are placed at the beginning of the surah were revealed.

The verses, especially ayah 13, were also predicting the opening of Makkah to Islam.

Main Lessons

1. The Business of Rewards is more Important than the Business of Dollars

When you have a business, you have some kind of product or service and you try to sell it to make money. If a person starts out with $1,000, and after a year they have nothing, then they have lost a lot of money on their dealings. If on the other hand a person starts with $1,000 and ends up with $10,000, then he has made a lot of money. In life the only thing we have is a limited amount of time. So Allah calls us to invest this time so that we will get the most benefit for it. If we invest it in the way Allah commands us to, we will see victory in this world, and more importantly, we will find ourselves in the highest levels of Paradise forever in the next world.

2. Faith and Jihad

These verses encourage the Muslims to believe in Allah and His Prophet, and perform jihad. As you learned earlier, jihad is exerting great effort and struggling in Allah's way against evil. Jihad can be fighting hostile enemies on the battlefield whenever needed. However, jihad can be performed without fighting at all. It can be a financial jihad by giving money to the needy, to good projects or to support the Muslim army. Jihad can also be against evil desires within one's self. Resisting the urge to say, see or do bad things is an important type of jihad. Exerting effort to learn Islam and other good knowledge is a type of jihad too. It is interesting to know that one of the best types of jihad does not involve fighting. The scholars call this type of jihad "Jihad-ul-Kalimah جهاد الكلمة , or Verbal Jihad. Prophet Muhammad says,

سُئل رسول الله ﷺ : أي الجهاد أفضل؟ قال:
"كلمة حق عند سلطان جائر." رواه النسائي وغيره

"The best form of jihad is a word of truth in front of an evil ruler." Reported by Nasai and others

The table below explains the various types of jihad in Islam.

Table: Types of Jihad

	Type of Jihad	Main Activities	Against	Done by
1	Military	Fighting	Hostile Enemy	Official and authorized army of the Muslim State
2	Financial	Charity and Donation	One's Greed	Everyone
3	Educational	Seeking and teaching knowledge	Ignorance	Everyone
4	Spiritual	Worshipping Allah	Shaytan and one's laziness	Everyone
5	Political	Speaking the truth and countering tyrants	Evil and Oppressive rulers	Qualified Scholars and Citizens
6	Moral	Leading moral life and avoiding immoral lifestyles	One's Desires	Everyone

You can infer from the table that jihad is a noble act that aims to maintain justice and peace on Earth. Some deviant Muslims murder innocent people in the name of jihad. They do that on their own and without the approval of righteous rulers and scholars of the Muslim society. Their actions are not forms of proper jihad, rather, it is mischief and murder.

3. Jannah is the Destination of True Believers

The description of Heaven in these verses is very encouraging to true believers. Gardens, rivers, palaces and, above all, eternal happiness are awaiting those who discipline themselves and struggle against evil throughout their lives.

Jannah, or Paradise, is the ultimate prize and the best ever reward one can receive. The Qur'an is full of great descriptions of Jannah. It is described in the Qur'an as a great win, eternal joy, and pure entertainment. The people of Jannah will receive everything they wish to have in the blink of an eye. They will enjoy all kinds of food, drink and entertainment. The rivers there do not only flow with sweet water, but also with honey, milk, non-intoxicating wines and other refreshing drinks.

The people of Jannah will live in magnificent palaces and castles made of gold, silver, pearls and other precious metals and stones. They will wear fine outfits made of silk and other luxurious materials. All of them will enjoy beautiful looks and physical bodies. The age of the people in Jannah is thirty three, which was the age of Prophet Isa when Allah elevated him to the Heavens. They never grow older but will live forever and experience no physical discomfort at all.

Allah will bless the people in Jannah with the companionship of all prophets and messengers, sahabah, great scholars and leaders from throughout history. The best entertainment the people can ever receive in Jannah is seeing Allah سبحانه وتعالى with their eyes. They will enjoy seeing Him like we see the full moon at night or the sun in day time. In Jannah, Allah will unite people with their husbands, wives, parents, children, family members and friends, as long as they were admitted to Jannah.

The above description is only a glimpse of what the believers will enjoy in Jannah. Allah says in the hadeeth Qudsi,

"I prepared for my pious servants what no eye has ever seen, no ear has ever heard and no mind has ever thought of."

Allah reminds us that the real victory is Paradise. However, if we do our part and if we are willing to perform proper jihad, united in Allah's path, then we will win victory against any evil enemy in this world also.

4. Learning from Al-Hawariyyeen: Supporting Allah's Cause Sincerely

The disciples of Prophet Isa are called, "Hawariyyoon." This word originally meant "to purify." It is said that they were originally called this because they had pure intentions in supporting Prophet Isa عليه السلام. It is also said that they were called this because they kept their clothes very clean.

In the last verse, Allah commands us to support His cause the same way the disciples of Isa supported Allah's religion. Initially they were weak and small in number, and the disbelievers had the larger numbers. Then Allah gave those who believed in Isa victory over everyone else. Allah called upon Muslims to support Prophet Muhammad when Muslims were very few. Now Islam is the fastest growing religion in the world. It is expected to be the most followed religion in the world within one century insha'Allah.

When Rasoolullah was chased around in Makkah, a delegation came from Madinah to pledge allegiance to him. Muslims then were less than two hundred people. He asked the Madinah delegation to elect twelve of them to be in charge on his behalf like Isa had his disciples. Nine years later, the supporters of Islam became more than ten thousand Muslims. They rallied into Makkah under the leadership of Prophet Muhammad, liberated Makkah from idol worshipping and declared the great victory of Islam.

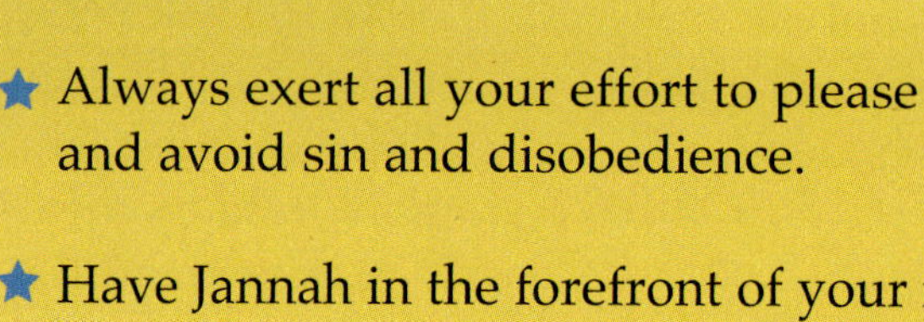

FAITH IN ACTION

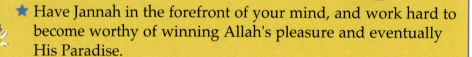

- Always exert all your effort to please Allah and avoid sin and disobedience.
- Have Jannah in the forefront of your mind, and work hard to become worthy of winning Allah's pleasure and eventually His Paradise.
- Always struggle against your inner self desires to do bad deeds.
- Always be a supporter of Allah's religion through your sincere actions.

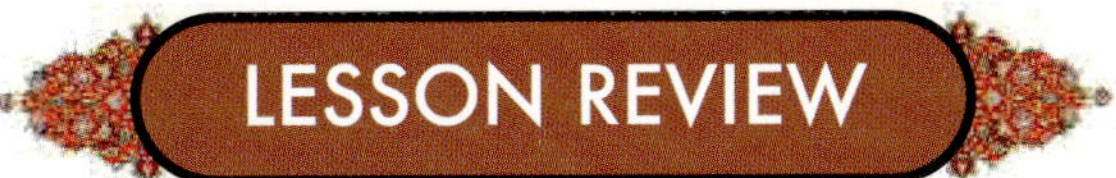

LESSON REVIEW

Projects and Activities

1. Read a short book about Jannah.

2. Create a poster in which you present three groups of ayaat and three ahadeeth about Jannah.

Stretch Your Mind

1. Why did Allah mention the stories of Prophets Musa and Isa in this surah?

2. How can a person become a true supporter of Allah? Mention five examples.

Study Questions

1. What "business" did Allah describe to the believers in this surah?
2. What is jihad?
3. Describe five types of jihad?
4. Can a person fight others whenever he or she wants? Why or why not?
5. What is the best type of jihad that doesn't involve fighting? Support your answer with a hadeeth.
6. Describe seven enjoyments the believers will receive in Jannah? And what is the best of them?
7. What was the last instruction Allah gave to the believers in this surah?

بِسْمِ اللَّهِ الرَّحْمَٰنِ الرَّحِيمِ

الم ۞ ذَٰلِكَ الْكِتَابُ لَا رَيْبَ ۛ فِيهِ ۛ هُدًى

لِّلْمُتَّقِينَ ۞ الَّذِينَ يُؤْمِنُونَ بِالْغَيْبِ وَيُقِيمُونَ

الصَّلَاةَ وَمِمَّا رَزَقْنَاهُمْ يُنْفِقُونَ ۞ وَالَّذِينَ

يُؤْمِنُونَ بِمَا أُنْزِلَ إِلَيْكَ وَمَا أُنْزِلَ مِنْ قَبْلِكَ

Prayer is Light

Praying The Prophet's Way

CHAPTER OUTLINE

1. The place of salah in Islam.
2. The importance of salah for every Muslim.
3. Prayer times.
4. How to perfect prayers.
5. Important thikr and du'aa' during salah.

VOCABULARY

Al-Israa' Wal-Mi'raj	المِعْراج الإسْراء
Takbeerat-ul-Ihram	تَكْبيـرةُ الإحـرام
Rak'ah	رَكْعَة
Qiyam	قـيام
Rukoo'	رُكوع
Sujood	سُجود
Juloos	جُلوس
Salat-ul-Fajr	صَلاةُ الفَجر
Salat-uth-Thuhr	صَلاةُ الظُهرْ
Salat-ul-Asr	صَلاةُ العَصْرْ
Salat-ul-Maghrib	صَلاةُ المَغرِبْ
Salat-ul-Ishaa'	صَلاةُ العِشـاءْ

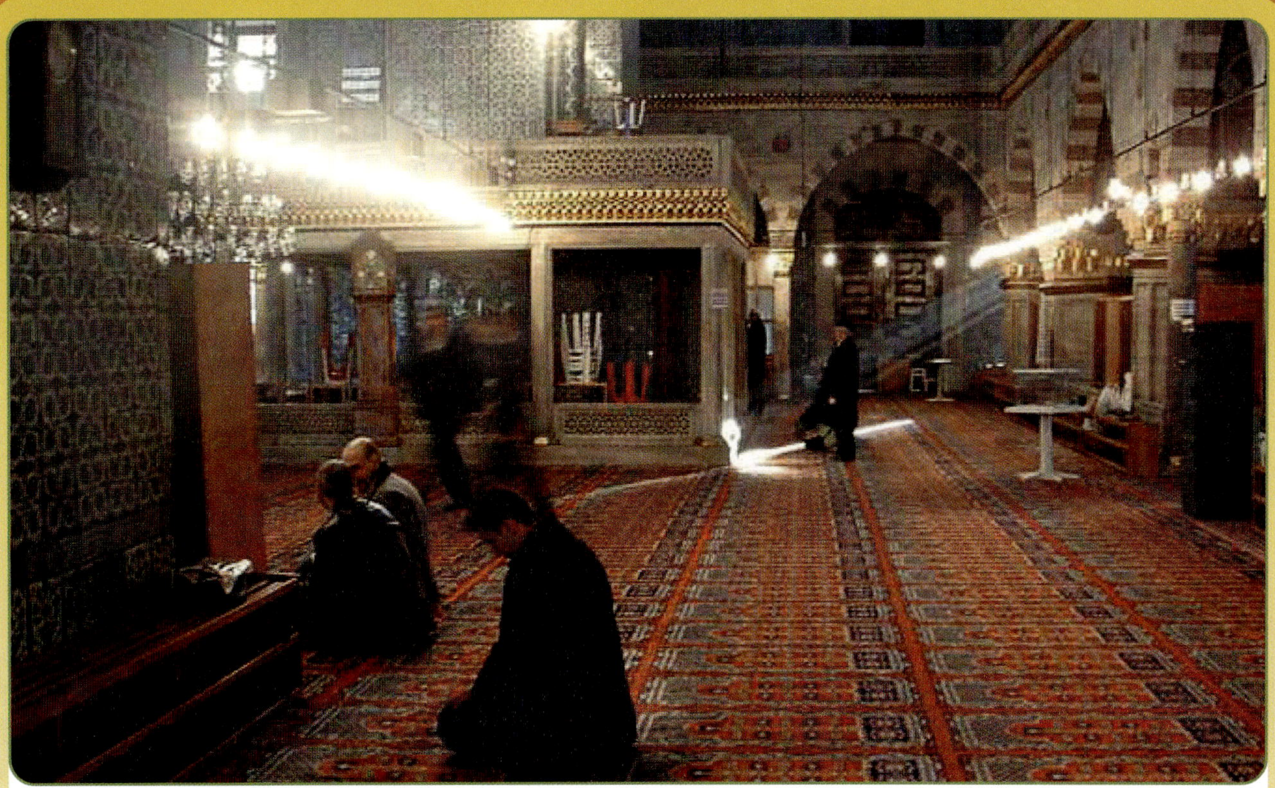

The Importance of Prayer

As you learned in your elementary years, salah is the second pillar of Islam, after shahadah, or declaration of faith. Salah, or prayer, was made obligatory when the Prophet ﷺ ascended to Heaven on the night of Al-Israa' Wal-Mi'raj الإسراء والمعراج . He was ordered by Allah to tell his followers to make fifty prayers a day. Prophet Muhammad ﷺ asked Allah to reduce it because that would be too difficult for the Muslims to do. So Allah finally reduced it to five prayers. However, the reward a Muslim gains for making five prayers is equivalent to that of fifty prayers. This means that if a Muslim keeps on praying five times a day, he or she will be rewarded as if praying fifty prayers a day.

Salah is of great significance in Islam as indicated by the following hadeeth, narrated by Mu'ath Ibn Jabal رضي الله عنه. The Prophet ﷺ said:

عن مُعاذ بن جَبَل رضي الله عنه قال : قال رسولُ اللهِ صَلى اللهُ عَليْهِ وَسَلم:
" رَأسُ الأمْر الإسْلام ، وعَمُودُهُ الصَّلاة ، وذِرْوَةُ سَنامِهِ الجهاد " السنن الكبرى للنسائي

"The head of this matter is Islam, its pillar is the prayer and the top of its hump is jihad in the way of Allah."

Reported in At-Tirmithi

The next hadeeth should serve as a warning of the dangerous consequences of skipping the salah.

عَنْ أمِّ أيْمَن رضيَ اللهُ عَنْها قالت: قالَ رَسولُ اللهِ صلى اللهُ عليه وسلم:
لا تَتْرُكِ الصَّلاة المكتوبة مُتَعَمِّداً ، فمن تركها مُتَعَمِّداً فَقَدْ بَرِئَتْ مِنْهُ الذِمَّة.

رَواهُ أحْمَد

"Do not knowingly neglect to observe a required prayer, for he who neglects the prescribed prayer on purpose will be deserted by Allah and His Messenger."

Reported in Ahmad

Indeed, salah is the most important act of worship in Islam. If one perfects it, it will help him or her greatly in this life and in the Hereafter. Otherwise, he or she may go through difficult times here and after death.

عن أبي هُرَيْرَةَ رضي الله عنه قال : قال رسولُ اللهِ صَلى اللهُ عَليْهِ وَسَلم:
إنَّ أوَّلَ ما يُحاسَبُ العَبْدُ عليْهِ يوم القِيامَةِ مِنْ عَمَلِه صَلآتُهُ ، فَإنْ صَلَحَتْ فَقَدْ أفْلَحَ وأنْجَحْ ، وإن فَسَدَتْ فَقَدْ خابَ وَخَسِرْ

رواهُ التِّرْمِذِيّ

"The first act that the servant will be accountable for on the Day of Judgment will be his salah. If it is good, then he will win the pleasure of Allah. And if it was poorly done, then he will lose in the Hereafter." Reported in At-Tirmithi.

Without question, salah is a must do, or fard, in Islam.

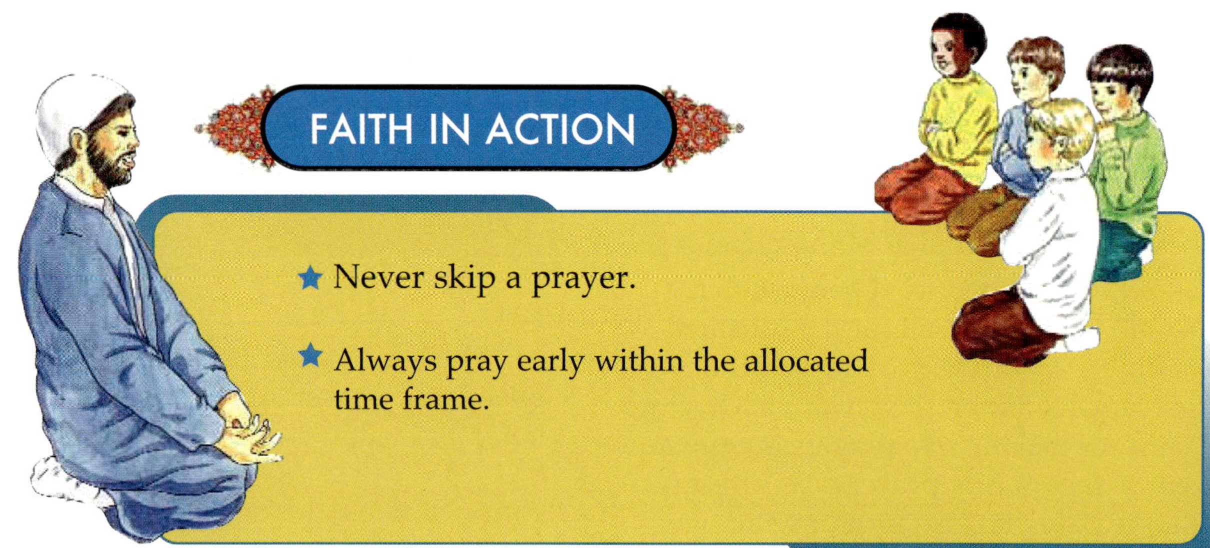

FAITH IN ACTION
Never skip a prayer.
Always pray early within the allocated time frame.

Prayer Times

Each prayer must be performed at a certain time. Allah ﷻ says in Surat-un-Nisaa':

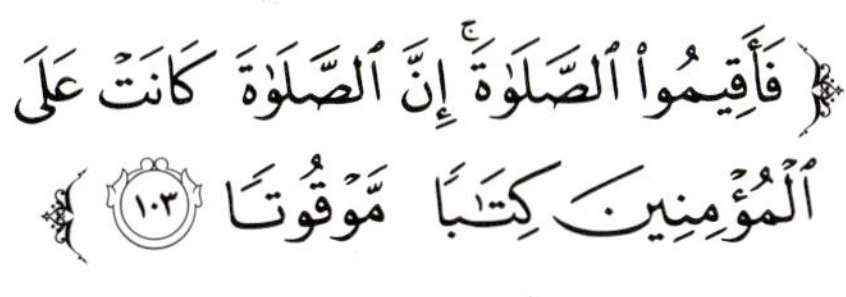

النساء: ١٠٣

"Set up prayer. For such prayers are mandated on the believers at assigned times." (4: 103).

Jareer Ibn Abdullah رضي الله عنه narrated that the Angel Jibreel (Gabriel) came to the Prophet ﷺ the day after 'Al-Israa' and said to him: "Stand and pray," and they prayed the noon prayer, Salat uth-Thuhr صَلاةُ الظُّهْرْ , when the sun had passed its meridian. He then came to him for the afternoon prayer, Salat ul-Asr صَلاةُ العَصْرْ , while the length of the shadow of an object was similar to its actual length. Then he came at sunset and said: "Stand and Pray," and they prayed the sunset prayer, Salat ul-Maghrib صَلاةُ المَغْرِب , just when the sun had disappeared. Then he came for the night prayer, Salat ul-'Ishaa صَلاةُ العِشاءْ , when twilight had passed. He returned at the break of dawn and they prayed the Fajr prayer, Salat ul-Fajr صَلاةُ الفَجْرْ .

Later, Jibreel came again at noon prayer and said: "Stand up and pray," and they prayed (Thuhr) when the shadow of something was as long as the length of the object. In the afternoon he came for Asr prayer, when the shadow cast from an object was twice its actual length. Then he came at the same time as the previous day for sunset prayer, Maghrib, without any change. Then he came for the night prayer, Isha, after half (or one-third) of the night had passed. Then he came when the sky was very yellowish and said:" Stand and pray', and then prayed the morning prayer, Fajr. Then Jibreel said:

"Between these points at each time are the times for the prayers."

Related by Ahmad, An-Nisa'i and At-Tirmithi.

What we have just read is a hadeeth that describes the times of the five daily prayers. At the time of the Prophet ﷺ, there were no clocks, watches, timetables, athan clocks etc. Therefore, Jibreel trained the Prophet ﷺ on using the sun as a measure of time. He taught him the earliest point and the latest point of each Salah. Of course now we are blessed with modern convenient methods of telling the time. Do we really have any excuse for not praying on time?

The best deed we can do in terms of prayer is to pray on time. This means praying at the very beginning of the designated prayer time. Once, Abdullah Ibn Mas'ood asked Rasoolulah ﷺ: What is the deed that Allah loves the most? The Prophet answered:

" الصَّــلاةُ عَلى وَقْـتِها "

رواه البخاري ومسلم

"To pray on time."

Reported in Al-Bukhari and Muslim

Perfecting Prayers

Salah is the most important aspect of worship for a Muslim. So it is necessary to perfect the way one prays. The best method of performing prayer is that demonstrated by Rasoolullah ﷺ.

عن مالك بن الحُويْرث رضيَ اللهُ عنهُ قال: قال رسولُ اللهِ صلى اللهُ عليْهِ وسلم:
" صَلوا كما رأيْتُموني أُصَلّي "
رواه البخاري

Malik Ibn Huwayrith related that the Prophet ﷺ said:

"Pray as you see me praying"
Reported in Al-Bukhari

Prophet Muhammad ﷺ was the best ever at performing prayer. Let's, then, explore how the Prophet ﷺ performed salah. We will examine how he prayed, and what he did at each of the positions of prayer.

Prayer involves four main positions;

1. Qiyam قيام Standing
2. Rukoo' رُكوع Bowing
3. Sujood سُجود Prostration
4. Juloos جُلوس Sitting

Each Rak'ah رَكْعَة, or unit of prayer, includes all of these positions. Different recitations and supplications are required during each position.

Abu Hurayrah رضي الله عنه reported: "A man entered the mosque and after praying, he went to greet the Prophet ﷺ and listen to him. The Prophet ﷺ greeted him back and said:"

" ارجِعْ فصَلِّ فإنَّكَ لَمْ تُصَلِّ "

"Go back and pray again, because you have not prayed."

This happened three times, and the man then said, "By the One who sent you with the Truth, I do not know any better than that, so teach me."

The Prophet ﷺ said: "When you stand for prayer, perform wudoo' well, then face Qiblah and make Takbeer and then recite Ummu-ul-Kitab (Surat ul-Fatihah) سورَةُ الفاتحة, and what you can recite more from Al-Qur'an. Then make rukoo' رُكوع (bowing) until you attain calmness in your rukoo' and raise from rukoo' until you straighten your back and attain calmness. Then make sujood سُجود (prostration) until you attain calmness in your prostration. Then sit until you attain calmness in your sitting. Do that during all your prayers." Related by Ahmad, Muslim, and Al-Bukhari.

The above hadeeth teaches us the importance of perfecting prayer. Salah is too important to be done in a sloppy or hasty manner. Unfortunately, many people do not perfect their prayers and perform them in a very poor way. They do them too fast, or move and look around, and even allow their minds to focus on worldly things during salah. Imagine if Rasoolullah ﷺ saw them praying like that! What would he say to them? You got it right! He would say to them:

"Go back and pray again because you have not prayed."

We usually do important things the best way we can. Should we not offer Salah to Allah ﷻ in the best way we can?

We must commit ourselves to performing the movements in a perfect way while connecting our hearts to Allah.

I Qiyam : The Standing Part of Salah:

Takbeerat-ul-Ihram: The Beginning Takbeer for entering Salah:

Prophet Muhammad taught us that the Muslim starts salah by saying the Takbeer statement "Allahu Akbar." This is called takbeerat-ul-Ihram تَكْبيرةُ الإحرام , the takbeer with which we enter the prayer. After this point only prayer is allowed. Eating, drinking, talking, looking around, laughing, and playing become haram. These things only become halal or permissible when we have made tasleem at the end of the prayer ,as the Prophet ﷺ said in the following hadeeth:

عن علي بن أبي طالبٍ رضيَ اللهُ عنهُ قال: قال رسولُ اللهِ صلى اللهُ عليْهِ وسلم:
" مِفْتاحُ الصَّلاةِ الطُّهورُ ، وتَحْريمُها التَكْبير، وتَحْليلُها التَسْليم " رواه الترمذي

The Prophet ﷺ said: "Wudoo' is the key to prayer, then salah starts with the beginning takbeer which prohibits [non-prayer related actions], and they become permissible at the tasleem (at

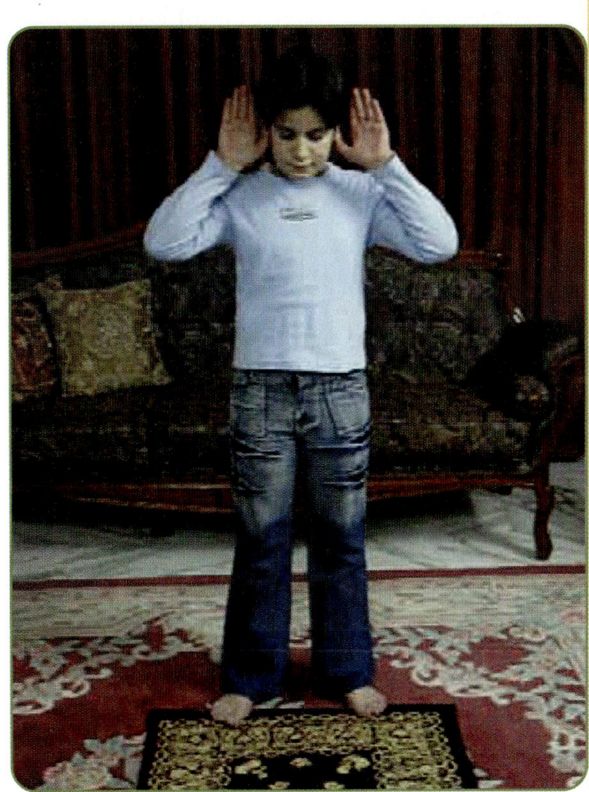

the end)." He also said:

عن أبي هُرَيْرَةَ رضيَ اللهُ عنهُ قال: قال رسولُ اللهِ ﷺ:
" إذا قُمْتَ تُريدُ الصَّلاةَ فتَوَضَّأْ فأحْسِنْ وُضوءَكَ ثم اسْتَقْبِلِ القِبلَةَ فَكَبِّر "
رواه البخاري ومسلم والنسائي

When the Prophet ﷺ used to stand for prayer, he faced Al-Qiblah and raised his hands by his ears and said "Allahu Akbar." Ibn 'Omar said that the Prophet ﷺ used to raise his hands leveling them with his shoulders when starting the prayer. He would then place the palm of the right hand on the left hand placing them on his waist.

Before the first takbeer, the Prophet ﷺ used to make sure that his body was properly covered with clean clothes. He ﷺ would clean his mouth and teeth so that he had fresh breath.

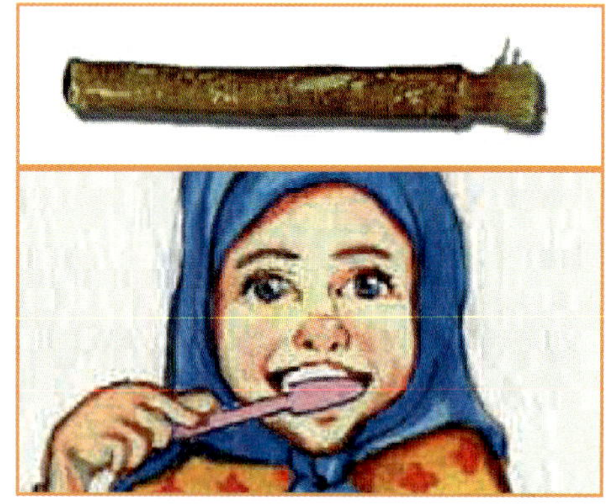

عن أبي هُرَيْرَةَ رضي الله عنه قال : قال رسولُ اللهِ صَلى اللهُ عَليْهِ وَسَلم:
" لولا أن أشُقَّ عَلى الناسِ لأمَرْتُهم بِالسِّواك مَعَ كلِّ صَلاة "

رواه البخاري ومسلم

"I wouldn't make it hard on people; otherwise, I would have ordered my followers to use the siwak at each prayer."

Reported in Al-Bukhari and Muslim.

Position of the Hands During Qiyam

There are twenty ahadeeth narrated by eighteen companions all saying that the people were ordered to place their right hand on their left forearm when in the standing position in prayer.

"I saw the Prophet ﷺ praying with his right arm over his left ."

Reported by Hulb at-Ta'i. It is also reported by Ahmad, and At-Tirmithi.

The Prophet was reported to place his hands on his chest, by the navel, and in between.

According to Maliki and Ja'fari schools of fiqh, one can leave his or her hands loose down to the sides during Qiyam. However, most sahabah and scholars believe that the Prophet used to position his both hands on the area between the navel and the chest as explained earlier.

The Maliki School favors the placing of the hands at the side during qiyam. This is also true in the Ja'fari school of fiqh which is followed by the Shi'ah community. The reason for that practice is a narration that describes Imam Malik as doing that.

Du'aa'-ul-Istiftah دُعاء الاسْتِفْتاح : The Opening Supplication:

Ali Ibn Abi Talib (R) reported that the Prophet ﷺ made this supplication after takbeer:

وجَّهْت وجْهيَ لِلّذي فَطَرَ السَّماواتِ والأَرْضَ حَنيفاً وما أنا مِنَ المشْرِكين ، إنَّ صَلاتي ونُسُكي ومَحْيايَ ومَماتي للهِ رَبِّ العالَمين لا شَريكَ لَهُ ، وبِذلِكَ أُمِرْتُ وأنا مِنَ المُسْلِمين

رواه مسلم

Wajjahtu wajhya lilathi fatar-as-samawati wal arda, hanifan Musliman wama ana minal Mushrikeen

Inna salatee wa nusukee wa mahyaya wa mamatee lillahi rabb-il-Aalameen

La shareeka lahu, wa bithalika umirtu wa ana min-al-Muslimeen

"I have turned my face to the One Who created the Heavens and Earth as a sincere servant, and I am not one of the polytheists. My prayers, my worship, my life and death are all for Allah, the Lord of the Worlds. He has no partner, that is what I have been ordered and I am of those who submit."

Al-Isti'athah الاسْتِعاذَة : Seeking Refuge from Shaytan:

It is a preferred act for one in prayer to seek refuge from Satan before reciting Surat ul-Fatihah. Allah Almighty says: "When you recite the Qur'an seek refuge in Allah from the outcast Satan." One should seek refuge silently, and in the first raka'ah only. Reported Abu Hurayrah.

Reciting Surat Al-Fatihah:

Surat-ul-Fatihah must be recited in every rak'ah of each prayer. Prophet Muhammad ﷺ made this point very clear in many ahadeeth.

عن عبادة بن الصامت رضي اللهُ عنهُ قال: قال رسول اللهِ صلى اللهُ عليهِ وسلّم:

" لا صَلاةَ لِمَنْ لَم يَقْرأْ بِفاتِحَةِ الكِتاب "

رواه البخاري ومسلم

Ubadah ibn us-Samit رضي الله عنه narrated that the Prophet ﷺ said: "The prayer would not be accepted from one who does not recite the opening of the Book (i.e. Al-Fatihah)."

In another hadeeth, he said: "It is also the Sunnah of the Prophet ﷺ to say "آمين Ameen" at the end of Surat-ul-Fatihah. This should also be said when praying in jama'ah, or in a group.

The word آمين Ameen means "Oh Allah respond."

According to Abu Hurayrah رضي الله عنه, the Prophet ﷺ said: "When the imam says : " waladdaalleen," say "Ameen," because whoever's 'Ameen' matches [in time and sincerity] that of the angels, he will be forgiven all his past sins." When the Prophet ﷺ used to conclude reciting Al-Fatihah in his loud prayers, he would raise his voice saying "Ameen"

After Al-Fatihah, Prophet Muhammad ﷺ would recite some more verses, a surah or even multiple suwar. This was in the first two rak'aat of each fard prayer.

Rukoo' رُكوع : The Bowing Part of Salah

There is one rukoo' in each rak'ah of the salah. The word "raka'h" is taken from the action of Rukoo'.

Making the Takbeer upon Moving from One position to Another:

The Prophet ﷺ would make the takbeer, Allahu Akbar, upon every movement in salah: before every rising, lowering, standing or sitting. However, when rising from the rukoo' position, he used to say: "Sami'allahu liman Hamidah (Allah hears him who praises Him)."

Abu Hurayrah رضي الله عنه described how the Prophet ﷺ used to perform one rak'ah of the salah. He reported that the Prophet used to make the first Takbeer after the 'Iqamah for Salah is made. Then he used to recite Al-Fatihah and some of the Qur'an. When he had done this, he would say the takbeer again while raising his hands, and then bow for rukoo'.

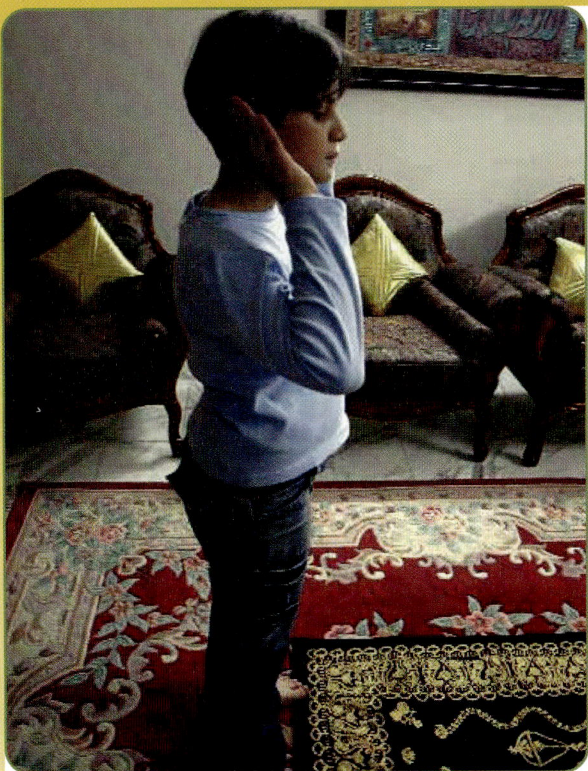

Before making rukoo', you may or may not raise your hands by your ears.

When making rukoo' make sure that your legs are straight, your back is flat parellel to the floor and you look at your Sujood spot.

How to Make Rukoo'

When the Prophet ﷺ was making rukoo', he used to place his palms firm on his knees while his legs are kept straight and a little apart. His back used to be almost parallel to the ground. It is the Sunnah to make the height of the head equal to that of the hips during rukoo'.

'Uqbah Ibn 'Aamir once bowed and kept his arms apart from his sides, his hands on his knees, and his fingers open beyond his knees. He said: "This is how I saw the Messenger of Allah ﷺ pray."

Tasbeeh During Rukoo'

Uqbah Ibn 'Aamir related that when the ayah 96 of Surat ul-Waqi'ah was revealed:

﴿ فَسَبِّحْ بِٱسْمِ رَبِّكَ ٱلْعَظِيمِ ٩٦ ﴾

الواقعة: ٩٦

"So praise be the name of your Lord, the Supreme." The Prophet said: "Make that tasbeeh during your rukoo'," That is why we say in Rukoo',

سُبْحَانَ رَبِّيَ الْعَظِيمِ

This is reported also by Ahmad, Abu Dawood, Ibn Majah and Al-Hakim.

More Du'aa' in Rukoo':

Du'aa'

اللّهم لكَ رَكَعْتُ ، وبِكَ آمَنْتُ ، ولَكَ أَسْلَمْتُ ، خَشَعَ لَكَ سَمْعِي وبَصَري ومُخّي وعَظْمي وَعَصَبي

Oh Allah, I bow to you, I believe in you and I submit to you. All my hearing, seeing, brain, bones and nerves fall in humbleness to you.

After the rukoo', Rasoolullah used to raise his back again to a complete standing position. When rising from rukoo', the Prophet ﷺ would say:

سَمِعَ اللهُ لِمَنْ حَمِدَه

Sami'allahu liman Hamidah (Allah hears he who praises Him)

Then he would say one of the following,

١. رَبَّنا وَلَكَ الحَمْد (البخاري ومسلم)

1. Rabbana wa lak-al-hamd.
1. Our Lord, we praise You (Bukhari and Muslim)

٢. رَبَّنا وَلَكَ الحَمْد كما يَنْبَغي لِجلالِ وجْهِكَ وعَظيم سُلْطانِكَ (ابن ماجه)

2. Rabbana wa lak-al-hamd kama yanbaghi lijalali wajhika wa atheemi sultanik
2. Our Lord, we praise You as Your glorified face and kingdom deserve. *(Ibn Majah)*

٣. رَبَّنا وَلَكَ الحَمْد حَمْداً كَثيراً طَيِّباً مباركاً فيه (أبو داود)

3. Rabbana wa lak-al-hamd hamdan katheeran tayyiban mubarakan feeh
3. Our Lord, we offer You a great, pure and blessed praise. (Abu dawood)

He would say this while raising his hands. Abu Hurayrah رضي الله عنه described the Prophet's ﷺ rising from rukoo' as follows:

"He would raise his head from rukoo', then stand straight until all of his backbones returned to their place."

However, one can straighten up from rukoo' without raising hands.

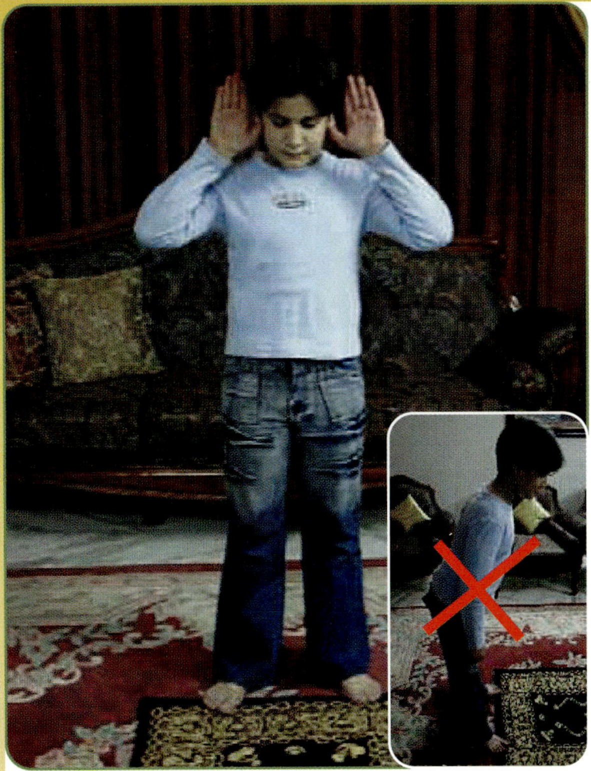

When raising your back up from rukoo', make sure that your back is up straight. You may or may not raise your hands by your ears.

When making sujood, your forehead, palms, knees and inner toes must be firm on the floor. Elbows must be apart from the floor.

III Sujood سُجود : The Prostration Part of Salah

Some scholars have said that sujood, or prostration, is the most important part of the prayer. The Prophet ﷺ said that the Muslim is closest to his Lord while in sujood. There are two prostrations in every rak'ah during salah.

How to make Sujood?

From the standing position after rukoo', the Prophet ﷺ used to make takbeer and kneel down for sujood. He would kneel first, then place his palms down, and finally his face.

Wa'il Ibn Hajr reported that when the Prophet ﷺ prostrated, he would place his forehead between his palms and separate his arms from the sides of his body. Abu Humaid added that when the Prophet ﷺ prostrated, he would place his nose and forehead upon the floor, keep his arms away from his sides and place his hands parallel to his shoulders. This was related by Khuzaymah and Al-Tirmithi.

عن عبدالله بن عَبَّاس رضيَ اللهُ عَنه قال: قال رسولُ الله صلَّى اللهُ عَلَيه وسَلَّمَ: "أُمِرْتُ أنْ أسْجُدَ عَلَى سَبْعَةِ أعْظُمٍ: الجَبْهَةِ، وأشَارَ إلى أنْفِهِ، واليَدَيْنِ والرُّكْبَتَيْنِ وأطْرَافِ القَدَمَيْنِ"

رواه البخاري وسلم

According to Al-Bukhari, Abdullah Ibn Abbas narrated that Rasoolullah said:

"I was ordered to make sujood on seven bones: the forehead, and he pointed to his nose, the two hands, the two knees and the two feet by the toes.

Here the Prophet ﷺ would raise his back up and say the following du'aa':

" رَبِّ اغْفِرْ لِي "

My Lord forgive me (Rabbighfirlee)

The Prophet ﷺ used to make the second sujood like the first one, then he would raise his back saying takbeer again, while standing for the second rak'ah. He would do this in all his prayers.

Tasbeeh and Du'aa' During Sujood:

'Uqbah Ibn 'Aamir and Wa'il Ibn Hijr related that on receiving the revelation of Surat Al-A'la, whose first ayah is, "Praise the name of your Lord, the Most High," (Qur'an 87:1)

﴿ سَبِّحِ اسْمَ رَبِّكَ الْأَعْلَى ۝ ﴾

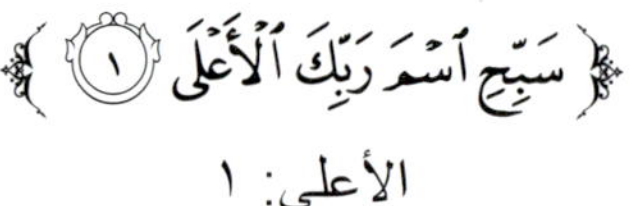

الأعلى: ١

The Prophet ﷺ said:

"Make that tasbeeh in your sujood." Therefore we should say in our Sujood:

سُبْحَانَ رَبِّيَ الْأَعْلَى

Subhana Rabbiyal A'la

This is also related by Ahmad, Abu Dawud, Ibn Majah and Al-Hakim. This must be repeated at least three times.

According to Huthayfah Ibn-ul-Yaman رضي الله عنه, the Prophet ﷺ used to say tasbeeh three to nine times in each rukoo' or sujood. The more tasbeeh you do, the more rewards you get.

However, the Prophet ﷺ used to make other kinds of tasbeeh and du'aa' during rukoo' and sujood.

The Two Knees

4

5

The Two Feet

7

6

1 The Forehead

3 2

The Two Hands

More Du'aa' in Sujood:

Du'aa'

اللَّهُم لكَ سَجَدْتُ ، وبِكَ آمَنْتُ ، ولَكَ أَسْلَمْتُ ، سَجَدَ وَجْهي لِلَّذي خَلَقَهُ وَشَقَّ سَمْعَهُ وبَصَرَهُ ، تَبارَكَ اللهُ أَحْسَنُ الخَالِقين .

Oh Allah, I prostrated to you, I believed in you and I submitted to you. My face prostrated to its Creator, the One who made its ears and eyes. Blessed is Allah the best of creators.

IV Juloos جلوس : The Sitting Part of Salah

As you learned earlier, there is a brief sitting period between the two prostrations in each rak'ah. However, there are longer juloos positions during salah.

Sitting, or juloos, is one main part of every prayer. Salat ul-Fajr and other two rak'aat prayers have one juloos at the end of the prayer. The other four prayers; Thuhr, Asr, Maghrib and Ishaa' have two sittings, the first is performed after the second rak'ah, and the second juloos is performed at the end of each prayer.

According to Al-Bukhari and Muslim, Abdullah Ibn Mas'ood رضي الله عنه narrated that Rasoolullah ﷺ taught the Sahabah to say the following Tashahhud statement during the first juloos:

التحيّات

At-Tahiyyat
The Greetings

التَّحيّاتُ للّهِ والصَّلواتُ والطَّيّبات ، السَّلامُ عليكَ أيُّها النَّبيُّ ورحمَةُ اللهِ وبركاته
السَّلامُ علينا وعلى عِبادِ اللهِ الصّالحين ، أشْهَدُ أن لا إلهَ إلاالله وأشْهَدُ أنَّ محمَّداً
عَبْدُهُ ورَسولُه

At-Tahiyat lillah, Wassalawatu wattayyibat, As-Salamu Alayka Ayuhan-nabiyyu Wa Rahmatullahi wa barakatuh, As-Salamu Alayna Wa 'Ala 'ibadullah-is-saliheen. Ash-hadu Anna La Illaha Illallah, Wa Ash-hadu Anna Muhammadan Abduhu wa Rasooluh."

Greetings, prayers and good deeds are due to Allah. May peace, Allah's mercy and blessings be upon you oh Prophet. May peace be upon us and the pious servants of Allah. I bear witness that there is no god but Allah and Muhammad is His servant and Prophet.

Again, the above should be said during the first juloos in all prayers, except Salat-ul-Fajr, which has only one juloos at the end of the prayer. Abdullah Ibn Mas'ood also reported that during the final juloos in all other prayers, the Prophet ﷺ used to recite the above tashahhud and the following As-Salat ul-Ibraheemiyyah, or the Abrahamic Prayer:

الصَّـلاة الإبراهيميَّة

As-Salat-ul-Ibraheemiyyah
The Abrahamic Prayer

اللهمَّ صلِّ على مُحَمَّدٍ وعَلى آلِ محمَّدٍ كما صَلَّيْتَ على إبراهيمَ وعلى آلِ إبراهيم
وبارِكْ على مُحَمَّدٍ وعَلى آلِ محمَّدٍ كما بارَكْتَ على إبراهيمَ وعلى آلِ إبراهيم
في العالَمين إنّكَ حَميدٌ مَجيد

Allahumma salli ala Muhammadin wa ala aali Muhammad, kama sallayta ala Ibraheema wa ala aali Ibraheem, wa barik ala Muhammadin wa ala aali Muhammad, kama barakta ala Ibraheema wa ala aal Ibraheem, fil aalameena innaka Hameedun Majeed.

Oh Allah make peace upon Muhammad and his family like you made peace upon Ibraheem and his family. Also, make blessings upon Muhammad and his family like you made blessings upon Ibraheem and his family. Among all the creation, you are worthy of praise and glory.

While sitting, Rasoolullah ﷺ used to have his back upright and place his left hand flat on his left thigh and fold the palm of the right hand, except the index, for pointing when making Tashahhud. The Prophet ﷺ used to sit on the sole of his left foot and erect his right foot with his toes facing Qiblah.

When sitting for the tashahhud make sure that your back and head are up straight. You should sit on your left foot and set your right foot up. When making shahadah during saying At-Tahiyyat, it is the Sunnah to point your right sabbabah (index finger) toward the Qiblah as shown in the small picture.

Du'aa' Before Tasleem:

After reciting At-Tashahhud and As-Salat ul-Ibraheemiyyah during the final juloos, the Prophet ﷺ used to say few du'aa's before tasleem:

اللهمَّ إني أعوذُ بكَ منْ عَذابِ جهَنَّم ، ومنْ عَذابِ القَبْرِ ، ومنْ فتْنَةِ المَحْيا والمَماتِ ، ومن فِتْنَةِ المَسيحِ الدّجال

Allahuma innee a'oothu bika min 'athabi jahannam, wa min 'athab-il-qabr, wa min fitnat-il-mahya wal-mamat, wa fitnat-il-maseeh-id-dajjal

Oh Allah protect me from the punishment of Hellfire, the punishment in the grave, the trial of life and death, and the trial of the false messiah.

This is reported in Muslim

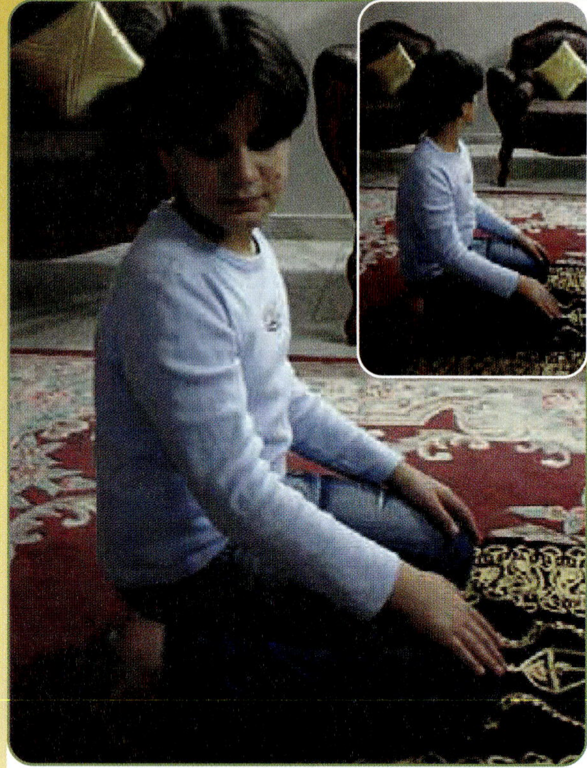

Turn your face completely to the right and say tasleem, then to the left.

Remember, you have to pray with your heart not only with your body.

The First Tasleemah and the Intention to End Salah

As you learned earlier, Prophet Muhammad ﷺ said that salah is unwound with tasleem. Therefore, he would end the prayer by turning his face to the right and saying tasleem:

السَّلامُ عَليكمْ وَرَحمَةُ اللهِ

"Assalamu Alaikum warahmatullah,"

May peace, blessings of Allah and His mercy be upon you

Then he would turn his face to the left and say the same.

...And finally:

* Perform salah with sincerity and khushoo'. Recognize that you are in the presence of your Lord, subhana wa ta'ala.
* Make each salah at the prescribed time.
* Plan your life around salah, not the other way around. For instance, don't just try to squeeze salah into a busy day. Plan your busy day around the prescribed times for salah and make the salah your priority.

Enjoy your salah!

When Rasoolullah used to ask Bilal, his Mu'thin, to make iqamah, he would say, " يا بلال أقِمِ الصَّلاة ، أرِحْنا بـها "

رواه أبو داود

"Oh Bilal, let's go ahead and have comfort in salah ."

Reported in Abu Dawood

DU'AA' AND THIKR AFTER THE PRAYER

After having ended his Salah the Messenger of Allah ﷺ used to ask for forgiveness three times then he would say:

"Allah humma antas salamu wa minkas salamu tabarakta ya thalijalali wal ikram."
(Reported by Bukhari, Muslim and At-Tirmithi)

It is reported by way of the Messenger of Allah ﷺ that he said:

"Whoever makes tasbeeh after each Salat 33 times, tahmeed 33 times, takbir 33 times, and completes a hundred by saying: 'La ilaha illa Allahu wahdahu la shareeka lahu, lahul mulku wa lahul hamdu, wa huwa 'ala kulli shay'in qadeer.' His sins would be forgiven even if they were as plentiful as the foam of the sea."
(Reported by Imam Muslim)

DU'AA' AND THIKR AFTER OBLIGATORY PRAYERS

Recite the following aloud or silently:

أَسْتَغْفِرُ اللهَ الْعَظِيمَ الذي لا إِلهَ إلا هوالْحَيُّ الْقَيّومَ وأتوبُ إليه

Astaghfirrullah Al-Athemm Al-Lathi La Ilaha Illa huwal-Hayyu-ul Qayyoom Wa-Atoobu Alayh. (3 times),
(I ask Allah to forgive me, there is no god but Him, the Alive, the all , and I repent to Him.

Then recite this du'aa silently:

اللهُمَّ أنتَ السَّلامُ ومنك السلامُ تباركْتَ يا ذا الجلال والإكرام

Allahumma antas-salamu wa mink-as-salamu tabarakta ya thaljalali wal ikram."
Oh Allah, You are the Peace, and You are the Source of Peace, You are Blessed, Oh Possessor of Glory and Honor)

Then recite the following Tasbeeh silently:

سُبْحانَ الله "Subhan-Allah" (Glory be to Allah) (33 times)

الْحَمْدُ لله "Alhamdu-lillah" (Praise be to Allah) (33 times)

اللهُ أَكْبَر "Allahu Akbar" (Allah is the Greatest) (33 times)

لا إِلهَ إلا الله وحده لا شَرِيكَ له ، له المُلكُ ولهُ الحَمْدُ وهُوَ عَلى كُلِّ شَيْءٍ قَدِير

"La ilaha illa Allahu wahdahu la shareeka lahu, lahul mulku wa lahul hamdu, wa huwa 'ala kullee shay'in qadeer"
There is none worthy of worship except Allah alone, no associate does He have, His is the Kingdom, to Him is All-Praise, and He is well able to do all things.

There are other du'aa's which Prophet Muhammad ﷺ used to say and teach to his companions. You can look for them in the books of hadeeth.

A Poem

SALAH

Salah is a basic pillar of Islam
It is mentioned again and again in the Qur'an
Praying in the mosque gives 27 times the reward
Pray with the intention that you're pleasing your Lord
When you walk to the mosque, just remember
You gain a reward and you're losing a sin
For every step towards your destination
This is a blessing from Allah swt to His creation
The Qur'an has foretold, that before you are dead
"say your prayers before your prayers are said"
Say Salah punctually, say it with care
On Judgment Day, we will be asked about prayer
That's the first question, so take this advice
Salah is the key to Paradise
Spread this word to Muslim sisters and brothers
Salah will separate Muslims from others
Salah is a blessing which Allah swt gave
It will intercede and protect us in the grave
When it comes eventually, to the day of rising
The believers body washed by wudoo' will be shining
For the believers who are regular in offering salah
It becomes a light of guidance on the siraat
Don't miss the Asr prayer at any cost
It will be like your family and wealth is lost
The Ayat-ul-Kursi after fard, should be read
It will lead you to paradise (insha Allah) after you're dead
Not reading salah will lead you to Hell
Surrounded by sinners in a deep well
So embrace Islam with all your heart
And remember the key is perfecting salah

source: http://members.tripod.com/islamickids/id99.htm

CHAPTER REVIEW

Projects and Activities

1. Record a video of an imam or a knowledgeable adult praying a four rak'aat prayer. The adult should explain how the Prophet ﷺ performed the different parts of prayer.
2. Create a Power Point presentation that illustrates with pictures how a four Rak'aat prayer is performed according to the Sunnah of the Prophet (P).

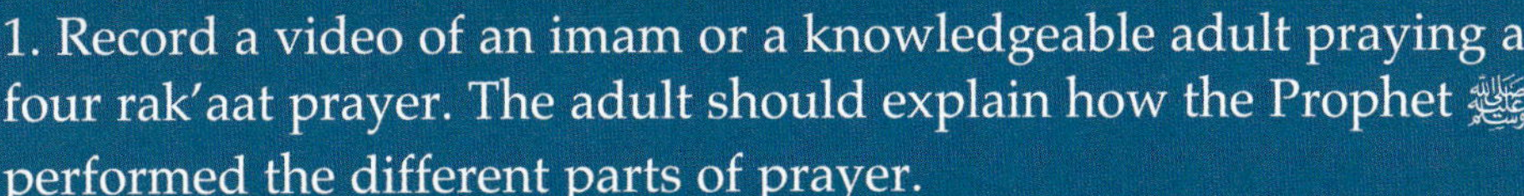

Stretch Your Mind

Compare and contrast the way you currently pray and the way prayer is explained in this chapter.

Study Questions

1. Define: a. Takbeerat-ul-Ihram b. Qiyam c. Du'aa'-ul-Istiftah d. Rukoo' e. Sujood f. Juloos g. At-Tashahhud
2. What are the main positions of salah?
3. Describe how salah should be started.
4. Describe how the qiyam position should be observed in prayer.
5. Describe how the rukoo' position should be observed in prayer.
6. Describe how the sujood position should be observed in prayer.
7. Describe how the juloos position should be observed in prayer.
8. How should salah be properly ended?

Salat-us-Sunnah: Voluntary Prayer in Islam

CHAPTER OUTLINE

1. The different types of recommended or voluntary prayers.
2. The importance and beauty of recommended prayers.
3. Apply your knowledge by performing recommended prayers as often as you can.

VOCABULARY

- Sunnah سُنَّة
- Sunan سُنَن
- Nafl نَفْل
- Nawafil نوافِل
- Tatawwu' تَطَوُّع
- Sunnah Ratibah سُنَّة راتِبة
- Sunna Mu'akkadah سُنَّة مُؤكَّدة
- Duha ضُحى
- Taraweeh تَراويح

Loving and Obeying the Prophet

We all have people in our lives whom we love and admire. We love our parents, so we obey them and take care of them. We love our friends and family, so we visit them and spend time with them. We love our teachers, so we show them respect and learn from them. We may have an older sibling or cousin whom we love and admire and therefore try to act and dress like him or her. In these ways, we make each person that we love a part of our lives. But, the person we should love the most and who should be the greatest part of our life is the Prophet Muhammad. This is clear in the Prophet's teachings:

The Prophet has said, "None of you

will have [complete] faith until I am more beloved to him than his children, his parents, and all people." (Bukhari).

One day, 'Umar ibn al-Khattab said to the Prophet, "I love you more than anything except my own self." The Prophet replied, "None of you will [truly] believe until I am dearer to him than his own self." 'Umar said, "However, now, by Allah, I love you more than my own self." The Prophet said, "'Umar, now you have it!" (Bukhari).

The Prophet, peace and blessings be upon him, sacrificed his entire life to teach us the message of Islam. Everything he did was for our benefit. He had a deep and abiding love for the believers. In the Qur'an, Allah says about the Prophet that "it makes him sad when you suffer, ardently anxious and worried is he over you, and he is most kind and merciful to the believers." (9:128). As Muslims, we should love him and place him above all else in our lives. The companions of the Prophet did so by serving and obeying him and giving up everything in order to be with him. They followed him in everything that he did and risked their lives for him. In our time, it may be easy to claim that we love the Prophet, however, the test comes when we have to choose between following the Prophet or following our worldly desires. The way to express our love for the Prophet is by learning about his life, character, and example; striving to follow his Sunnah and guidance; and sending peace and blessings upon him. By doing so, we make him a part of our lives now and hope to be with him in the afterlife.

The Prophet, peace and blessings be upon him, is the best of creation and the most beloved by Allah. We should love the Prophet and follow him for the sake of Allah. As Allah informs us in the Qur'an, the Prophet had the best morals and character. There is no one better than the Prophet to follow in order to reach Paradise. Allah tells us in the Qur'an, "Indeed you have in the Messenger of Allah an excellent example." (33:21). Allah commands the Prophet to say to the believers, "If you love Allah, follow me, and Allah will love you and forgive you your sins." [Surat-Al-Imran 3:31].

The Importance of Performing Salat-ul-Sunnah

One important way to follow the Prophet and draw closer to Allah is by performing voluntary prayer. In the Hadith Qudsi, the Prophet tells us that Allah has said, "My slave approaches me with nothing more beloved to Me than what I have made obligatory upon him, and My slave continues to draw nearer to Me with voluntary works until I love him." (Bukhari). This means that the best way to obey Allah is by performing the obligatory or fard prayers. After fulfilling this obligation, one keeps coming closer to Allah by performing the voluntary or recommended prayers that the Prophet used to perform. The voluntary or recommended prayers are known in Arabic as "Salat-us-Sunnah." When a person follows the Prophet by praying Salat-us-Sunnah, Allah will love him or her, just as He promised in the Hadeeth Qudsi and in the above Qur'anic verse.

Furthermore, the Sunnah prayers will help makeup for the mistakes and shortcomings of our fard prayers. The Prophet Muhammad, peace and blessings be upon him, has told us that "a prayer that is not complete is added to from the voluntary prayer that is associated with it until it is complete." This means that if, for example, we forgetfully miss a rak'ah, make a mistake in our recitation of Qur'an, or are absentminded during our fard prayer, Allah will look to our Sunnah prayers to take the place of our fard prayers. Being that we are all humans who make many mistakes, we should be grateful for Allah's generosity by making sure we always pray our Sunnah prayers.

Types of Prayers

Prayer is a broad word that refers to a way to worship and glorify Allah. In Islam, there are many ways to worship and pray to Allah. Since Islam is a way of life, prayer is not restricted to a specific time and place, but should be a part of our entire life. The following are different types of prayer:

1. Salat-ul-Fard: Obligatory Ritual Prayer

The obligatory ritual prayer has been established by Allah and His Messenger five times a day. It is fard, or obligatory, to perform these prayers on time and haram, or forbidden, to miss them. This means that every accountable Muslim must perform these prayers. Performing the obligatory prayers makes one deserving of reward and missing them makes one deserving of punishment.

2. Salat-us-Sunnah: Voluntary Prayer

The voluntary or recommended ritual prayer was performed by the Prophet at certain times. This prayer is also known as Salat-ut-Tatawwu' in Arabic and sometimes referred to as "supererogatory prayer" in English. Performing voluntary prayers makes one deserving of much reward and the love of Allah and His Messenger. The voluntary prayer can be classified into two major types:

a. As-Sunnah Ar-Ratibah: Regular Sunnah

The regular Sunnah is also known in Arabic as As-Sunnah Al-Mu'akkadah, or the "confirmed recommended prayer." The Prophet, peace and blessings be upon him, performed this type of recommended prayer regularly either before or after fard prayers, and rarely missed it. Consistently missing the regular sunnah shows disrespect to the Prophet, peace and blessings be upon him, and is therefore sinful.

b. Salat-un-Nafl: Extra Sunnah Prayer

The extra sunnah prayer can be performed at anytime. There are certain times in the day when the Prophet would occasionally perform extra Sunnah prayers. These times are known to have more baraka or blessing, but one can perform extra Sunnah prayers anytime he or she likes.

As-Sunnah Ar-Ratibah

The regular or confirmed recommended prayers according to the Sunnah of the Prophet, peace and blessings be upon him, are as follows:

- 2 Rak'aat before Fajr
- 2 or 4 Rak'aat before Thuhr and 2 after Thuhr
- 2 Rak'aat after Maghrib
- 2 Rak'aat after 'Ishaa' and Salat-ul-Witr (1 to 11 Rak'aat).

Table: Regular Sunnah prayers

	Prayer	Number of Rak'aat of Sunnah
1	Fajr	2 Rak'aat Before Fard
2	Thuhr	2 or 4 Rak'aat before Fard and 2 after
3	Asr	No Regular Sunnah
4	Maghrib	2 after Fard
5	Ishaa'	2 after Fard

Witr Prayer

Another important confirmed sunnah prayer is the Witr prayer. "Witr" literally means "odd number," and so the Witr prayer is any number of odd Rak'aat, usually three. The Witr Prayer is usually performed after, the Sunnah prayer that follows Ishaa, however, it can be, performed anytime between Ishaa and Fajr.

The Witr prayer is considered by many scholars to be the most important confirmed sunnah prayer. In the Hanafi school of fiqh, the Witr prayer is so important that it is considered to be wajib, which means that it is an obligation that is only slightly lower than a fard prayer. Ali رضي الله عنه has told us that, "The Witr prayer is not required like your obligatory prayers, but the Prophet, peace and blessings be upon him, would perform the Witr prayer

and say, ‘O you people of the Qur’an, perform the Witr prayer, for Allah is One and He loves the Witr prayer.’”
(Reported by Ahmad, Nasa’ee, Abu Dawud)

One should strive to perform all of the confirmed recommended prayers. Performing all of the confirmed recommended prayers will lead a person to great reward and to the love of Allah and His Messenger. The Sunnah prayers will also make up for deficiencies in one’s fard prayers.

" عن أبي هريرة رضي الله عنه قال : أوصاني خليلي بِثلاث ، لا أدعَهُنَّ حتّى أموت: صَوْم ثَلاثَة أيام مِنْ كُلِّ شَهْر وَصَلاةِ الضُّحى ونَوْم على وِتْر "

رواه البخاري ومسلم

Abu Hurayrah رضي الله عنه said: My beloved friend (Rasoolullah) advised me to do three things, and I am not leaving them till I die; to fast three days of every month, to pray Salat-ud-Duha, and to pray Salat-ul-Witr before I sleep”

Reported in Al-Bukhari and Muslim

Salat-un-Nafl

Salat-un-Nafl are extra Sunnah, or voluntary prayers, that the Prophet, peace and blessings be upon him, performed, but did not emphasize as much as regular recommended prayers. The following are examples of extra Sunnah prayers:

1. Qiyam-ul-Layl: The Late Night Prayer

The late night prayer is at least two Rak’aat and is usually performed in the late part of the night. Allah refers to the devout people, who are regular in praying at night, by saying:

﴿ وَٱلَّذِينَ يَبِيتُونَ لِرَبِّهِمۡ سُجَّدٗا وَقِيَٰمٗا ٦٤ ﴾

“And those who spend the night before their Lord prostrating and standing.” [Surat-Al-Furqan: 64]

The Prophet also said,

" أفضل الصلاة بعد الفريضة صلاة الليل "

رواه مسلم

“The best prayer after the obligatory ones is the night prayer.”
Reported by Imam Muslim

The time of Qiyam-ul-Layl starts after Ishaa’ prayer, and ends at the time of fajr prayer. However, the best time to perform Qiyam-ul-Layl is to wake up at the last third of the night, which is a time of great barakah, or blessing, and pray. This is called tahajjud. Allah says in Surat-ul-Israa’,

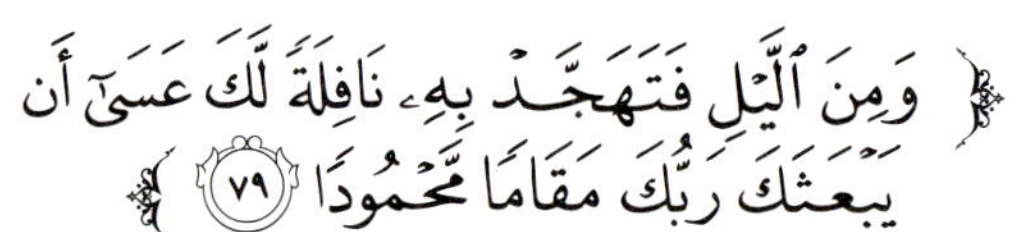

“And during a part of the night, pray tahajjud as an extra [prayer] for you; maybe your Lord will raise you to a position of great glory.” [17:79]

The Prophet, peace and blessings be upon him, tells us that in the last third of the night, Allah says: "Who shall call upon Me, that I may answer him? Who shall ask Me, that I may give to him? Who shall seek My forgiveness, that I may forgive him?" (Bukhari). The Late night prayer is an intimate meeting with Allah while most of the world is asleep and quiet. To rise from one's sleep to tell Allah one loves Him, thank Him, and pray for forgiveness is a great act of worship.

In fact, tahajjud was obligatory for the Prophet, peace and blessings be upon him However, out of mercy, it is voluntary for all believers other than the Prophet. The person who performs this prayer voluntarily out of love for Allah receives a multitude of blessings from Allah.

2. Salat-ud-Duha: The Midmorning Prayer

This refers to a prayer that is performed after sunrise is complete and before the time of Dhuhr comes very close. The midmorning prayer is at least two rak'aat and at most twelve rak'aat, while it is best to perform four or eight rak'aat, divided into two-rak'a units. The Prophet, peace and blessings be upon him, has taught us that the Duha prayer is better than or equal to more than 360 charities. He said, "Charity is required from every part of your body daily. Every saying of 'Glory be to Allah' is charity. Every saying of 'Praise be to Allah' is charity. Every saying of 'There is no God but Allah' is charity. Every saying of 'Allah is the Greatest' is charity. Ordering the good is charity. Forbidding the evil is charity. And what suffices for those (as a charity) are the two rak'at of Duha."

3. Two or Four Rak'aat before 'Asr

There are many narrations regarding the performance of either two or four rak'aat before the 'Asr prayer. Additionally, the Prophet's ﷺ companions, as well as pious men that came after them, performed these prayers regularly.

عن ابن عمر رضي الله عنه قال:
" رَحِمَ اللهُ امْرَءً صَلّى قبلَ العَصْرِ أرْبعاً "
رواه أحمد وأبو داود والترمذي

Ibn Umar narrates, "May Allah have mercy on a person that prays four rak'aat before 'Asr prayer."

Reported bu Ahmad and Tirmithi

4. Two Rak'aat before Maghrib and Ishaa' prayer

These are two units of prayer before the Maghrib, or sunset prayers. It has also been narrated that the Prophet and his companions prayed these two units of prayer before the Ishaa' prayer. Ibn Zubair reports the following regarding two units of prayer before Ishaa', "There exists no obligatory prayer without there being, immediately preceding it, two rak'at." *(Reporteted by Ibn Hibban)*

5. The Taraweeh Prayers

This prayer is a special prayer that is performed after the Ishaa' prayer and before the Witr, during the month of Ramadan. It includes eight rak'aat, according to the majority of imams, and scholars. Other imams believe it should include twenty rak'aat.

Abu Hurairah (R) narrated that the Prophet ﷺ would encourage people to pray taraweeh without commanding it as obligatory. He would say,

"من قام رمضان إيماناً واحتساباً غفر له ما تقدَّم من ذنبه"

رواه البخاري ومسلم

"Whoever prays (Taraweeh) during the nights of Ramadan with a firm belief and hoping for reward, all of his previous sins would be forgiven."
Reported by Imams Al-Bukhari and Muslim

6. Salat-ul-Istkharah: The Guidance Prayer

The Prophet ﷺ has taught us to perform the Guidance Prayer whenever we are faced with a matter in which we have to make a decision between two choices. He said, "When a matter concerns one of you, pray two nonobligatory (voluntary) rak'aat and say: 'O Allah, I ask You to show me what is best through Your knowledge, and bring it to pass through Your power, and I ask You of Your immense favor; for You are all-powerful and I am not, You know and I do not, and You are the Knower of the Unseen. O Allah, if You know this matter (here you mention what matter you need to ask Allah about) to be better for me in my religion, livelihood, and final outcome (or the short term and the long term of my case), then bring it about and facilitate it for me, and bless me with abundance therein. And if You know this matter to be worse for me in my religion, livelihood, and final outcome (or the short and long term of my case), then keep it from me, and keep me from it, and bring about the good for me whatever it may be, and make me pleased with it,' and one should mention the matter at hand."

(Reported by Imam Al-Bukhari)

اللَّهُمَّ إنِّي أَسْتَخِيرُكَ بِعِلْمِكَ ، وَأَسْتَقْدِرُكَ بِقُدْرَتِكَ، وَأَسْأَلُكَ مِنْ فَضْلِكَ الْعَظِيمِ فَإِنَّكَ تَقْدِرُ وَلا أَقْدِرُ، وَتَعْلَمُ وَلا أَعْلَمُ ، وَأَنْتَ عَلامُ الْغُيُوبِ ، اللَّهُمَّ إنْ كُنْتَ تَعْلَمُ أَنَّ هَذَا الأَمْرَ (هنا تسمي حاجتك) خَيْرٌ لِي فِي دِينِي وَمَعَاشِي وَعَاقِبَةِ أَمْرِي أَوْ قَالَ: عَاجِلِ أَمْرِي وَآجِلِهِ ، فَاقْدُرْهُ لِي وَيَسِّرْهُ لِي ثُمَّ بَارِكْ لِي فِيهِ ، اللَّهُمَّ وَإِنْ كُنْتَ تَعْلَمُ أَنَّ هَذَا الأَمْرَ (هنا تسمي حاجتك) شَرٌّ لِي فِي دِينِي وَمَعَاشِي وَعَاقِبَةِ أَمْرِي أَوْ قَالَ : عَاجِلِ أَمْرِي وَآجِلِهِ، فَاصْرِفْهُ عَنِّي وَاصْرِفْنِي عَنْهُ وَاقْدُرْ لِي الْخَيْرَ حَيْثُ كَانَ ثُمَّ ارْضِنِي بِهِ . وَيُسَمِّي حَاجَتَهُ) وفي رواية (ثُمَّ رَضِّنِي بِهِ)

رَوَاهُ الْبُخَارِيُّ

"Allahumma innee astakheeruka bi 'ilmika wa astaqdiruka bi qudratika, wa as-aluka min fadlikal 'adheem, fa inaka taqdiru wa la aqdir, aw ta'lamu wa la a'lam, wa anta 'allamul ghuyoob. Allahumma in kunta ta'lam anna hadhal amra khayrun lee fi deenee wa ma'ashee wa 'aqibati amree, faqdurhu lee wa yassirhu lee, thumma barik lee feeh, wa in kunta ta'lamu anna hadhal amrua sharrun lee fi deenee wa ma'ashee wa 'aqibati amree, fasrifhu 'annee wasrifnee 'anhu, waqdur liyal khayra haythu kana, thumma raddinee bih."

When we perform the Guidance Prayer, we are asking Allah to guide us in making the best decision. We are also affirming our reliance on Allah to give us what is best for us. After praying the Guidance Prayer, we may have a dream showing us the best decision, or we may have a feeling about what we should do. Or, maybe Allah will open up one course of action and make another difficult for us. If we do not experience any of these things, at least we know that we have left our decision to Allah, for He knows what is best for us and He is the only One who decides in the end.

These are just a few of the many extra Sunnah prayers that the Prophet ﷺ encouraged Muslims to perform. We should strive to perform these prayers as often as possible out of love for the Prophet, peace and blessings be upon him, and out of seeking the reward of Allah. However, remember that the most beloved act to Allah is the constant one. It is better to take one of these prayers and make it your habit then to perform all of these prayers for just a few days. Start step by step in order to make sure that you remain consistent, rather than burdening yourself all at once so that you are unable to continue.

The following hadeeth describes Allah's love for the Muslim who strives hard to draw near to Allah by obeying Him and performing obligatory and voluntary acts of worship, such as prayer. Allah tells us in this hadeeth Qudsi how He will guide and support such a Muslim in everything he says and does by being his hearing, his sight, his hands, and his feet. Allah is also showing us that someone who is close to Allah remembers Allah in everything he does, so that he cannot disobey Allah with his hearing, sight, hands, or feet. Such a Muslim worships Allah as though he sees Him and remembers that Allah is always watching him.

hadeeth Qudsi:

عَنْ أَبِي هُرَيْرَةَ ـ رَضِيَ اللهُ عَنْهُ ـ قَالَ : قَالَ رَسُولُ الله صَلَّى اللهُ عَلَيْهِ وَسَلَّمَ ـ إِنَّ اللهَ تَعَالى قَالَ : "مَنْ عَادَى لِي وَلِيًّا فَقَدْ آذَنْتُهُ بِالْحَرْبِ ، وَمَا تَقَرَّبَ إِليَّ عَبْدِي بِشَيْءٍ أَحَبَّ إِلَيَّ مِمَّا افْتَرَضْتُ عَلَيْهِ ، وَلَا يَزَالُ عَبْدِي يَتَقَرَّبُ إِلَيَّ بِالنَّوَافِلِ حَتَّى أُحِبَّهُ ، فَإِذَا أَحْبَبْتُهُ كُنْتُ سَمْعَهُ الَّذِي يَسْمَعُ بِهِ وَبَصَرَهُ الَّذِي يُبْصِرُ بِهِ ، وَيَدَهُ الَّتِي يَبْطِشُ بِهَا وَرِجْلَهُ وَيَمْشِي بِهَا وَإِنْ سَأَلَنِي لَأُعْطِيَنَّهُ، وَلَئِنِ اسْتَعَاذَنِي لَأُعِيذَنَّهُ،
رَوَاهُ الْبُخَارِي .

Abu Hurayrah رضي الله عنه reported that the Prophet ﷺ said:

"Allah Most High says, 'Whomever is hostile to a friend of Mine I declare war against. My slave approaches Me with nothing more beloved to Me than what I have made obligatory upon him, and My slave continues to draw nearer to Me with voluntary works until I love him. And when I love him, I am his hearing with which he hears, his sight with which he sees, his hand with which he seizes, and his foot with which he walks. If he asks Me, I will surely give to him, and if he seeks refuge in Me, I will surely protect him. I do not hesitate from anything I shall do more than My hesitation to take the soul of the believer who dislikes death; for I dislike displeasing him."

Reported by Imam Al-Bukhari

CHAPTER REVIEW

Projects and Activities

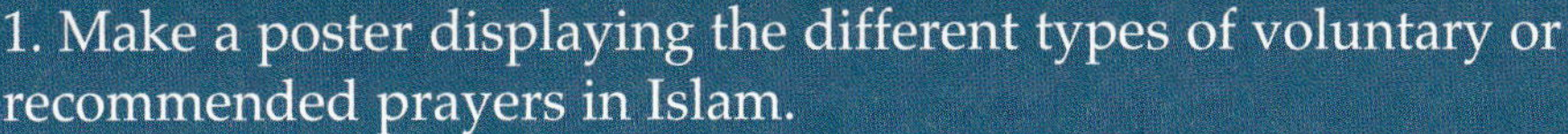

1. Make a poster displaying the different types of voluntary or recommended prayers in Islam.
2. Come up with a daily checklist of the fard and Sunnah prayers that you should do every day. Use this checklist on a daily basis to keep track of your consistency and progress.
3. Count how many Sunnah ratibah prayers you perform for one week confirmed.

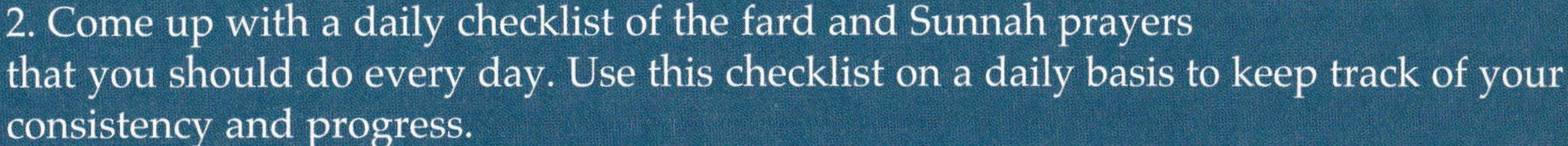

Stretch Your Mind

1) How does performing Sunnah prayers show our love for the Prophet?

2) Why should we love the Prophet more than anyone, even ourselves?

3) What is the difference between Tahajjud and Qiyam-ul-Layl?

Study Questions

1. Define: a. Sunnah Ratibah b. Sunan c. An-Nawafil d. Duha e. Qiyam-ul-Layl f. Taraweeh
2. How many Rak'aat are there in each confirmed Sunnah prayer? Make a table to answer the question?
3. How can our Sunnah prayer help make up for mistakes in our fard prayer?
4. What are the extra Sunnah prayers, other than the regular Sunnah prayers, that we may pray daily?
5. What is Salat-ul-Istikharah? Describe how it is performed?

LESSON ONE

Congregational Prayers in Islam
1. Salat-ul-Jama'ah صلاة الجماعة : The Daily Congregational Prayers

CHAPTER OUTLINE

1. The different types of congregational prayer in Islam.
2. Obligatory and recommended congregational prayer.
3. The importance of Salat-ul-Jama'ah and other congregational prayers.

VOCABULARY

- Salat-ul-Jama'ah صلاة الجماعة
- Salat-ul-Jumu'ah صلاة الجمعة
- Salat-ul-Eid صلاة العيد
- Salat-ul-Masbooq صلاة المسبوقة

Performing the five obligatory prayers (Fajr, Thuhr, 'Asr, Maghrib, and 'Isha) in jama'ah or, in a group, is itself a Sunnah mu'kkadah, or confirmed Sunnah. Some scholars, like Imam Ahmad Ibn Hanbal and others, consider Salat-ul-Jama'ah in the masjid an obligatory ritual on men. The Prophet ﷺ always prayed in the masjid with the Sahabah, or companions. The Prophet ﷺ emphatically encouraged the Muslims to pray in a group or congregation whenever possible. The Prophet gave women the choice to come to the masjid for Salat-ul-Jama'ah, or to pray at home.

hadeeth Shareef

عن عبدِ الله بن عمر رضي الله عنه قال:

"صلاةُ الجَماعَةِ أفضلُ مِنْ صَلاةِ الفرد بِسَبْعٍ وَعِشْرين دَرَجة"

رواه البخاري ومسلم

Abdullah Ibn Umar narrates, "The prayer in congregation is superior to a prayer performed individually by twenty-seven degrees."

(Reported by Al-Bukhari and Muslim)

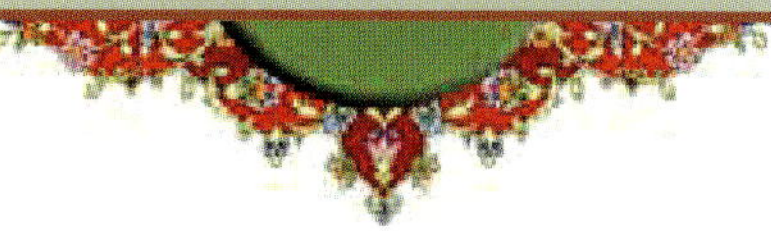

By the example and sayings of the Prophet ﷺ, we come to understand the importance of attending the obligatory prayers in the masjid and performing them in a group. We should all aspire to perform the obligatory prayers in congregation and encourage others to do so. When we are at home we should politely ask our parents or the adults in our family to take us to the masjid in order to pray. If no one is able to drive us there, we should ask them to pray in a group with us at home.

Do you think that Allah commanded Muslims to build masajid all over the world only for Salat-ul-Jumu'ah or the Friday prayer once a week? The image of a large, beautiful masjid that is empty all week long is a sad one. Allah wants us to visit His house, the masjid every day. Here is a story about the importance of visiting the masjid and praying in congregation every day:

A blind man once came to the Prophet, peace and blessings be upon him, and said: "O Rasoolullah ﷺ, I am a blind man and my house is a little far from the masjid. Would you allow me not to come to the masjid every day?" The Prophet ﷺ first said: "Yes." As the man started walking away, the Prophet ﷺ quickly called him back and asked:

"Do you hear the call to prayer (from your house)?" "Yes," the man replied. The Prophet then said:

"Then, you should answer the call," meaning that it is better to come to the masjid for the congregational prayers every day.

Although the man was blind and it may have taken him some time to find his way to the masjid five times a day, the Prophet ﷺ told him to answer the call to prayer and come to the masjid for every prayer. This is how important it is to center one's life around praying in the masjid and to put all of one's efforts into doing so consistently. Every step one takes towards the masjid will be rewarded immensely.

Later, Abdullah Ibn Umm Maktoom, the blind man, was to become a great Muslim. The Prophet came to trust Abdullah greatly and he made him the mu'athin of the masjid, so that Abdullah would give the call to prayer. Abdullah was also sometimes chosen as the leader of Medina, when the Prophet was traveling outside the city. Had the Prophet allowed Abdullah to stay home instead of coming to the masjid everyday, Abdullah would never have become such an important Muslim in the community.

When we go to the masjid to perform Salat-ul-Jama'ah in congregation, we receive much reward. We please Allah and gain the barakah, or the blessing of praying in His house. We come to know the Muslims in our community and gain a sense of unity. In Salat-ul-Jama'ah, the rich man prays next to the poor man and they are both equal as they stand before Allah. Furthermore, at the masjid, we are surrounded by other people who are struggling to be good Muslims. By getting to know one another and attending Islamic classes together at the masjid, we can help each other to become great Muslims.

The Prophet ﷺ, always checked to make sure that his Sahabah, or companions, came to Salat-ul-Jama'ah, or the congregational prayers, everyday. He would be upset with those who were always absent without good reason, such as being sick or traveling outside Madinah.

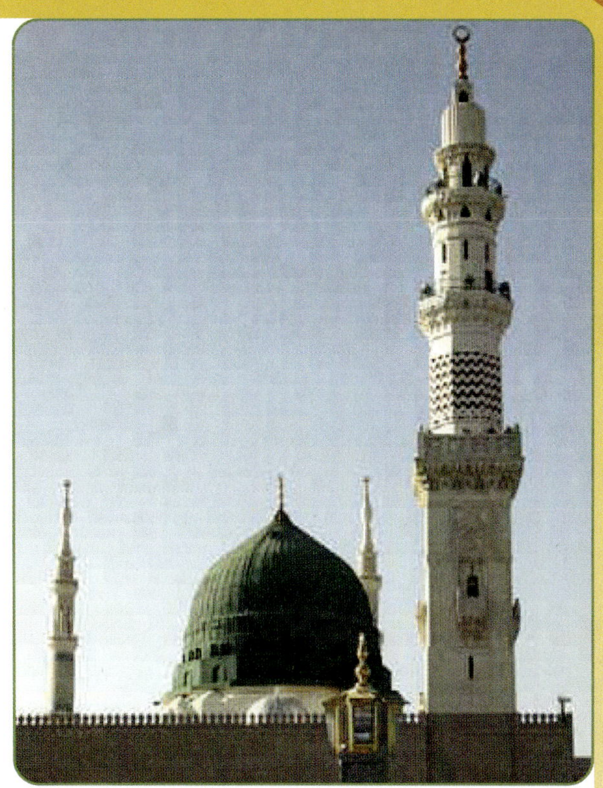

How to Pray Salat-ul-Jama'ah

Where Do We Pray Salat-ul-Jama'ah or Congregational Prayer?

Usually Salat-ul-Jama'ah takes place at the masjid. The Prophet and the Sahabah used to pray in the masjid five times a day. However, a Muslim can pray Salat-ul-Jama'ah in a group with other Muslims at school, work, or at home, when he is unable to go to the masjid because of a good reason. Of course, Salat-ul-Jama'ah is most rewarded in the masjid.

When Do We Pray Salat-ul-Jama'ah?

Five times a day, Muslims pray Salat-ul-Jama'ah in the masjid shortly after the prayer time starts and the adhan or call to prayer is given.

Who Should Pray Salat-ul-Jama'ah?

The Prophet ﷺ encouraged all Muslims to pray Salat-ul-Jama'ah at the masjid. However, while men are only excused if they are sick, traveling, or have a valid excuse, women are generally excused from praying at the masjid if they are busy at home. When a woman is unable to pray in the masjid because she has young children, Allah gives her great reward for praying at home and taking care of her children.

How Do We Perform Salat-ul-Jama'ah?

1. Where to Stand

The imam usually stands in the middle of the front line. Men line up behind the imam; then the boys line up; then the girls, leaving a gap between themselves and the boys; and then the women. So, if you are praying in a large congregation, make sure to stand in the appropriate line.

- If there is a male imam and one male ma'moom, or person following the imam, the ma'moom stands to the right of the imam. The same goes for a female Imam and one female ma'moomah.

- If there is a male Imam and one female ma'moomah, the female ma'moomah stands behind the imam.

2. How to Follow the Imam

- Follow the Imam in every move that he makes during the prayer.
- When the imam says "Allahu-Akbar" out loud, you should say it quietly to yourself.
- Some Muslims recite Al-Qur'an quietly to themselves, even when the imam is reciting out loud. They wait a moment and make every movement right after the imam. This is the correct way to pray in a congregation according to the shafi'i school of Fiqh.
- Some Muslims listen silently when Al-Qur'an is being recited, even when the imam is reciting quietly to himself. They make every movement with the

Position of imam and people behind him in Salat-ul-Jama'a

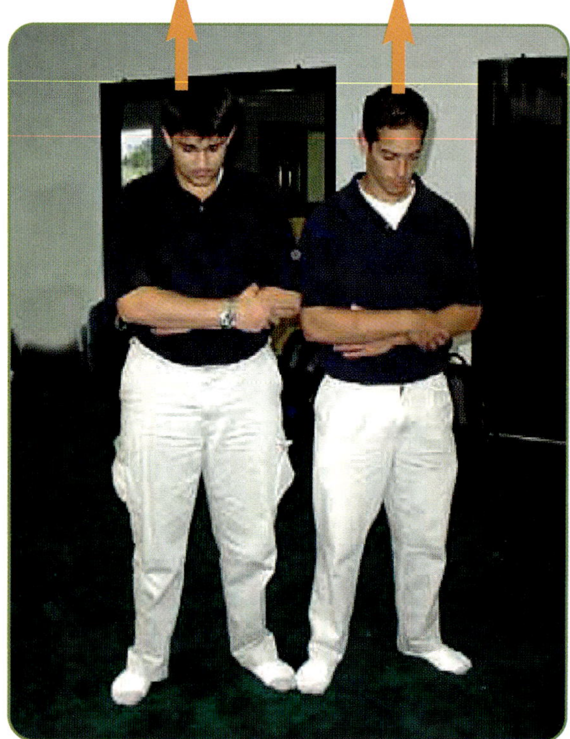

The positions of imam and ma'moom when only 2 males pray together.

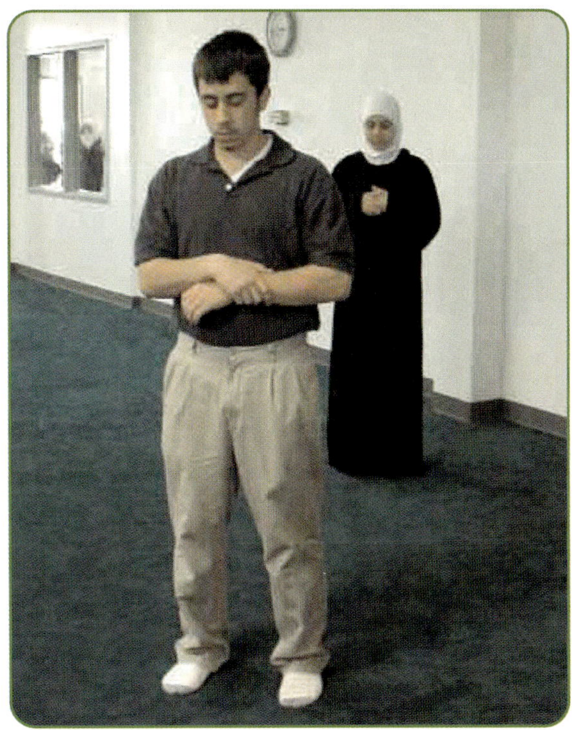

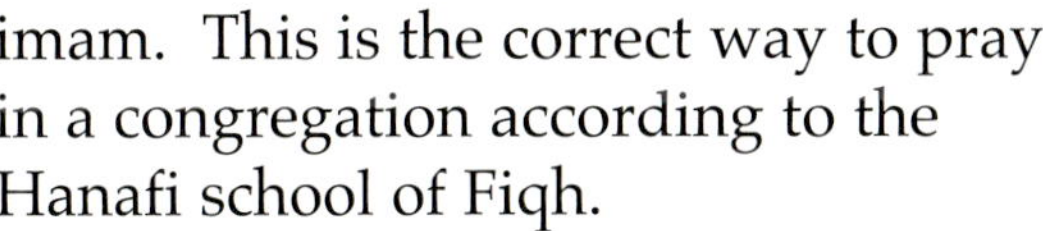

The positions of imam and ma'moom when a male and female pray together.

imam. This is the correct way to pray in a congregation according to the Hanafi school of Fiqh.

-You should never make a movement before the imam.

- When you are praying, remember that you are standing before Allah. Try not to make unnecessary movements and try to be respectful to those praying beside you by not being loud in your prayer and by not taking up too much space.

3. Salat-ul-Masbooq: Joining a Group in Prayer after the Imam has Started

When you join a group in prayer after the imam has finished the first rak'ah, it is called Salat-ul-Masbooq. If you arrive late for prayer at the masjid and you have already missed at least one Rak'ah of the prayer, you should walk in calmly and join the group with respect. Join the last line of the congregation in order not to disrupt the prayer. Immediately raise your hands and say "Allahu akbar," and follow the imam.

After the imam makes tasleem by turning to his right and left sides and saying "Assalamu 'alaykum wa rahmatullah," you may stand up to complete your prayer by performing any parts that you may have missed. If you join the group in prayer anytime before the imam stands up after completing rukoo,' or the bowing position, you count that as a rak'ah, or unit of prayer, that you have prayed with the imam.

If you happen to join the congregation while the imam is still in rukoo' position, then you have observed the rak'ah. But if you miss the rukoo' with the imam, then you have missed the rak'ah and you have to make it up.

The following are possible scenarios for Salat-ul-Masbooq:

- If you join the group for 'Asr prayer after the imam has started, and you pray three rak'aat with the group, then you know that you have missed one out of the four rak'aat of the 'Asr prayer. After the imam makes tasleem, you stand up to pray one more rak'ah, then you end your prayer as usual, by making juloos, or the seated position, tashahhud, and tasleem.
- If you pray two rak'aat of the 'Asr prayer with the group, then you know that you have missed two rak'aat. After the imam makes tasleem, you stand up to pray two more rak'aat, and end your prayer as usual.
- If you pray one rak'ah of the 'Asr prayer with the group, then you know that you have missed three rak'aat. After the imam makes tasleem, you stand up to pray three more rak'aat. You make juloos and read the first tashahhud after one rak'ah. Then, you pray two more rak'aat and end your prayer as usual, by making the second juloos, reciting the final tashahhud, and making tasleem.
- If you realize that you have not prayed any rak'aat of the 'Asr prayer with the group, then you know that you have missed all four rak'aat. After the imam makes tasleem, you stand up to pray four rak'aat as you usually would and end your prayer as usual. Even though you did not pray any rak'aat with the group, insha Allah you got the reward and blessing of praying in congregation.

CHAPTER REVIEW

Projects and Activities

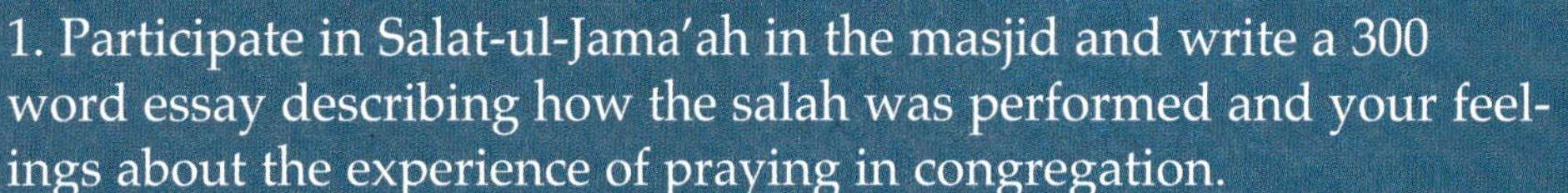

1. Participate in Salat-ul-Jama'ah in the masjid and write a 300 word essay describing how the salah was performed and your feelings about the experience of praying in congregation.
2. Make a poster illustrating how Salat-ul-Jama'ah is performed. Draw a group of people performing Salat-ul-Jama'ah. The group should include men, women, and children.

Stretch Your Mind

1. How can Salat-ul-Jama'ah make our Muslim society stronger?
2. Why are Muslim women not obliged to pray Salat-ul-Jama'ah and Salat-ul-Jumu'ah in the masjid?

Study Questions

1. Why is Salat-ul-Jama'ah better than praying alone? Support your answer with a hadeeth.
2. How should people stand if the ma'moom is:
   a. One male. b. One female. c. More than one follower.
3. What is Salat-ul-Masbooq?
4. What should a Muslim do in the following situations?
   a. He came to the Masjid and realized that he missed one rak'ah of the Thuhr prayer with the jama'ah.
   b. She came to the masjid and realized that she missed two rak'aat of the Thuhr prayer with the jama'ah.
   c. He came to the masjid and realized that he missed two rak'aat of the Fajr prayer with the jama'ah.
   d. She came to the masjid after the imam had said the tasleem.
5. Indicate if the following actions of a Muslim are right or wrong. If the action is wrong, write down the correct action.
   a. He came to the masjid and joined the group while the imam was in the sujood of the first rak'ah. He assumed that he had caught the first rak'ah of the prayer and did not make it up at the end.
   b. She came to the masjid and joined the line of men behind the imam.
   c. He came to the masjid and found the imam making tasleem. He found an empty corner of the masjid, made iqamah, and started another Jama'ah with a group of people who also came late.
   d. She came to the masjid and found that the imam had already started the prayer. She dropped all of her things on the floor and quickly ran to join the prayer, bumping into people as she got in line.
   e. He decided not to join the imam since he missed a few rak'aat with the group.

LESSON TWO

Congregational Prayers in Islam
2. Salat-ul-Jumu'ah صلاة الجمعة : The Friday Prayer

VOCABULARY

- Jumu'ah الجُمُعَة
- Salat-ul-Jumu'ah صلاة الجُمُعَة
- Khutbah خُطْبَة
- Khutbat-ul-Jumu'ah خُطْبَة الجُمُعَة
- Khateeb خَطيب
- Ghusl غُسْل

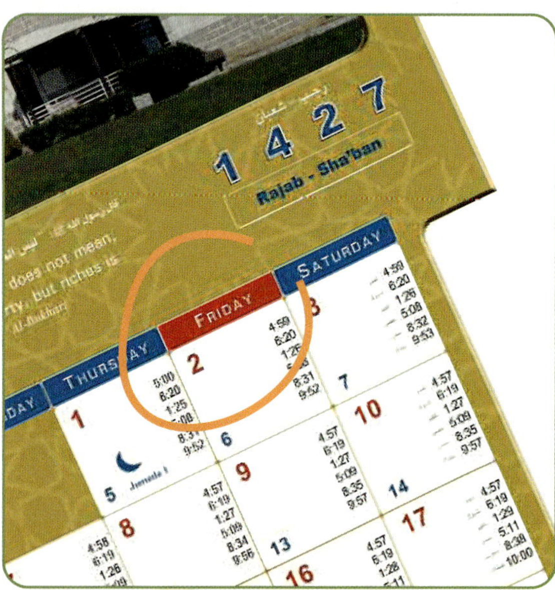

For Muslims, Friday is the best day of the week. The Arabic word for Friday is "الجُمُعَة Al-Jumu'ah," which literally means "the gathering". Al-Jumu'ah is like a little holiday. Some people even call it "Eid-ul-Muslimeen," or the "Holiday of the Muslims." In many Muslim countries, people usually get Fridays off in order to perform more acts of worship and spend more time with their friends and family.

Allah places much barakah or blessing in Fridays. There are many special things we do on Fridays. The most important thing that Muslims do on Friday is perform صلاة الجُمُعَة Salat-ul-Jumu'ah, or the Friday Prayer. The Friday Prayer is a weekly communal prayer, which means that Muslims pray together in a group as one united community.

Let us learn the following hadeeth about the importance of yawm-ul-Jumu'ah, or the day of Friday.

Masjid-ul-Jumu'ah in Madinah, built on the place where the Prophet made the first Jumu'ah prayer in Madinah

hadeeth Shareef

عن ابي هريرة رضي الله عنه قال: قال رسولُ الله ﷺ :
" خير يَوم طَلَعَتْ عليه الشَّمْسُ يَومُ الجُمُعَة ، فيهِ خُلِقَ آدَم وفيهِ أُدْخِلَ الجَنَّة وفيه أُخْرِجَ منها ، ولا تَقومُ الساعة إلا في يوم الجُمُعَة."

رواه مسلم وأحمد ومالك

Abu Hurairah narrated that the Messenger of Allah (saw) said: "The best day on which the sun rises is Friday. On it Adam was created, and on it he entered Jannah, and exited Jannah, and the Day of Judgment will not start except on Friday."

Reported in Muslim, Ahmad and Malik

Salat-ul-Jumu'ah:

Salat-ul-Jumu'ah, or the Friday Prayer is a special congregational prayer that takes place during Thuhr time on Fridays. Although the Friday Prayer takes the place of the Thuhr prayer, it is different than the Thuhr prayer in that it is two rak'aat, rather than four. The Friday Prayer begins after the time for prayer starts and the call to prayer is given. It consists of a خُطبة khutbah, or sermon, before the two Rak'aat of prayer. The khutbah is usually delivered by the imam or a knowledgeable, righteous Muslim. The person who gives the khutbah is called a 'خطيب "khateeb." The outline of the khutbah follows specific rules and is meant to teach us important lessons about Islam. The khutbah is actually part of Salat-ul-Jumu'ah and it is therefore forbidden to speak after it starts. During the khutbah, we should listen respectfully and attentively. The person who attends Salat-ul-Jumu'ah will be forgiven for all of the minor sins that he or she has committed since the last Jumu'ah.

Salat-ul-Jumu'ah is a fard or obligatory for every Muslim man. Allah has commanded that Muslim men should leave their work and go to the masajid to pray during the time of Salat-ul-Jumu'ah. This means that it is haram, or forbidden for men to miss Salat-ul-Jumu'ah to work or do other things. This was revealed in Surat -ul-Jumu'ah, as we see in the story below.

Story From The Life Of The Prophet

One time, Prophet Muhammad was delivering Khutbat-ul-Jumu'ah, or the Friday sermon, in the masjid. The Muslims sat, listening attentively to his great speech, when a caravan suddenly drove noisily through the streets of Madinah. There was a man with the caravan beating his drum and singing, calling the people to come and buy many beautiful products and ornaments.

When the Muslims in the masjid heard the caravan coming, many of them got up and left the Prophet as he was speaking. They hurried towards the caravan to buy things. Twelve Muslims remained, including Abu Bakr and Umar, to listen to the rest of the Prophet's sermon.

Prophet Muhammad was saddened by the Sahabah's preference for wealth and trade over Salat-ul-Jumu'ah. Allah was also displeased by this, as He revealed in Surat-ul-Jumu'ah. In these verses, Allah commands the Muslims to leave work and business in order to attend Salat-ul-Jumu'ah, and He criticizes those who are distracted from Salat-ul-Jumu'ah by worldly pursuits. From these verses, we see that it is a fard, or obligatory, for Muslim men to attend Salat-ul-Jumu'ah, and haram, or forbidden, to miss it unless one has a valid excuse, such as being sick. It is also clear from these verses that Muslim men may go back to work after they have completed Salat-ul-Jumu'ah. Allah tells us that if we obey Him and leave our business to pray Salat-ul-Jumu'ah, it will be better for us and He will provide for us.

سورة الجمعة

Surat-ul-Juma'ah (62:9-11)

﴿ يَٰٓأَيُّهَا ٱلَّذِينَ ءَامَنُوٓاْ إِذَا نُودِيَ لِلصَّلَوٰةِ مِن يَوۡمِ ٱلۡجُمُعَةِ فَٱسۡعَوۡاْ إِلَىٰ ذِكۡرِ ٱللَّهِ
وَذَرُواْ ٱلۡبَيۡعَۚ ذَٰلِكُمۡ خَيۡرٞ لَّكُمۡ إِن كُنتُمۡ تَعۡلَمُونَ ٩ فَإِذَا قُضِيَتِ ٱلصَّلَوٰةُ فَٱنتَشِرُواْ
فِي ٱلۡأَرۡضِ وَٱبۡتَغُواْ مِن فَضۡلِ ٱللَّهِ وَٱذۡكُرُواْ ٱللَّهَ كَثِيرٗا لَّعَلَّكُمۡ تُفۡلِحُونَ ١٠ وَإِذَا رَأَوۡاْ
تِجَٰرَةً أَوۡ لَهۡوًا ٱنفَضُّوٓاْ إِلَيۡهَا وَتَرَكُوكَ قَآئِمٗاۚ قُلۡ مَا عِندَ ٱللَّهِ خَيۡرٞ مِّنَ ٱللَّهۡوِ وَمِنَ ٱلتِّجَٰرَةِۚ وَٱللَّهُ
خَيۡرُ ٱلرَّٰزِقِينَ ١١ ﴾

Understood Meaning

[9] O you who believe, when the call is made for prayer on Friday, then come quickly to prayer and leave all business. That is best for you if you only knew!
[10] And when the prayer is finished, then you may go throughout the land and seek the bounty of Allah. And remember Allah frequently that you may prosper.
[11] But when they see some business or amusement, they break up for it and leave you standing. Say: What is with Allah is better than amusement and better than business and Allah is the Best of Providers!

Salat-ul-Jumu'ah is an Obligatory Weekly Congregational Prayer

Missing Salat-ul-Jumu'ah is such a grave matter that the Prophet ﷺ has said, "I would ask a man to lead the people in prayer so that I may burn the houses of those men who did not attend the Friday Prayer with us." He also said, "Either they stop neglecting Friday prayers or Allah will set a seal on their hearts so they cannot find the right path again." (Reported by Imams Muslim, Ahmad and An-Nasa'ee). In another authentic hadeeth reported by Abu Dawod, Tirmidhi, An-Nasa'ee, and Ibn-Majah, that the Prophet ﷺ said, "Whoever does not attend three Friday prayers [without a valid excuse], Allah will set a seal on his heart."

Work, business, and entertainment are prohibited during the Friday prayer time.

Proper Manners of Salat-ul-Jumu'ah

Let us learn some Sunan and adaab, or proper manners of the Friday Prayer

1. Ghusl on Fridays

It is a Sunnah to make غُسل ghusl or wash oneself by taking a special bath or shower, on Friday before the Jumu'ah Prayer. Ghusl is a purifying ritual that is similar to a bath or shower, but contains a few additional steps.

2. Reading Surat-ul-Kahf

Reciting Surat-ul-Kahf every Friday is another Sunnah with much reward. The Prophet, peace and blessings be upon him, said that whoever recites the first ten ayaat of Surat-ul-Kahf before Jumu'ah prayer will be protected from Ad-Dajjal and the punishment of the grave. The Prophet ﷺ also said, "Whoever recites (the entire) Surat-ul-Kahf on Friday, Allah will give him a light till the next Friday." (Imams Al-Baihaqee and Al-Hakim).

3. Wearing Neat Clothes and Perfume.

It is also the Sunnah of Prophet Muhammad to wear the best clothes he owned and to put on perfume or musk for Salat-ul-Jumu'ah.

4. Going Early to Salat-ul-Jumu'ah.

Muslims should go early to Salat-ul-Jumu'ah. Imams Al-Bukhari and Muslim reported that the Prophet Muhammad ﷺ said, "If one washes himself and then goes to Friday Prayer, it is considered as if he donated a camel for the sake of Allah. However, if he goes in the second hour, then it is considered as if he donated a cow; and, if in the third hour, then as if he donated a big sheep; and, if in the fourth hour, then as if he donated a chicken; and, if in the fifth hour, then as if he donated an egg. Then, when the imam starts delivering the sermon, the angels come and listen to it."

5. Listening Attentively to the Khutbah

The khutbah is meant to remind us of Allah and teach us something of our religion. It is important that Muslims go early to Salat-ul-Jumu'ah and listen attentively to the khutbah from the very beginning. During the khutbah, a Muslim should focus on the lessons of the Khutbah and avoid distractions. It is forbidden to speak, sleep, or do other things while listening to the khutbah. According to Imams Al-Bukhari, Muslim, and others, the Prophet once said, "If you tell your friend to pay attention on Friday, while the imam is delivering the sermon, then you have committed vain talk (which is sinful)."

6. Behaving Respectfully in the Masjid.

Muslims should be respectful to others, especially during Salat-ul-Jumu'ah. For example, it is disliked to walk between people who are sitting during the Friday gathering, unless there is an empty spot to fill. In an authentic hadeeth reported by Imam Abu-Dawod, Al-Nisai, and Ahmad, a man was walking between people during the Friday gathering while Prophet Muhammad ﷺ was delivering his sermon, so the Prophet told him, "Sit, because you caused harm to other people and you came in late."

7. Making Thikr and Du'aaDduring the Special Hour

The Prophet ﷺ said that there is a special hour on Friday, during which Allah will respond to those who make du'aa' to Him. The Prophet ﷺ encouraged Muslims to remember Allah and make du'aa' to Him at this time.

Scholars have different opinions as to the specific time of this special hour. Some say that it is during Salat-ul-Jumu'ah, but the stronger opinion is that this hour is the last hour of the day on Friday, meaning the hour just before Maghrib on Friday.

It is also recommended that we send abundant peace and blessings upon the Prophet on Fridays. We do this by saying :

صَلى الله عَلى مُحَمَّدٍ وَعَلى آلِهِ
وَصَحْبِهِ وسَلَّم

Sallallahu-Ala Muhammad wa Ala Alihi wasahbihi wa Sallim.

Benefits of Salat-ul-Jumu'ah

Salat-ul-Jumu'ah has many benefits for us, including the following:

- We obey Allah and please Him.
- We receive much reward and blessing.
- We are forgiven for our minor sins from one Jumu'ah to the next.
- We are reminded of Allah and learn things about our religion from the khateeb during the Jumu'ah khutbah.
- We stay in touch with our community and meet new Muslims every time we go to the masjid.

CHAPTER REVIEW

Projects and Activities

Participate in Salat-ul-Jumu'ah in the Masjid and write a 500 word essay describing the following:

a. How Salat-ul-Jumu'ah was performed.
b. What the imam said in his khutbah.
c. How do you feel about your experience of Salat-ul-Jumuh'ah.

2. Make a poster illustrating how Salat-ul-Jumu'ah and the Khutbah are performed.

Stretch Your Mind

1. Why do you think Allah made Salat-ul-Jumu'ah obligatory on all male Muslims?
2. Why is Salat-ul-Jumu'ah shorter than the regular Thuhr prayer?
3. Why do you think the Prophet recommended that we make ghusl on Fridays?

Study Questions

1. What day of the week is Jumu'ah? What do some people call this day?
2. What is the best day of the week for Muslims? Why? Support your answer with a hadeeth.
3. Name three special things Muslims do on Fridays.
4. What is the Jumu'ah khutbah?
5. Can Muslim men miss Salat-ul-Jumu'ah? Why or why not?

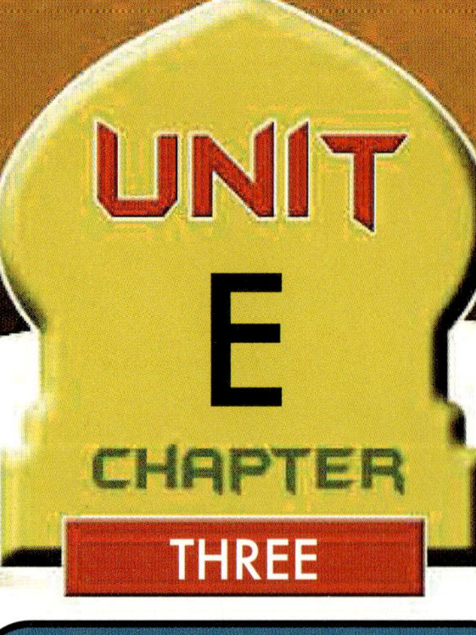

LESSON THREE

Congregational Prayers in Islam
3. Eid Prayers

VOCABULARY

Eid	عيد
Eid-ul-Fitr	عيدُ الفِطـر
Salat-ul-Eid	صَلاة العيد
Zakat-ul-Fitr	زكاة الفِطـر

It was the 29th day of Ramadan. The class was buzzing with excitement. Ramadan was almost over, and that meant Eid عيد might be the next day! Eid would be on the first day of Shawwal, the month after Ramadan.

Some students wanted Eid to be the next day. They were excited about all of the fun activities, games, gifts, and yummy food.

Other students were looking forward to Eid, but they wanted just one more day of fasting to earn more good deeds. After all, Ramadan comes only once a year.

WHAT DO YOU THINK THEY FOUND OUT? TOMORROW WAS EID!

In Arabic, "eid" means "celebration."

All About Eid

Eid-ul-Fitr is a celebration after the end of Ramadan, which means it occurs on the first day of the month of Shawwal. Eid celebrates the end of fasting in Ramadan, and it is one of the two festivals Allah made for Muslims.

Muslims celebrate this joyous occasion they have received from Allah سُبحانه وتعالى. It is a time of togetherness when Muslims meet with family members and friends. Eid is also a time of giving. Each family is required to donate a small amount of money to the poor before the Eid prayer. This charity is called Zakat-ul-Fitr زكاة الفطر, or "charity of the breakfast."

On the day of Eid, it is Sunnah for all Muslims to take a special bath called ghusl غسل , and then gather for the Eid prayer. This prayer can be offered in a masjid, in a big hall, or outside. Prophet Muhammad ﷺ used to pray Salat-ul-Eid with all the Muslims outside.

After the prayer, family and friends visit each other and enjoy themselves. We should always remember the needy, who may not get to have many of the nice treats that we get on Eid. For example, parents give their children money or gifts in celebration of Eid-ul-Fitr. Children may send each other Eid greetings on the Internet or make each other cards.

Is Salat-ul-Eid the same as the five daily prayers?

Before the Eid prayer, one should recite the takbeer:

Activity: Recite this takbeer with your class!

اللهُ أكبر ، اللهُ أكبر ، اللهُ أكبر ،
لا إلهَ إلا الله

[Transliteration] "Allahu akbar Allahu akbar, Allahu akbar, la ilaha illalllah. Allahu akbar Allahu akbar, Allahu akbar, wali llah il hamd.

اللهُ أكبر ، اللهُ أكبر ، ولله الحَمْد

[Translation] "Allah is Greater, Allah is Greater, Allah is Greater there is no one worthy of prayer but Allah. Allah is Greater, Allah is Greater, all praise be to Allah."

Salat-ul-Eid begins with two rak'aat. However, once the rak'aat are over, an Imam delivers a khutbah. It is very important to listen to the khutbah, because it is a part of the prayer, just like at Jumu'ah time. Unlike the five daily prayers, the prayer of Eid-ul-Fitr has no athan or an iqamah to call upon the Muslims. There is no standard time to pray; it can be offered anytime between sunrise and noon in the Eid day. The Eid prayer is also Sunnah.

The 'Eid prayer consists of two rak'aat just like Salat-ul-Jumu'ah or Salat-ul Fajr. However, there is a difference between the two prayers. During the first rak'ah of Salat-ul-Eid, it is Sunnah for the imam to say "Allahu Akbar" seven times after the beginning takbeer. The Muslims behind the Imam follow by repeating the takbeers. During the second rak'ah, the imam says "Allahu Akbar" five times after the takbeer he made for standing after the prostration. Then, the takbeer is repeated seven times in the first rak'ah and five times in the second. This is the only difference between Salat-ul-Eid and other prayers.

The imam recites Qur'an after completing the seven takbeer in the first rak'ah and after the five takbeer in the second rak'ah. 'Aishah (R) said: the Prophet ﷺ would say the takbeer seven times in the first rak'ah and five times in the second rak'ah on the day of Eid-ul-Fitr and Eid-ul-Adha, the two festivals."

(Reported by Abu Dawood)

Projects and Activities

1. Perform Salat-ul-Eid with your classmates.

2. Develop a poster illustrating how Salat-ul-Eid and the khutbah are performed.

Stretch Your Mind

1. Why is Eid-ul-Fitr important in Islam?

2. Both Salat-ul-Eid and Salat-ul-Jumu'ah consist of two rak'aat and a khutbah, but what are the differences between the two rituals in the way they are performed?

Study Questions

1. What does Eid mean?
2. How do we know when Eid-ul-Fitr is?
3. What does Salat-ul-Eid include?
4. How is the Eid prayer different from the five daily prayers?
5. How do Muslims celebrate their Eid?

Prayer in Times of Difficulty

CHAPTER OUTLINE

1. Learn when a Muslim can shorten or combine two prayers together.
2. Appreciate Allah سبحانه وتعالى and his favors in making worship easier in times of difficulty.
3. Learn the Islamic rules of prayer in sickness, during travel, and severe weather.

VOCABULARY

- Salat-ul-Musafir صلاة المسافر
- Salat-ul-Mareed صلاة المريض
- Salatul-Qadaa' صلاة القضاء
- Jami' جمع
- Qasr قصر
- Sujood-us-Sahw سجود السهو

Easing and Reducing Prayers

Allah سبحانه وتعالى is the most merciful and loving. Therefore, he made his religion easy to learn, understand, and practice. Whenever there is a difficulty, there is a way to ease it in Islam.

As we learned in previous sections, the prayers have a number of conditions that are required to make it perfect. However, Muslims may go through difficult situations like sickness, travel, or inclement weather that warrant some ease. Under these circumstances, Islam allows us to shorten and/or combine our prayers as a mercy to us and a protection from hardship. In fact, Allah ﷻ intends for all of his creation to enjoy ease in this life and the Hereafter. Allah says in the Qur'an:

﴿ يُرِيدُ ٱللَّهُ بِكُمُ ٱلْيُسْرَ وَلَا يُرِيدُ بِكُمُ ٱلْعُسْرَ ﴾

البقرة: ١٨٥

"Allah intends for you ease, and He does not want to make things difficult for you." [Surat-ul-Baqara 2:185]

Keeping this in mind, we will learn in the following sections what warrants the reduction of prayers, in addition to the integrals of shortening the prayers. We will also look at the Sunaan of Allah's Messenger ﷺ in performing shortened prayers and how he shortened his prayers.

Salat-ul-Mareed صلاة المريض : The Prayer of the Sick

As mentioned earlier, Allah ﷻ intends for all of his creation ease in this life and the Hereafter. There are sometimes circumstances that befall an individual that requires that he shortens his prayers. If someone falls ill or fears that the exertion of prayer will make him more ill or slow his recovery, he can then offer prayer by sitting, lying, or in extreme cases, with his eyes.

Of course, this is only permissible under those circumstances and is not allowed for those who are of sound body and health. Imran bin Hussain narrates, "I had piles, so I asked the Prophet ﷺ about the prayer and he said, 'Offer the prayer standing and if you cannot do so, pray while sitting, and if you can't do that, then make salah while lying on your side.'" This is related by Bukhari, Tirmidhi, Abu Dawud, Ibn Majah, An-Nasa'i.

How should the prayer of the sick be performed?

The following will explain exactly how the prayer of the sick should be performed:

1. The person performing prayer who can't stand should sit while making prayer. He/She should make rukoo' and sujood by bowing the head making sure that the sajdah is lower than the rukoo'.
2. If prayer while sitting is still too overwhelming for the sick person, then he or she should pray while lying down.
3. The back of the person should be firmly fixed on the bed with the legs pointing towards the Qibla.
4. The legs should not be completely stretched, but the person's knees should be raised.
5. The head should rest at a high level with a pillow under it.

6. The prayer must be made using gestures, like bowing the head, with the sajdah being lower than the rukoo'.

7. If the knees can't be raised, then stretching them is overlooked, but the head of the person must be facing the Qibla.

If prayer cannot be made sitting, then it is permissible to pray on the side of the body, preferably the right side using head gestures for the rukoo' and sujood. If someone is so sick that he/she can't even make head gestures, then he or she can blink his or her eyes or just think the rukoo' and the sujood in his or her mind.

Combining Prayers During Illness

Sometimes it is necessary to combine prayers due to severe illness. This does not mean common cold or flu, but a sickness that would worsen or slow the healing process if one was to perform an individual prayer.

According to Hanbali and Shaf'i'ee schools, it is allowed to combine two prayers due to illness, either during the time of the earlier or later salah, as it is a greater hardship. Only the Thuhr and Asr prayers are combined with each other, and the Maghrib and Ishaa' prayers are combined with each other. Fajr is to be prayed by itself.

The Traveler's Prayer صلاة المسافر

In today's world travel is very important and sometimes unavoidable. Although we have many modern means of transportation designed to get us where we're going with relative comfort and ease, travel can still be very tiring and problematic. As a mercy, Allah سبحانه وتعالى has made prayer easy upon us during the tiring times of travel. He says in the Qur'an:

﴿ وَإِذَا ضَرَبْتُمْ فِي ٱلْأَرْضِ فَلَيْسَ عَلَيْكُمْ جُنَاحٌ أَن تَقْصُرُوا۟ مِنَ ٱلصَّلَوٰةِ ﴾

النساء: ١٠١

"When you travel throughout the Earth, there is no blame on you if you were to shorten your prayers."

According to most schools of fiqh, whenever someone wants to shorten his or her prayers during travel the following stipulations have to be followed:

- The distance traveled has to be at least 48 miles or more (77 kilometers).

- Someone travels the distance of 48 miles (77 kilometers) arriving at his destination, but doesn't intend to remain there for more than 15 days.

- A traveler that intends to stay at his destination for at least 15 days will be considered a traveler for the duration of his or her journey only.

However, according to a number of imams and scholars, a traveler can shorten his prayers as long as he is traveling away from his hometown. They say the Prophet ﷺ never set a number of days during which a traveler can shorten the prayer.

The act of shortening the prayers is known as qasr (قصر). Not all prayers are shortened, only those that are four units (4 rak'aat) in length. This is illustrated in the following table:

PRAYER	REGULAR	DURING TRAVEL
FAJR	2	2
THUHUR	4	2
ASR	4	2
MAGHRIB	3	3
ISHAA'	4	2

If you notice the table above, only the fard prayers that feature 4 units are shortened. The Fajr and Maghrib prayers are left the same. They are not to be shortened! Similarly, there is no shortening of the Witr, Sunnah, or Nafl prayers.

Should any traveler pray behind those who are residents in the location in which he is traveling, then he is required to follow the imam in full prayer. For example, if you were traveling to New York from Dallas for the duration of 10 days and wanted to pray in the local mosque, you would be required to pray four full units of prayer behind the imam that is praying a full salah. Therefore, if the imam prays 4 rak'aat of Thuhr, then the traveler praying behind him is obliged to pray 4 full rak'aat as well.

It is not encouraged to pray Sunnah prayers while traveling except for the Sunnah of Fajr prayer.

However, if a resident happens to line up in prayer behind a traveler, then the traveler is obliged to inform the resident that he is a traveler and that he needs to complete the full prayer. For example, a traveler that is journeying from Dallas to New York should inform those who have joined him in Salat-ul-Thuhr to complete four rak'aat of prayer, since he will pray only two because he is a traveler.

Combining the Prayers جمع الصلاه

Not only is it possible to shorten prayers during travel, it is also permissible to combine the prayers when traveling, and this act of combining prayers is known as jama' جمع It is important to note that the majority of scholars, including the Hanbalis, Shafi'is, and Malikis, consider combining the prayers valid throughout travel with minimal conditions. However, the scholars of the Hanafi school consider combining the prayers to only be valid during the Hajj season with the sultan or his deputy present. They hold the opinion that the Prophet ﷺ only performed his Thuhr prayer later in its allotted time and the Asr prayer early in its allotted time, giving the appearance that both of them were combined. However, the reality is that he made each prayer within its own special time.

Only the Thuhr and Asr prayers are combined with each other and the Maghrib and Ishaa'are combined with each other. Fajr is to be prayed by itself.

The Athan and Iqamah During Travel:

The athan and iqamah are always encouraged for a group of three or more individuals. However, if those people who are traveling in a group desire to pray while traveling, the athan and iqamah should be made. The mu'athin would recite the athan, a member from the group would give the iqamah, and then they would join in prayer. When combining the prayers, a new athan is not needed, only another iqamah is needed.

Rain and Severe Weather

Sahabi Abu Salamah ibn 'Abdurrahman said: "It is a Sunnah to combine the Maghrib and 'Ishaa' prayers when it is raining." Al-Bukhari records that the Prophet ﷺ combined the Maghrib and 'Ishaa' prayers on a rainy night in the masjid.

Therefore, Imams Shafi'i , Malik and Ahmad Ibn Hanbal hold that combining the Magrib and Ishaa' prayers is allowed for rain, snow, ice, and severe cold. Combining the prayers should happen during the time of the earlier prayer. If the rain continues during the start of the latter prayer, then the Imam can combine the prayer.

This concession is allowed only for one who prays with a congregation in the mosque. However, for one who prays alone or in a group in his house, it is not allowed for him to combine the salah.

Imam Shafi'ee allowed the combination of Thuhr and Asr Prayers for rain and inclement or severe weather.

Pressing Needs

It has also been narrated that the Prophet ﷺ combined prayers due to pressing and urgent needs. This was done under extreme circumstances, and should not be done under regular circumstances. Prayer in congregation should always be observed as should prayer in its allotted time. Let us not forget the words of Allah ﷻ when he says:

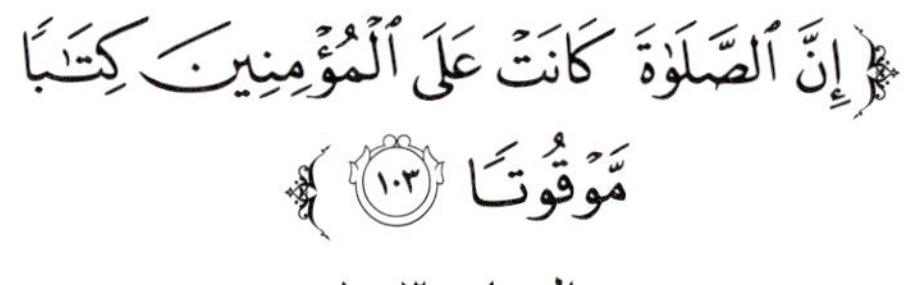

"Verily, the prayer is enjoined on the believers at fixed hours." (4:103)

Imam Muslim narrates the following regarding combined prayers due to pressing needs, "The Messenger of Allah ﷻ combined the Thuhr and 'Asr and then the Maghrib and 'Ishaa' in Madinah without there being any danger or rain." Ibn 'Abbas was asked: "What did he desire by that action?" He replied: "He did not want any hardship for his ummah." This is related by Muslim.

These few points illustrate the mercy shown upon us by Allah ﷻ. He desires that we do not fall under any hardships and has made worship for us easy. We should be extremely grateful and appreciative of the bounties that he has bestowed upon us, those that we know of and those that we don't! However, the Prophet ﷺ did this only one time, or just few times, to show Muslims that they can combine the prayer when there is a real need. Therefore, we should not make it a habit. In normal situations, the Prophet ﷺ used to perform the five prayers, each in its assigned time everyday.

Corrective Rituals in Prayer

Now we need to examine what should be done if we make a mistake in our prayers.

Mistakes happen, and we are only held accountable for the mistakes that we knowingly make. Islam has offered us two major ways to correct our prayers, should we make any mistakes: Qadaa', or making up, and Sujood As-Sahw, or the prostration of forgetting. In the following section, we will learn how we practice these two corrective methods.

Salatul-Qadaa'

(صلاة القضاء)

Qadaa' (قضاء) is a term used for missed prayers that need to be made up. One of the first actions that a Muslim will be responsible for on the Day of Judgment is his/her prayer. This gives us an idea of how important it truly is. Even in times of illness, travel, fear or inclement weather, salah must be performed. There is no excuse for prayers to be missed. Allah ﷻ has made it easy for us to complete our prayers, even in difficult situations. In fact, the determining factor between true faith and disbelief is the leaving of the prayers. Allah ﷻ said about missing prayers: "And then there came after them a later generation who wasted the prayers and followed their own lusts, but they will meet with destruction." He also mentions in another verse, "Woe unto the worshippers who are heedless of their prayers!" Therefore, it is imperative that the prayers be made, and during their allotted times!

How Missed Prayers Should be Made Up:

Missed prayers are made up in the same manner that the regular prayers are made. For example, if the Fajr prayer is missed, two rak'aat should be made up as soon as possible, preferably before the time of Thuhr prayer has begun. The same thing applies to the Asr prayer if it is missed; it should be made up before the Maghrib. If you miss more than one prayer, you should make them up as soon as possible, keeping the same order of the prayers. It is not befitting for us to change that order and make prayers out of place.

Sujood-us-Sahw

It is sometimes necessary to make up for mistakes during prayer. Even the Messenger of Allah ﷺ would forget during prayer. It is confirmed that the Prophet ﷺ sometimes forgot something in the salah. It is also true that he said: "I am a human being and forget like you forget. If I forget, remind me."

Therefore, what are the ways that we make up for mistakes during the prayer? We will examine those ways and discuss their details during the next section.

What is Sujood-us-Sahw?

Sujood-us-Sahw (سُجود السهو) refers to two prostrations made at the end of prayer for missing an obligatory act of prayer unintentionally. These two prostrations are made at the end of prayer.

Most of the scholars, including those from the Maliki, Shafi'i, and the Hanbali schools, are of the opinion that these two prostrations are made during the prayer before the tasleem (saying "Assalamu-Alaikum"). However, the Hanafi school holds that these two prostrations should be made after making one tasleem to the right.

The two prostrations made at the

end of prayer was a confirmed Sunnah of Rasoolullah ﷺ. It is recorded from Abu Sa'eed al-Khudri that the Prophet said: "If one of you has some doubts during his salah and he does not recall (the number of rak'aat) he has prayed, three or four, then he can put an end to his doubt by performing Salah according to what he was certain of [the lesser amount] and then making two sujood before the tasleem." In the story of Thul-Yadayn, in the two sahihs, we are told the Prophet ﷺ made the prostrations after the tasleem.

When should Sujood-us-Sahw be made?

Sujood-us-Sahw should be made under the following circumstances:

- If a person completes tasleem before actually finishing the prayer, like skipping one rak'ah or more. In this case, you stand up and make up the missed rak'aah or rak'aat, and then make Sujood-us-Sahw before tasleem.

- If an additional sujood, rukoo', rak'ah, or Rak'aat have been made to the prayer, you make Sujood-us-Sahw before tasleem.

- If the first tashahhud is forgotten along with any other wajib or Sunnah acts of prayer, you don't have to make up the first tashahhud or a Sunnah act of the prayer, but instead make Sujood-us-Sahw before tasleem.

- If you doubt whether you have prayed three or four units of prayer, you follow certainty. If you were more convinced that you prayed a rak'aah less, for example, then you make up what you think you missed and then you make Sujood-us-Sahw before tasleem. However, if you were more convinced that you prayed the right number of rak'aat, then you complete your salah without making Sujood-us-Sahw.

These cases show the importance of the performance of two prostrations after the prayer if someone forgets any wajib or Sunnah act during the prayer unintentionally. However, when mistakes such as these are made willfully and intentionally, prayers must be made up from the beginning, and it is not permissible to make Sujood-us-Sahw for any mistakes done intentionally.

CHAPTER REVIEW

Projects and Activities

1. Imagine that you were traveling and it is the time of Thuhr prayer. Make the Thuhr and Asr prayers in a combined and shortened manner.
2. Suppose you were praying Maghrib prayer and at the final Tashahhud position you remembered that you forgot to perform the first Tashahhud. Practice what should you do in this case.

Stretch Your Mind

1. Are you allowed to do qasr and jama' during travel, even if you are not tired?

2. Since you are allowed to shorten your prayer during travel time, are their other worships that are made easier for you during travel? What are they?

Study Questions

1. What does Salat-ul-Musafir mean?
2. What does qasr mean?
3. What does jama' mean?
4. What can you do if you are traveling and want to pray?
5. What are the prayers that you can shorten?
6. What are the prayers that you can combine together?
7. Should you pray the Sunnah prayers while during travel?
8. What are the Sunnah prayers that the Messenger of Allah (saw) used to keep praying even during travel?
9. What should you do when you miss a prayer until its time is out?